AF531173

Gill Books
Hume Avenue
Park West
Dublin 12
www.gillbooks.ie

Gill Books is an imprint of M.H. Gill & Co.

978 0 7171 8401 9

Printed by Printer Trento, Italy

This book is typeset in Bembo.

The paper used in this book comes from the wood pulp of managed forests. For every tree felled, at least one tree is planted, thereby renewing natural resources.

5 4

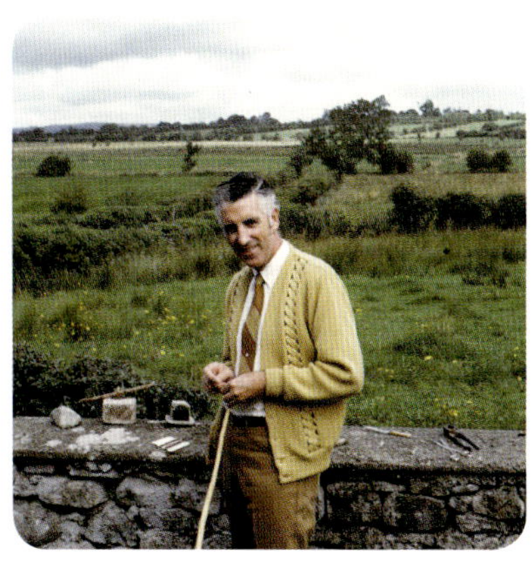

To my late father, Patrick Kelly, whose wit,
wisdom and love of Ireland I will treasure forever.

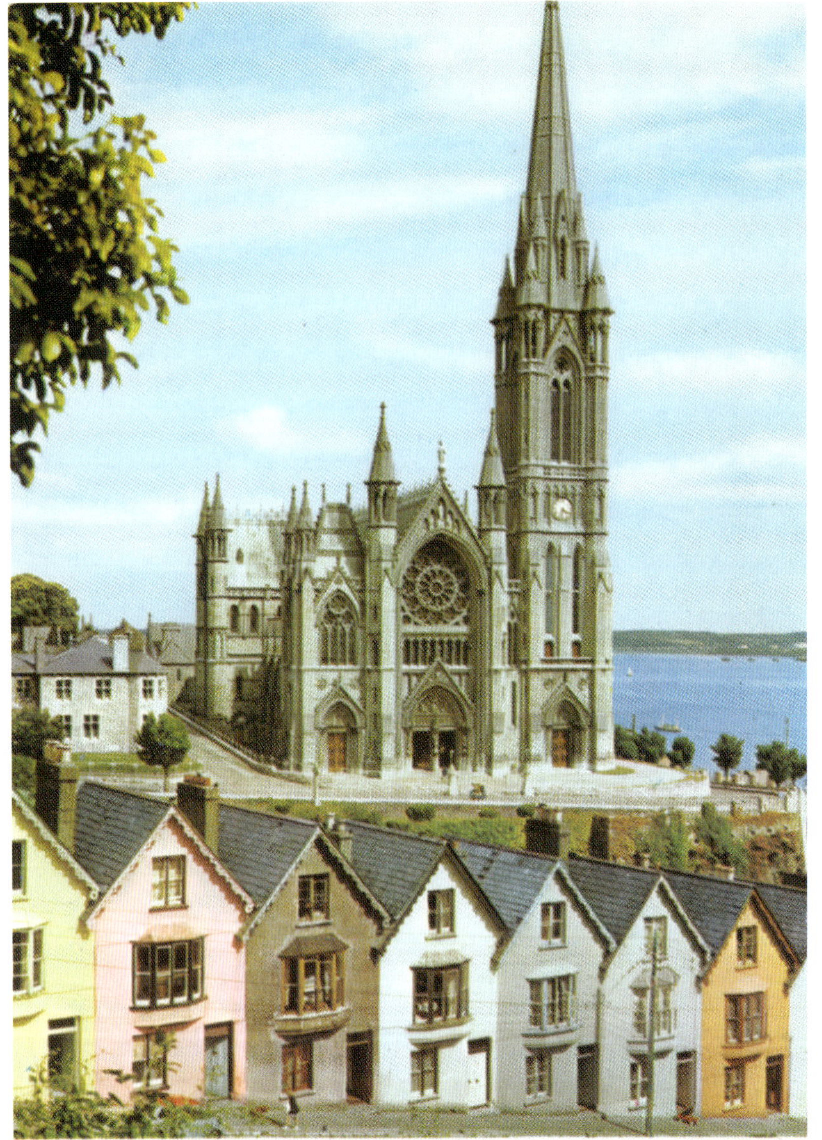

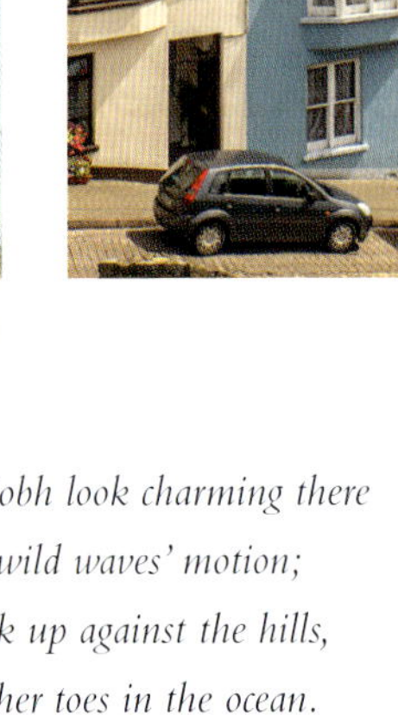

And doesn't old Cobh look charming there
Watching the wild waves' motion;
Leaning her back up against the hills,
And the tip of her toes in the ocean.
'Dawn on the Irish Coast', John Locke

ACKNOWLEDGEMENTS

Photographing and researching this book was more rewarding than I could have ever imagined – it was a dream come true. None of this would have been possible without the encouragement and support of Dana, Jensen and my dear friends. A special thanks to Edmund Nägele who provided me with illuminating stories and invaluable insight into the John Hinde experience. Arpy Shively for her professional advice and creative assistance. Also, thanks to the John Hinde Agency for preserving and providing the postcards seen here. A special thanks to Deirdre Nolan for taking a chance on my dream and everyone at Gill Books who were always supportive and reassuring. Finally, to the scores of people I had the privilege to meet up and down this great island of ours, I will forever remember your kindness and hospitality.

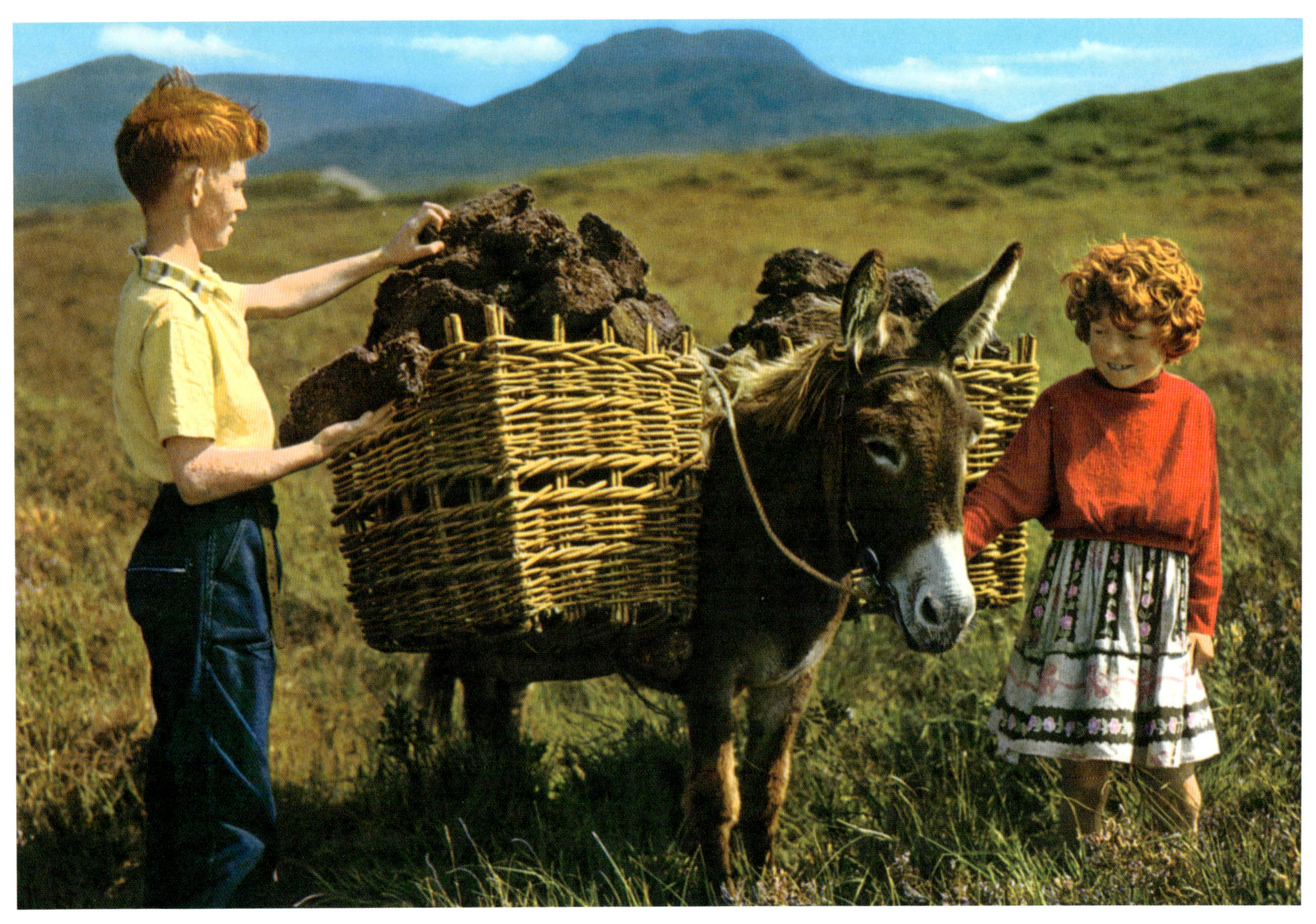

'We wished that the visitors who bought the postcard and then looked at it later would feel that this was in fact the actual impression that they recorded in their mind when they were on that particular spot.' John Hinde

INTRODUCTION

JOHN HINDE (1916–1997) was a pioneer of colour photography and one of the most successful and prolific postcard publishers in the world. His largest collection of postcards celebrated Ireland. In them, he portrayed an island brightened by his imagination: a place where children were red-haired and freckled, the sun always shining, and the sky forever blue. His idealistic images were to become the stereotypical portrayal of Ireland for many years, and to this day elicit nostalgia from viewers worldwide.

John Hinde's great success reflects the post-war expansion of the tourist industry in Ireland, particularly the growth of the American vacationer. Hinde promoted his romanticised scenes well before the development of digital imaging and social media. They depicted an Ireland people wanted to remember, but were in stark contrast with the realities of the stagnant economy and repressed society of the time.

Return to Sender pairs Hinde's iconic postcards of Ireland from the 1950s, '60s and '70s with corresponding contemporary photographs. The side-by-side contrast of these then-and-now photographs illustrates the ways Ireland's rural and urban landscapes have changed over the decades or, in some places, not changed at all.

From March to October 2018 I criss-crossed Ireland, retracing the steps of John Hinde and his small team of photographers. The exact dates of the postcards here are unknown, but they were taken some time between 1956 and 1970. In most cases, I tried to recapture each postcard by photographing the same spot where the original shot was taken. However, due to newly sprung shrubbery, trees or buildings, I was sometimes unable to access the precise location for my photographs. Where my view was blocked or hindered, I tried to find the closest, most accurate position from which to shoot.

John Hinde was not just a renowned photographer, he was an innovator and entrepreneur too. Like a film director, he would often stage-manage his photographs by adding people and flowers, as well as regularly painting transparencies to get a cottage, a car or a cardigan to the colour he wanted. For John Hinde this usually meant bright red pullovers, Mediterranean blue skies, and yellow cars. Why red or yellow? Very simply, it made the finished cards stand out on the rotating wooden stands on which they were displayed.

As the purpose of my photographs is to provide the reader with context, I did not intentionally place people or items in the shot; neither did I add or change the colour of objects or buildings. Most of Hinde's postcards were shot with Plaubel Junior 4×5 cameras using Ektachrome-x sheet film. I shot my photographs in RAW on a digital flashcard with my Nikon digital camera.

In addition to showcasing John Hinde's remarkable photography of Ireland, I hope I've given the reader the chance to reminisce about an idyllic and vanishing Ireland and to show a little of what has, or hasn't, changed over the past 60 years.

WHAT MADE HINDE'S POSTCARDS SO SPECIAL?

John Hinde created a sense of nostalgia in each of his postcards. His surreal intensification of colour was intended to make the audience form an idealised memory of Ireland. At the time, most serious photography was presented in black and white. Hinde wanted to make perfect colour photographs. Kate Burt, writing in the *Independent*, wrote that it was Hinde's creative use of colour that made his postcards different from others:

> *Hinde was an innovator in a world where serious photography was black and white, and where colour photography was poor – because neither Ireland nor Britain had the technological capabilities to reproduce the vibrant hues Hinde dreamed of. So he sent his transparencies to Italy, where technology was more advanced. Not only could the images be produced in far lusher shades than was possible over here, they also got additional help with extensive retouching, which would turn insipid sweaters, mousey heads of hair, faded sun-loungers and dull skies into dazzling points of interest. (And, more importantly, according to those who knew him, into hard cash.)*

John Hinde became one of the most successful postcard publishers in the world, although critical acclaim only began in 1993 with a retrospective exhibition at the Irish Museum of Modern Art.

Today, Hinde is widely regarded as an influential figure in fine arts, design and pop culture, as well as an outstanding social documentarian. His bright, dream-like postcards have become a vibrant resource for a better understanding of the social and cultural history of Ireland in the 1950s and '60s.

WHO WAS JOHN HINDE?

> *I had this sort of vision thing, of the top of the ladder when I was at the bottom, of fantastic colour photographs that I have never seen and that nobody else had ever seen and my whole aim was all the time how to get there, how to achieve it. You ever visualise Heaven? John Hinde*

John Hinde was born in Somerset in 1916, the great-grandson of James Clark, the founder of C. & J. Clark Ltd, the famous shoemakers. At the age of three, he developed an illness that left him with permanent disability in his left leg. After a brief apprenticeship in the family shoe business, and then with a Bristol architect, Hinde went to study colour photographic printing at the Reimann School of Art and Design in London. He became a member of the Royal Photographic Society in 1943.

During World War II, Hinde was a war photographer covering scenes of the Blitz, and for the rest of the 1940s was pre-occupied with the reproduction of colour photographs in books. Of particular interest was his work with Adprint, where he photographed for *Britain in Pictures*, a series published by William Collins, as well as *A Fire Guard Life* (1944), *Citizens in War – and After* (1945), *Exmoor Village* (1947) and *British Circus Life* (1948).

Throughout his career, Hinde's essential trademarks were his attention to detail, his intensive use of colours and his mastery of photographic technique. His work in the 1940s was groundbreaking, with his colour photographs being recognised by London's Imperial War Museum as the only examples of such photography from the war.

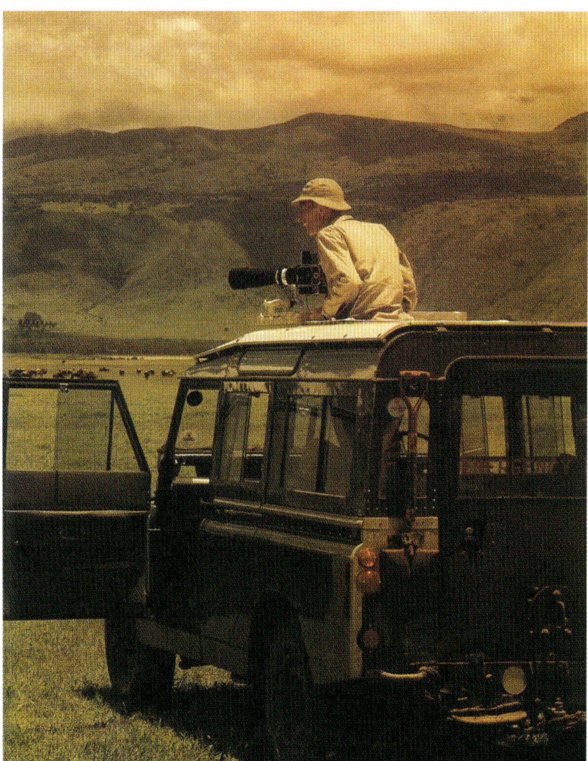

One of the few known photographs of John Hinde, on safari in East Africa, 1966.

After the war, Hinde briefly diverted into circus management and became publicity manager for a circus in Ireland. It was here he met his wife Jutta Falnoga, a trapeze artist. In 1955, they founded a travelling circus called the John Hinde Show, but it failed after a year due to Hinde launching it during one of Ireland's wettest years ever. Near bankruptcy and desperate for work, he decided to go back to photography.

Encouraged by the recently opened Shannon Airport, teeming with Irish-American tourists looking for souvenirs, Hinde launched John Hinde Ltd in Bullock Harbour, Dublin in 1956. Within a decade his portfolio of Irish postcards increased from 30 to 300. The collection was produced by a team of six photographers, including Hinde himself, at his studios between 1956 and 1972. The John Hinde Collection at the National Library of Ireland's photographic archive alone consists of 441 colour, A6-size postcards, and 47 large, 9'×6.5' colour postcards.

By 1965, Hinde had employed two young German photographers, Elmar Ludwig and Edmund Nägele, as well as an Englishman, David Noble, to carry on his work.

Following his success in Ireland, Hinde expanded his postcard empire into Britain, producing a famous series of images for Butlin's popular holiday camps, and then into Africa, Australia, Jamaica, Malaysia, Singapore and Canada. The company expanded rapidly until it was sold in 1972 to Waterford Glass. By then, sales had reached in excess of 50 million postcards worldwide. During his retirement, Hinde concentrated on landscape painting. A father of five, he died in Dordogne, France in 1997.

AUTHOR'S NOTE

Throughout my childhood, the sender of these postcards was my father, Patrick Kelly. Born in Co. Roscommon, he emigrated to California in the early 1950s. Throughout his life he revisited Ireland often and sent his young family a steady stream of postcards, glossy milestones to measure his quest for historic and natural wonders in the country he always held dear.

When I was nine years old I started travelling with my father on many of his visits back home. Westport House in Co. Mayo; the stern beauty of Bunratty Castle in Co. Clare; grey Kylemore Abbey in Connemara, Co. Galway, wreathed in green; he wanted to show me the places and tell me the legends, to build memories that would last a lifetime.

My father died in 2015 and in 2018 I came back to live in Ireland with my family. *Return to Sender* is my tribute to John Hinde, whose jewel-bright Ireland was the stuff of my childhood dreams. It's also a tribute to my father, who instilled in me an almost mystical feeling for Ireland's beauty. Revisiting these scenes, it doesn't matter that the skies are often slate-grey, the grass rarely deep emerald, or that sunshine-yellow cars are as rare as flaming-red pullovers. Without artifice, transformed and yet true to its past, the magic of Ireland is still there for me.

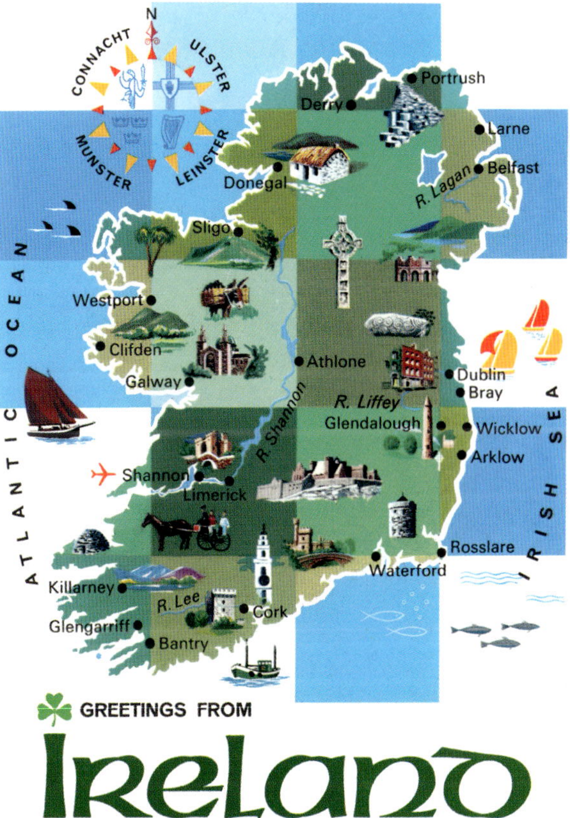

02

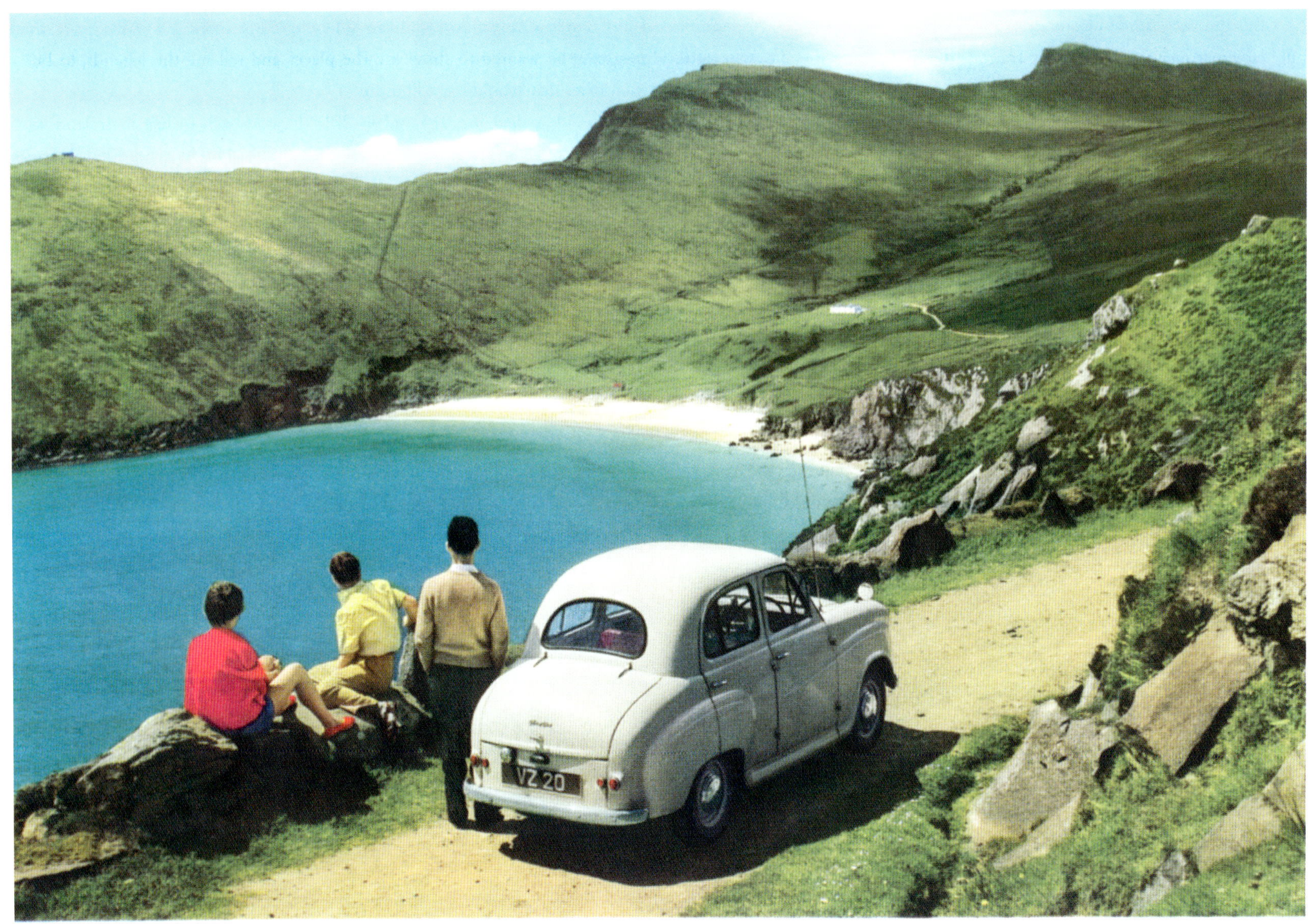

On the road to Keem Strand, Achill Island, Co. Mayo, Ireland.

Colour Photo by John Hinde, F.R.P.S.

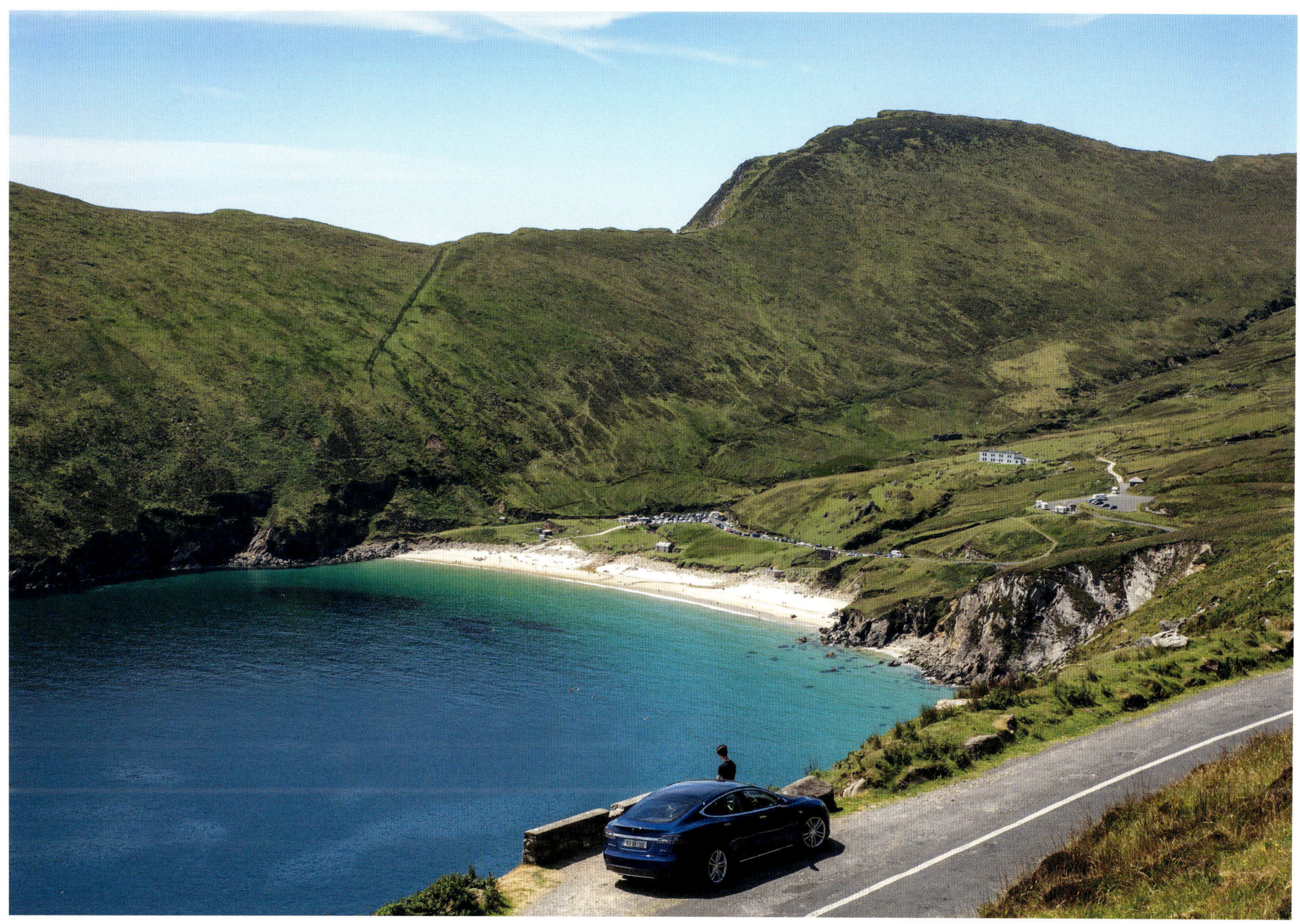

Along the Wild Atlantic Way coastal touring route, Keem Bay on Achill Island is often found listed amongst the top ten beaches in the world. On this glorious summer's day, the intense natural blue of water and sky rivals that of the highly coloured original.

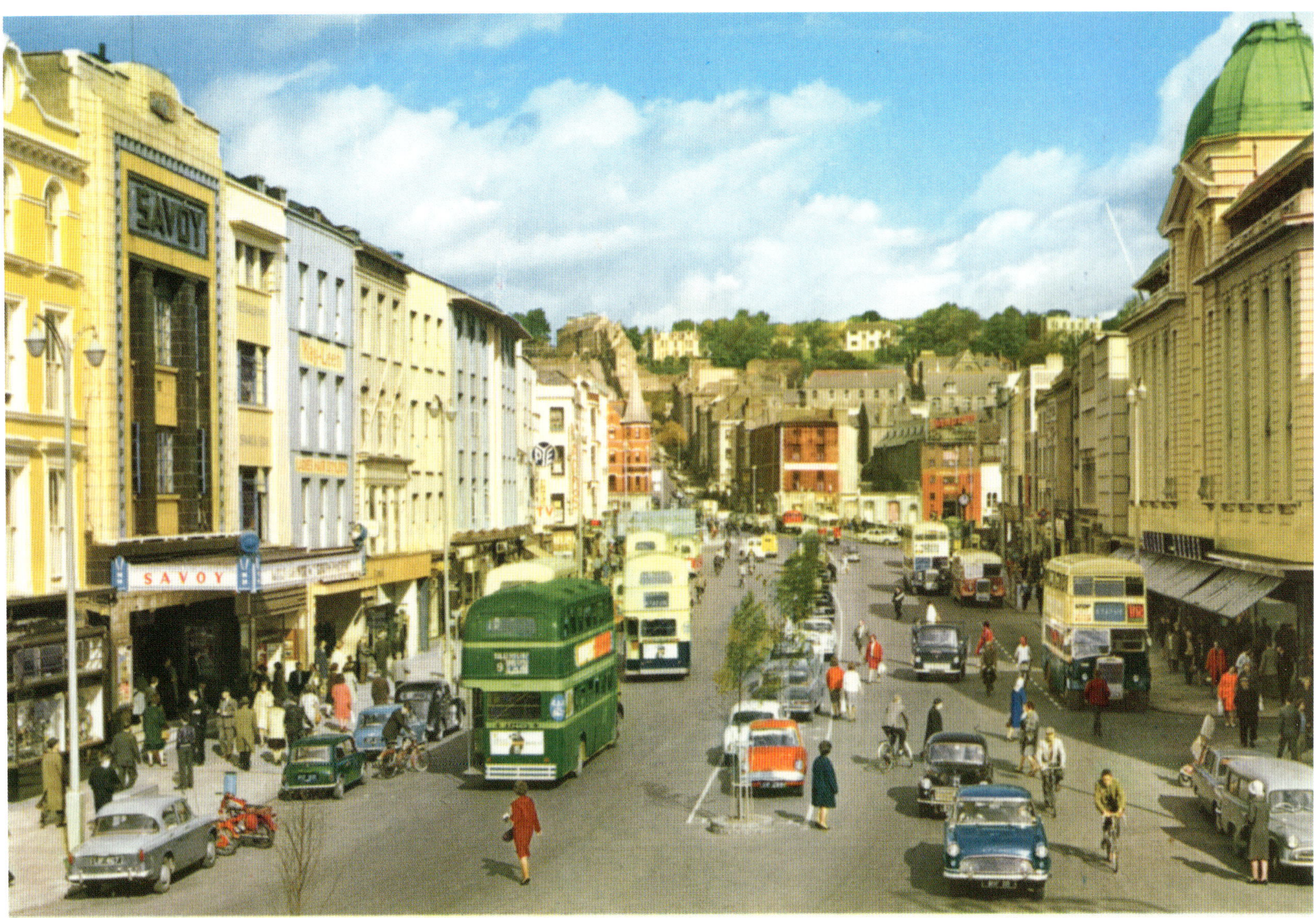

St. Patrick's Street, Bridge and Hill, Cork City, Ireland. *Photo : E. Nägele, John Hinde Studios.*

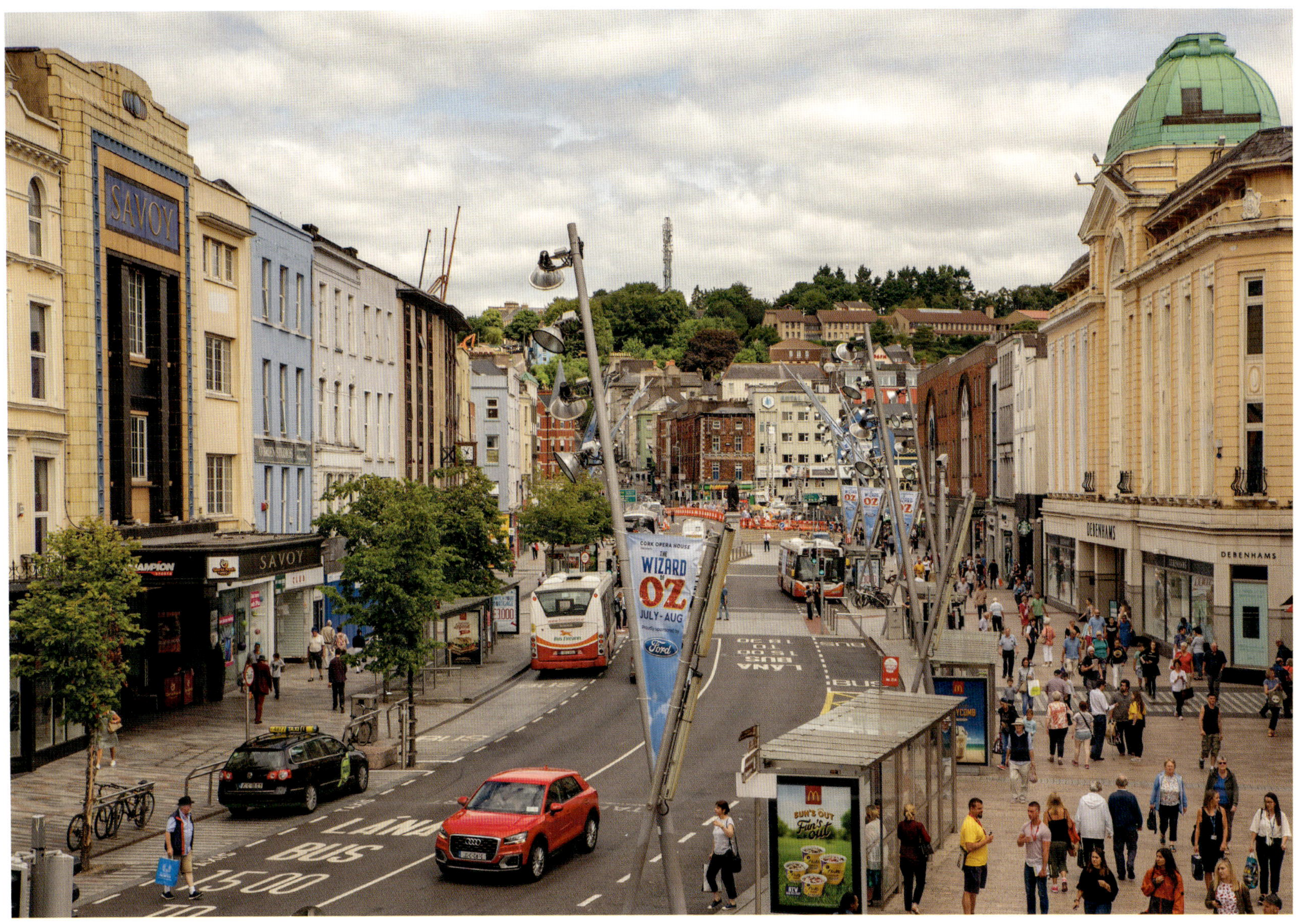

I found this postcard location on the first floor of Fitzgerald Menswear. They have been at this St Patrick's Street location since 1944. Cork is always so bustling. As the clever street art graffiti I found read: '*Ireland is like a bottle, it would sink without a Cork*'.

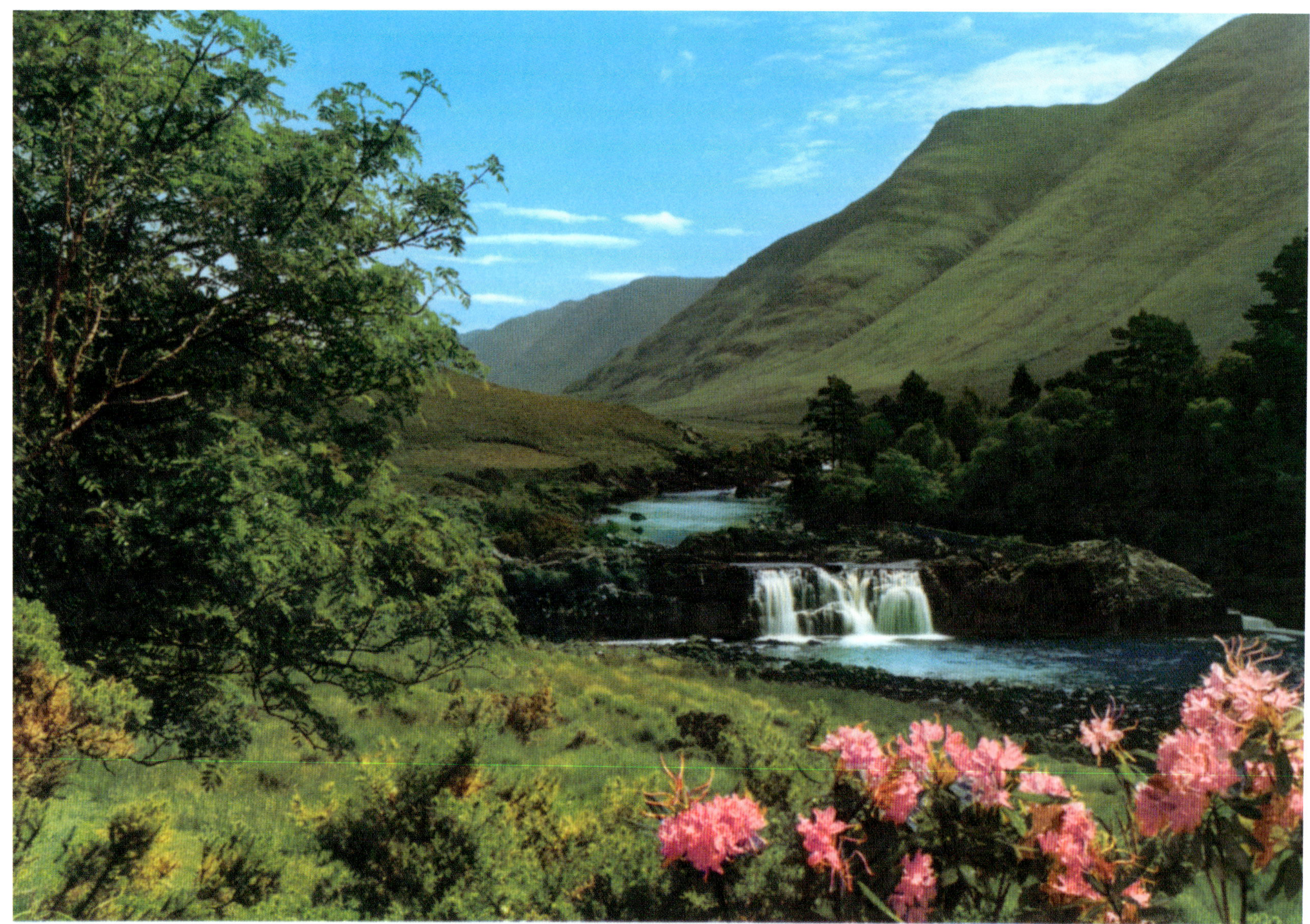

Aasleagh Falls near Leenane, Connemara, Co. Galway, Ireland.

Colour Photo by John Hinde, F.R.P.S.

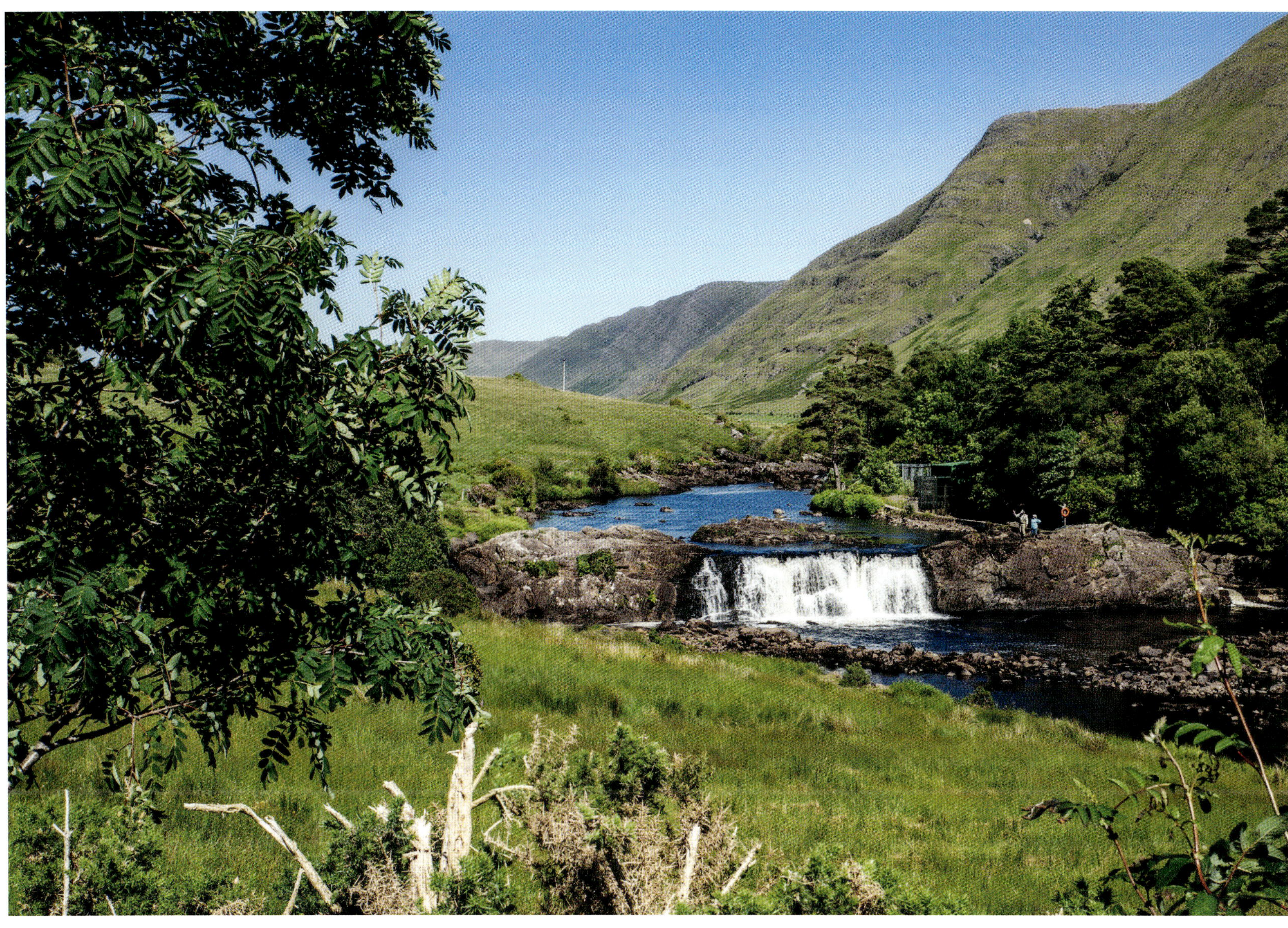

Just outside the village of Leenane and near the Galway–Mayo border is this picturesque waterfall. I was here around the summer solstice. Anglers brave the rock's edge, fishing for salmon and sea trout as these noble fish make their way back up the river Erriff from the Atlantic.

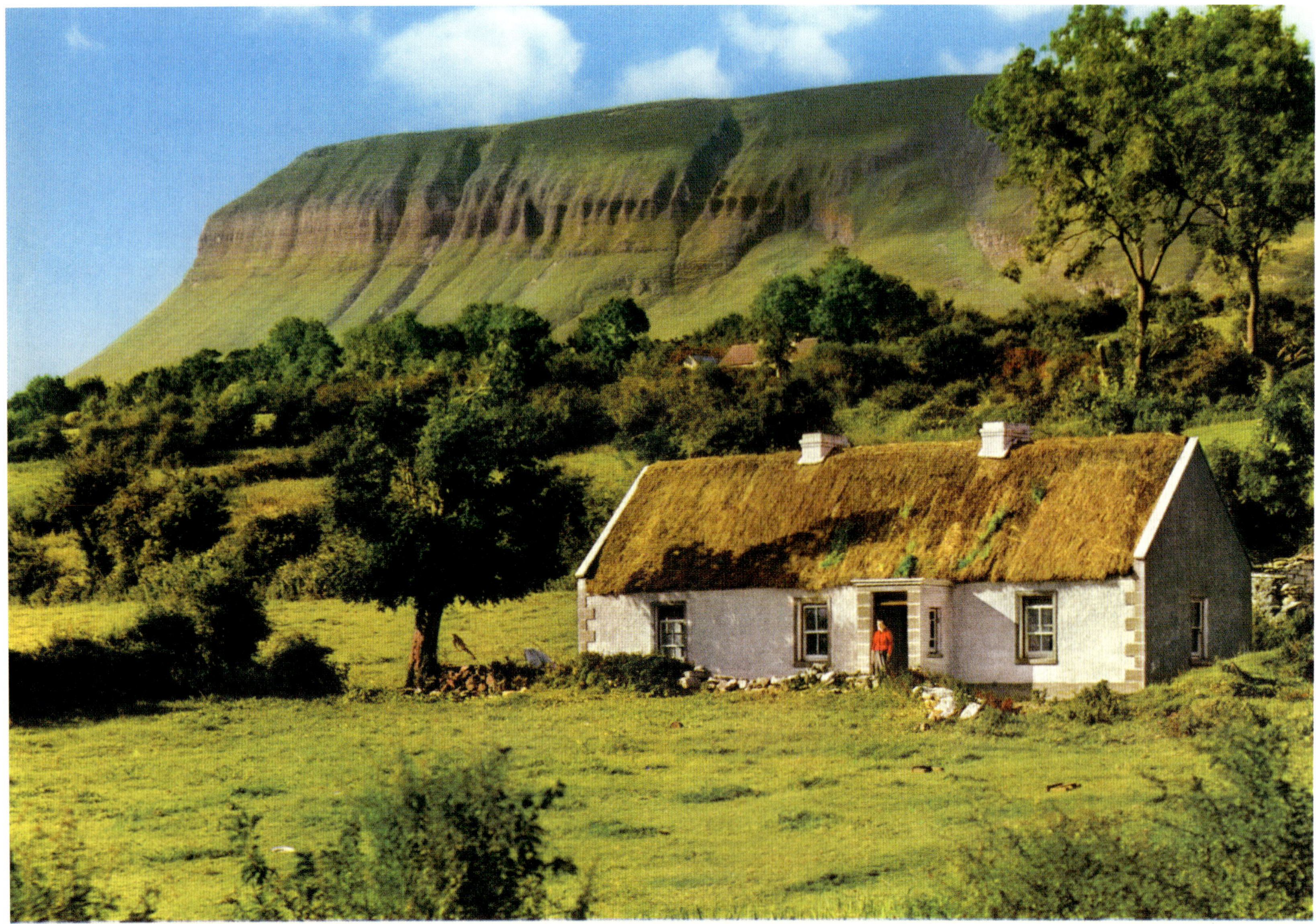

Thatched Cottage in the Yeats Country, Ben Bulben Mountain, Co. Sligo, Ireland. Colour Photo by John Hinde, F.R.P.S.

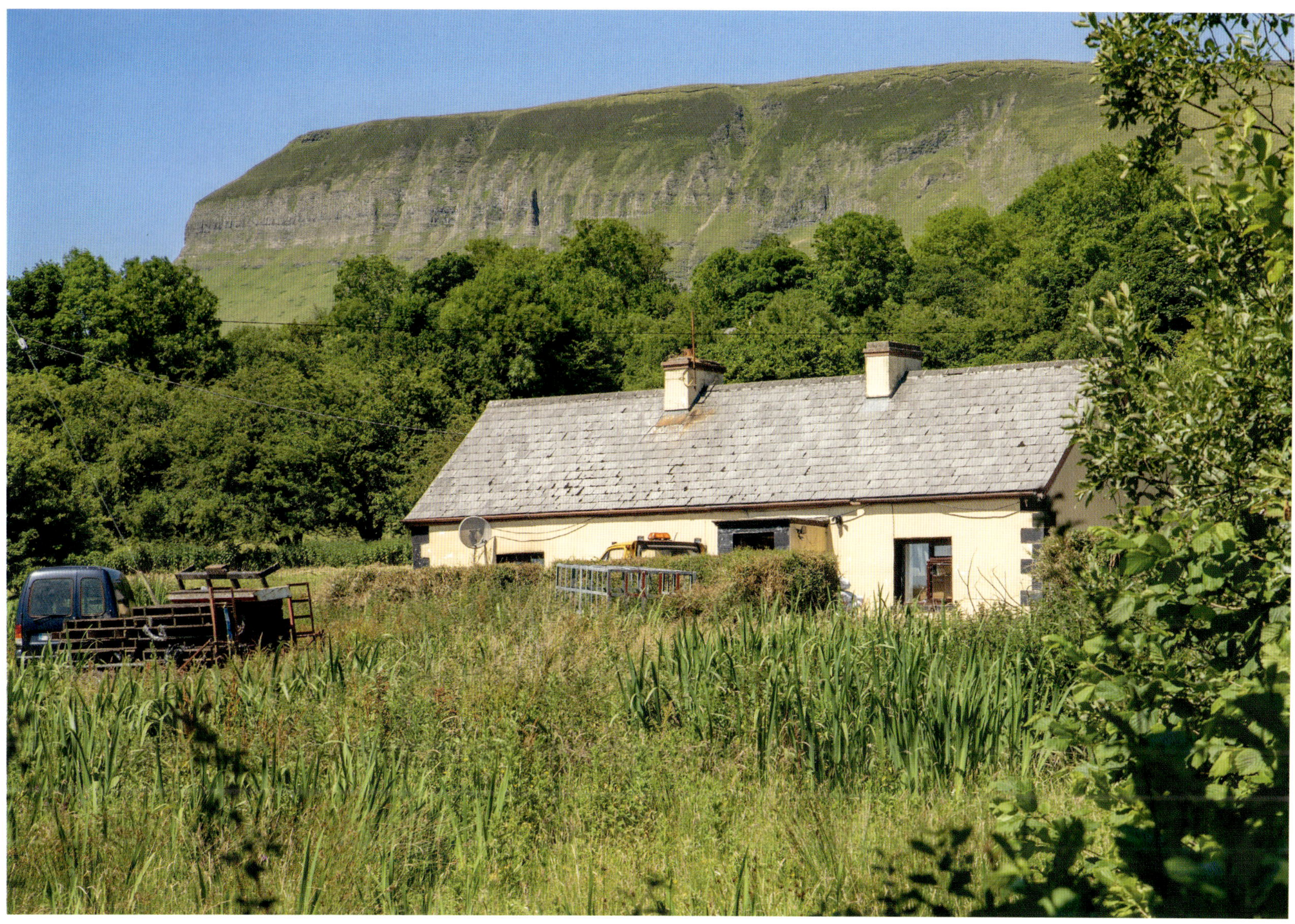

On a summer's day in 1958, young Mary Brandley was busy making hay near her family's cottage. John Hinde stopped his car and asked if he could take her picture in the doorway of the house.

'I remember it so well,' she told me in the doorway of her current home, less than a kilometre from the old cottage, 'as if it were yesterday.'

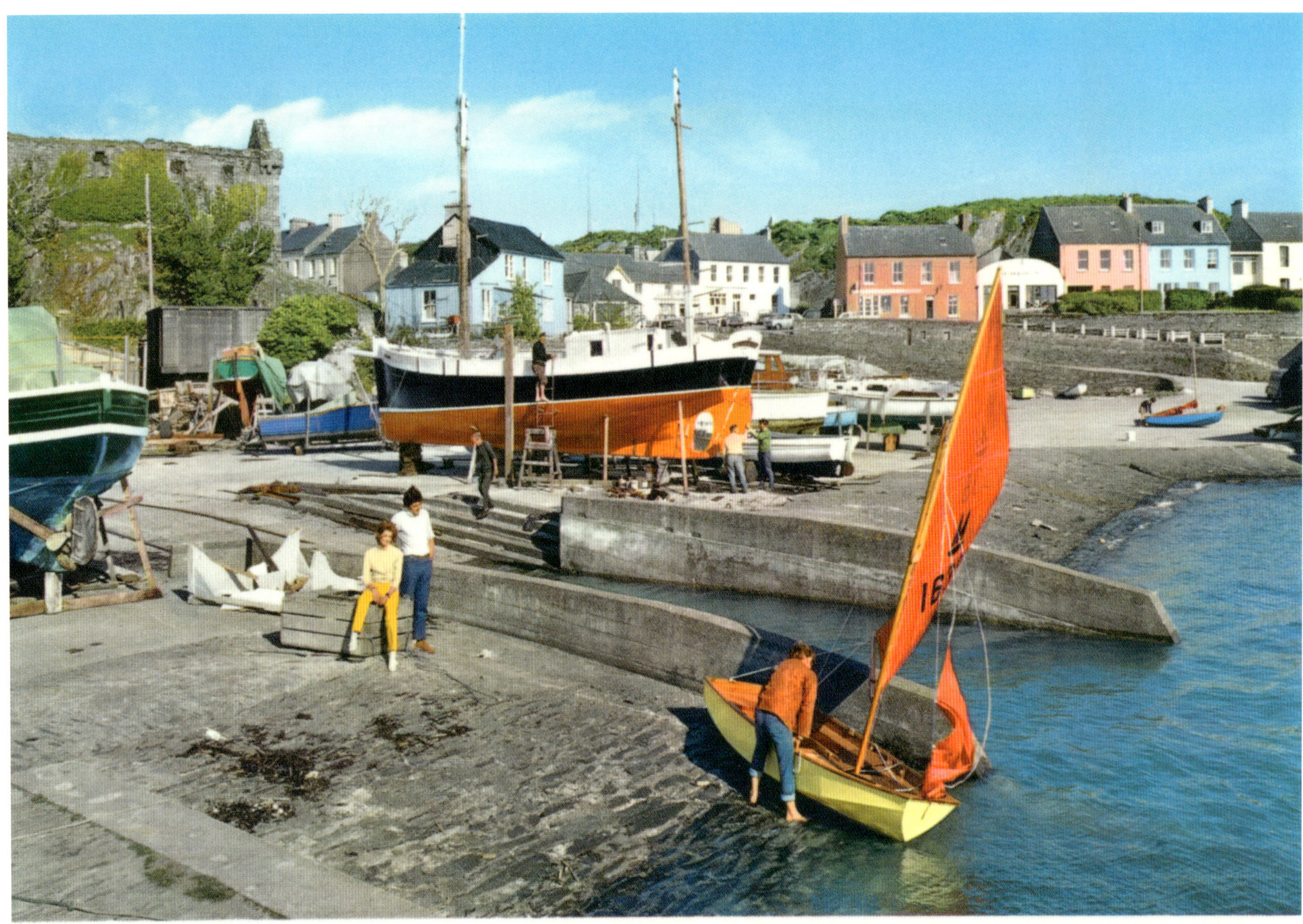

The Fishing Village of Baltimore, West Cork, Ireland. Photo: D. Noble, John Hinde Studios.

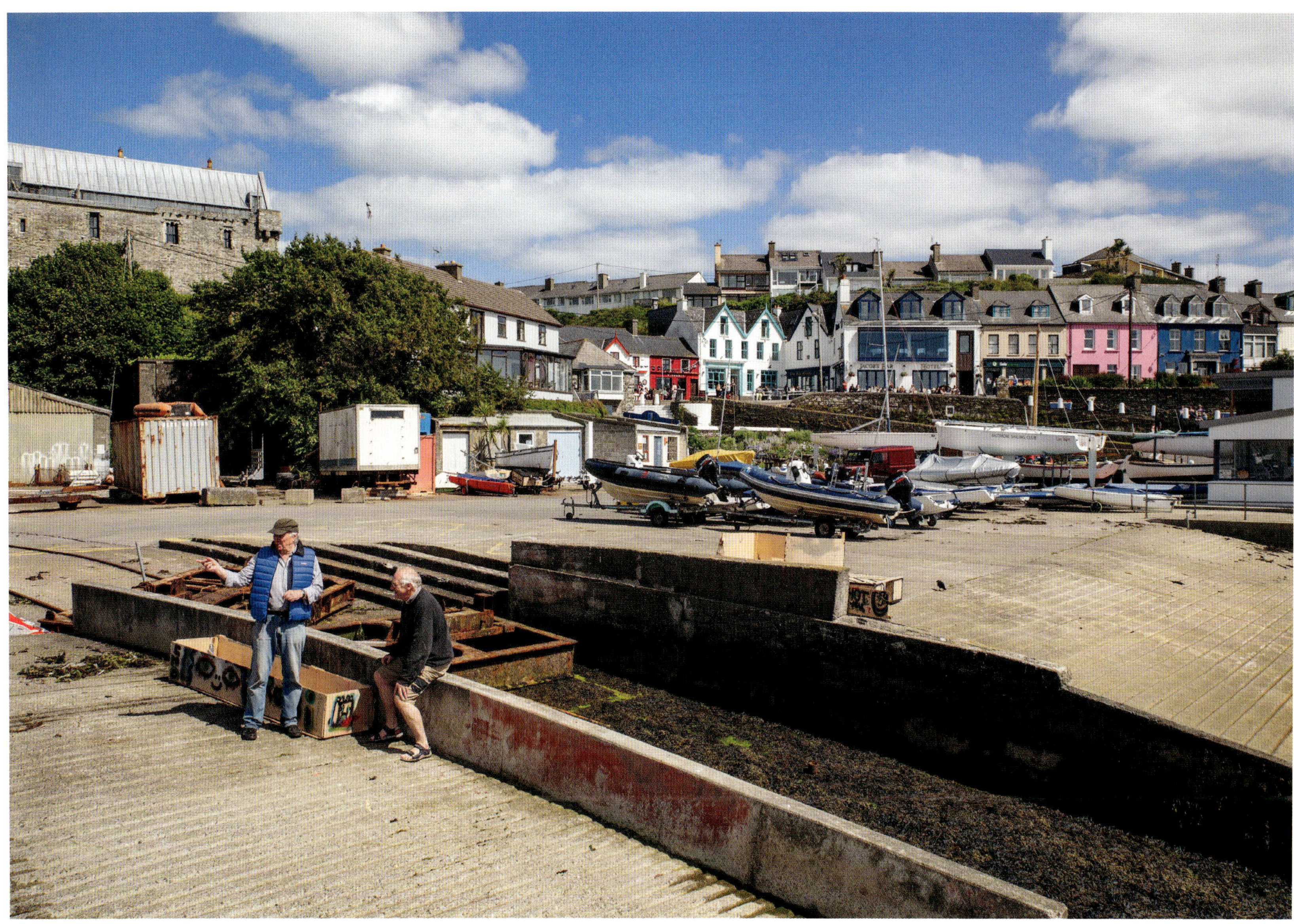

In 1631, Baltimore fell victim to an attack by Barbary pirates from Algiers. More than 100 inhabitants were captured and shipped from the coves of West Cork to the slave markets of North Africa. The Sacking of Baltimore was the worst such attack by Barbary corsairs in the British Isles. Today, the most vivid colour is provided by the charming houses along the bay.

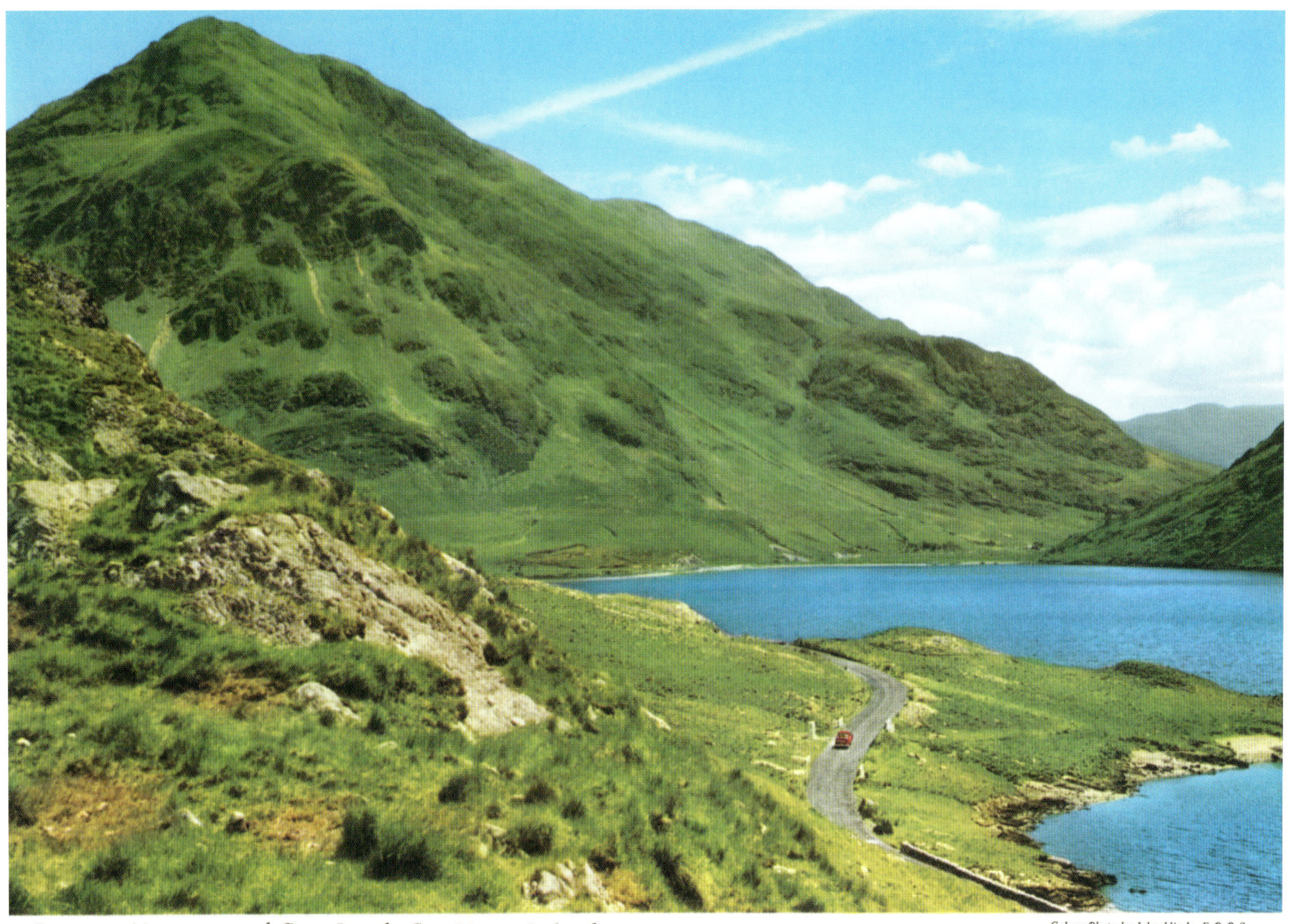

Bengorm Mountain and Doo Lough, Co. Mayo, Ireland.

Colour Photo by John Hinde, F.R.P.S.

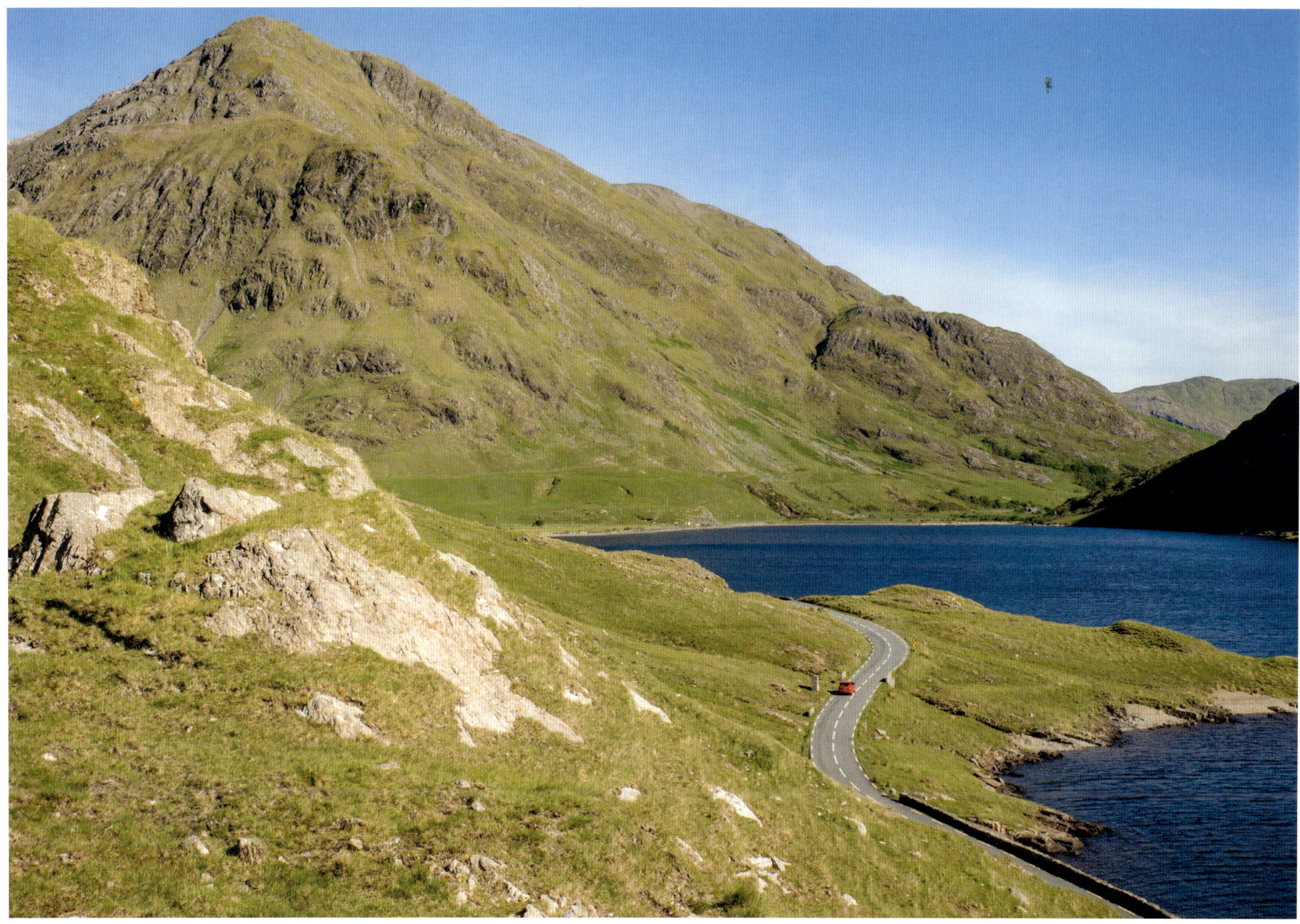

Scrabbling up the steep hillside, my son Jensen and I were out of breath when we finally reached this spot. Surrounded by Mayo's finest Blackface mountain sheep, Jensen asked, 'Do you think that ram might charge at us?' With my tripod securely in place and camera mounted, we waited for almost an hour. It felt longer. Finally, a single red car appeared in the frame.

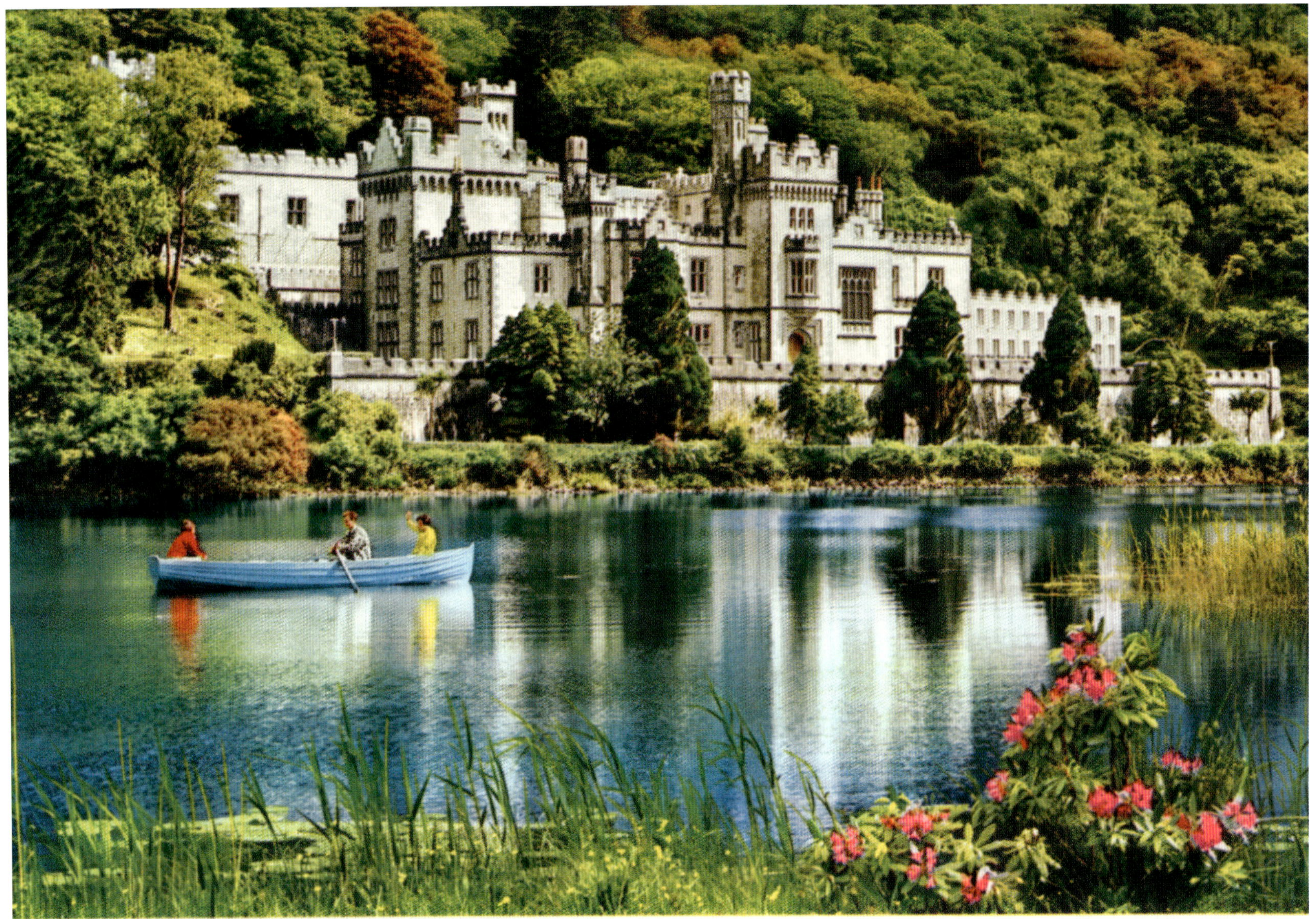

Kylemore Abbey, Connemara, Co. Galway, Ireland.

Photo: E. Nägele, John Hinde Studios.

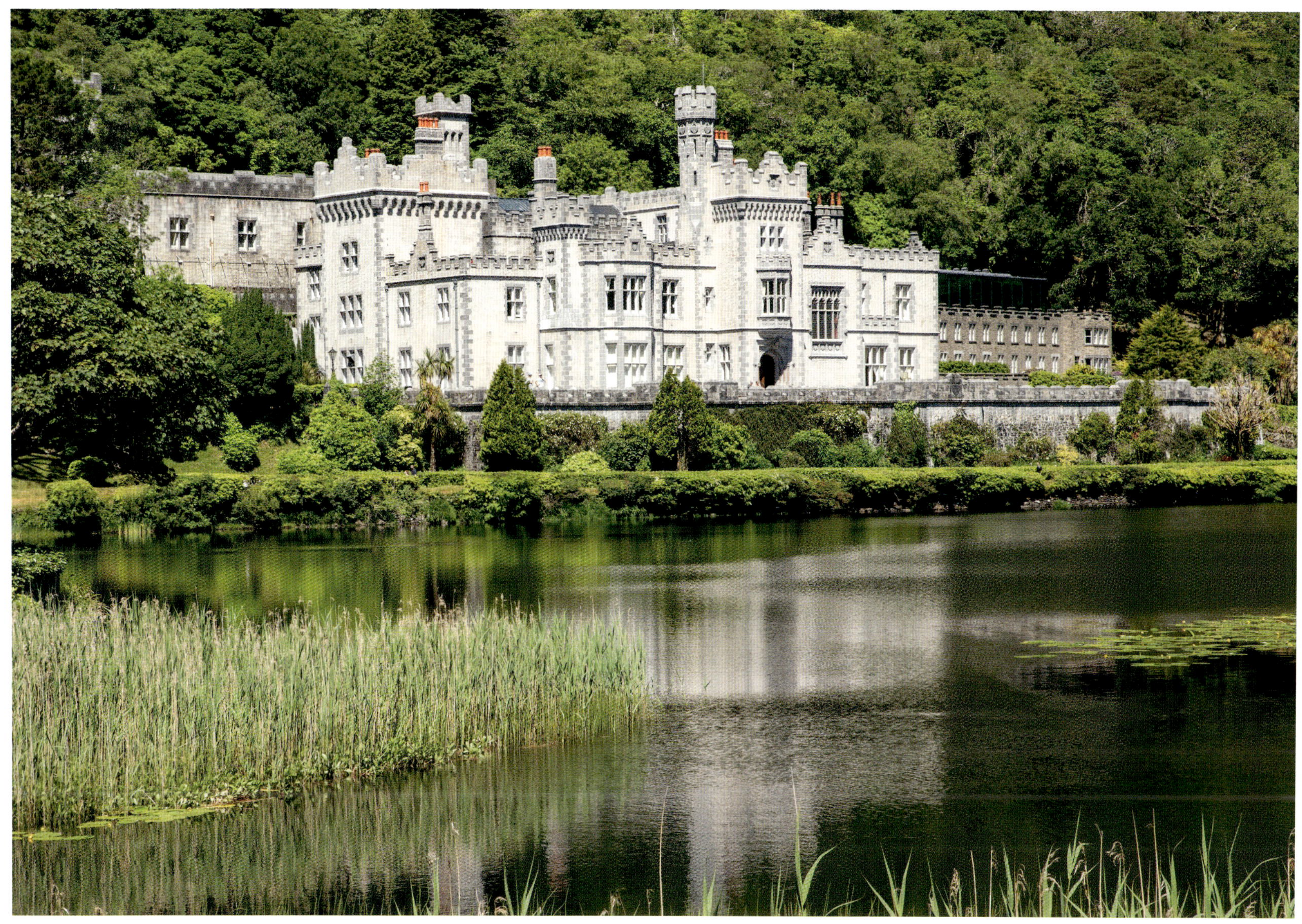

This was a favourite stop for both me and my father. Back in the early 1970s, we were often the only visitors. Nowadays you'll have to fight off coachloads. Despite its venerable appearance, Kylemore was founded in 1920 by Benedictine nuns fleeing wartime Belgium. Still, the scene remains timeless.

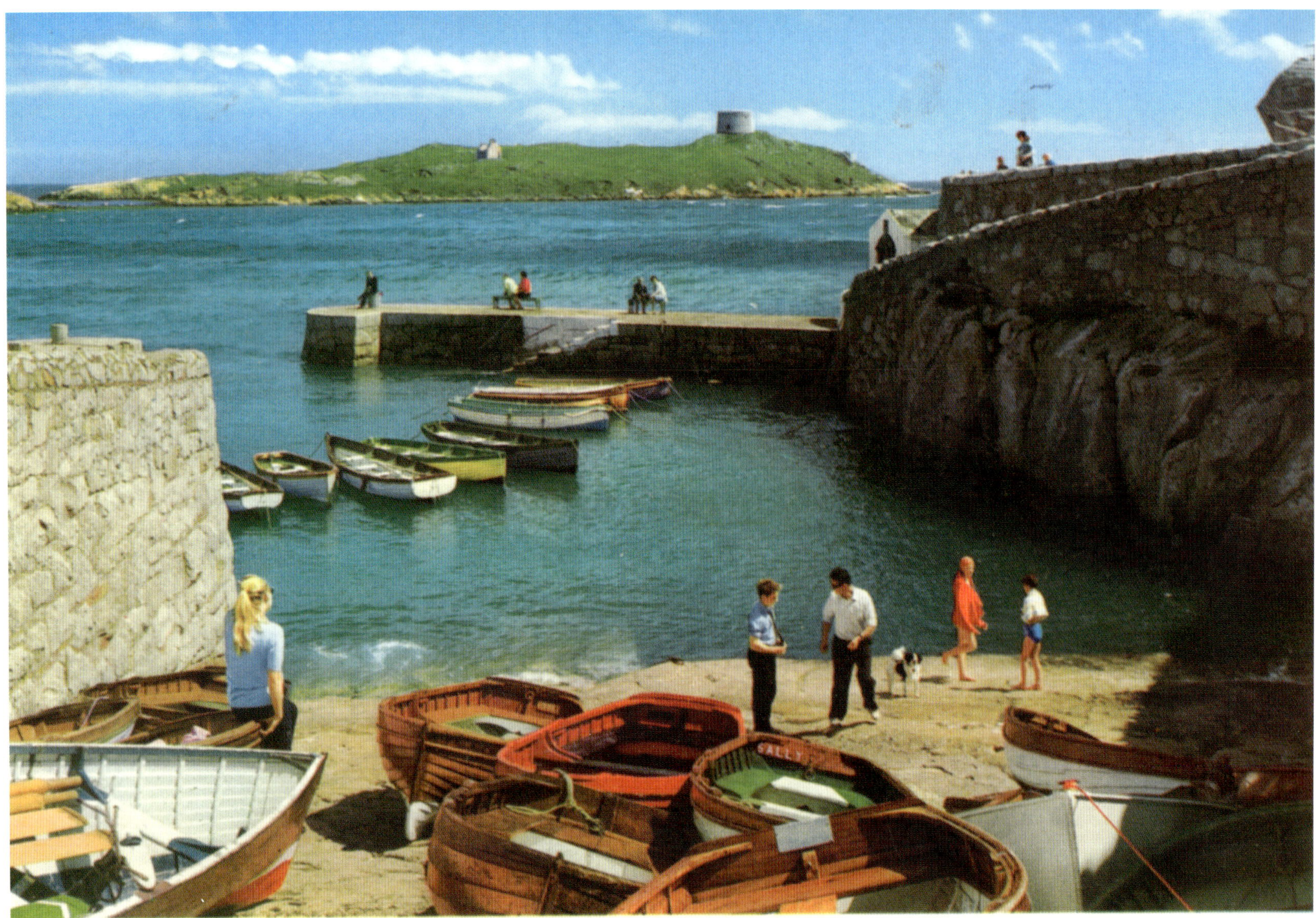

Coliemore Harbour, Dalkey, Co. Dublin, Ireland.

Photo: E. Ludwig, John Hinde Studios.

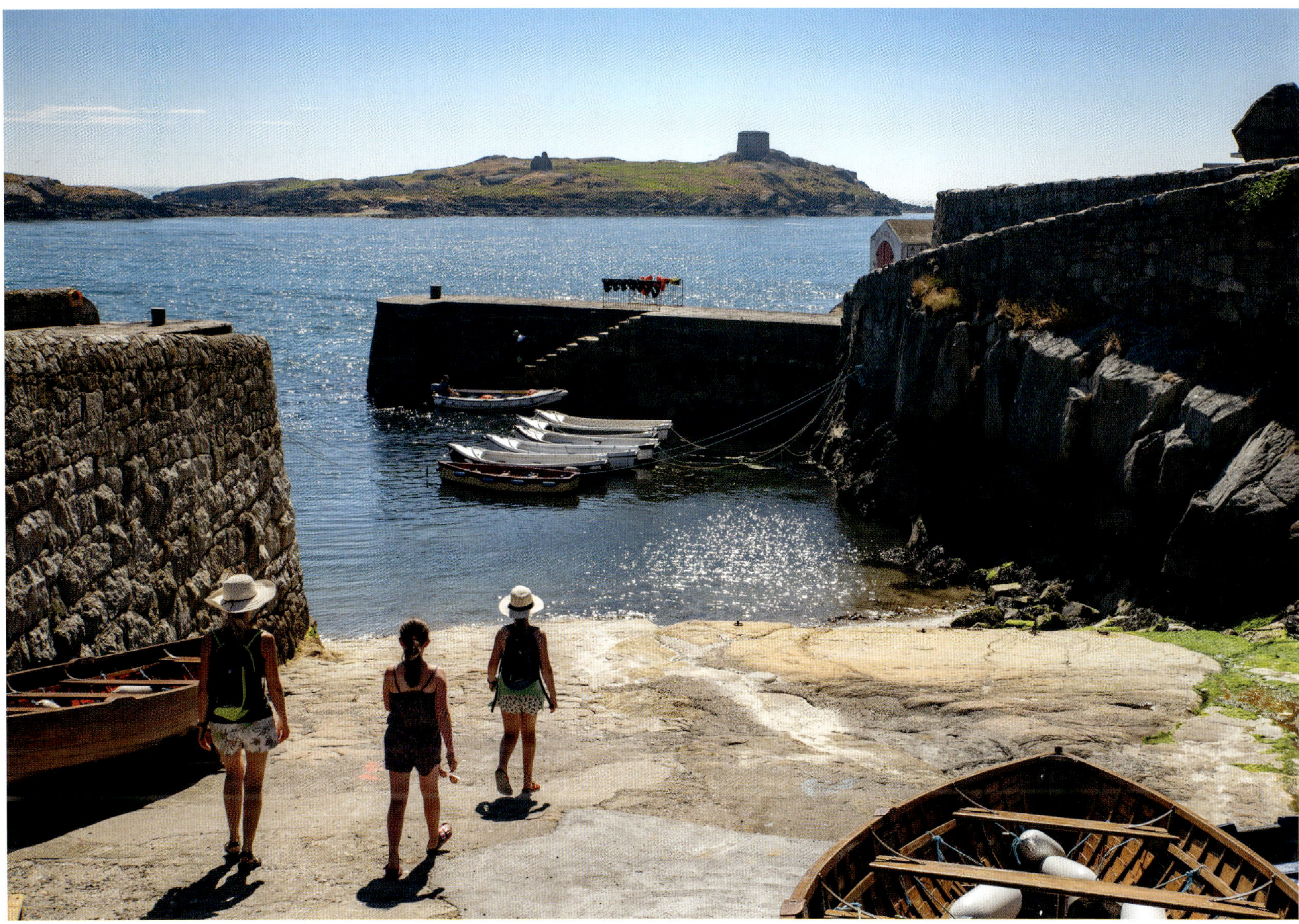

What I love about this pair of images of Coliemore Harbour, with spectacular views of Dalkey Island, is that there is very little difference between them. Yet Dalkey, one of the most affluent suburbs of Dublin, has witnessed significant changes in the roughly 50 years between both shots.

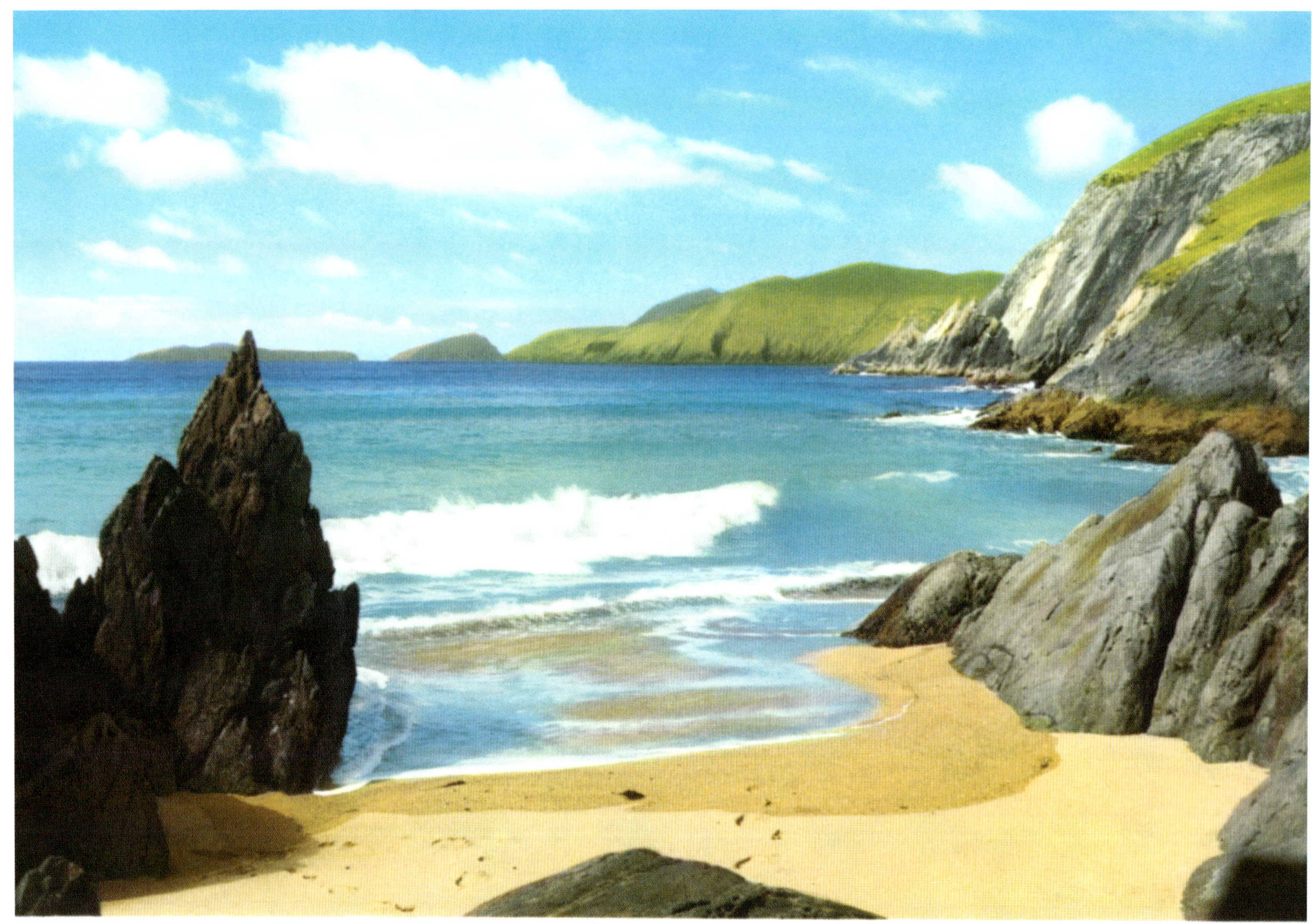

Blasket Islands from Dingle Peninsula, Co. Kerry, Ireland.

Colour Photo by John Hinde, F.R.P.S.

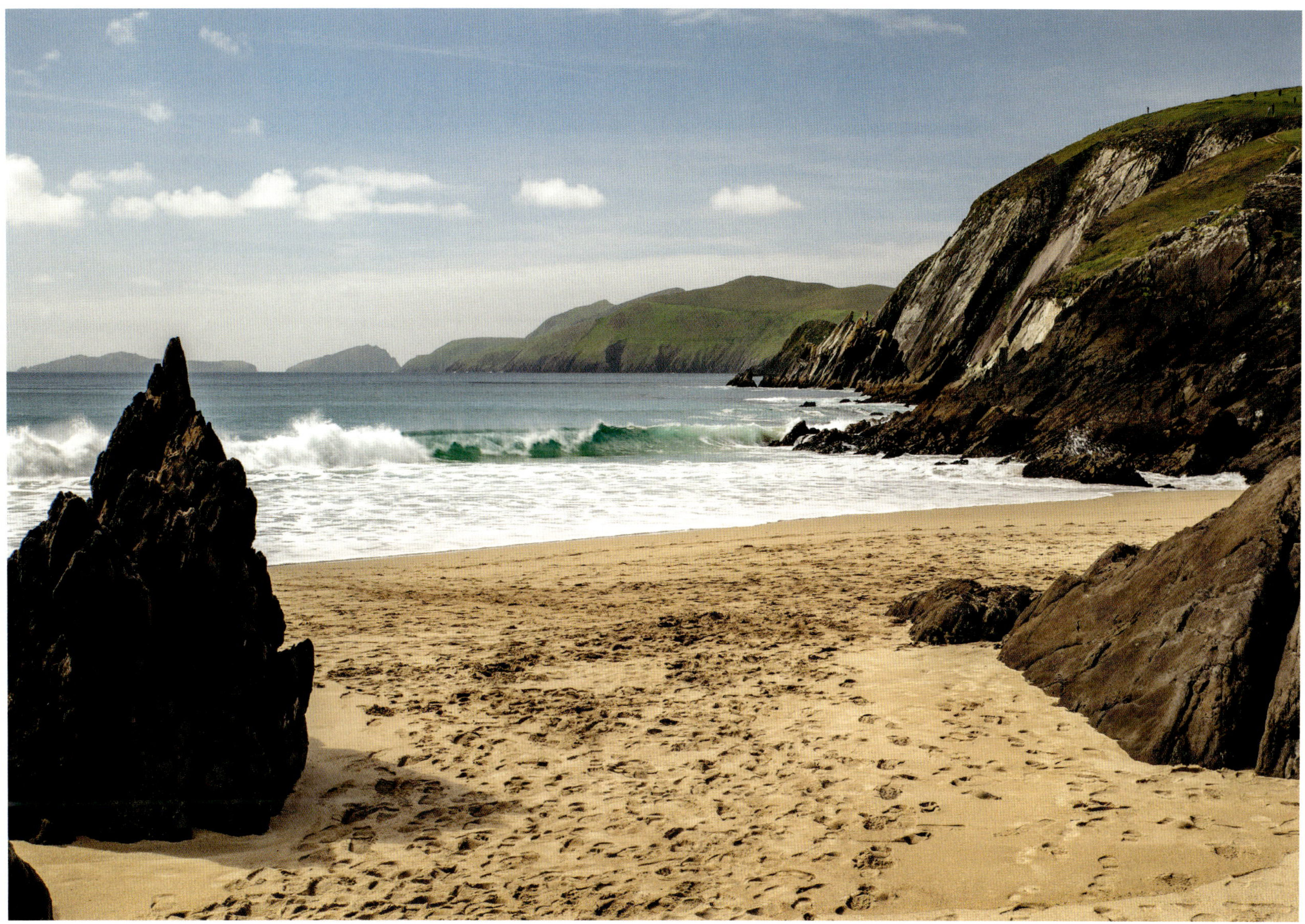

When I arrived, the beach was busy with sunbathers, walkers and several surfers. I had to wait this many footprints to take the shot. In the foreground of the photo, a family from Poland was enjoying a picnic. I set up my tripod and camera and was considering my next move when the father walked over to me and politely said, 'Would you like us to move?'

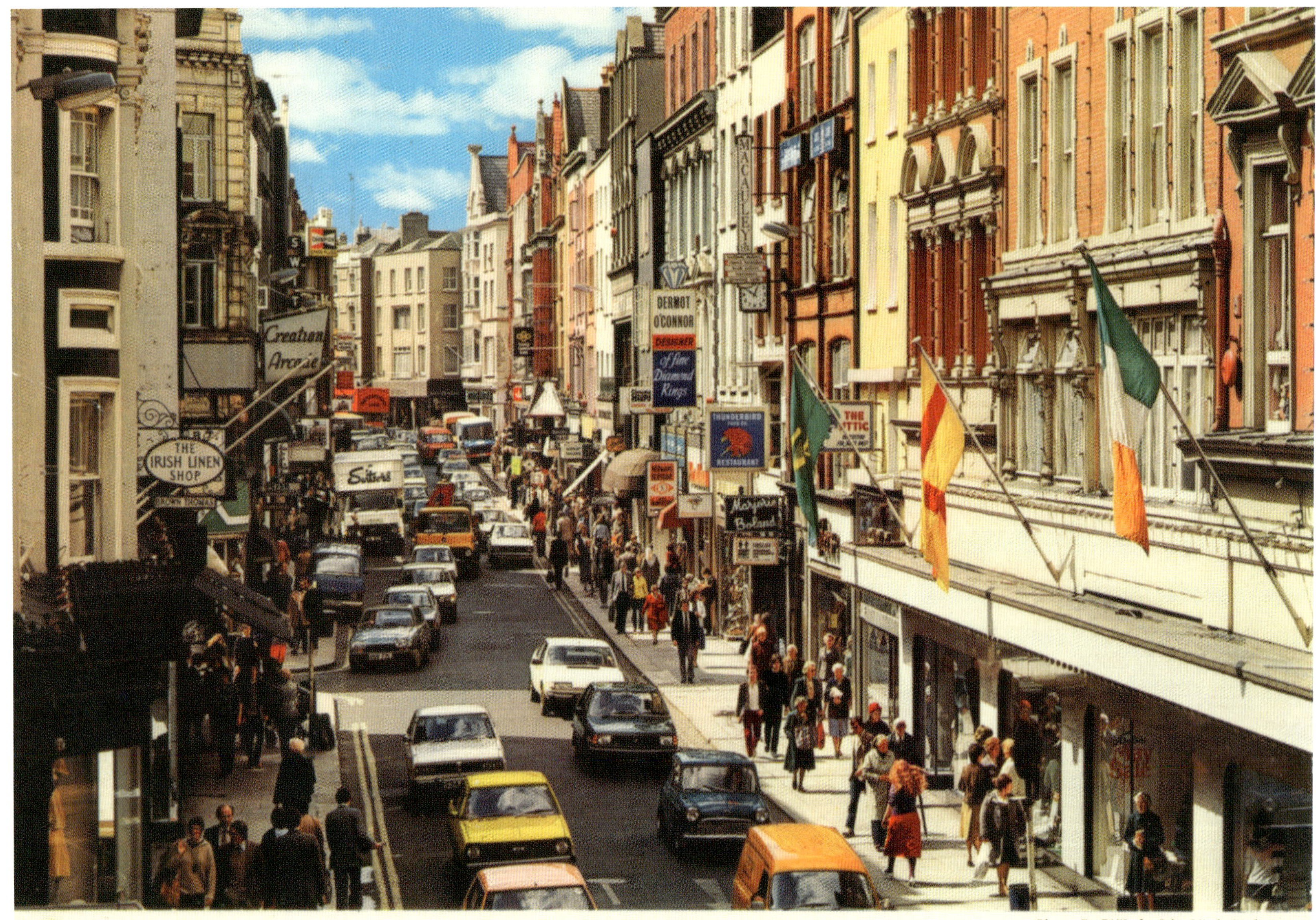

Grafton Street, Dublin, Ireland.

Photo: P. O'Toole, John Hinde Studios.

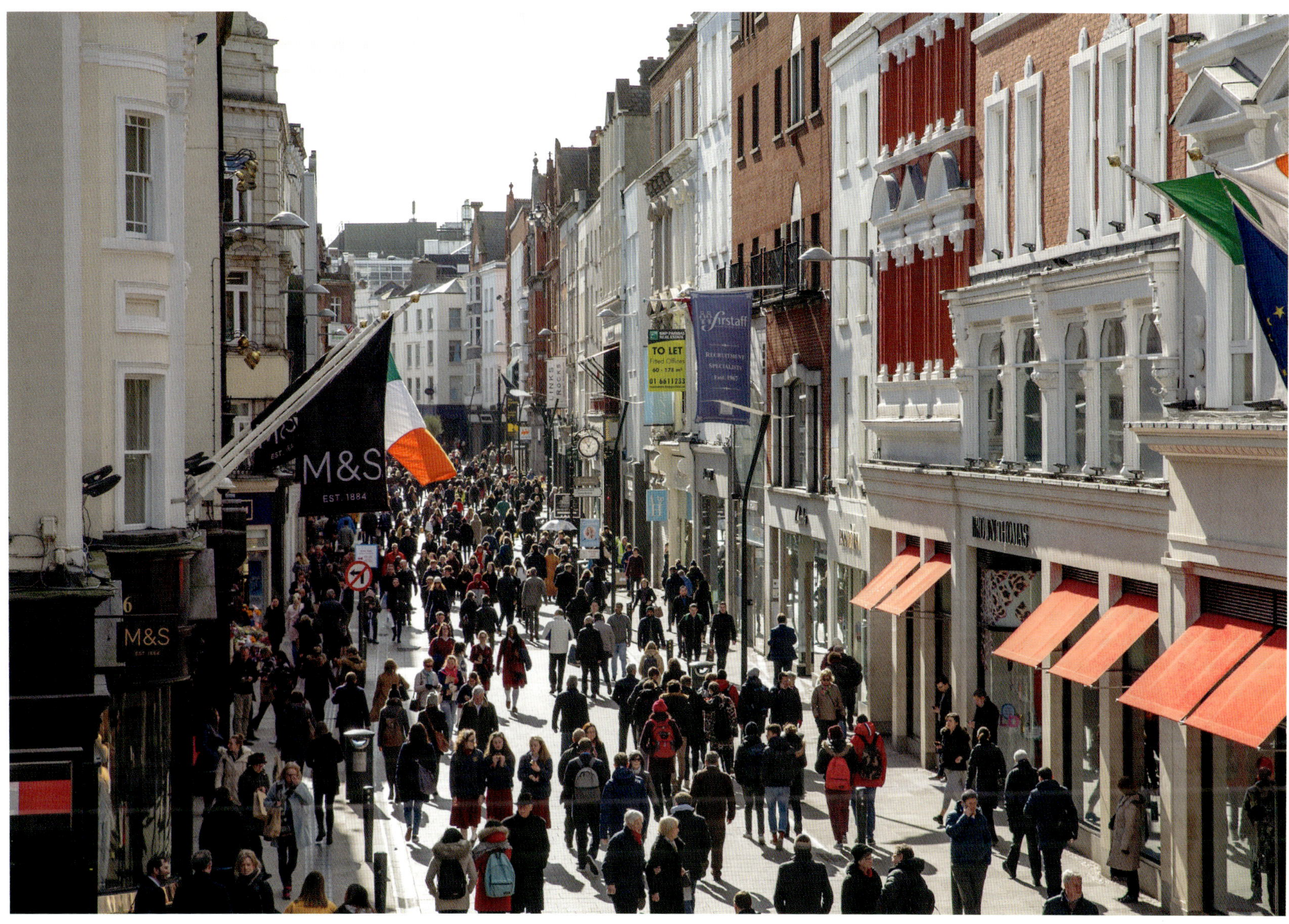

Grafton Street has been home to some of our most beautiful historic buildings, housing iconic Irish businesses such as Brown Thomas, Weir & Sons and Bewley's Oriental café, and launching the careers of some of Ireland's most successful musicians who busked along the footpath. It was formally pedestrianised in 1982.

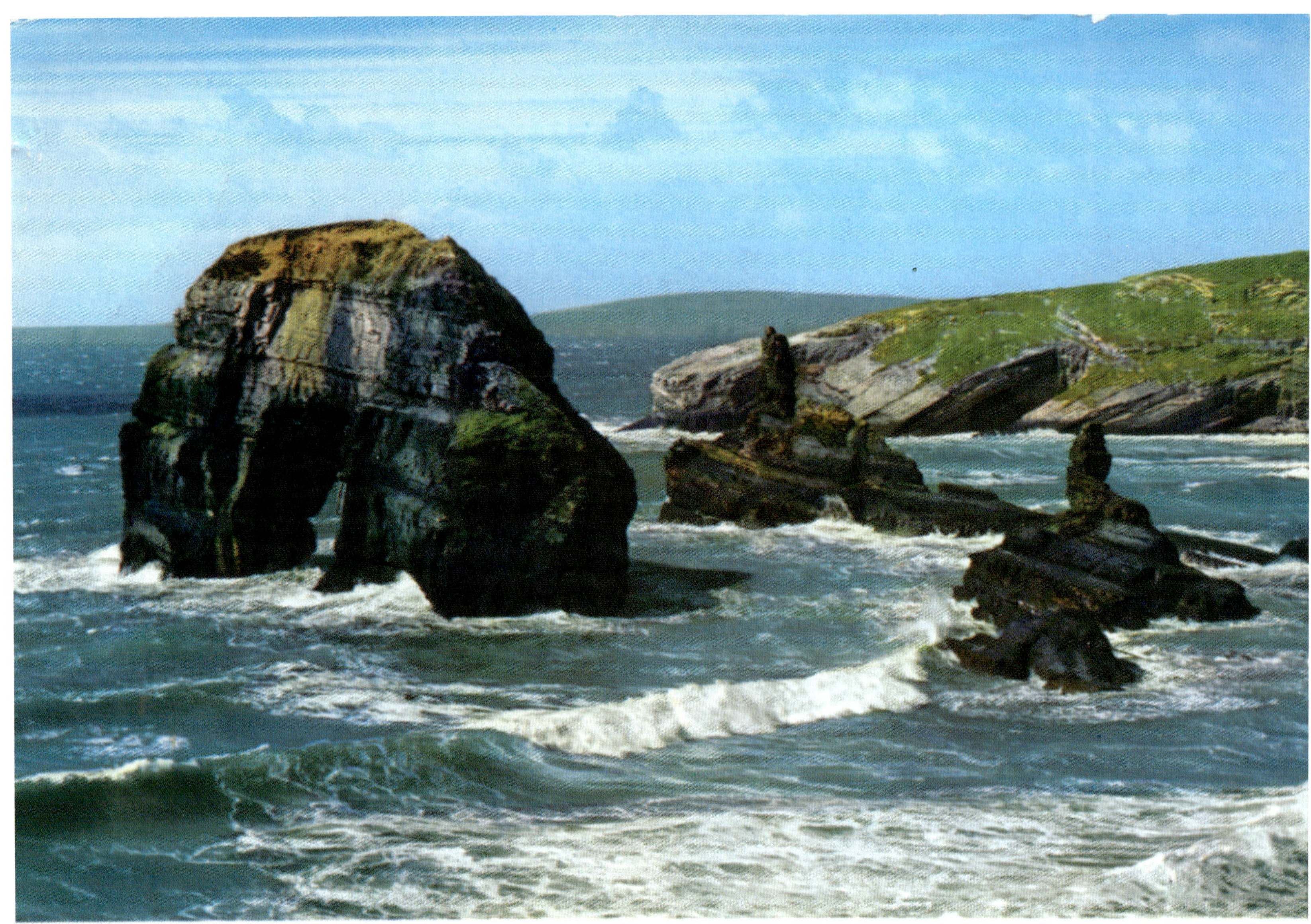

Virgin Rock, Ballybunion, Co. Kerry, Ireland.

Colour Photo by John Hinde, F.R.P.S.

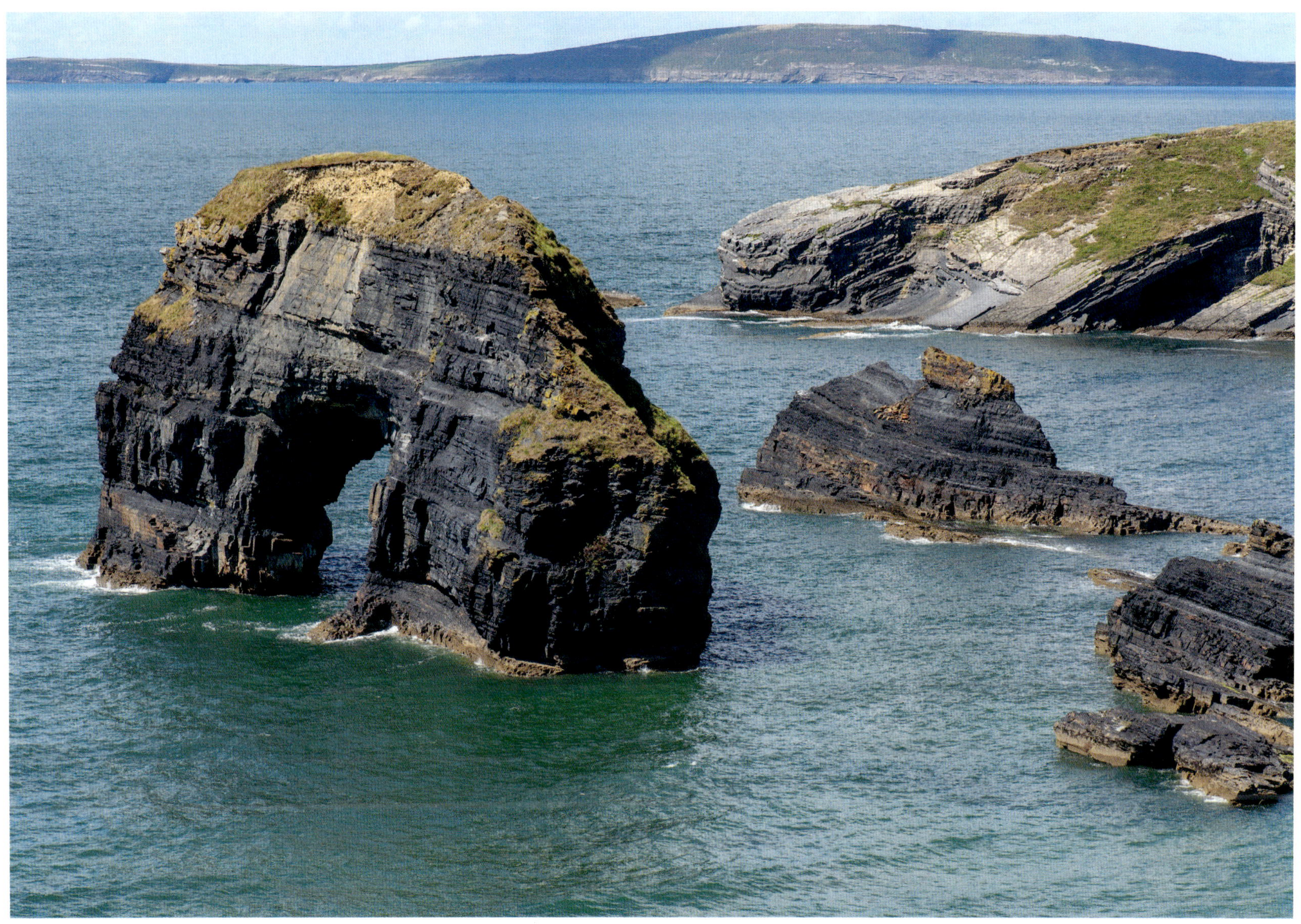

For breathtaking views, set off on the cliff walk from Ballybunion to the Virgin Rock at Nun's Beach, overlooked by the ruins of a convent. Invoke heavenly assistance, then use the conveniently placed rope handrail to get down the steep slope to this beautiful sandy beach.

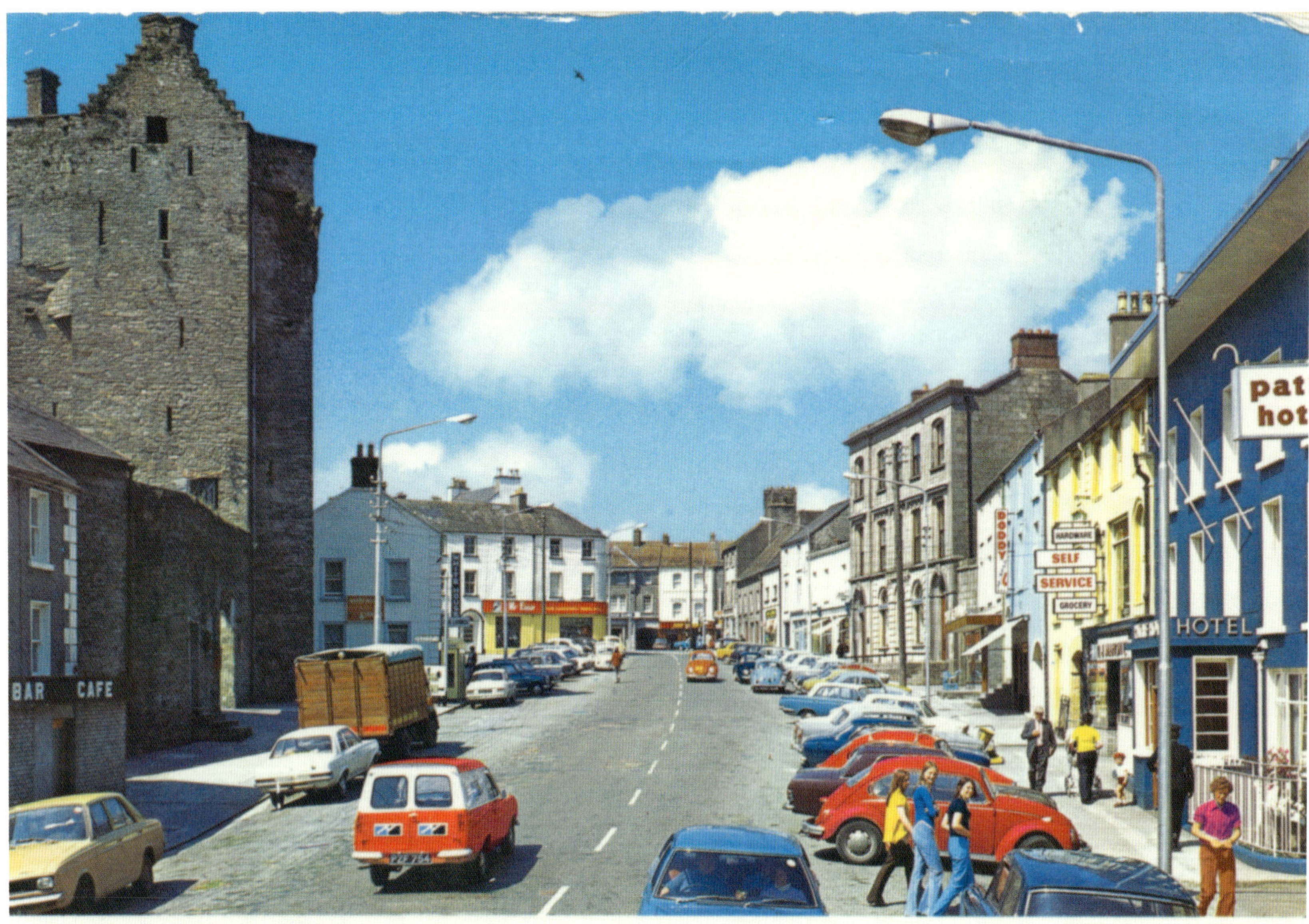

Roscrea, Co. Tipperary, Ireland.

Photo: D. Noble, John Hinde Studios.

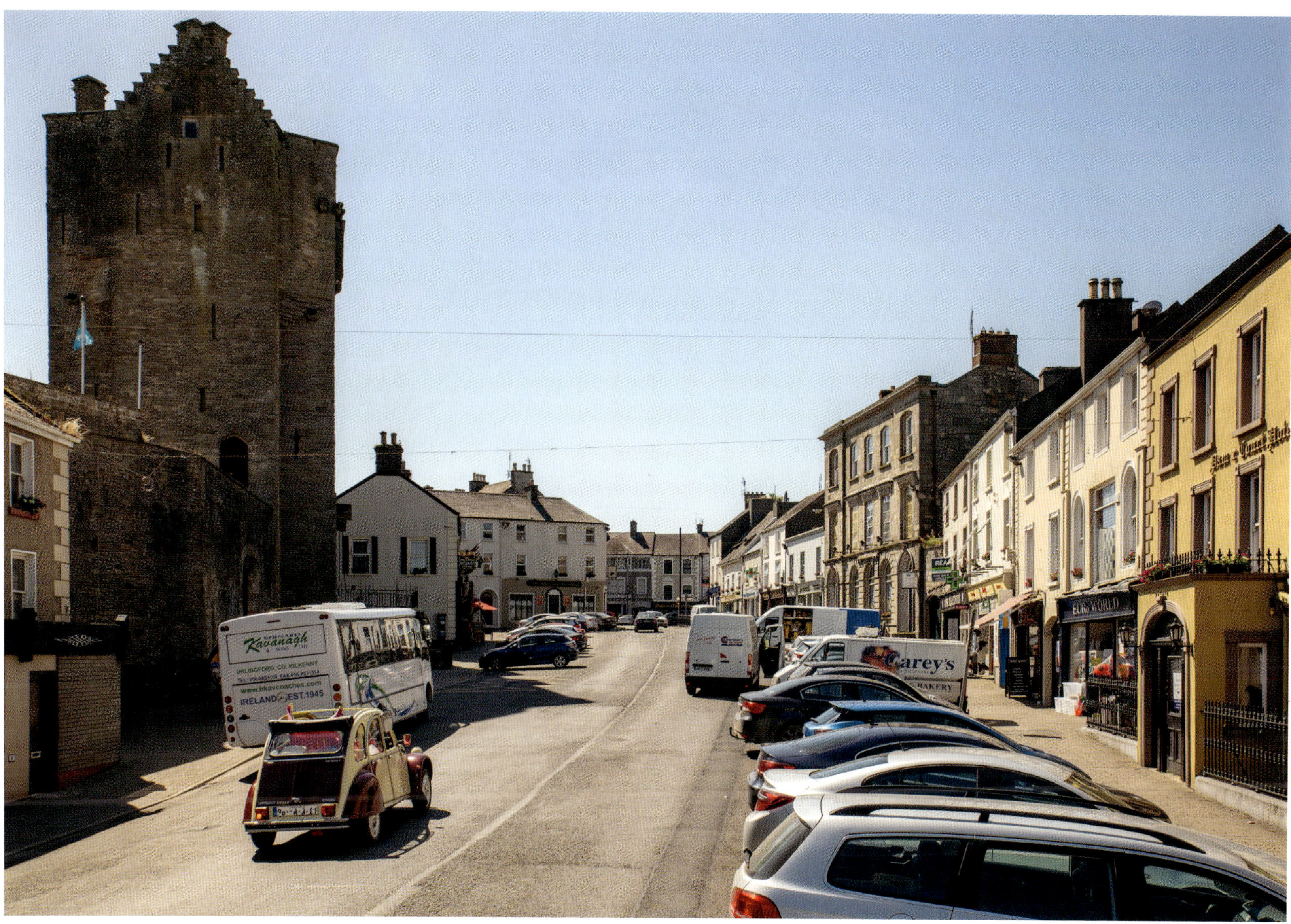

Roscrea, Co. Tipperary, is one of the oldest and most historic towns in Ireland. The 13th-century castle dominates the town's skyline. John Hinde's glorious technicolour version is somewhat tempered in today's remake, but Roscrea remains a handsome, solid market town.

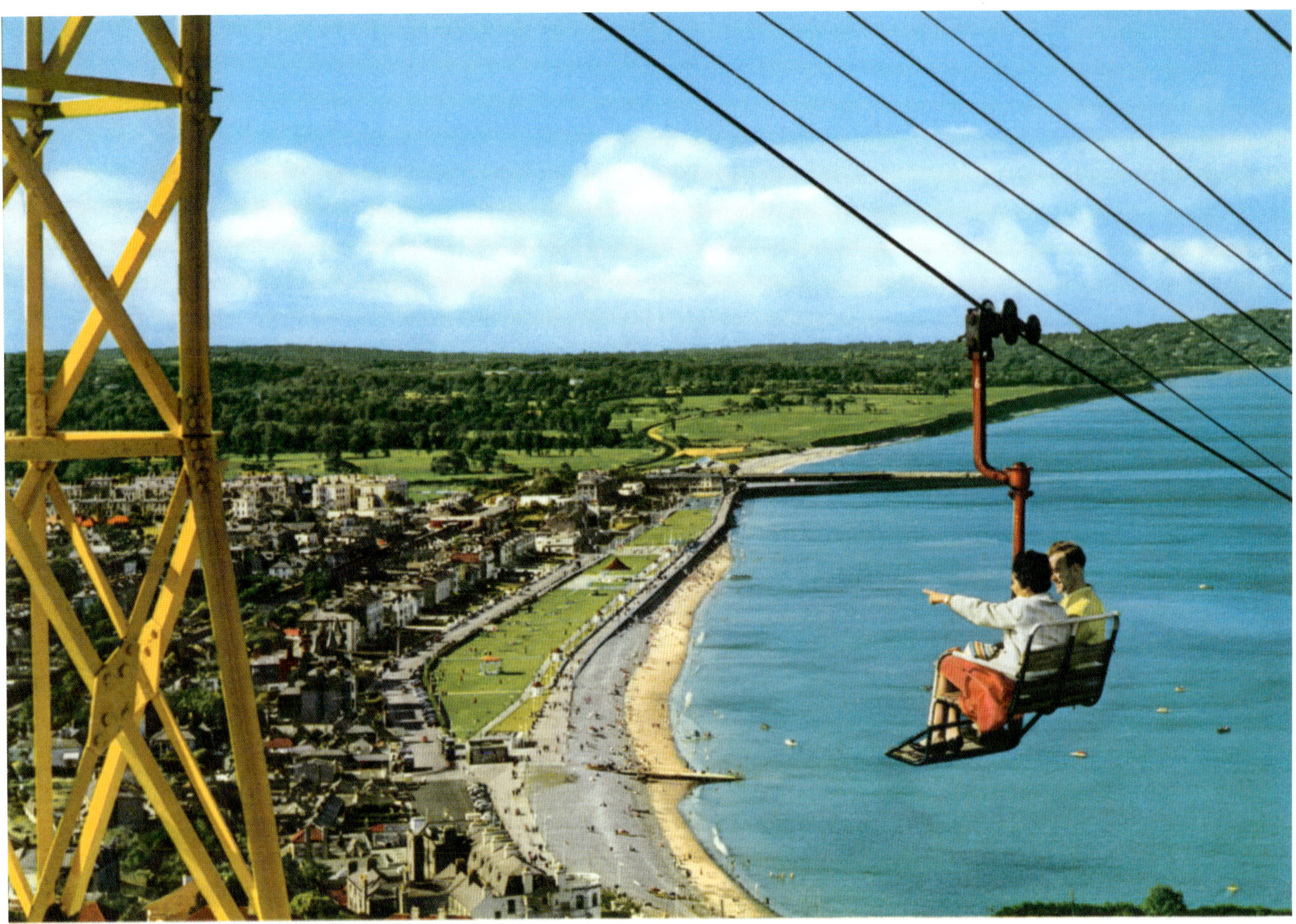

Aerial Chair Lift to Eagle's Nest, Bray, Co. Wicklow, Ireland.

Colour Photo by John Hinde, F.R.P.S.

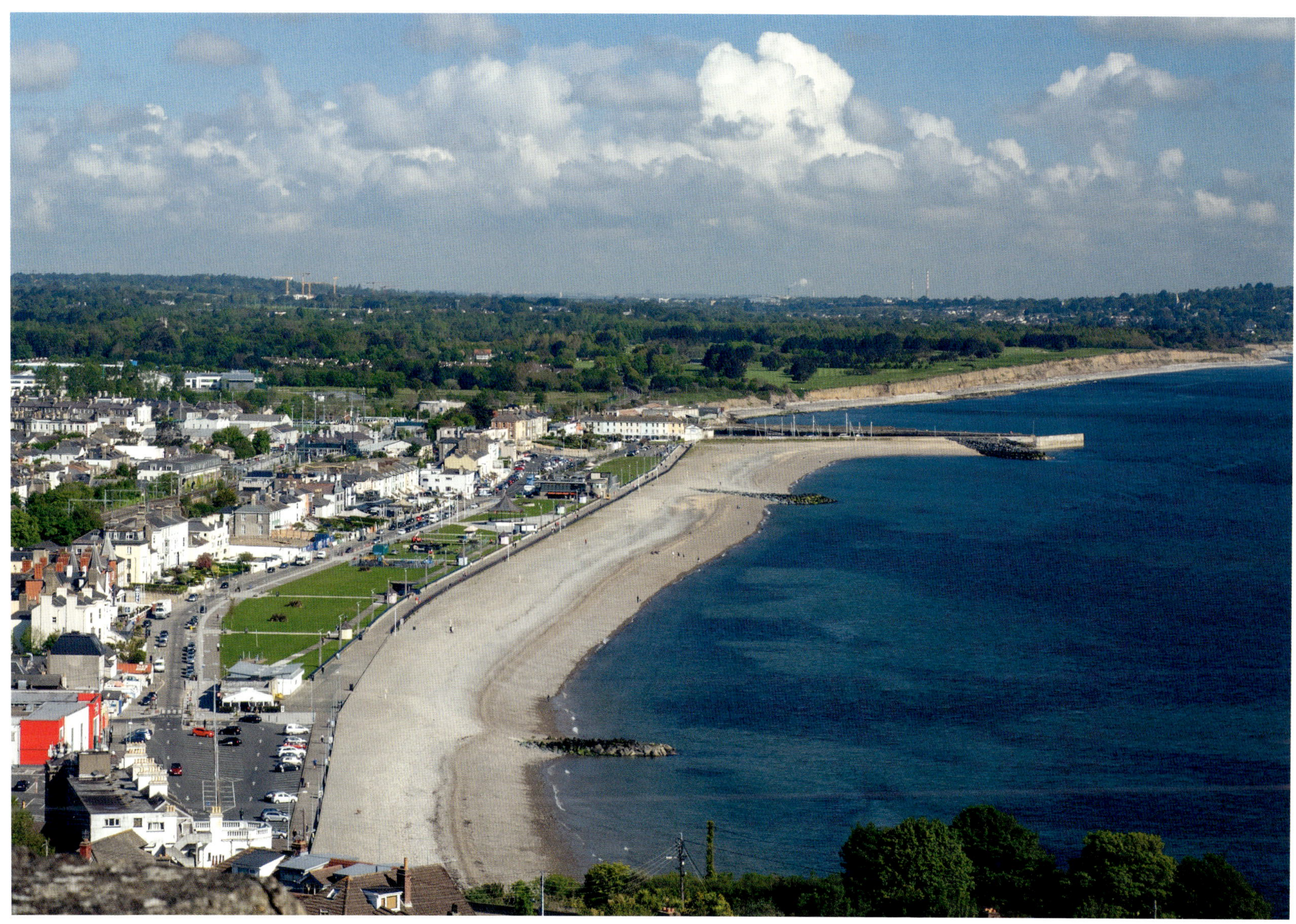

Opened in 1952, the aerial cableway or chairlift took visitors from the foot of Bray Head up to the Eagle's Nest restaurant and ballroom, high on the northern side. It closed in the early 1970s. Bray old-timers still reminisce about their adventures, and misadventures, on the cableway, floating above the sapphire ocean in an electric-blue sky.

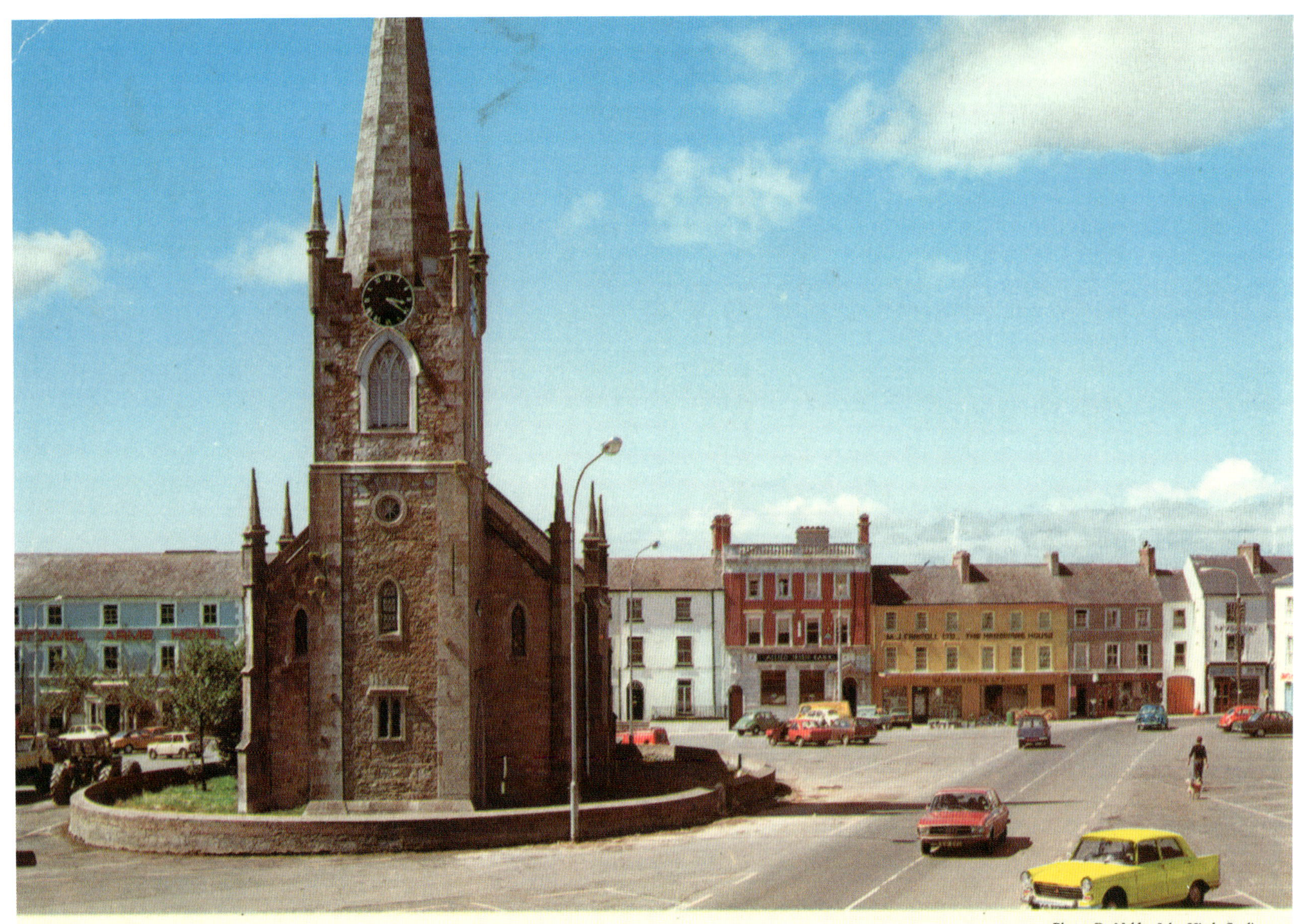
Listowel, Co. Kerry, Ireland.
Photo: D. Noble, John Hinde Studios.

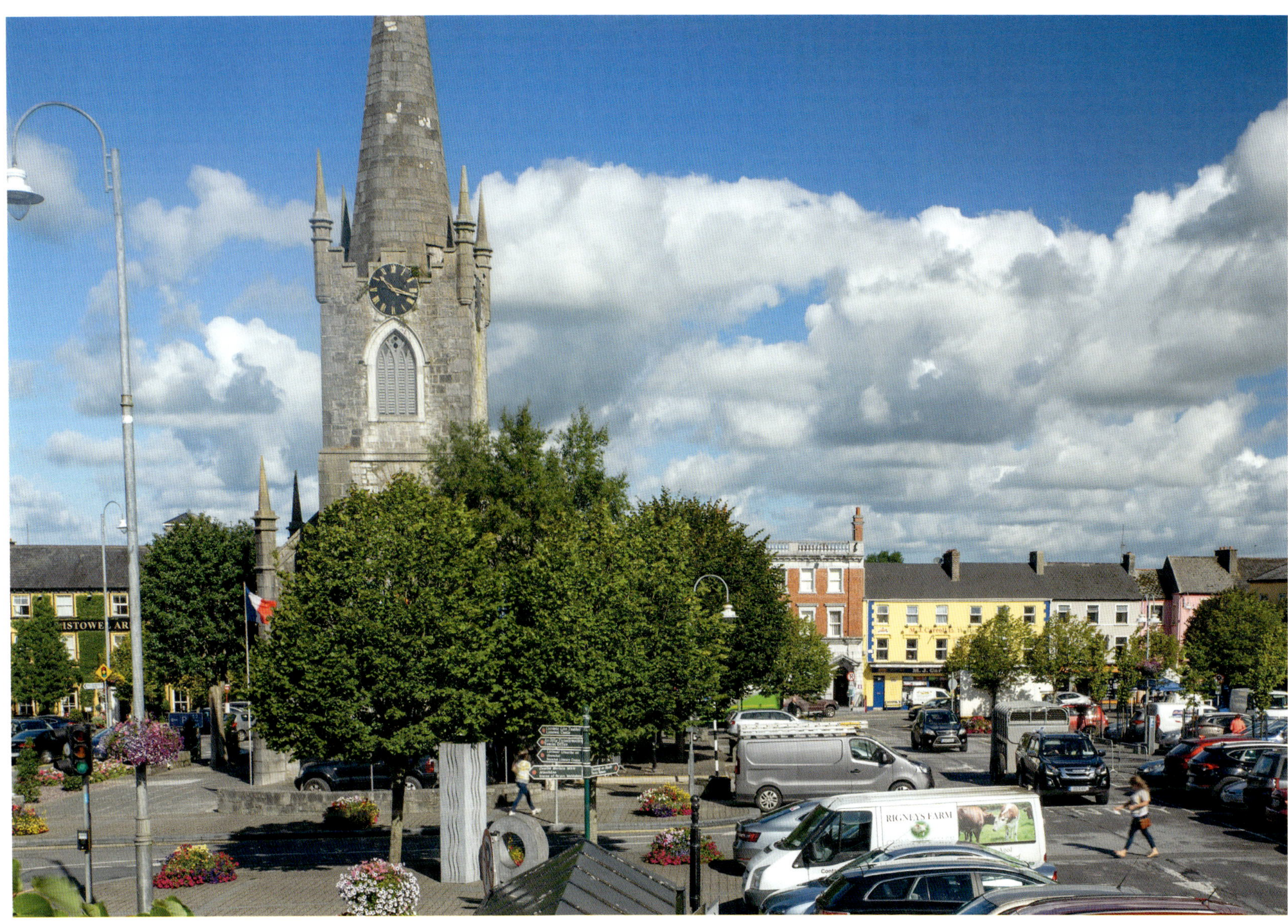

Under romantic skies in the new photograph, Listowel remains poised despite untrammelled tree growth, having been named Ireland's tidiest town of 2018. This former Church of Ireland building is now the St John's Theatre and Arts Centre, a premier visual and performing arts venue.

30

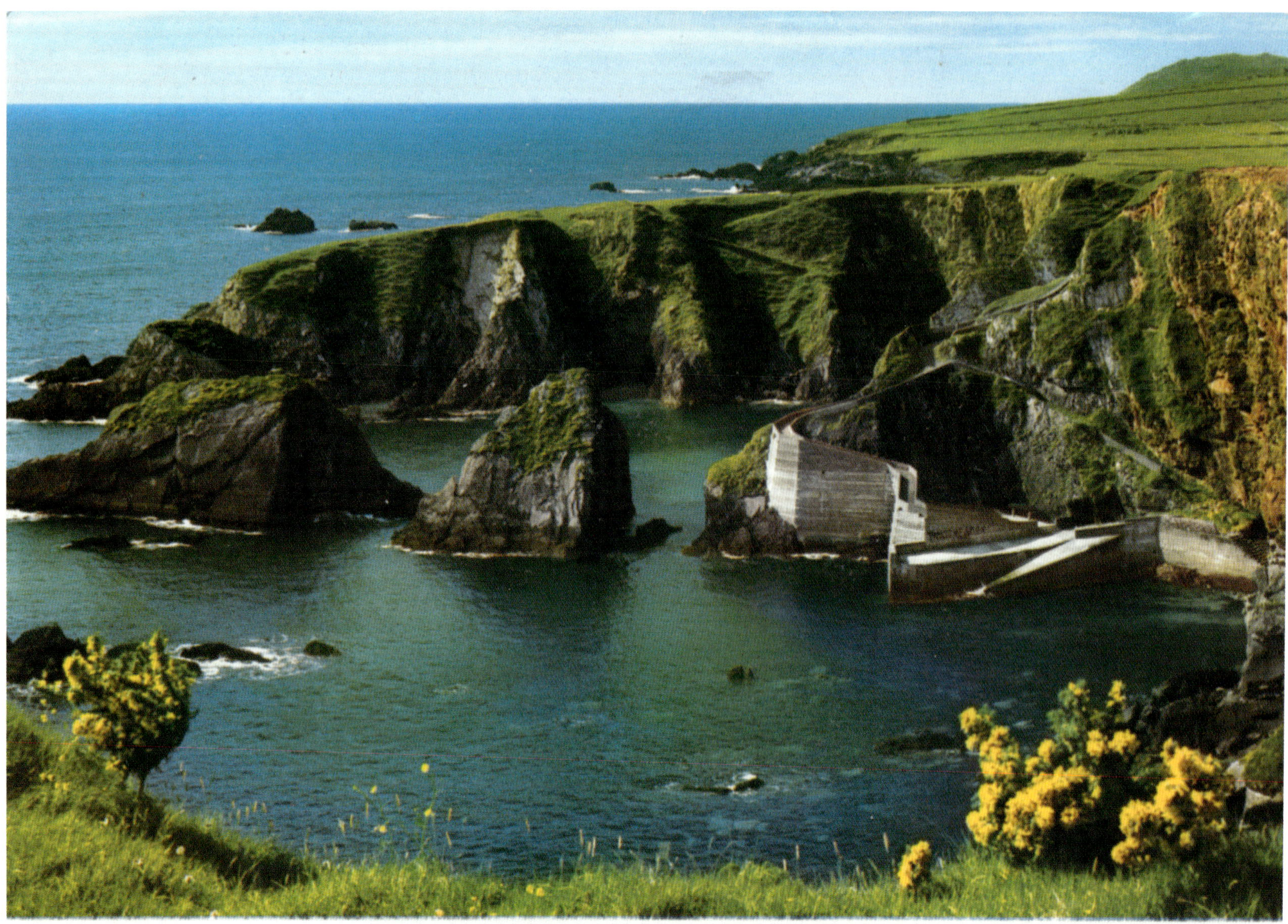

Dunquin Harbour, Dingle Peninsula, Co. Kerry, Ireland

Photo: E. Ludwig, John Hinde Studios.

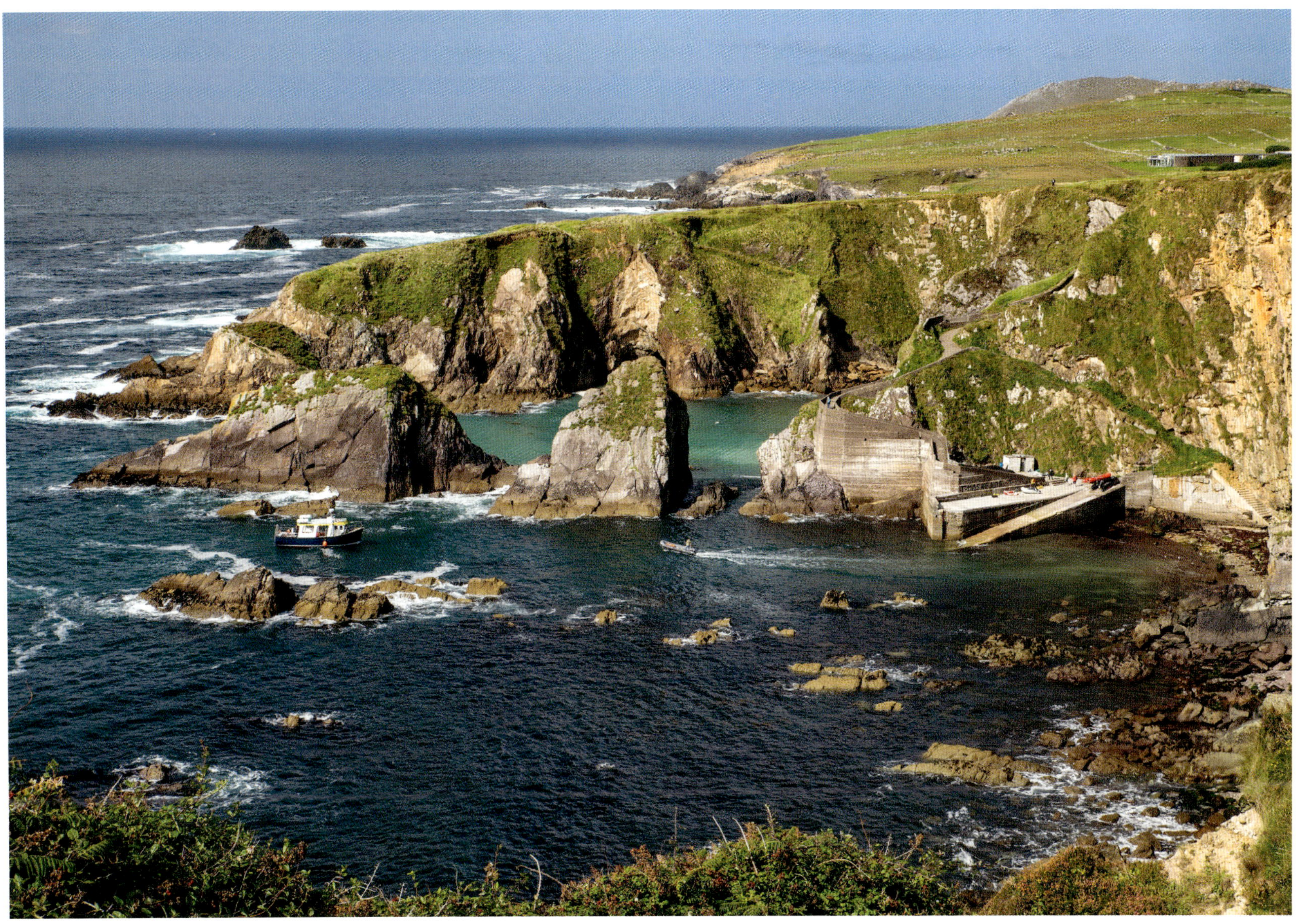

This pathway leads to the harbour and ferry services, used to transport people and sheep to the Blasket islands when they were inhabited. The most westerly lands in Europe, known simply as the Blaskets, the islands have been uninhabited since 1953. Today, visitors can travel by ferry to experience this remote and wildly beautiful place.

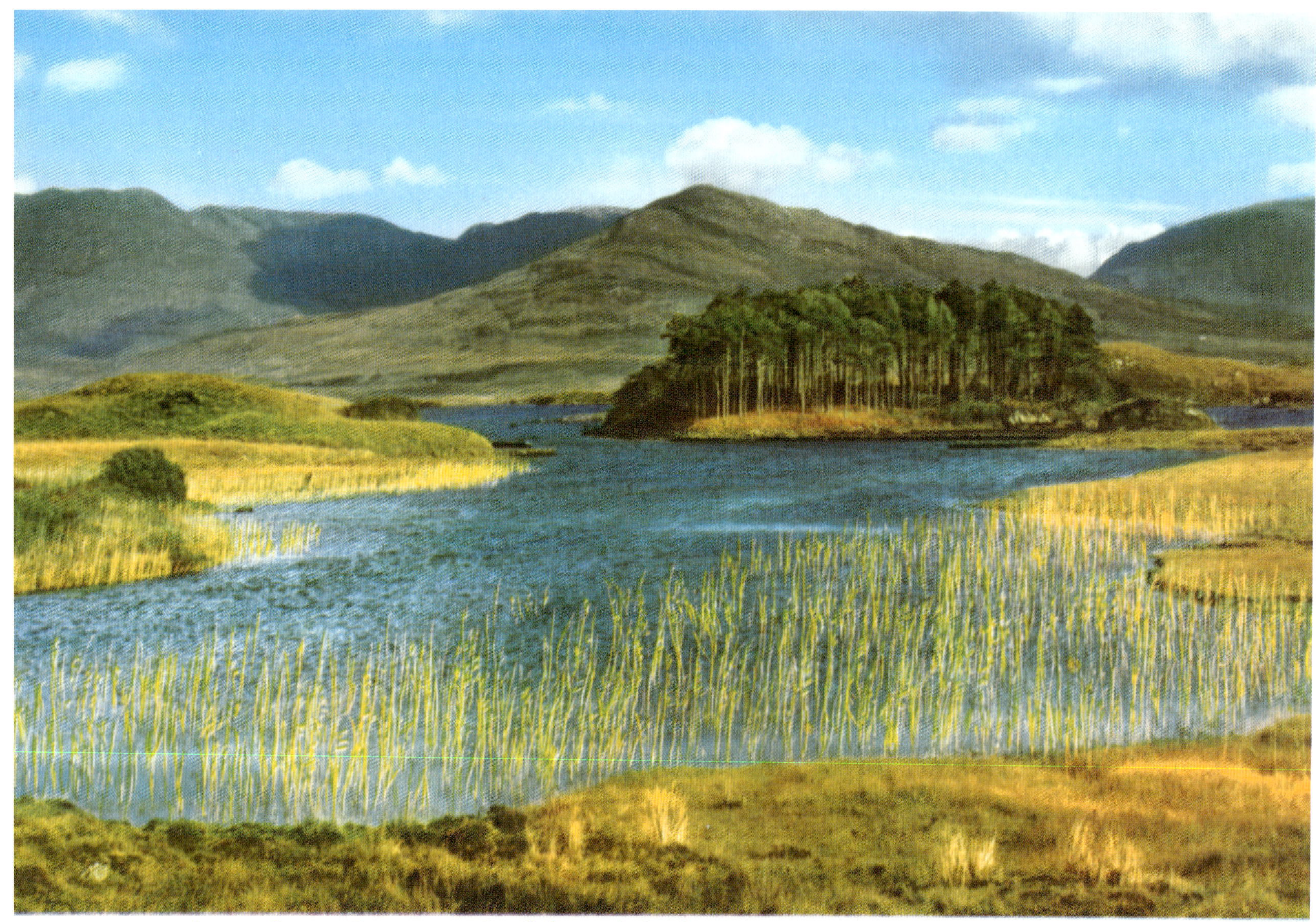

Derryclare Lough near Recess, Connemara, Co. Galway, Ireland. *Colour Photo by John Hinde, F.R.P.S.*

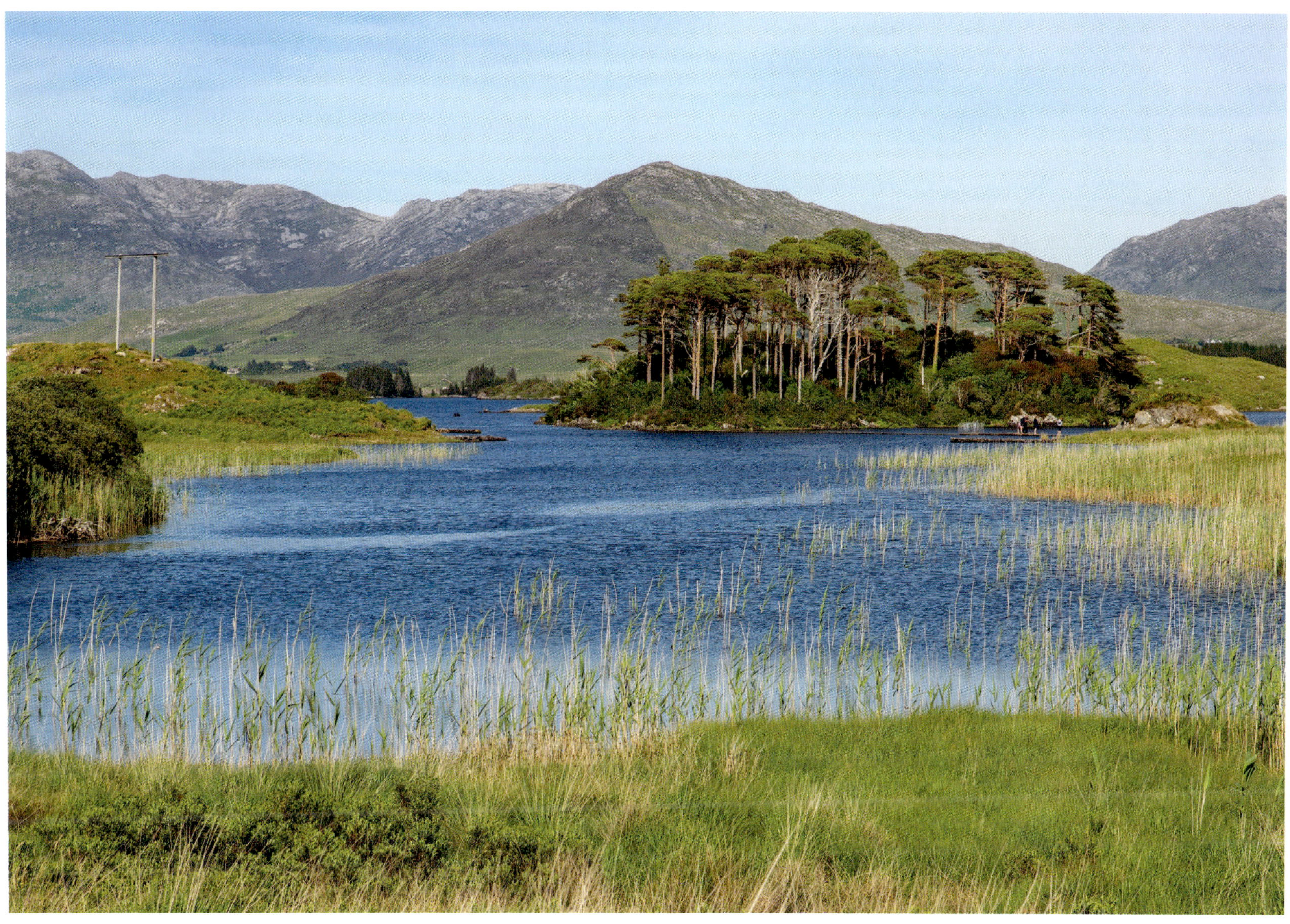

The magnificent stand of Scots pines on Pine Island, Derryclare Lough, makes this one of the many popular tourist stops in the Connemara region. I took this shot on the longest day of the year and one of the warmest of 2018. I had the place mostly to myself – just me and 100,000 midges.

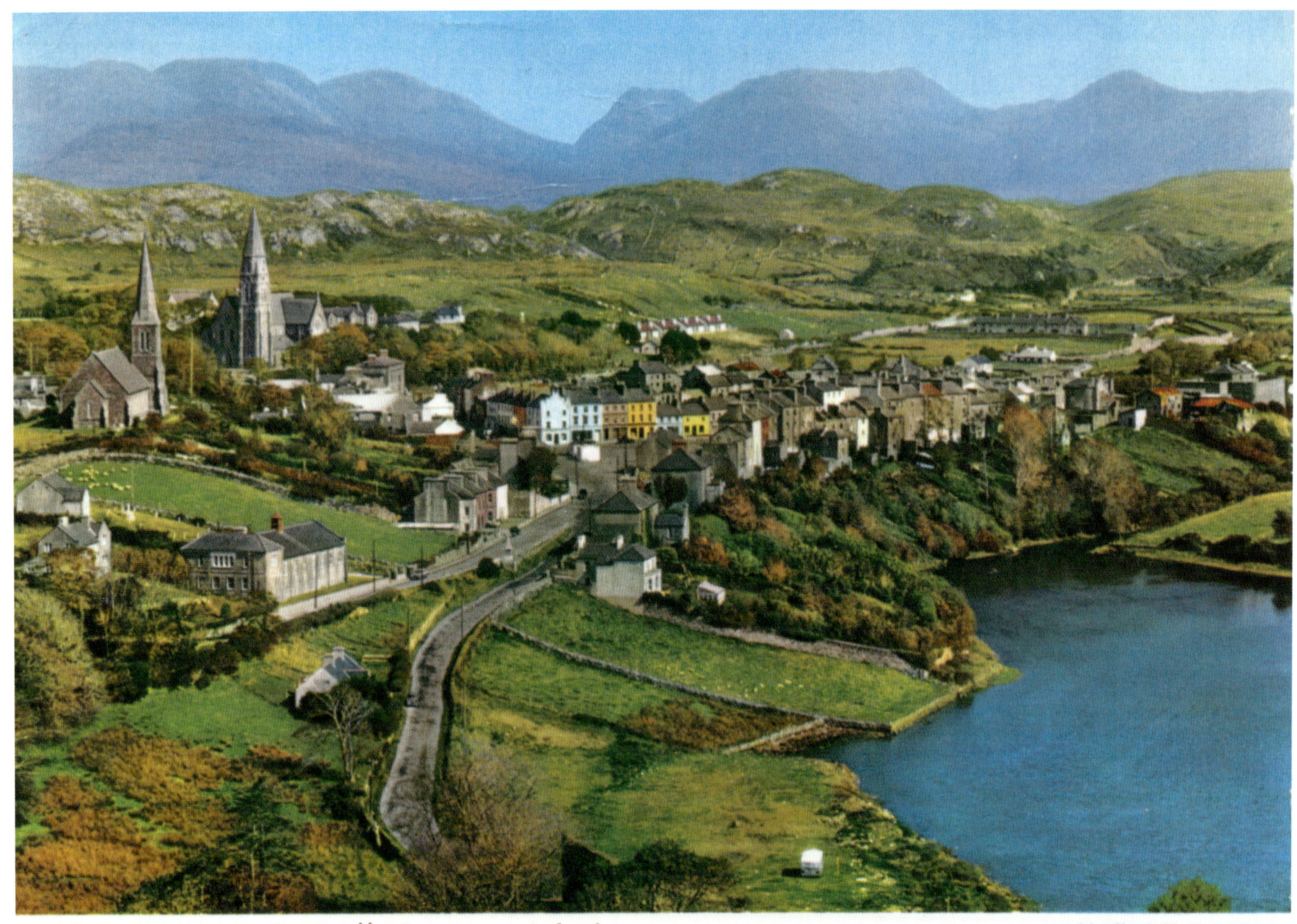

Clifden, and the "Twelve Pins", Connemara, Ireland.

Colour Photo by John Hinde, F.R.P.S.

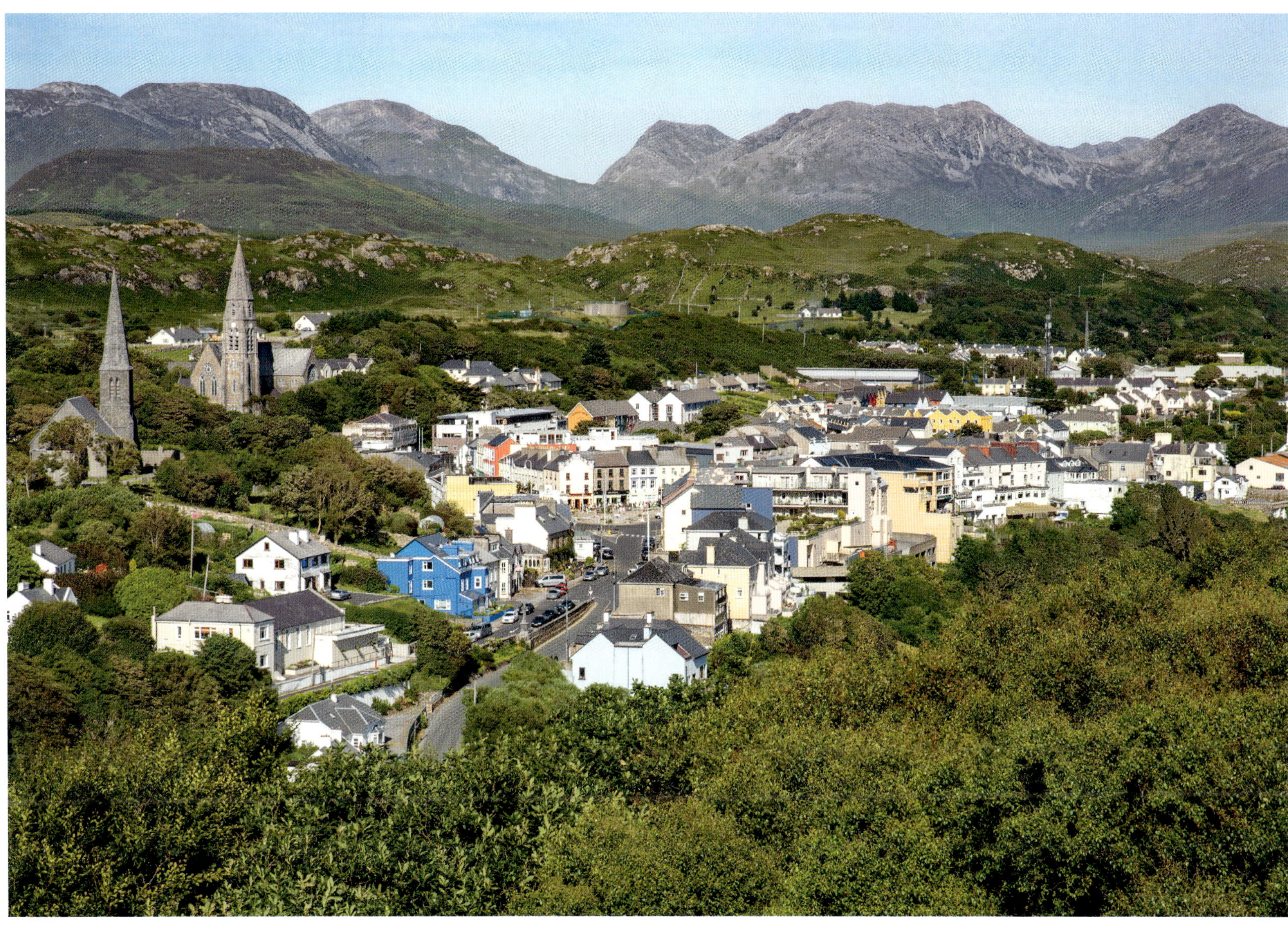

Nestled between the sparkling quartzite peaks of the Twelve Bens mountain range and the Atlantic is Clifden. These shots were both taken on Monument Hill. The John D'Arcy Monument, which crowns the hill, is a tribute to the town's founder.

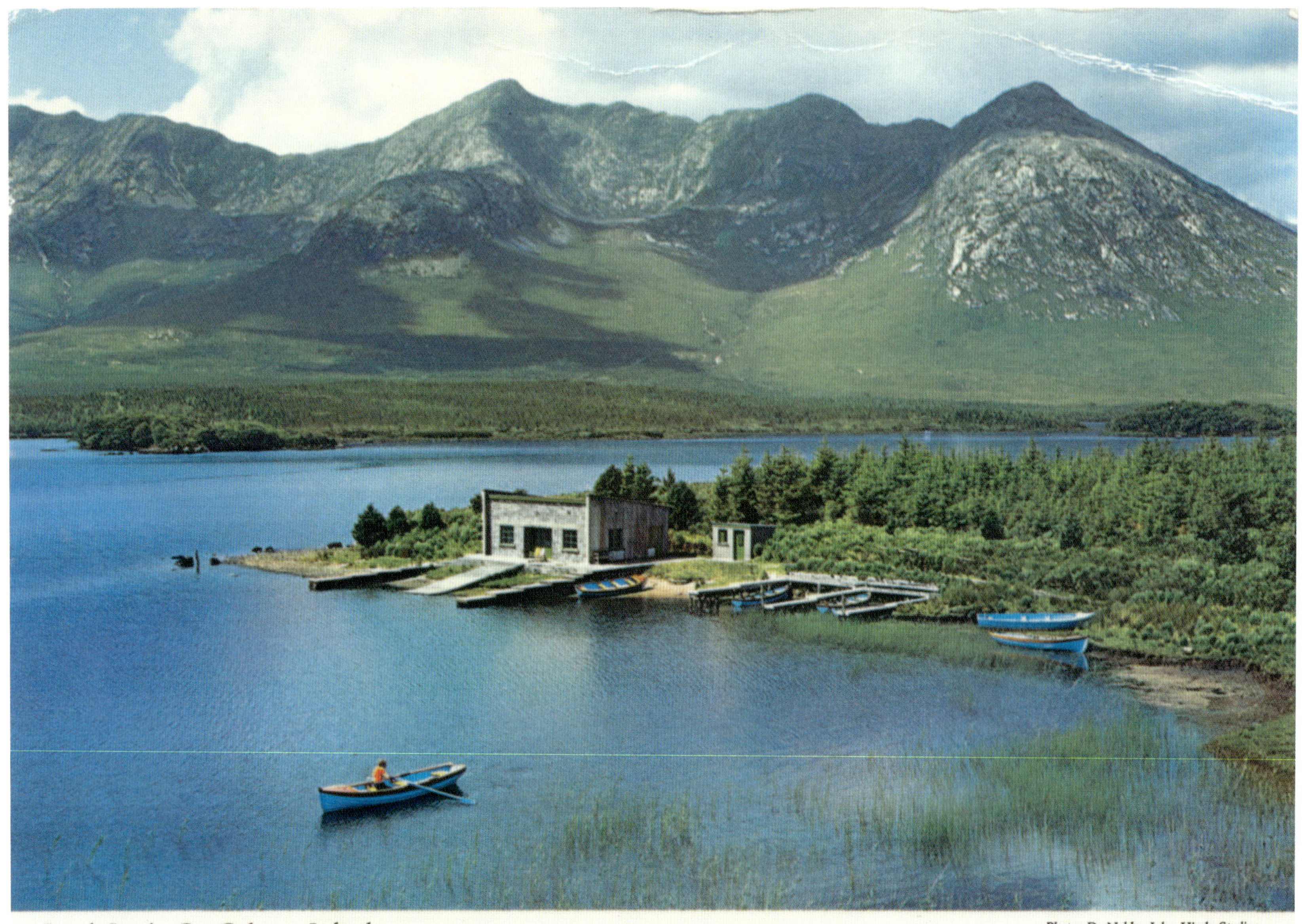
Lough Inagh, Co. Galway, Ireland.
Photo: D. Noble, John Hinde Studios.

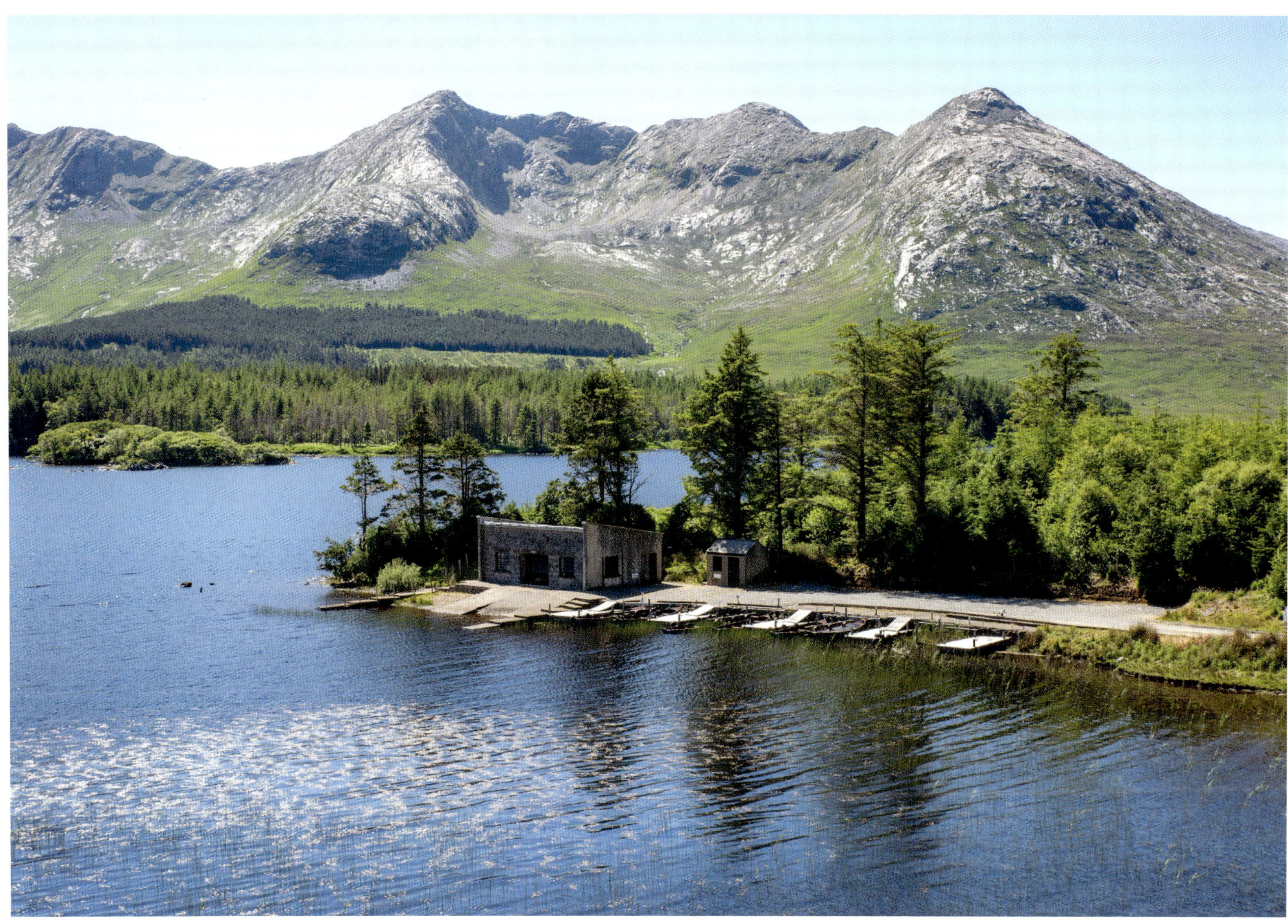

Not much has changed since John Hinde stood on this spot in the stunning Inagh Valley some 50 years ago. But if you look closely on the far shore, you'll see a significant increase of pine trees. Forestry is, literally, a growth industry in Ireland.

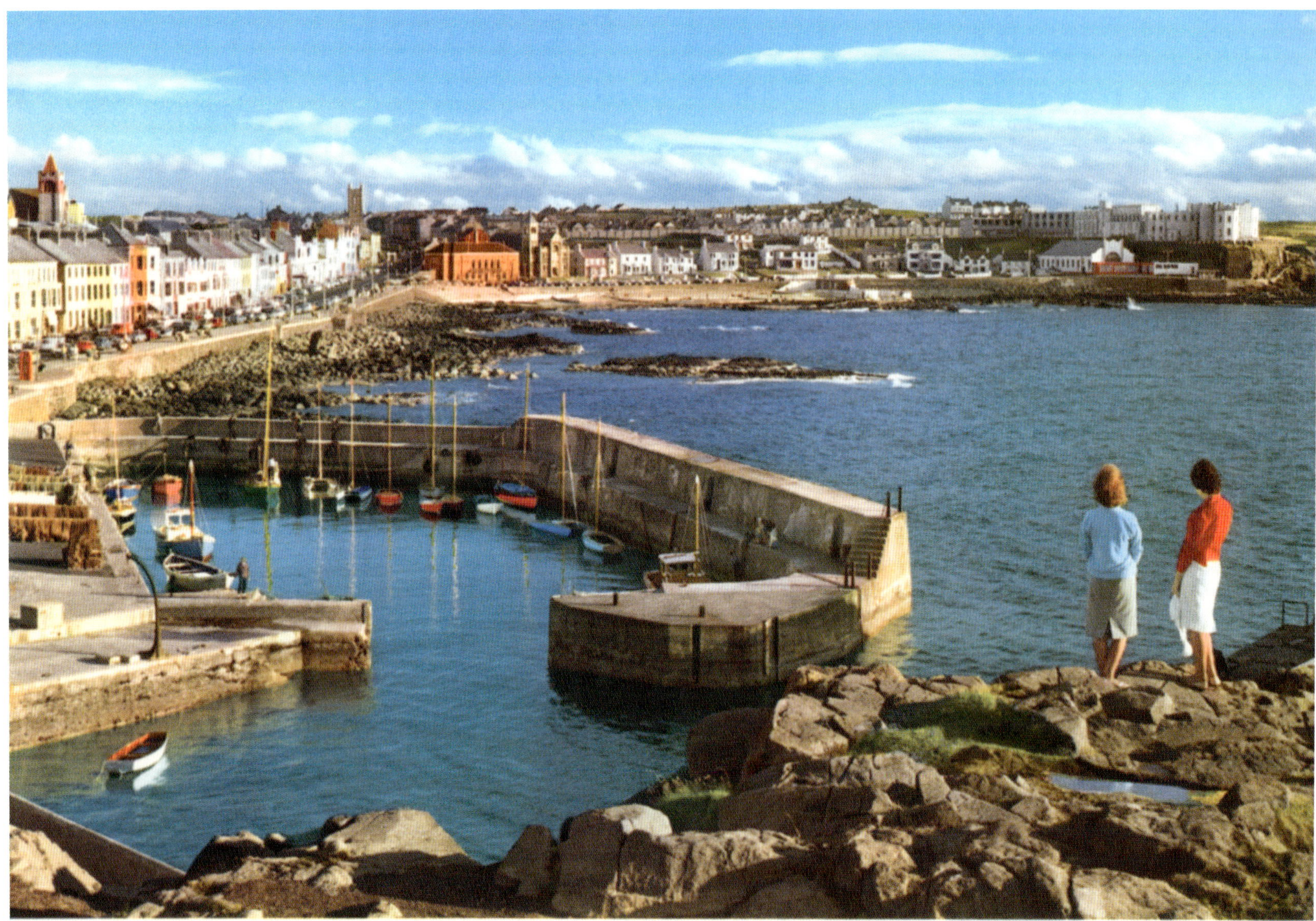

The Harbour and Promenade, Portstewart, Co. Londonderry, N.I. *Photo : E. Nägele, John Hinde Studios.*

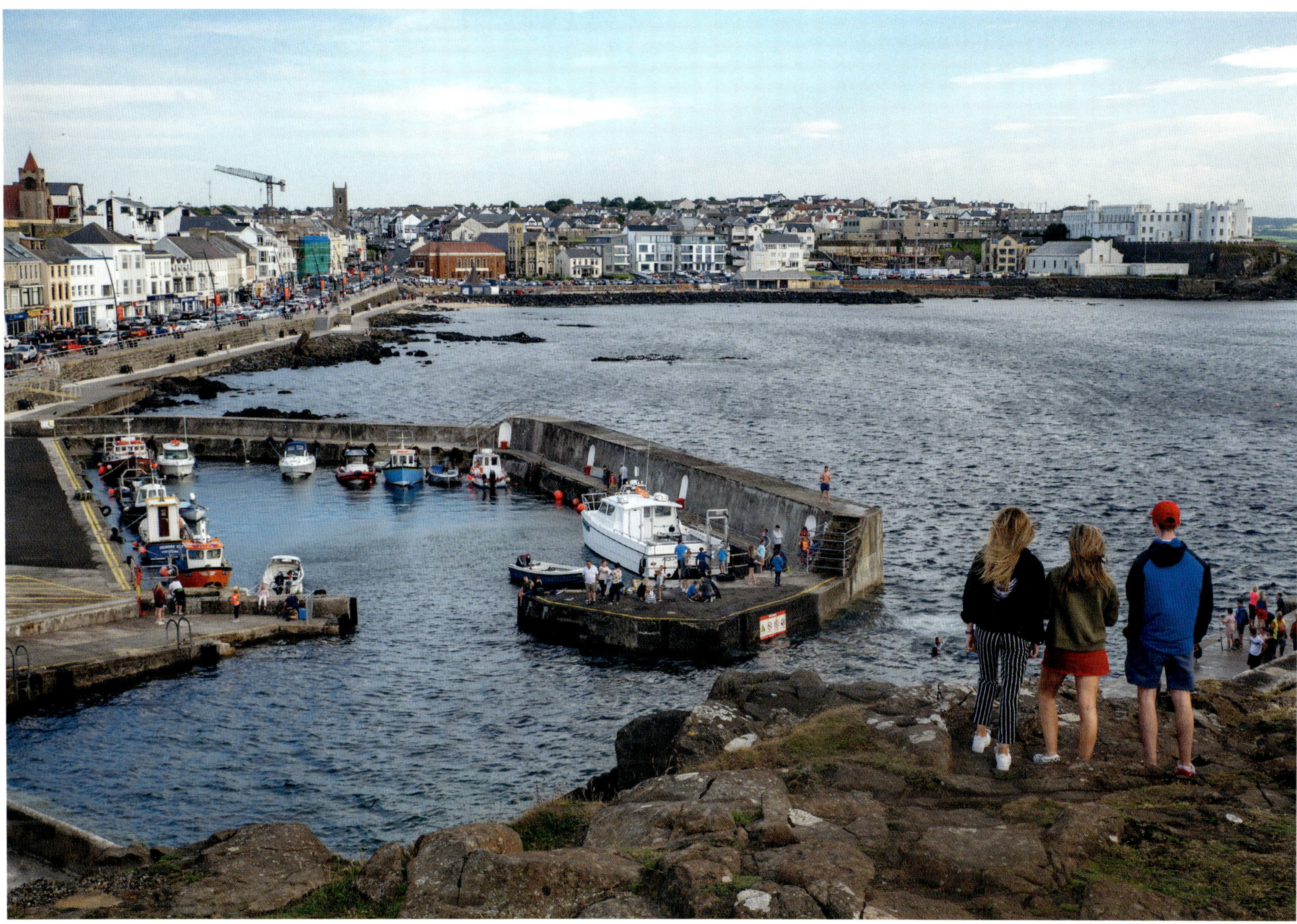

When my wife and I arrived in Portstewart one July evening, the townspeople were out enjoying the summer air. We reached the top of Harbour Hill; I quickly identified this shot location and set up my equipment. Anxious not to lose the light, I shouted out, 'Stay where you are, don't move and don't turn around', to the terrified teenagers standing below.

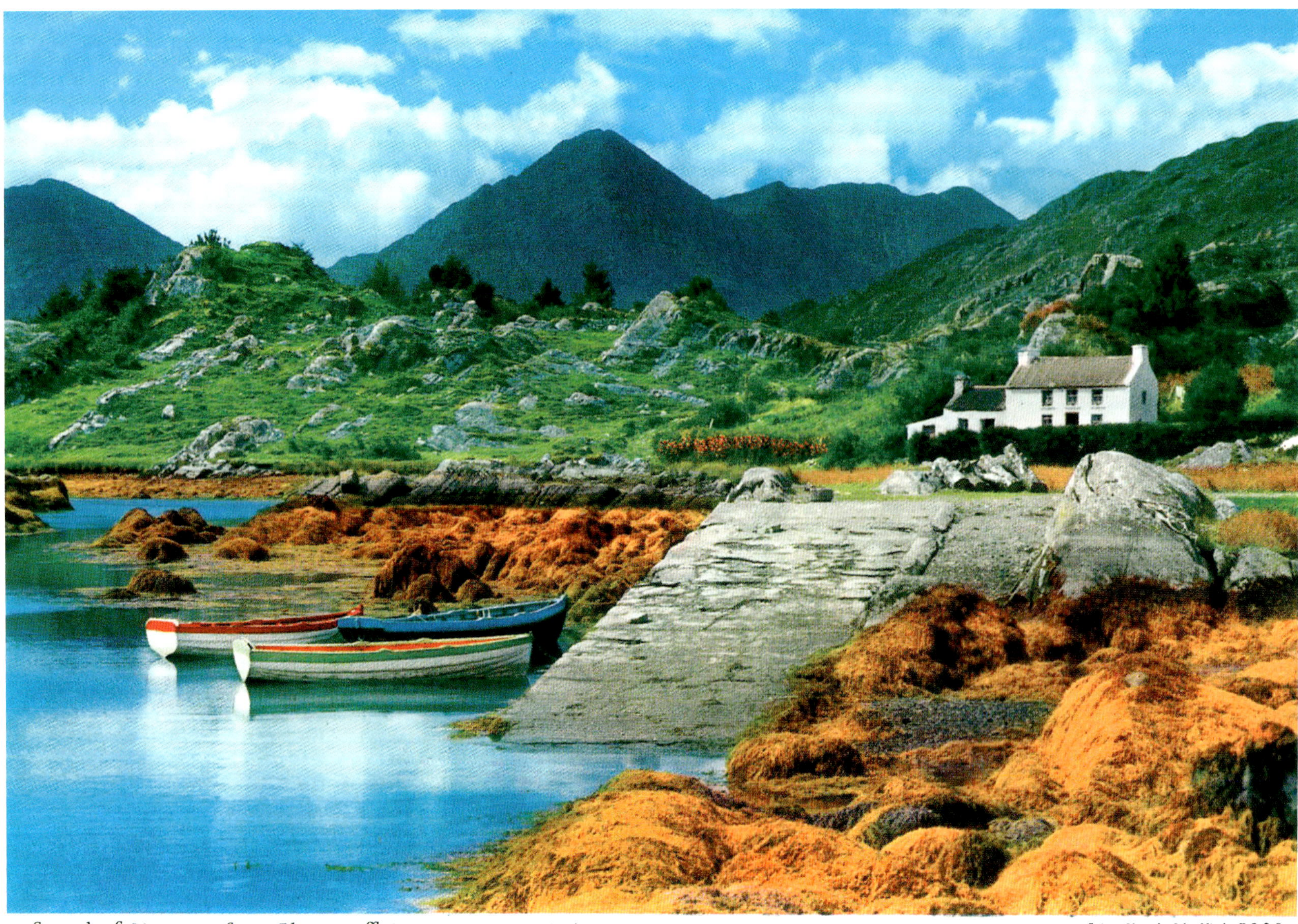

Sugarloaf Mountain from Glengarriff, Bantry Bay, Co. Cork, Ireland.

Colour Photo by John Hinde, F.R.P.S.

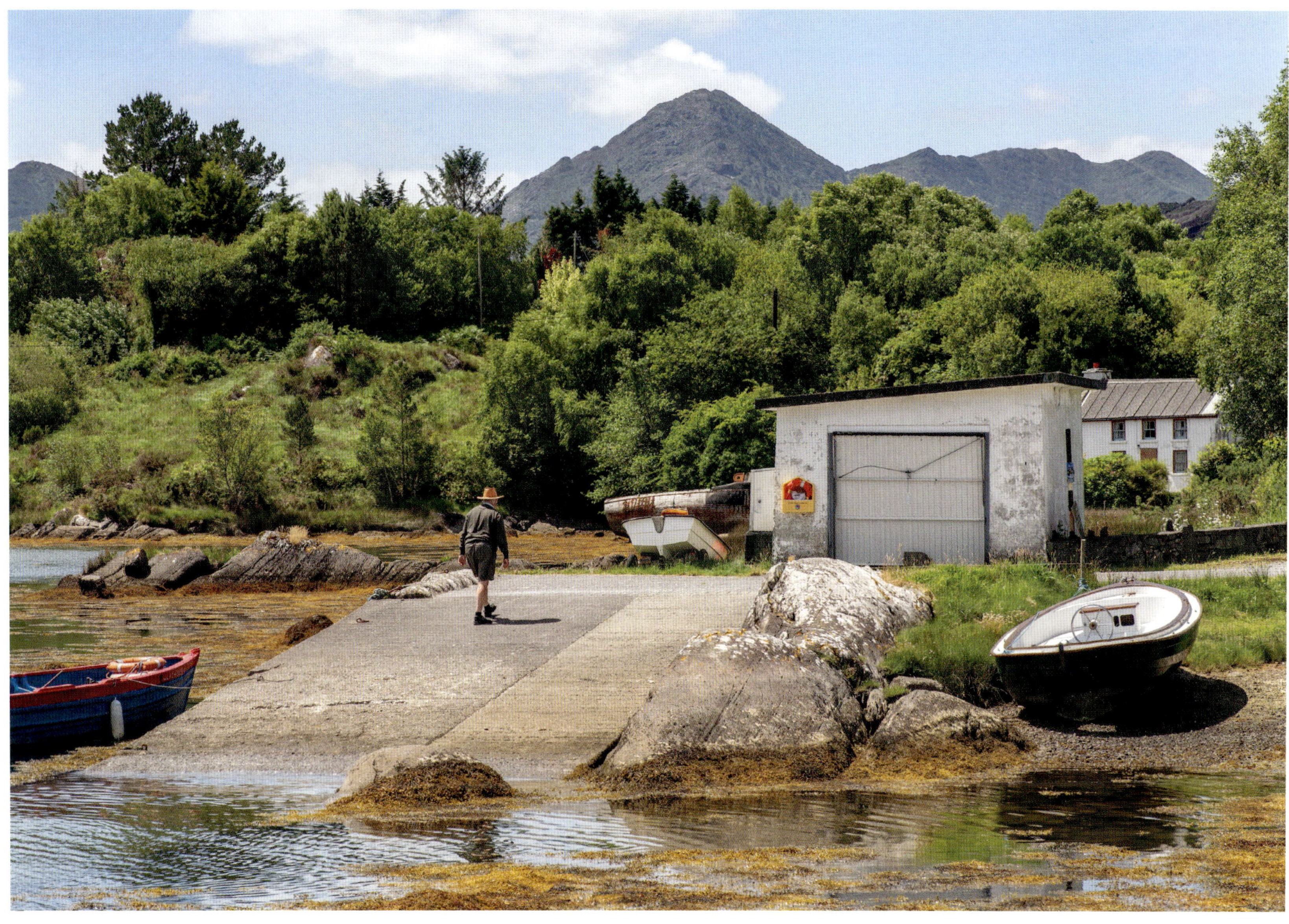

The man in my photo runs a small boat service taking visitors to the lush gardens on nearby Garnish Island. He told me that the white house in the postcard had been vacant for years. Through trial and error, and a few slips and falls, I finally found the spot, but was unable to get to the precise location, beaten back by a solid wall of brambles.

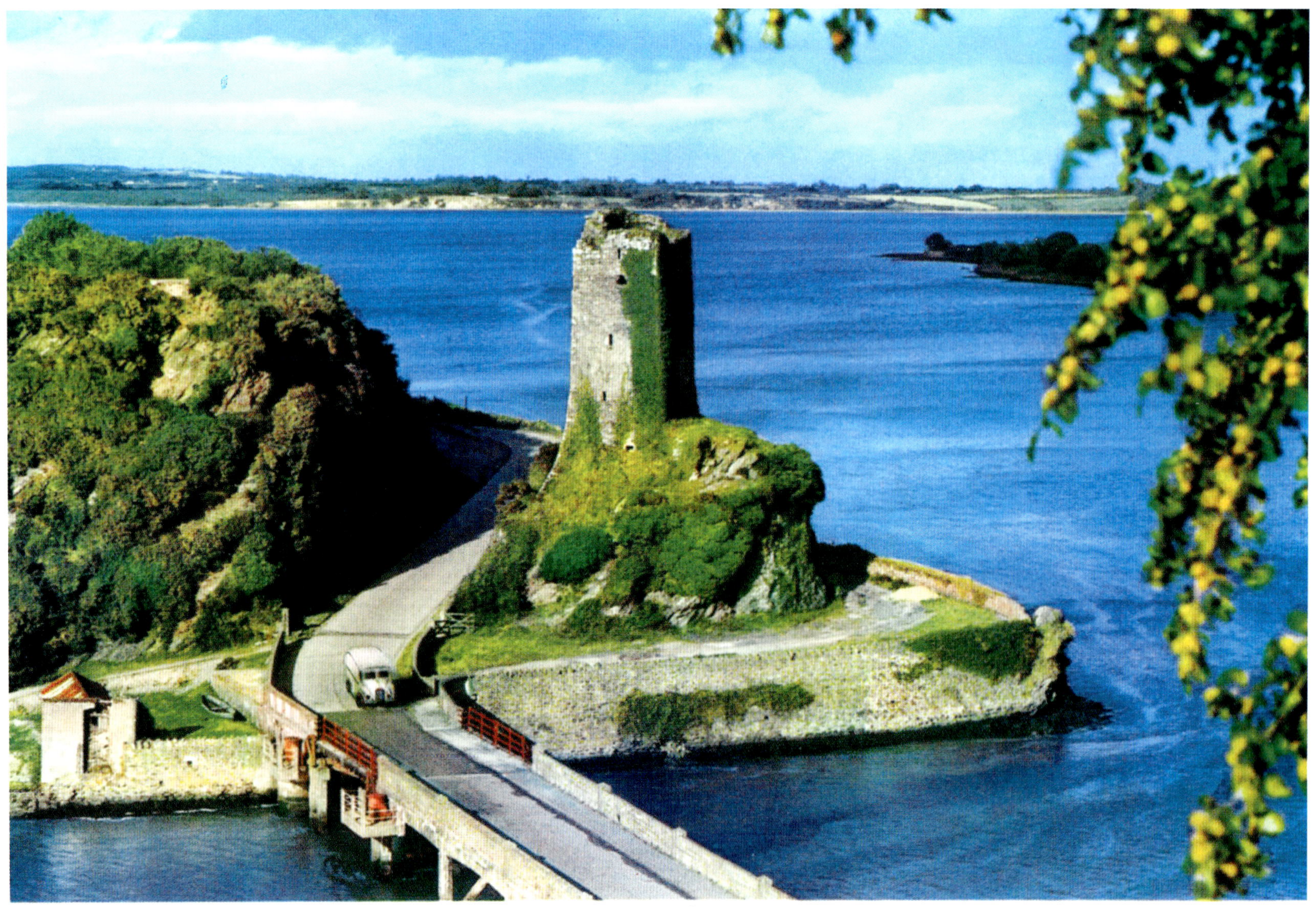

Norman Castle (1169 A.D.), River Slaney, Ferrycarrig, Wexford, Ireland.

Colour Photo by John Hinde, F.R.P.S.

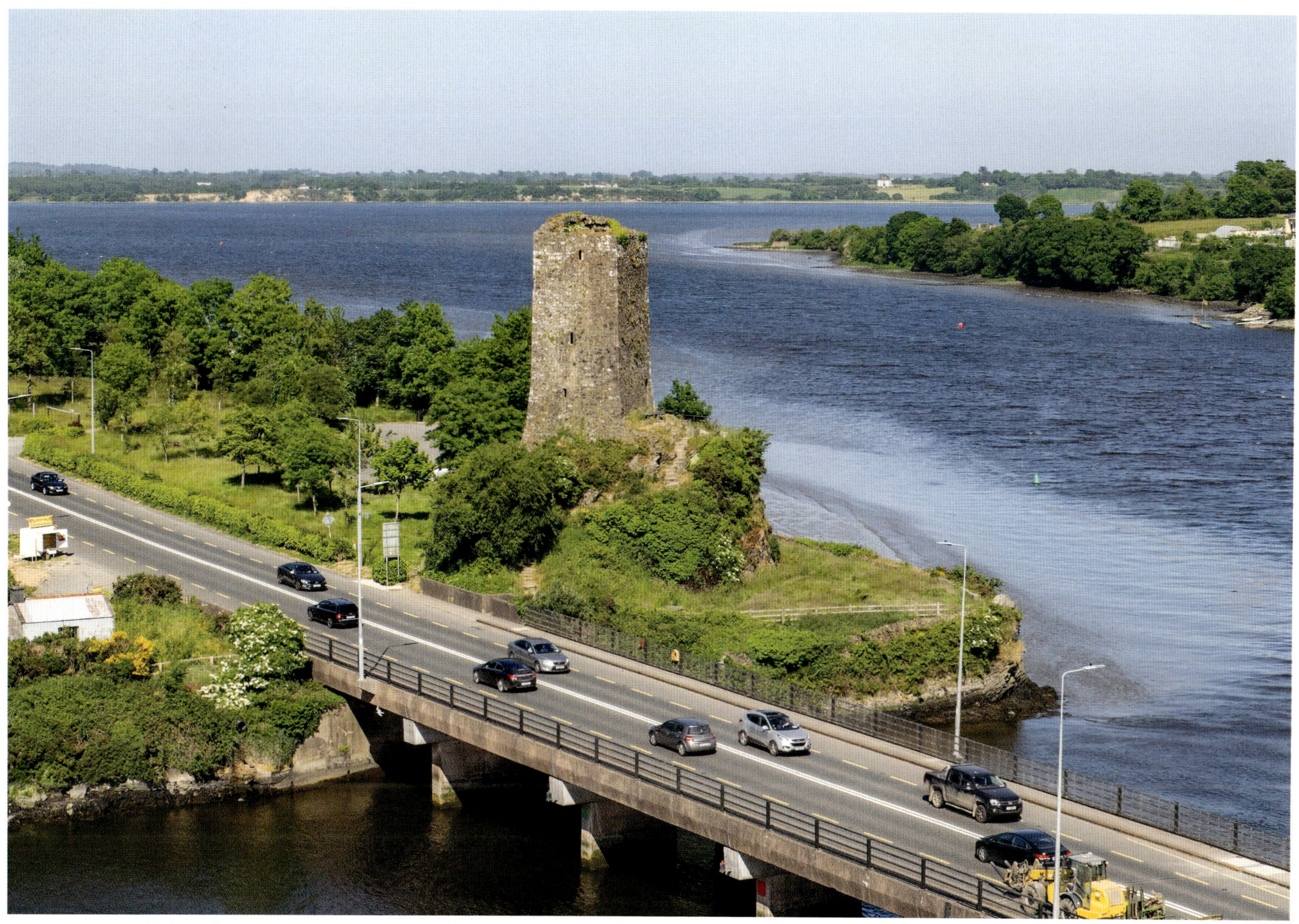

I walked the length of the Irish National Heritage Park to recapture Hinde's scene. This is Roche's Tower House, built in the 15th century to protect expanding trade and traffic on the river Slaney. Unmoved by time, the tower house gazes out over today's sleek ribbon of road, carrying 21st-century traffic across the new bridge.

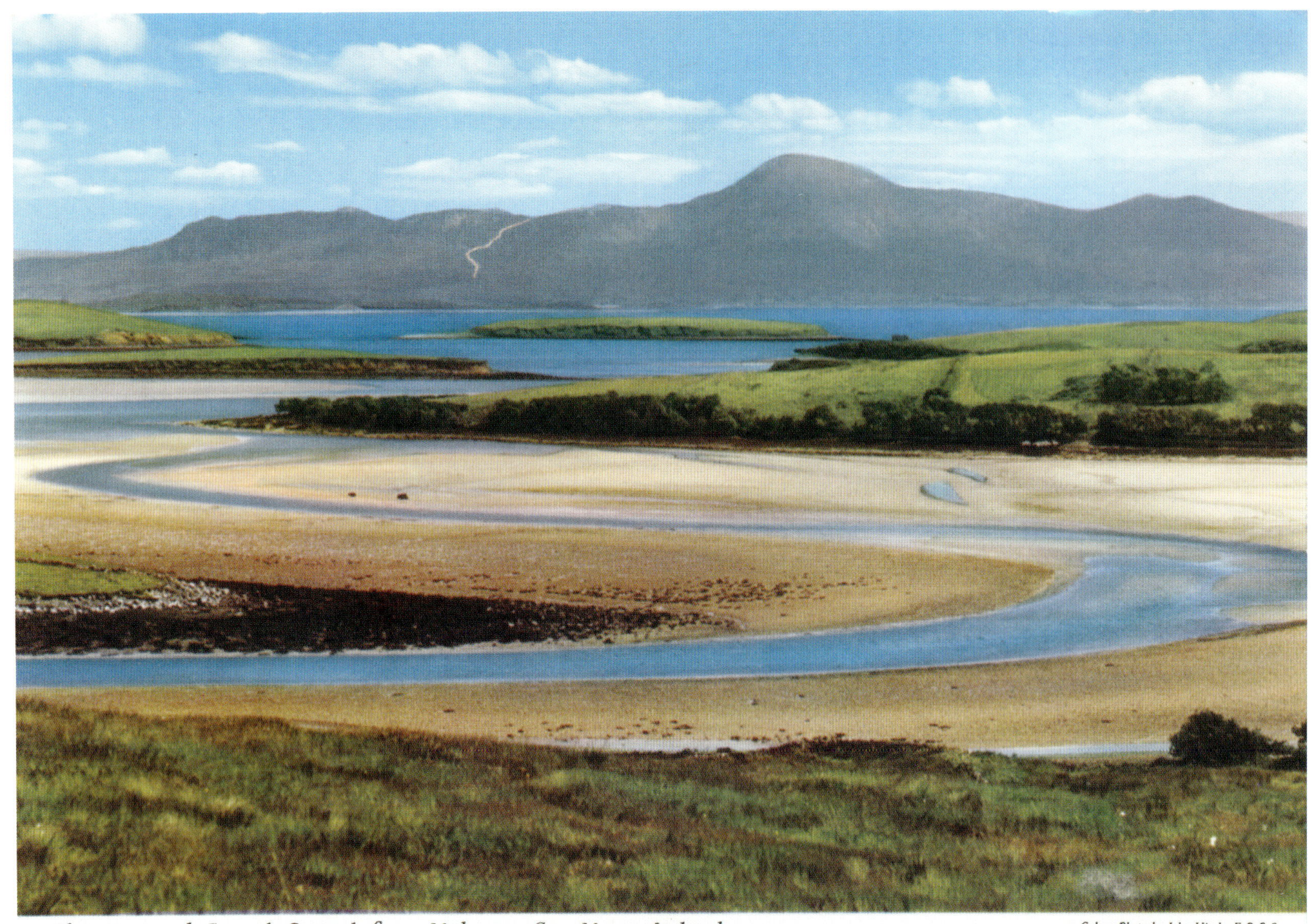

Clew Bay and Croagh Patrick from Mulrany, Co. Mayo, Ireland.

Colour Photo by John Hinde, F.R.P.S.

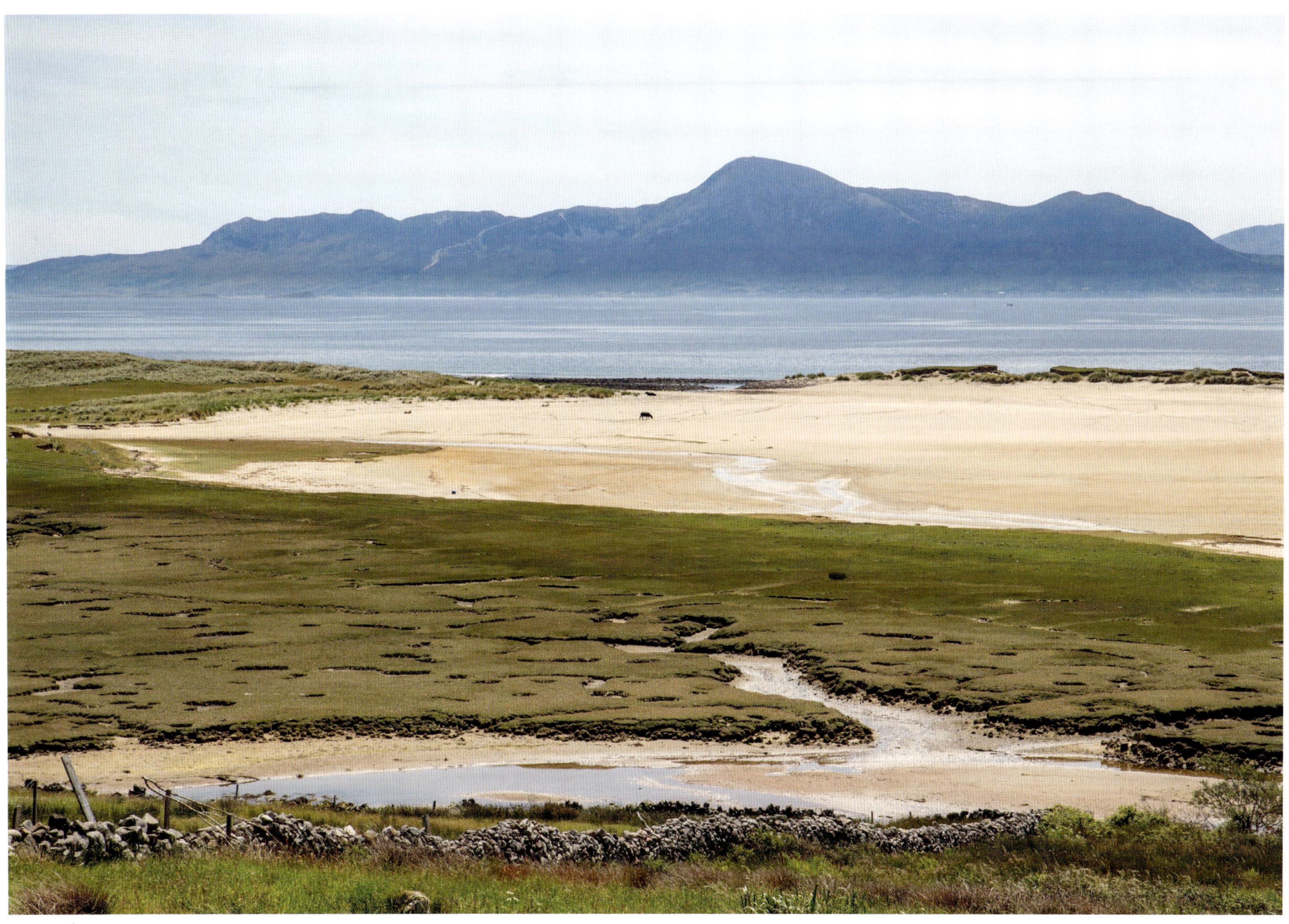

In Irish, Mulranny, or 'an Mhala Raithne', means 'the hill of the ferns', a natural resting point on the Great Western Greenway cycling and walking trail from Westport to Achill. Apart from cycling, Mulranny is now renowned for its exceptional outdoor activities such as golf, sea kayaking and fishing.

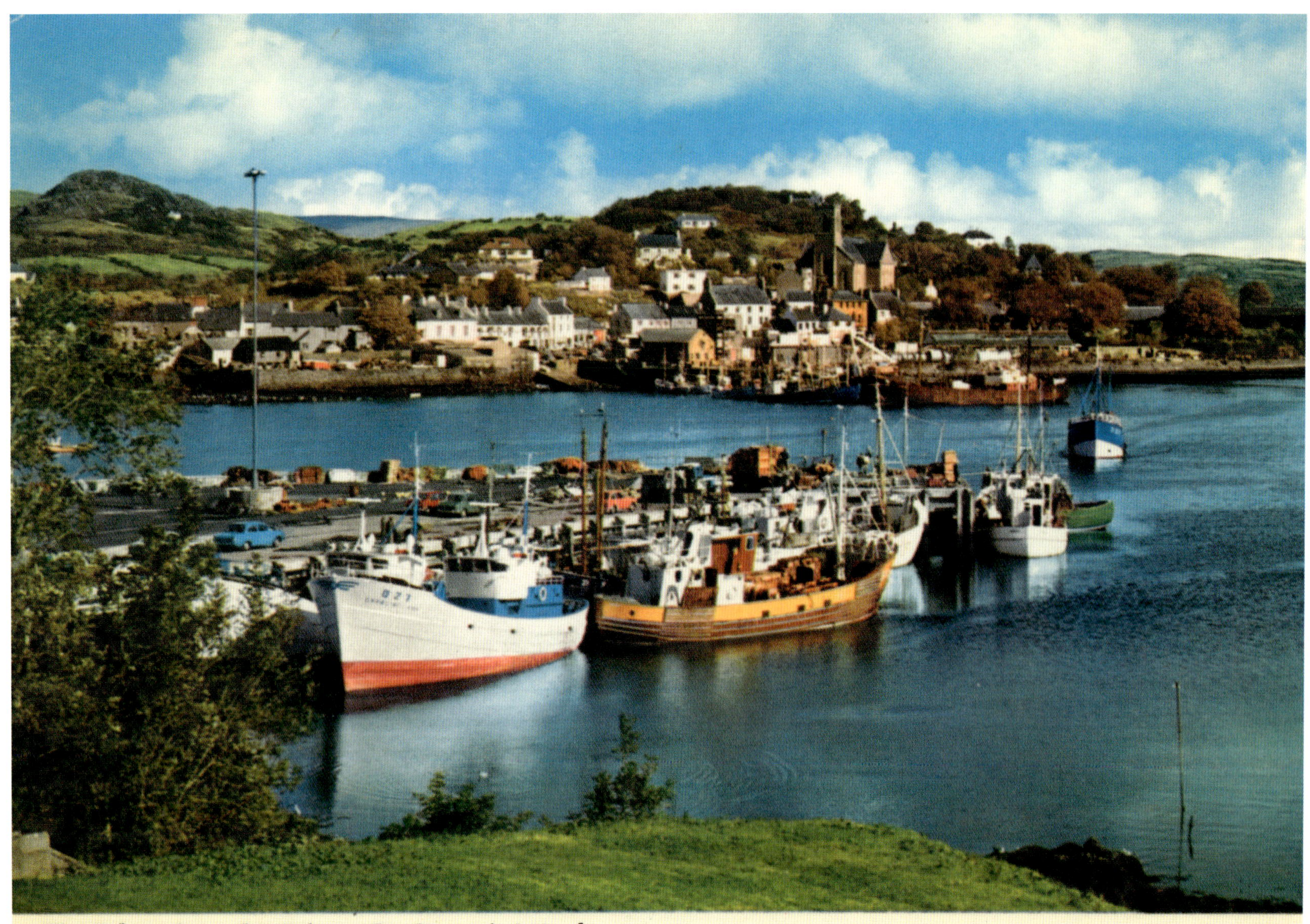

The Fishing Port of Killybegs, Co. Donegal, Ireland. Photo: D. Noble, John Hinde Studios.

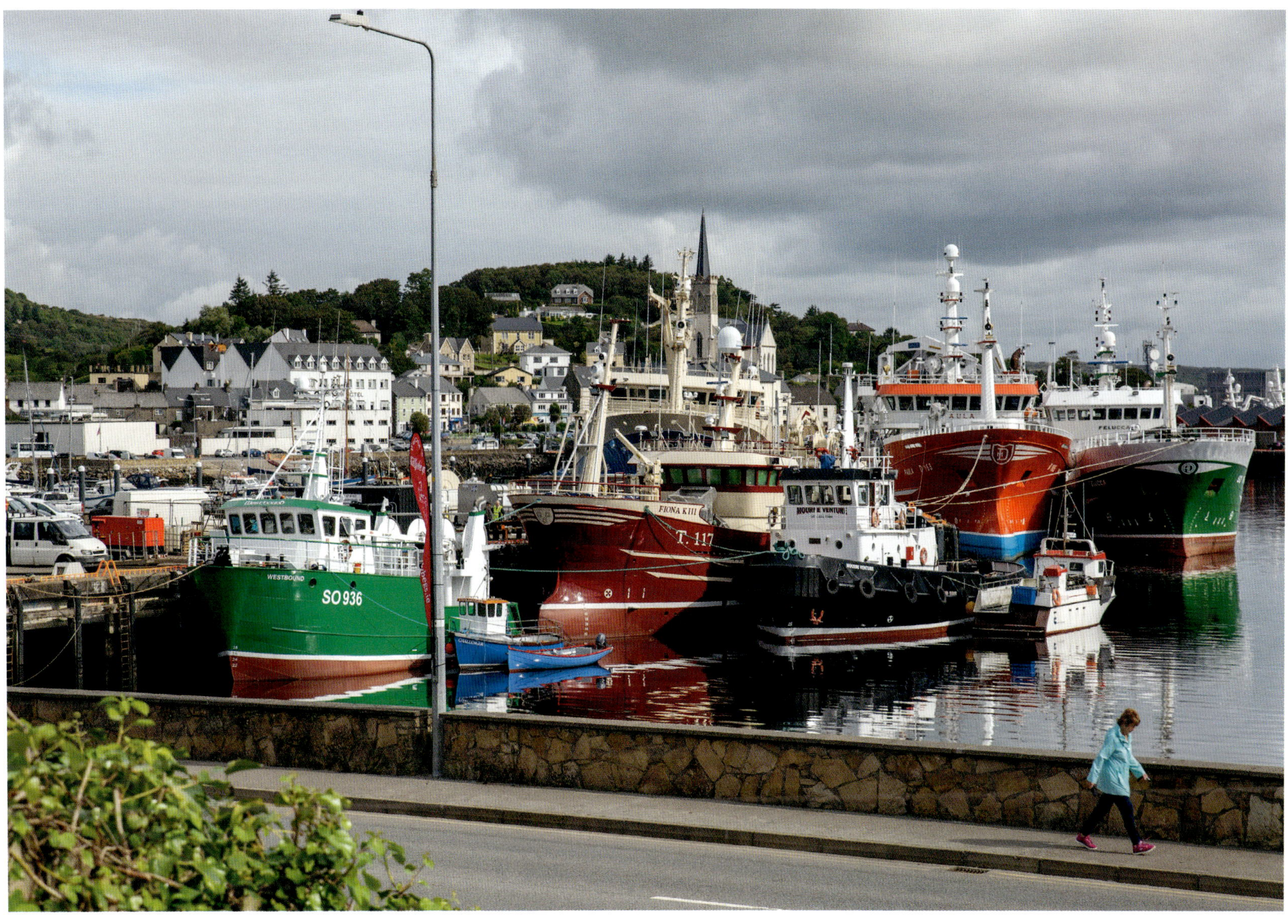

I shot this from the car park of LyIT's School of Tourism in Killybegs. A fitting viewpoint this, as tourism, depicted and promoted in Hinde's postcards, has transformed Ireland. The college also offers courses in culinary arts. Put together a renowned cookery school full of keen chefs, and a beautiful Irish town whose waters teem with tasty fish, and what have you got? The perfect recipe for a delicious destination.

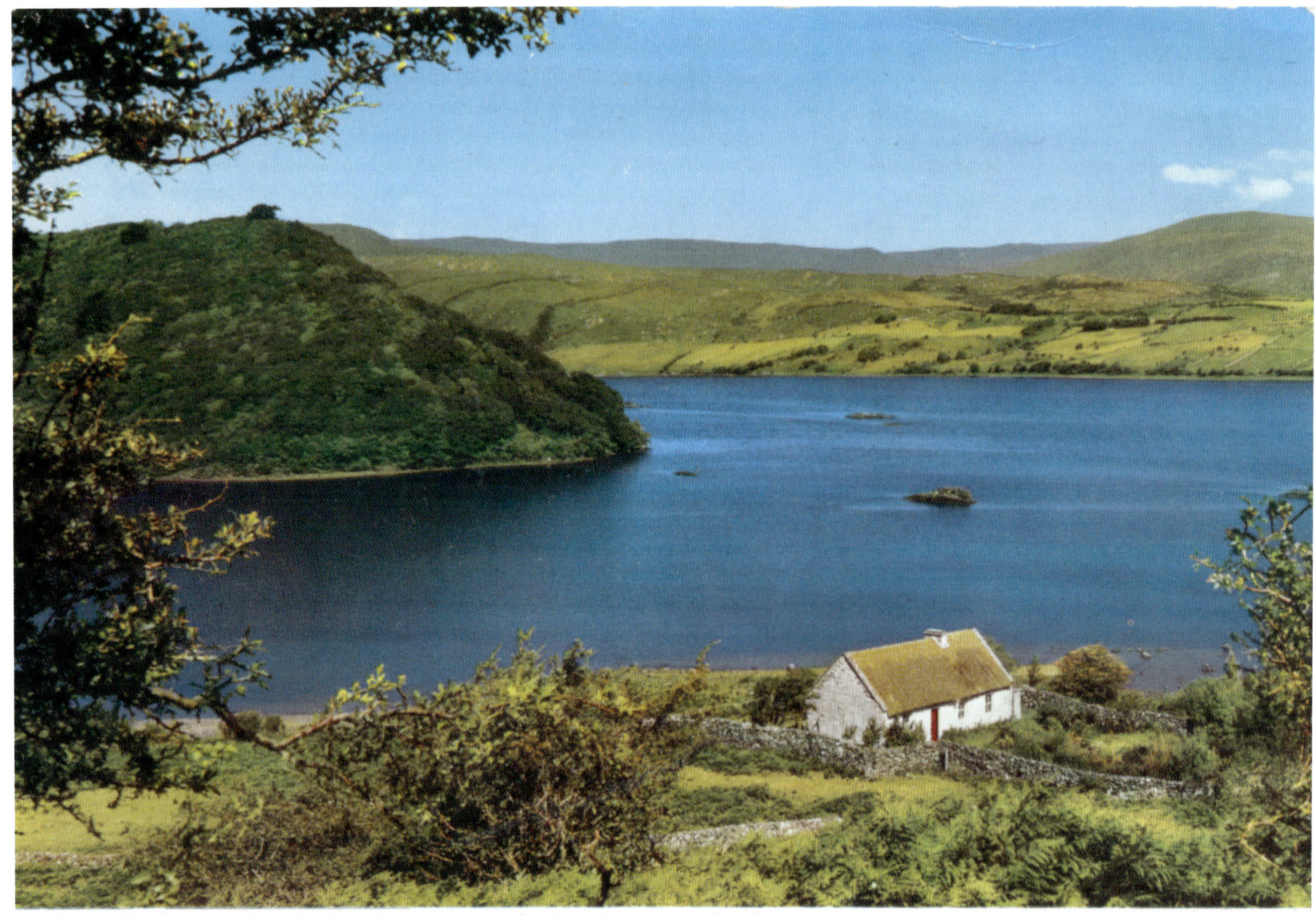

The Hill of Doon, Lough Corrib, Oughterard, Co. Galway, Ireland. Colour Photo by John Hinde, F.R.P.S.

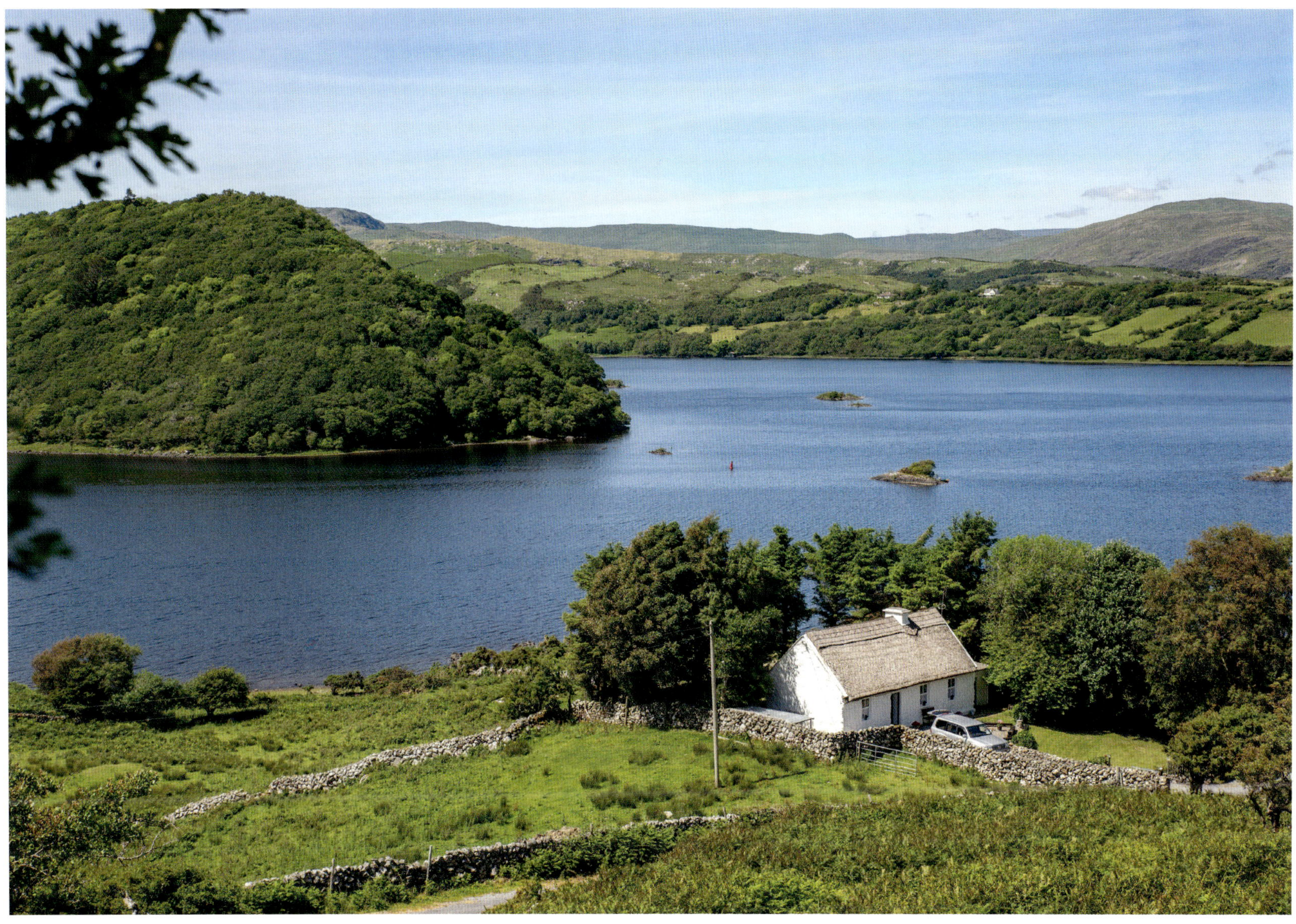

One of John Hinde's most iconic postcards, the essence of idyllic, pastoral Ireland. Comparing his postcard with today's photo, and other then-and-now photos in the book, tree and shrub foliage appears to be flourishing anew, especially in the Irish countryside. Which, of course, only makes it even more idyllic.

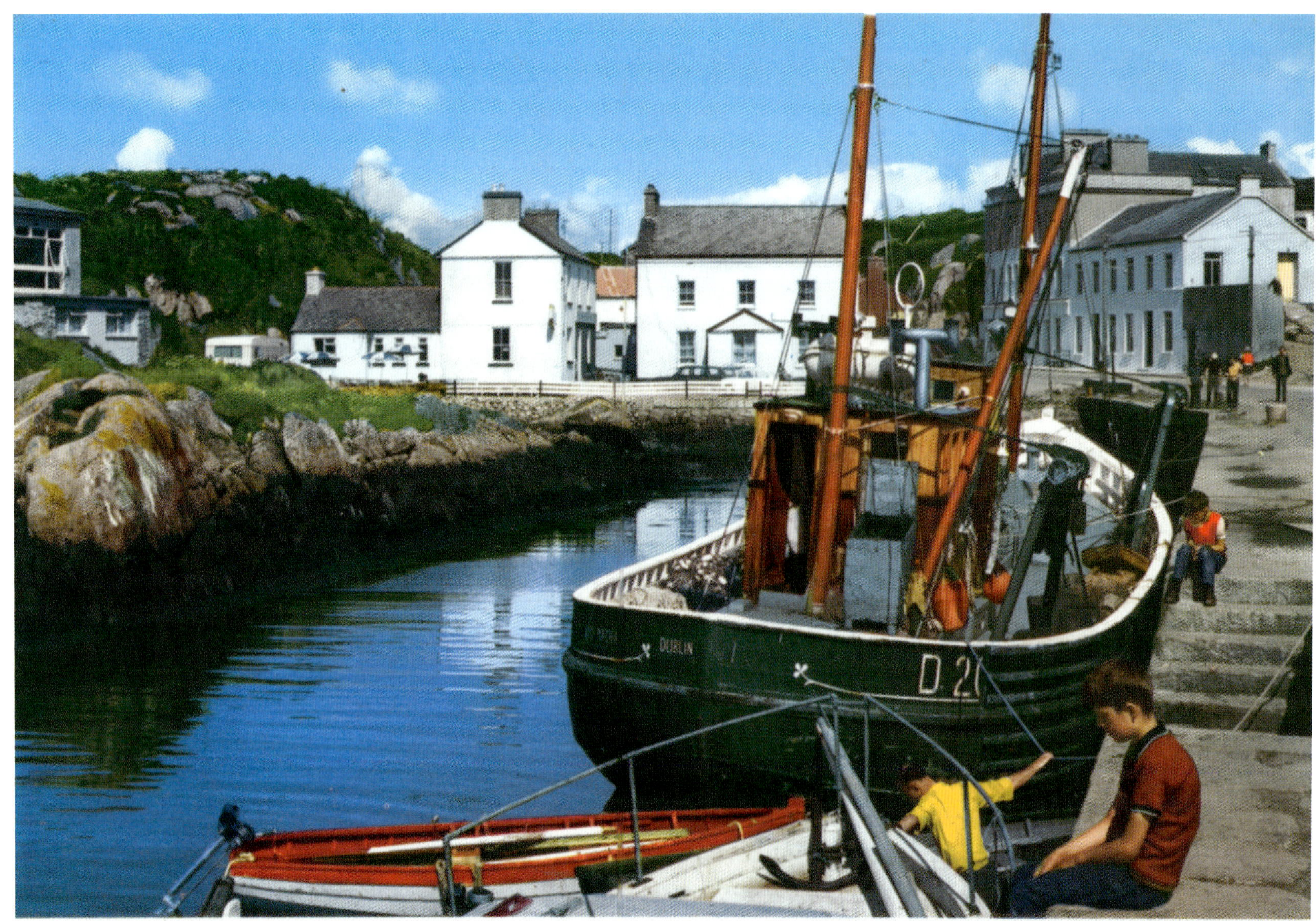

The Fishing Village of Burtonport, Co. Donegal, Ireland.

Photo : Joan Willis, John Hinde Studios.

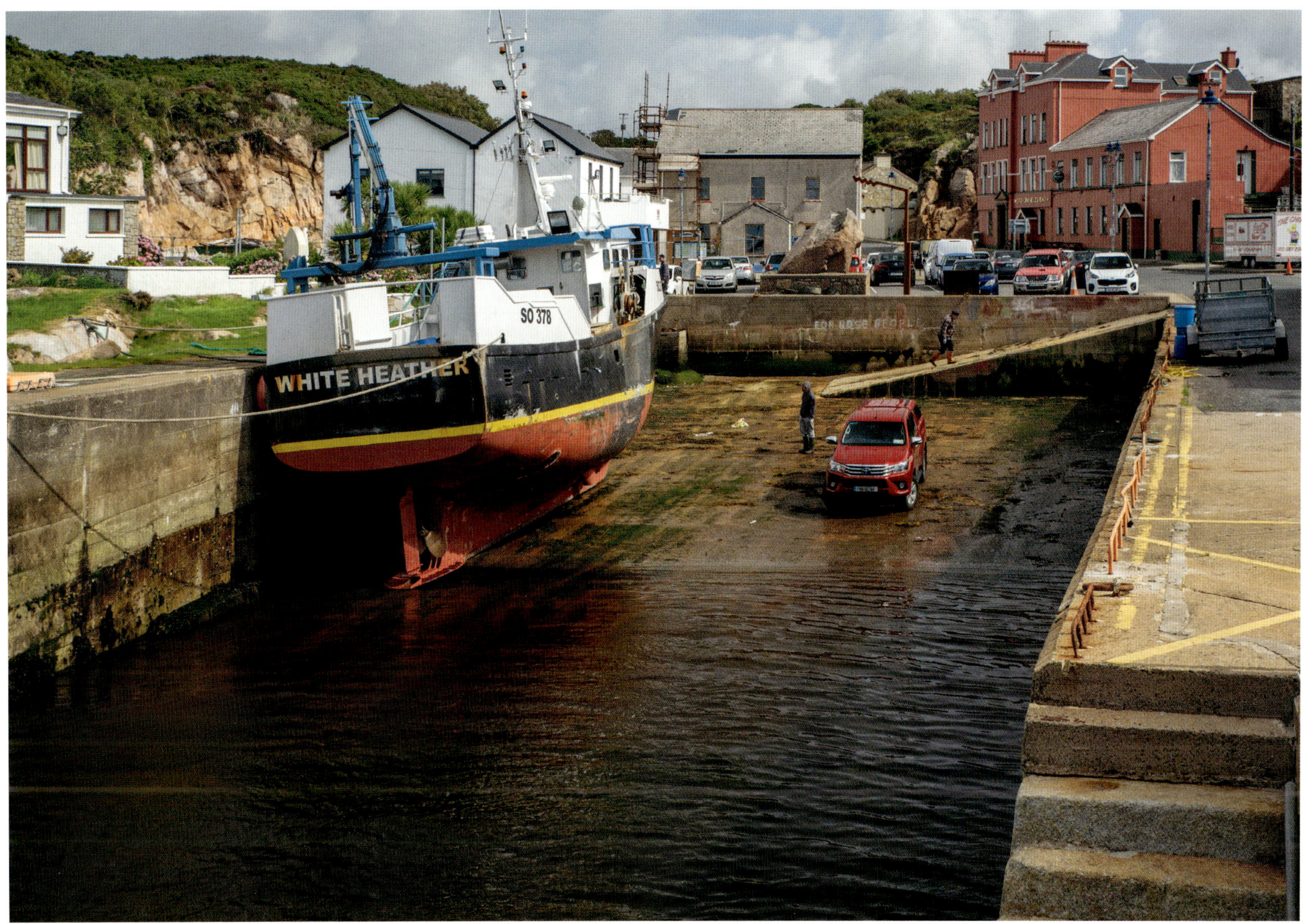

The Burtonport Welcome Centre states that this postcard dates from 1970: '*The fishing boat, the* Ard Macha D21, *was owned by skipper Joe McGinley, who lived in the house on the left with his wife, Bridget. The nearest boy sitting down is Gerry O'Donnell, and the boy sitting on the steps further away is Joe Greene.*'

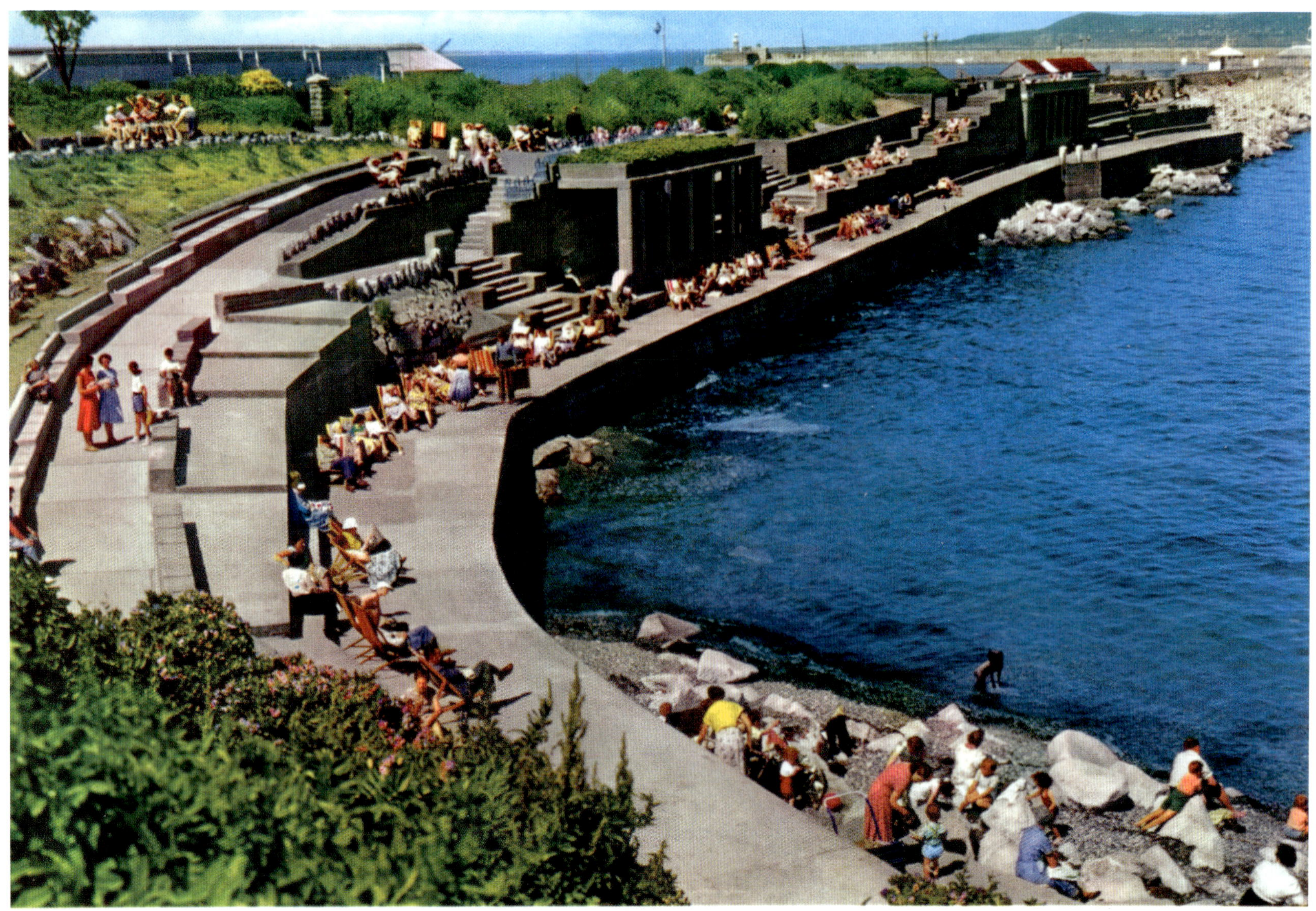

Sun Terraces, Dun Laoghaire, overlooking Dublin Bay, Ireland.

Colour Photo by John Hinde, F.R.P.S.

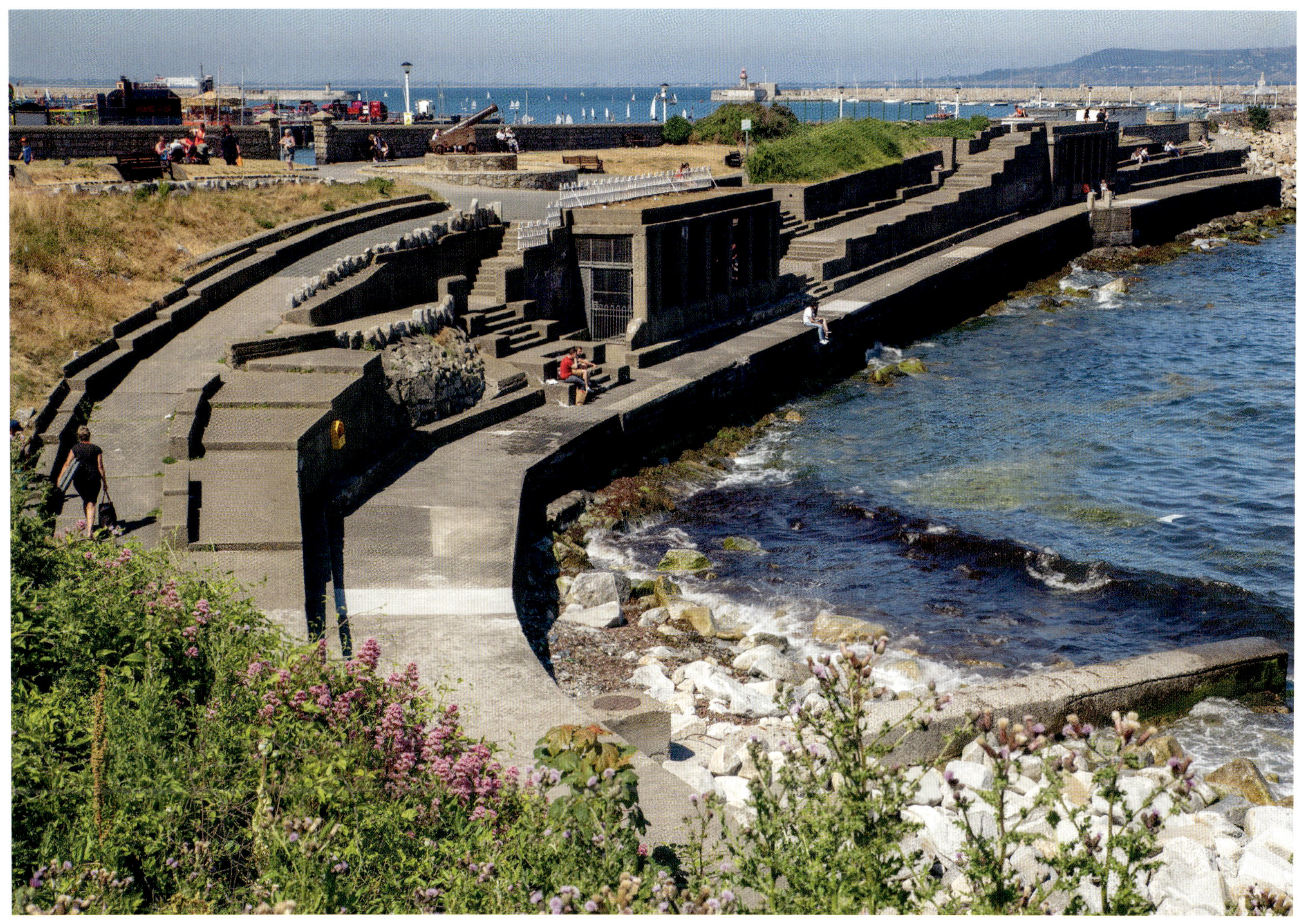

This postcard's caption reads in part: '*Dún Laoghaire is eight miles from Dublin city, and an important gateway to Ireland, the terminus of the daily cross-channel service from Holyhead. It is a delightful place to bathe, or just sit and watch the hundreds of brightly coloured yachts sailing gracefully in the bay.*'

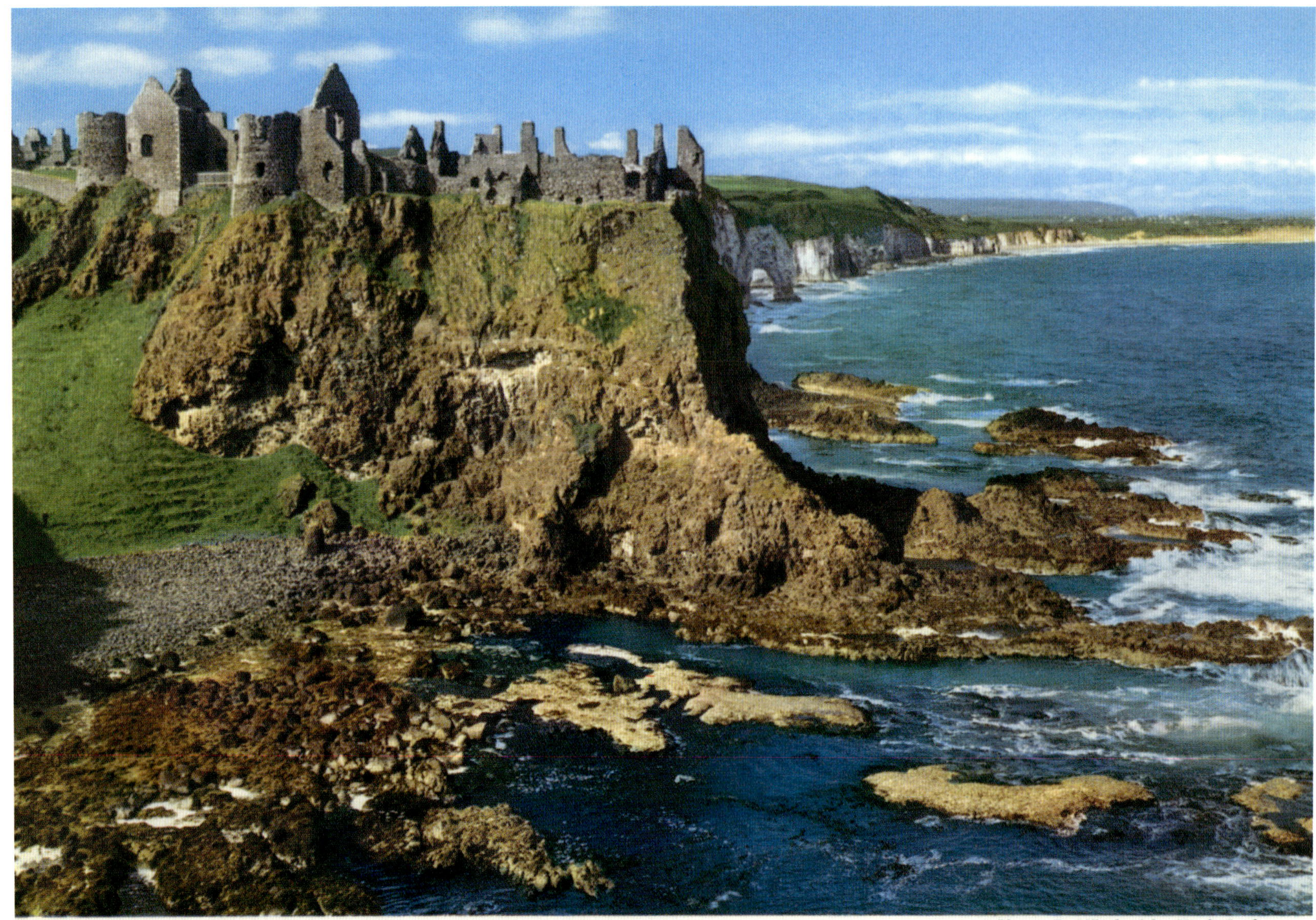

Dunluce Castle and White Rocks of Portrush, Co. Antrim, N.I. Photo : E. Nägele, John Hinde Studios.

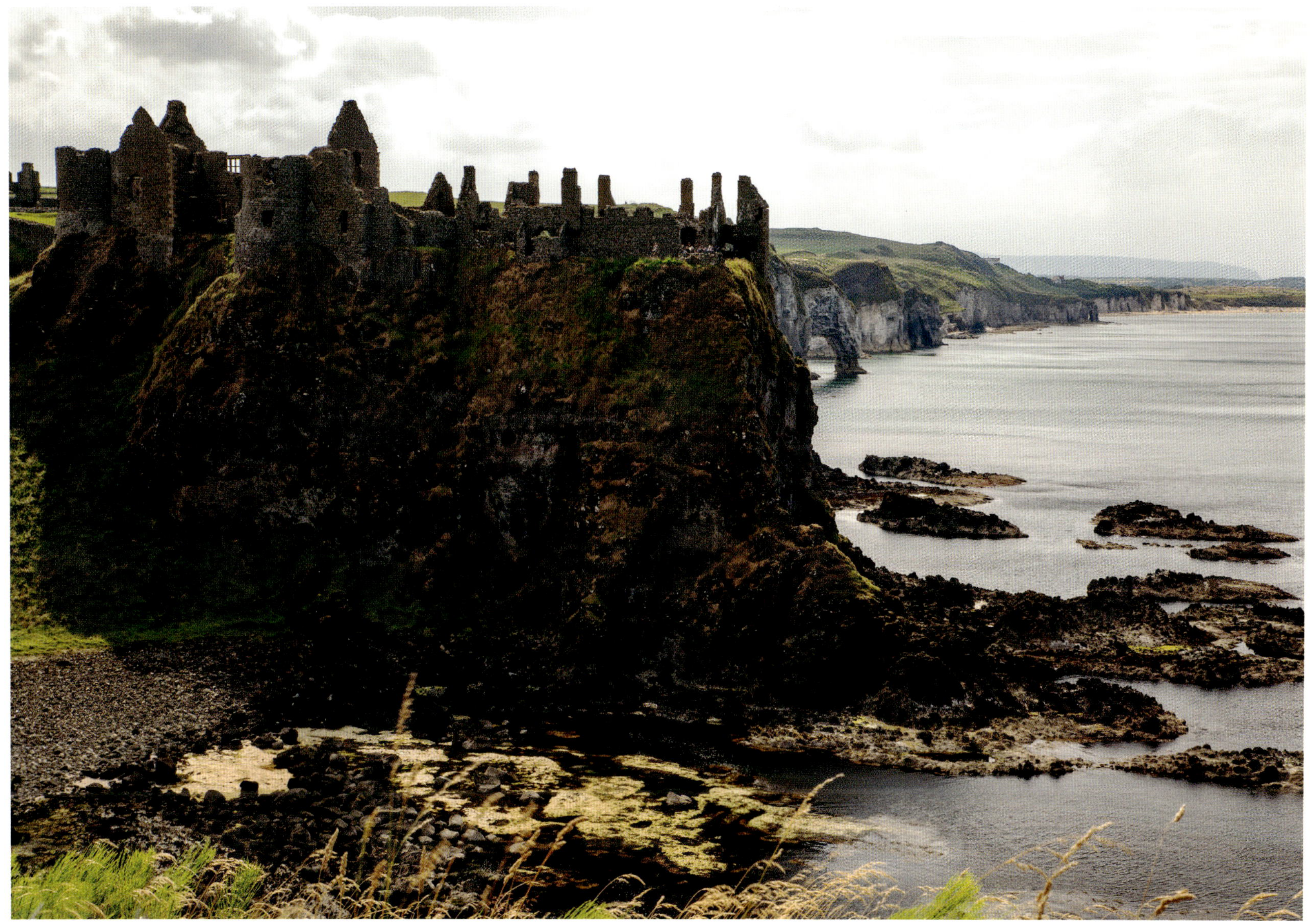

Recognise the cruel pinnacles of Dunluce Castle on the north Antrim coast? Fans of the epic fantasy series *Game of Thrones* will know it as the seat of the House of Greyjoy. Today, the ruined castle is one of the area's main attractions, but for me the breathtaking views that frame it are even more spectacular.

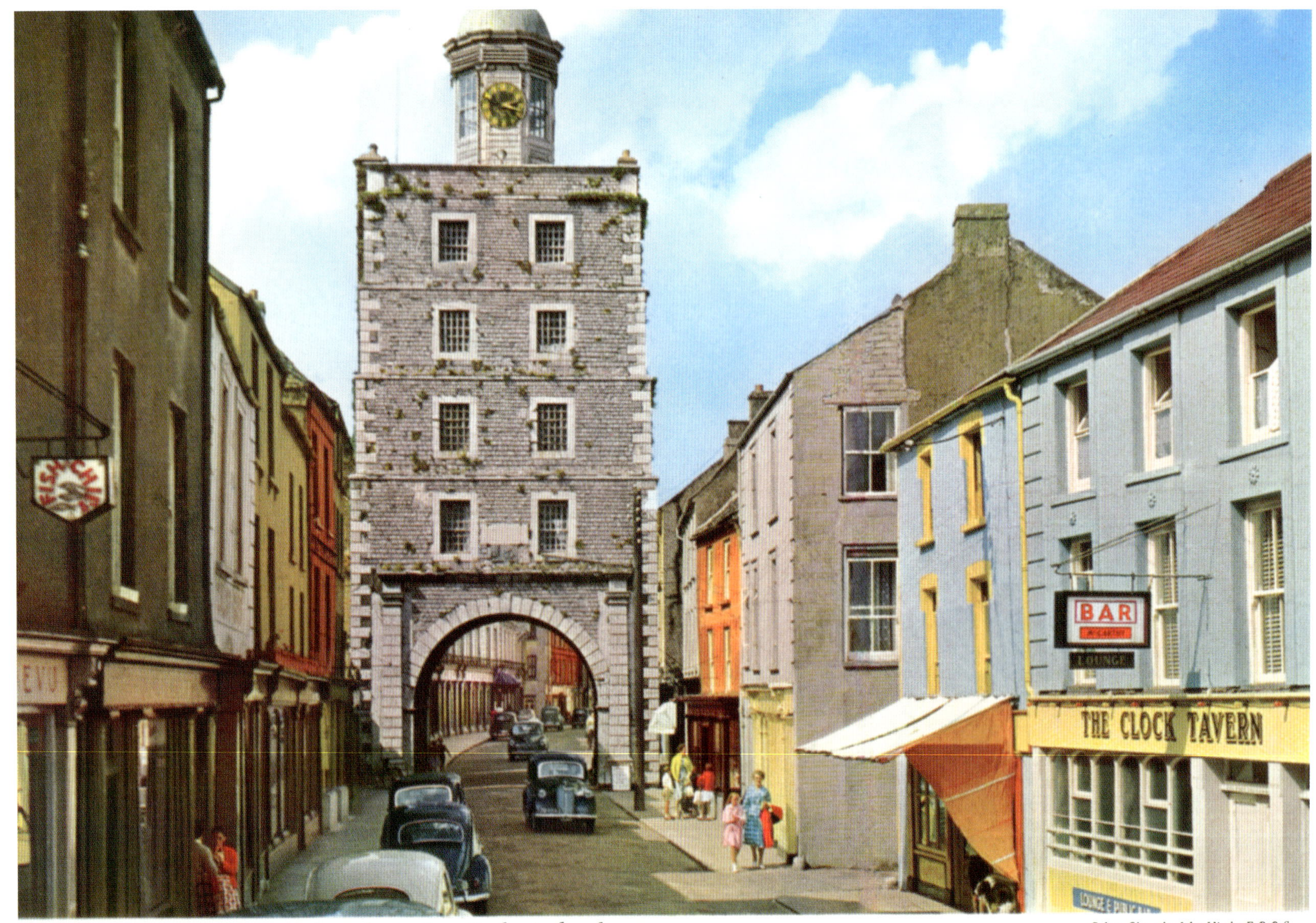

Clock Gate, Main Street, Youghal, Co. Cork, Ireland.

Colour Photo by John Hinde, F.R.P.S.

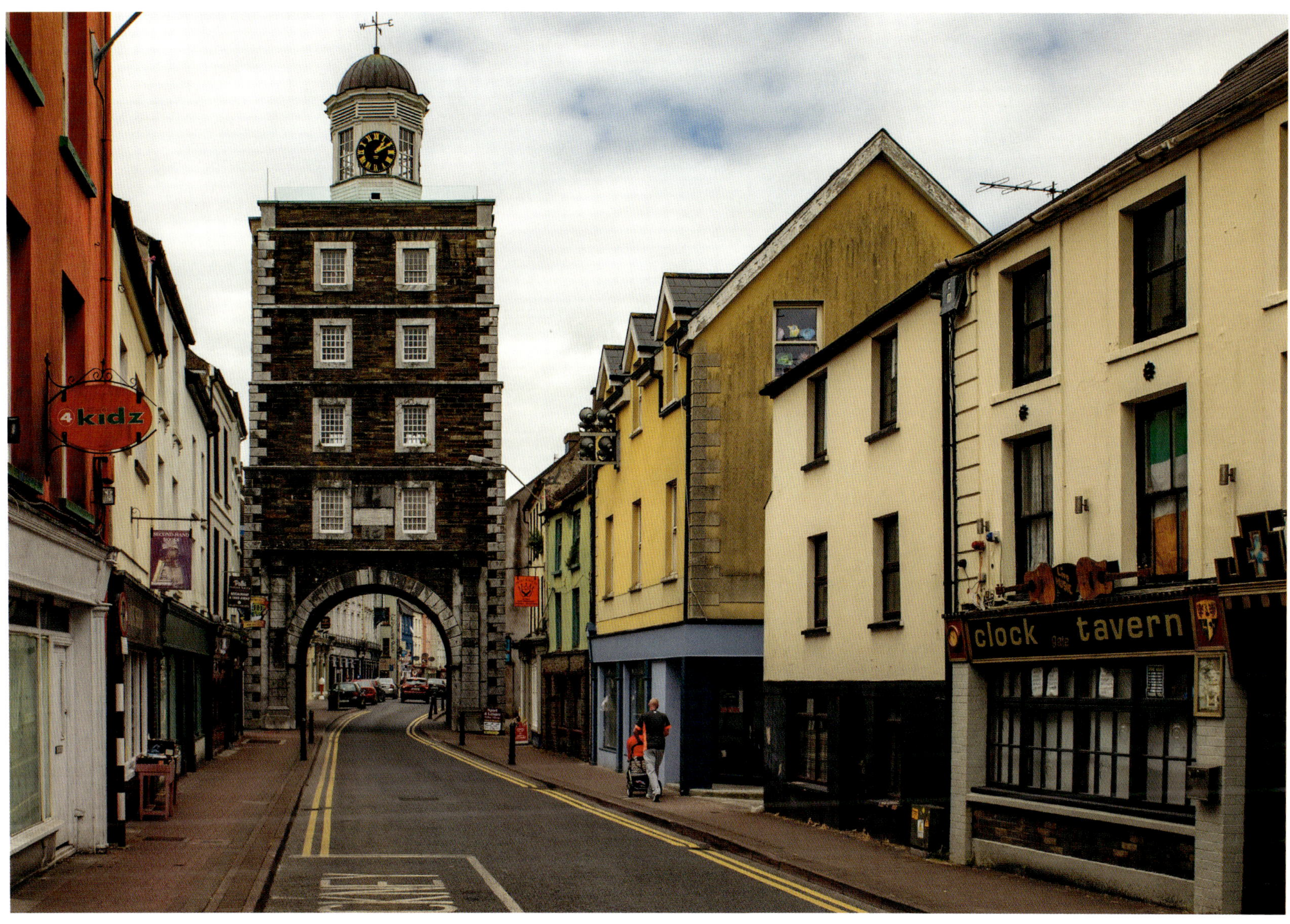

The Clock Gate Tower was built on the site of Trinity Castle, one of five principal fortifications in late 14th-century Youghal. The tower itself was built in 1777 as a gaol, and was a prison for many years, a scene of torture and execution. Nowadays it is the city's most recognisable landmark and a popular tourist attraction.

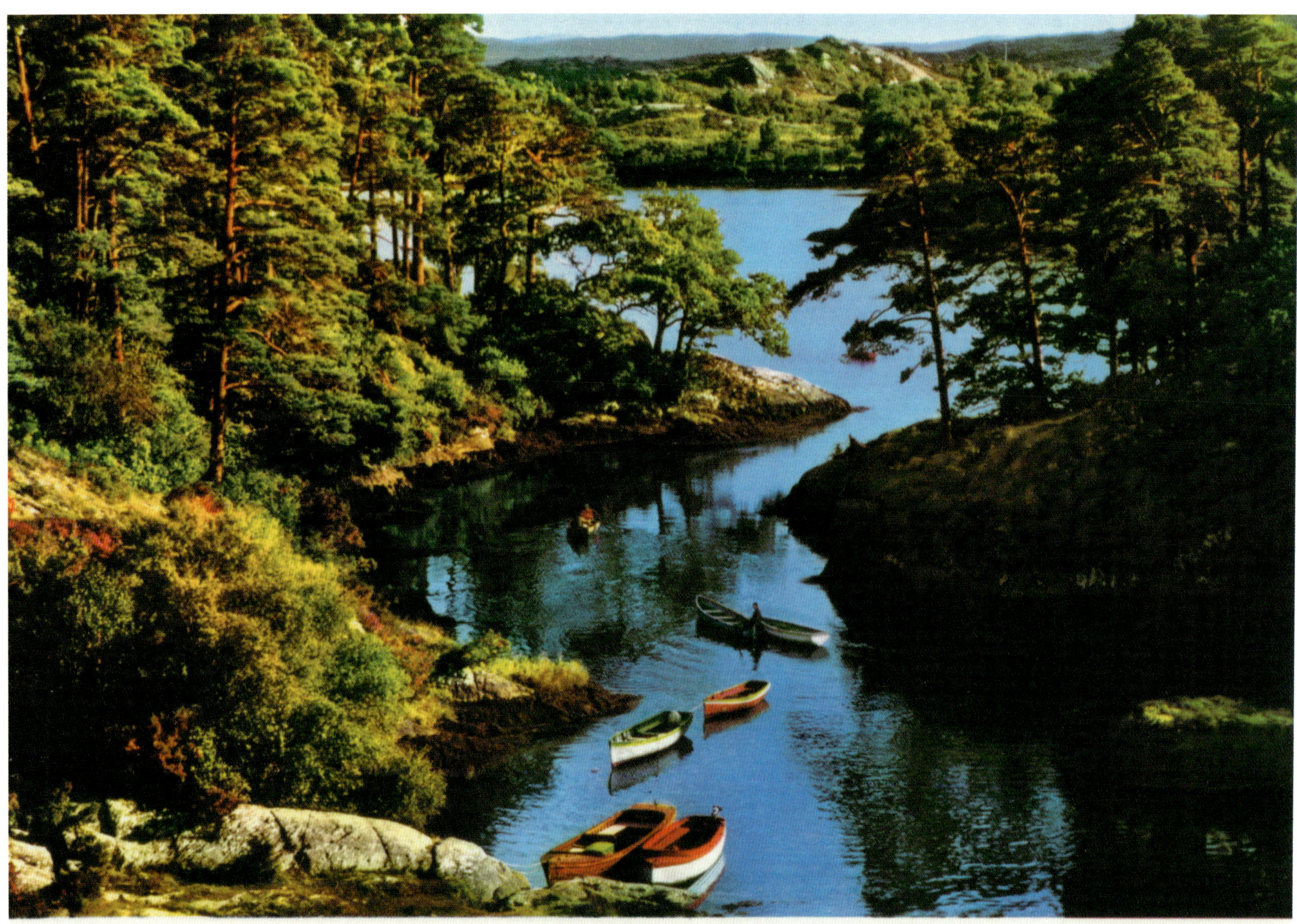

The Blue Pool, Glengarriff, Bantry Bay, Co. Cork, Ireland.

Colour Photo by John Hinde, F.R.P.S.

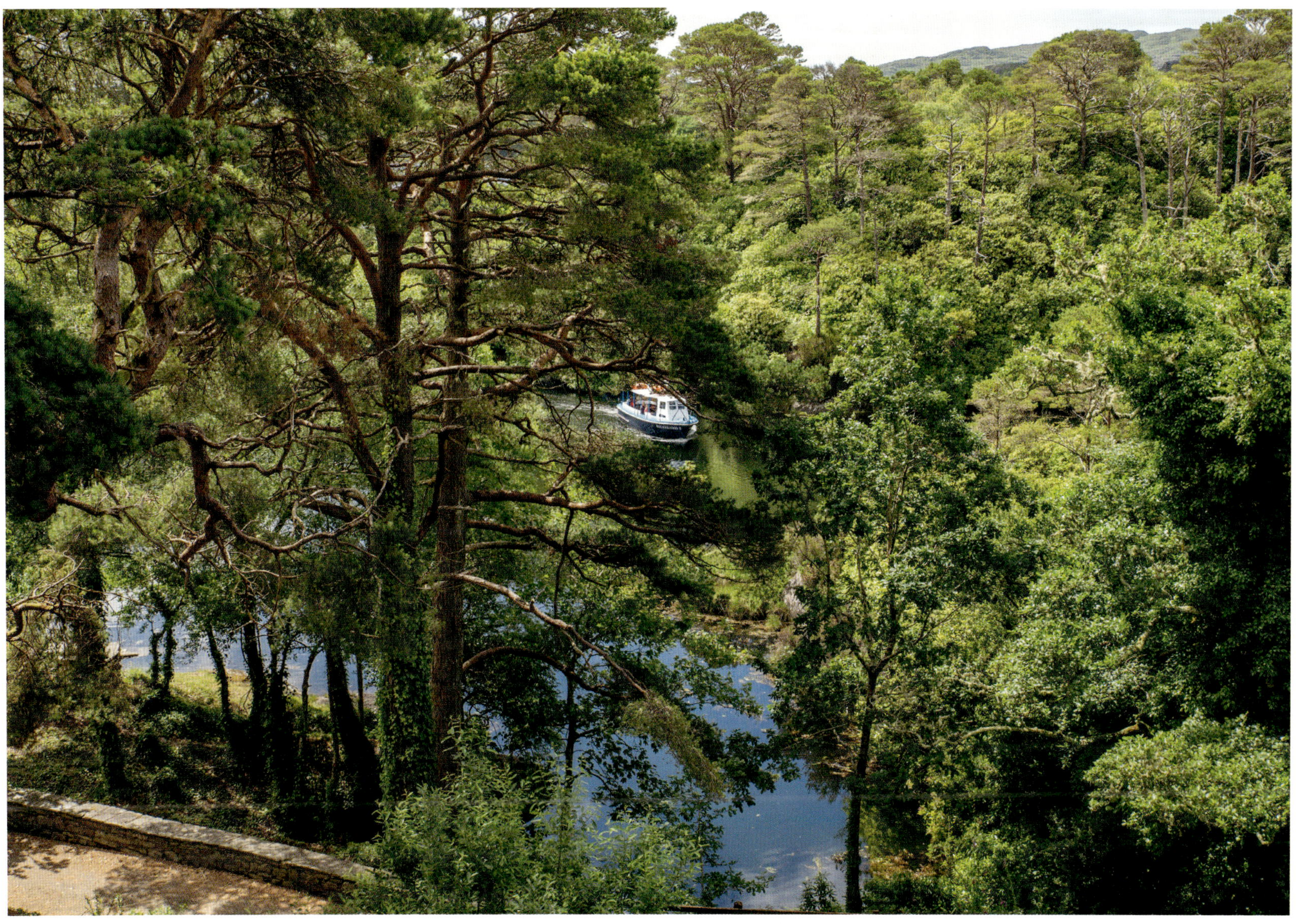

That's a Blue Pool ferry coming into Blue Pool and one of the many places from which to get a boat to Garnish Island. The blue pool is formed where river and sea meet, forming a magical tidal harbour overflowing with lush vegetation.

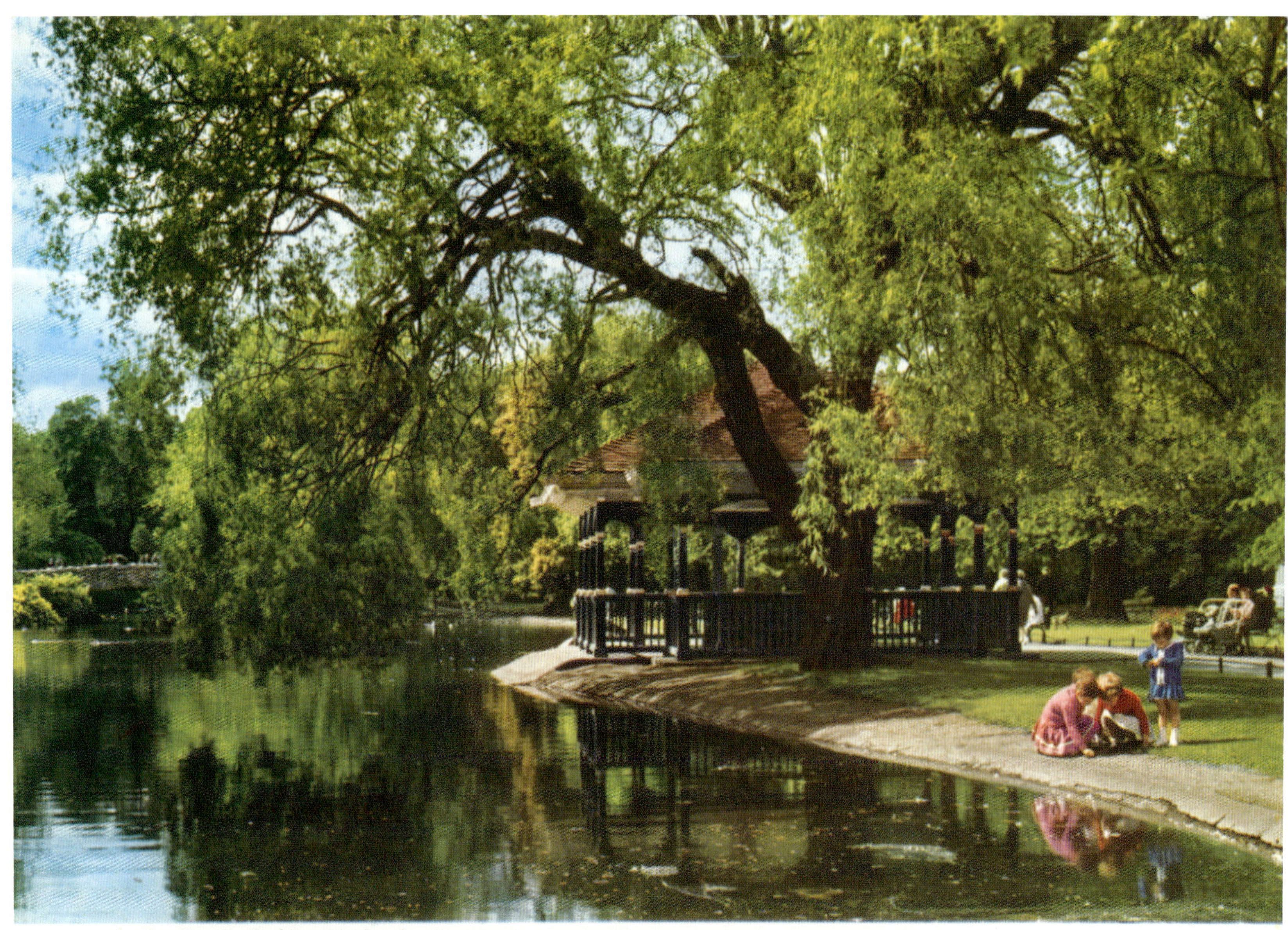

St. Stephen's Green, Dublin, Ireland.

Photo: E. Ludwig, John Hinde Studios.

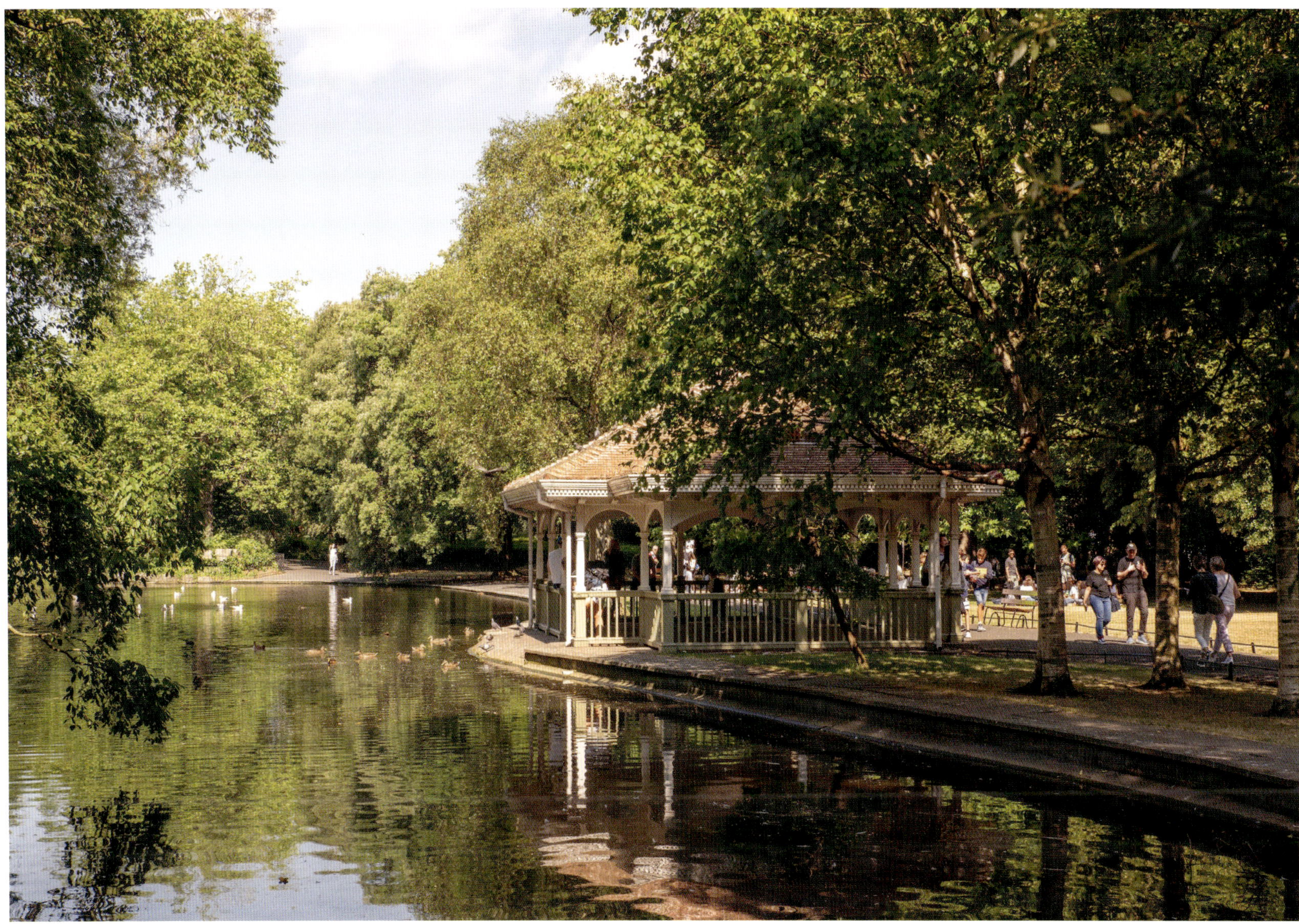

'The Green' became a public park in 1880 after a grant from Sir Arthur Edward Guinness, who grew up in what is now Iveagh House. Ten years later, this bandstand was added, paid for by the Dublin Metropolitan Police to commemorate Queen Victoria's jubilee. Statues and memorials include those of James Joyce, W.B. Yeats, James Clarence Mangan, Thomas Kettle, Wolfe Tone, Robert Emmet, Countess Markievicz and, of course, Arthur Guinness.

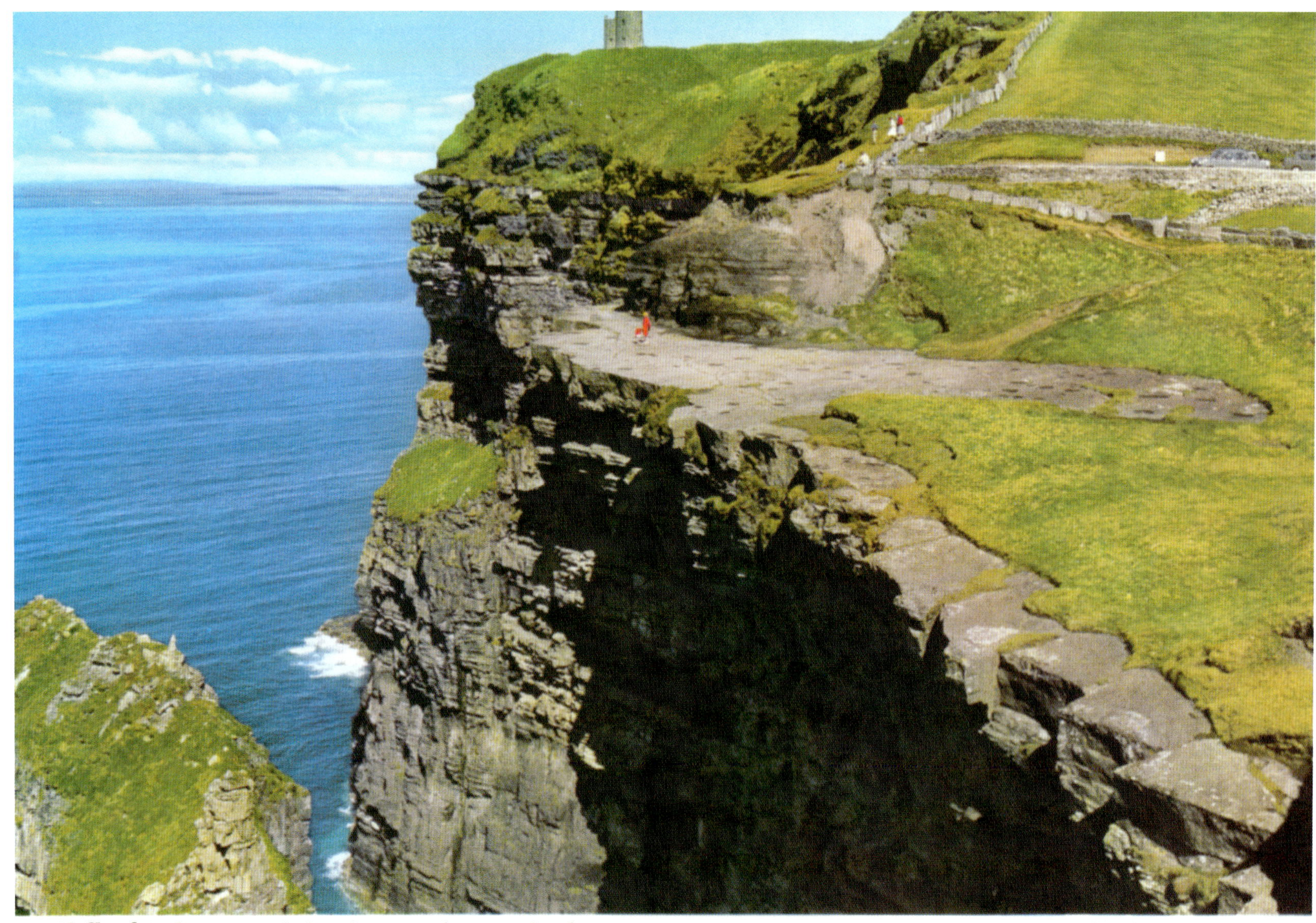

Cliffs of Moher, near Lahinch, Co. Clare, Ireland.

Colour Photo by John Hinde, F.R.P.S.

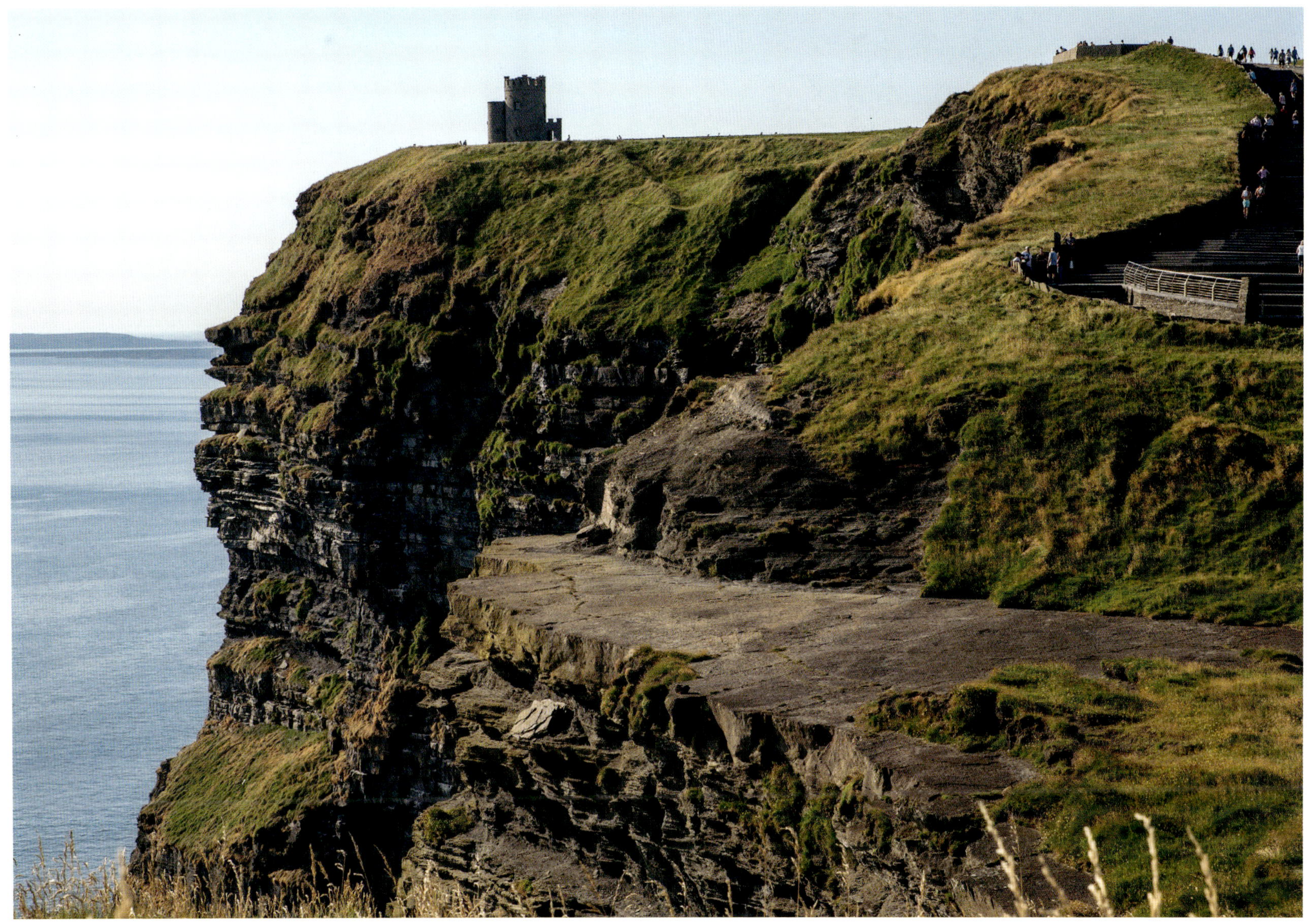

When I came here with my son Jensen in July, I explained to the man at the visitor centre my desire to reshoot this iconic postcard.

'What? No way can you take that same shot. Out of the question.' He spoke of 'health and safety concerns' he must enforce; how the area is fenced off; how visitors can no longer roam free. 'Stay to the designated path,' he told me, 'and no drones, either.'

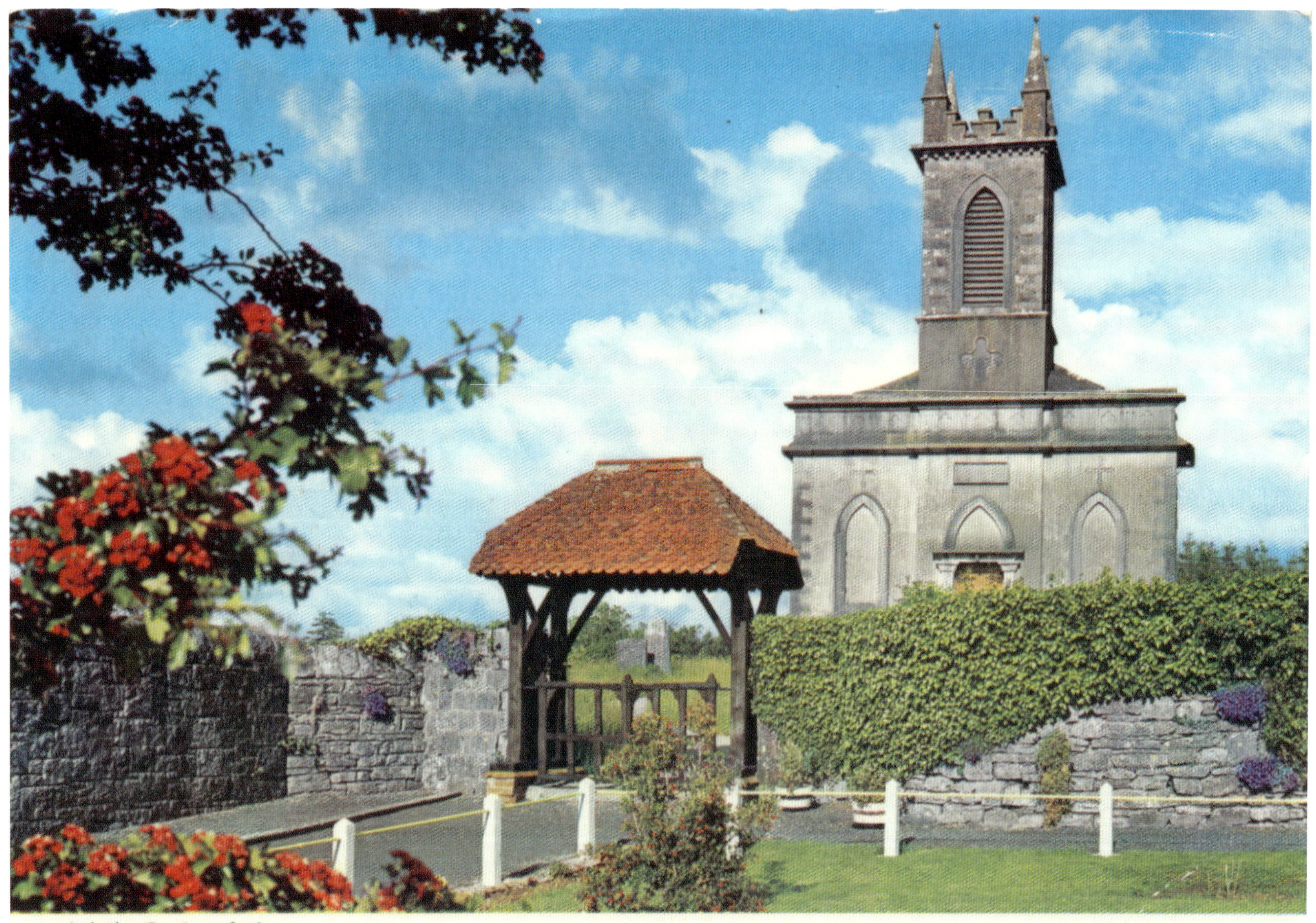

Ardagh, Co. Longford.

Photo: D. Noble, John Hinde Studios.

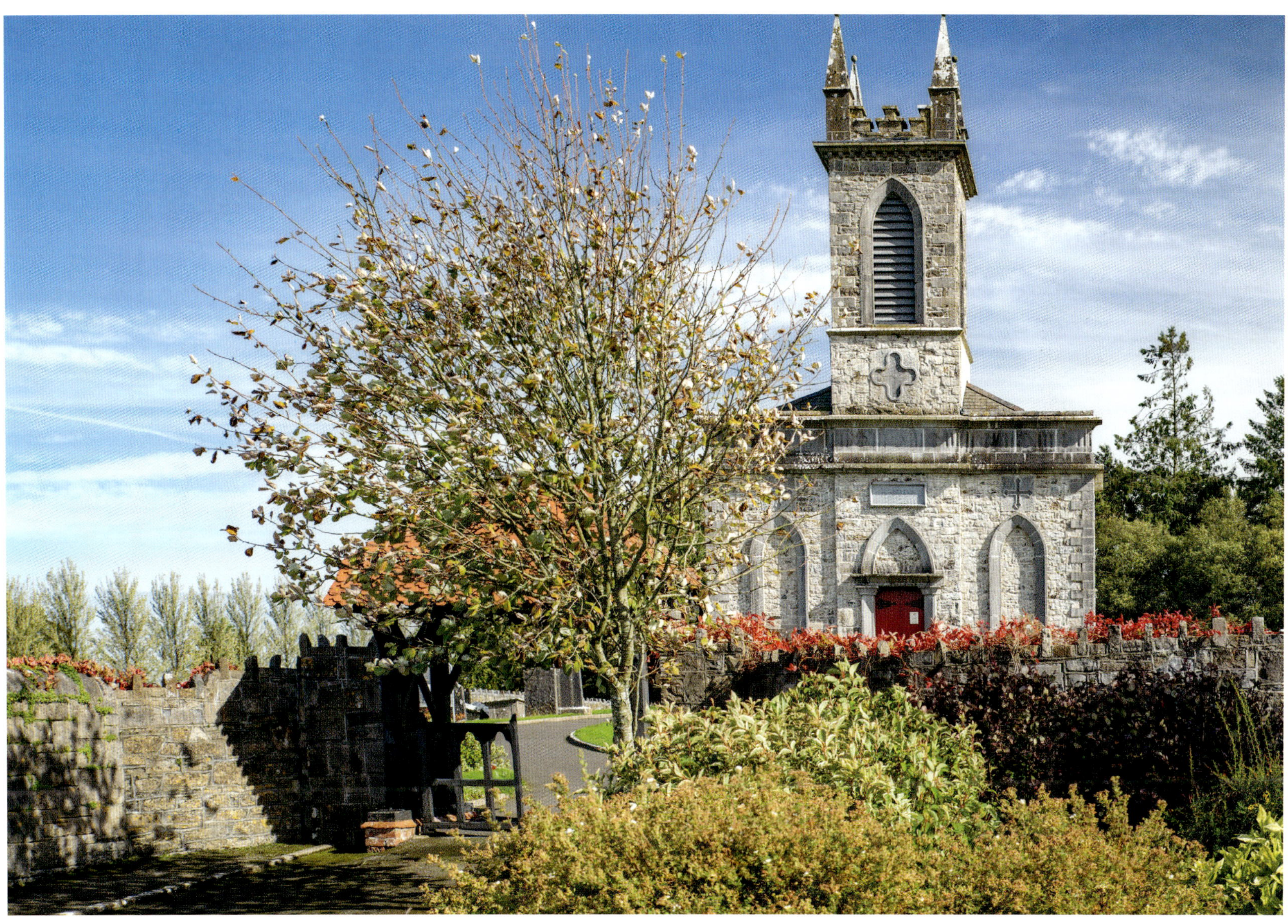

The Irish novelist, playwright and poet Oliver Goldsmith was born nearby in 1728, and the village of Ardagh featured in his comedic play, *She Stoops to Conquer*. St Patrick's Church features a lychgate, commonly found in England but very unusual for Ireland.

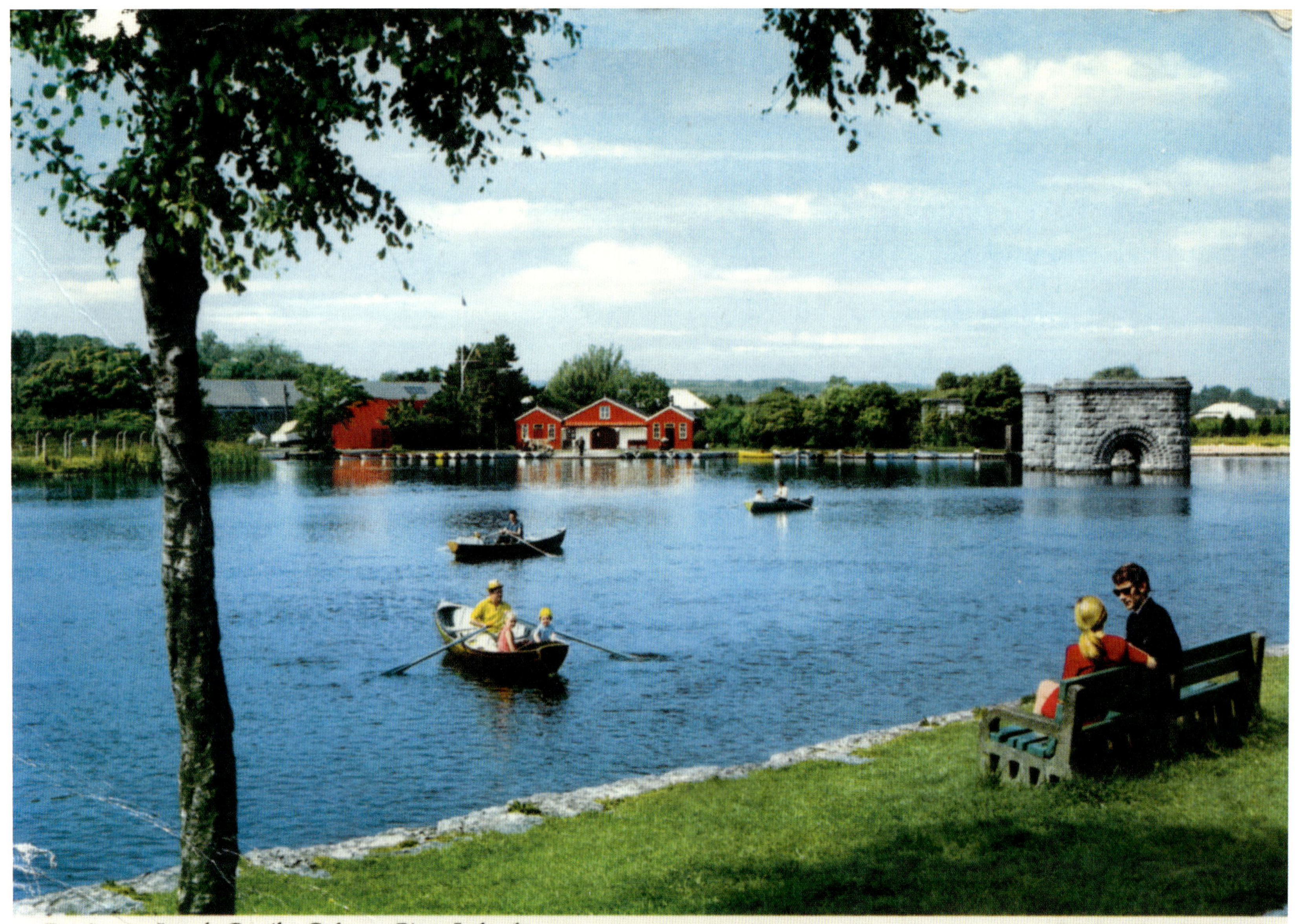

Boating on Lough Corrib, Galway City, Ireland

Photo: D. Noble, John Hinde Studios.

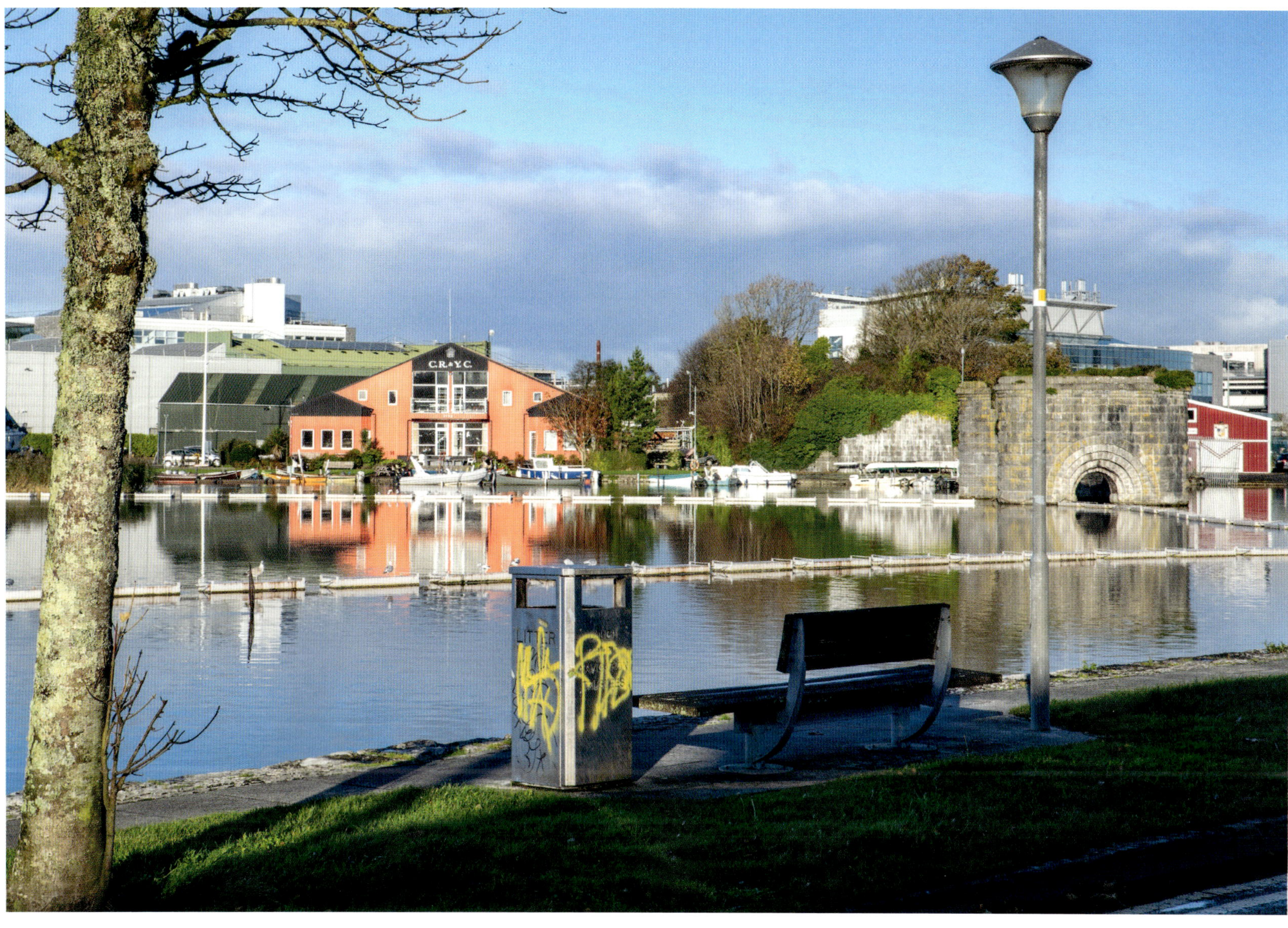

Across the river Corrib and adjacent to the salmon weir is the Corrib Rowing and Yachting Club. Founded in 1864, it is recognised as one of the oldest clubs in Ireland. Bright if unlovely graffiti is a 21st-century addition to the original shot.

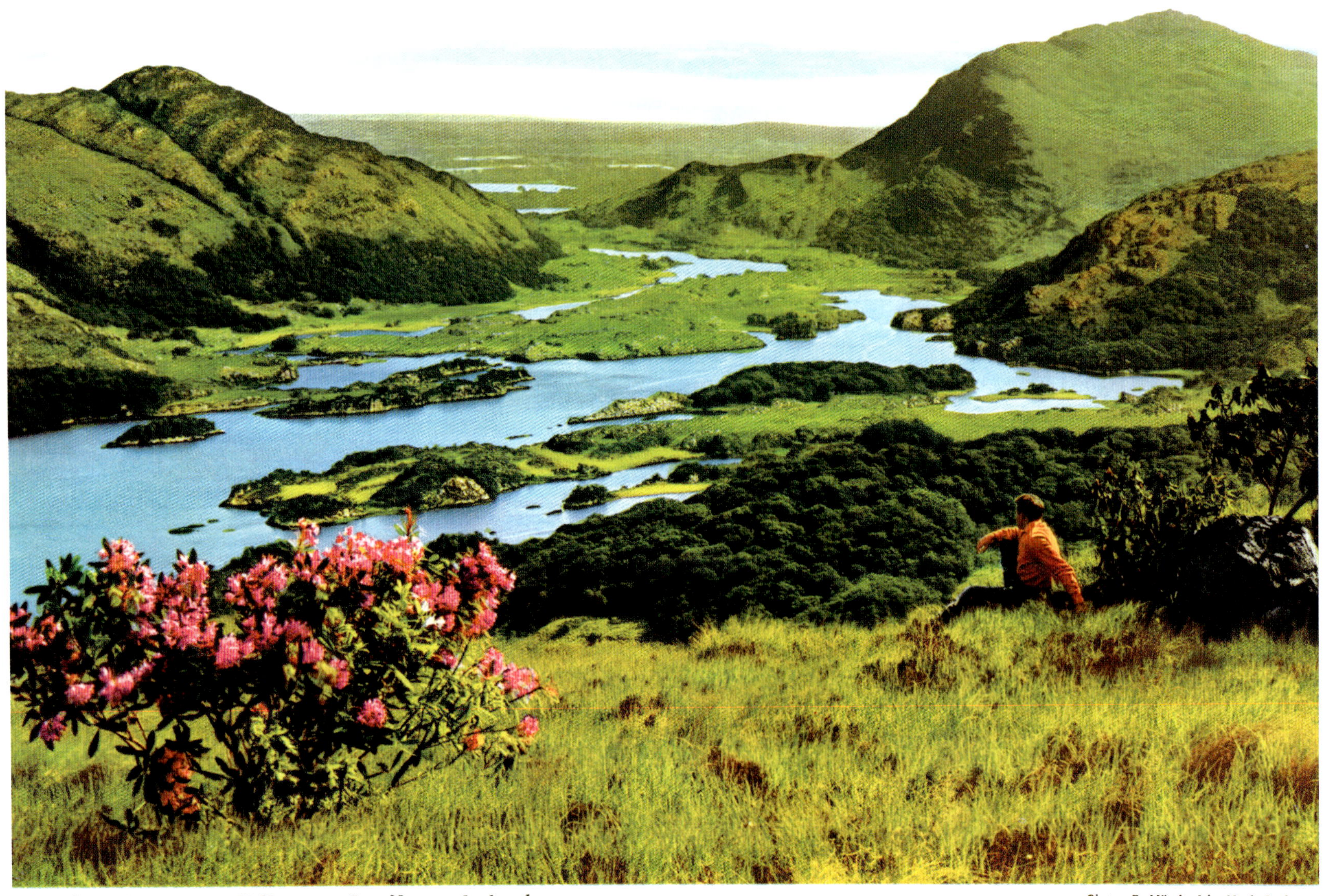

Ladies' View, near Killarney, Co. Kerry, Ireland.

Photo : E. Nägele, John Hinde Studios.

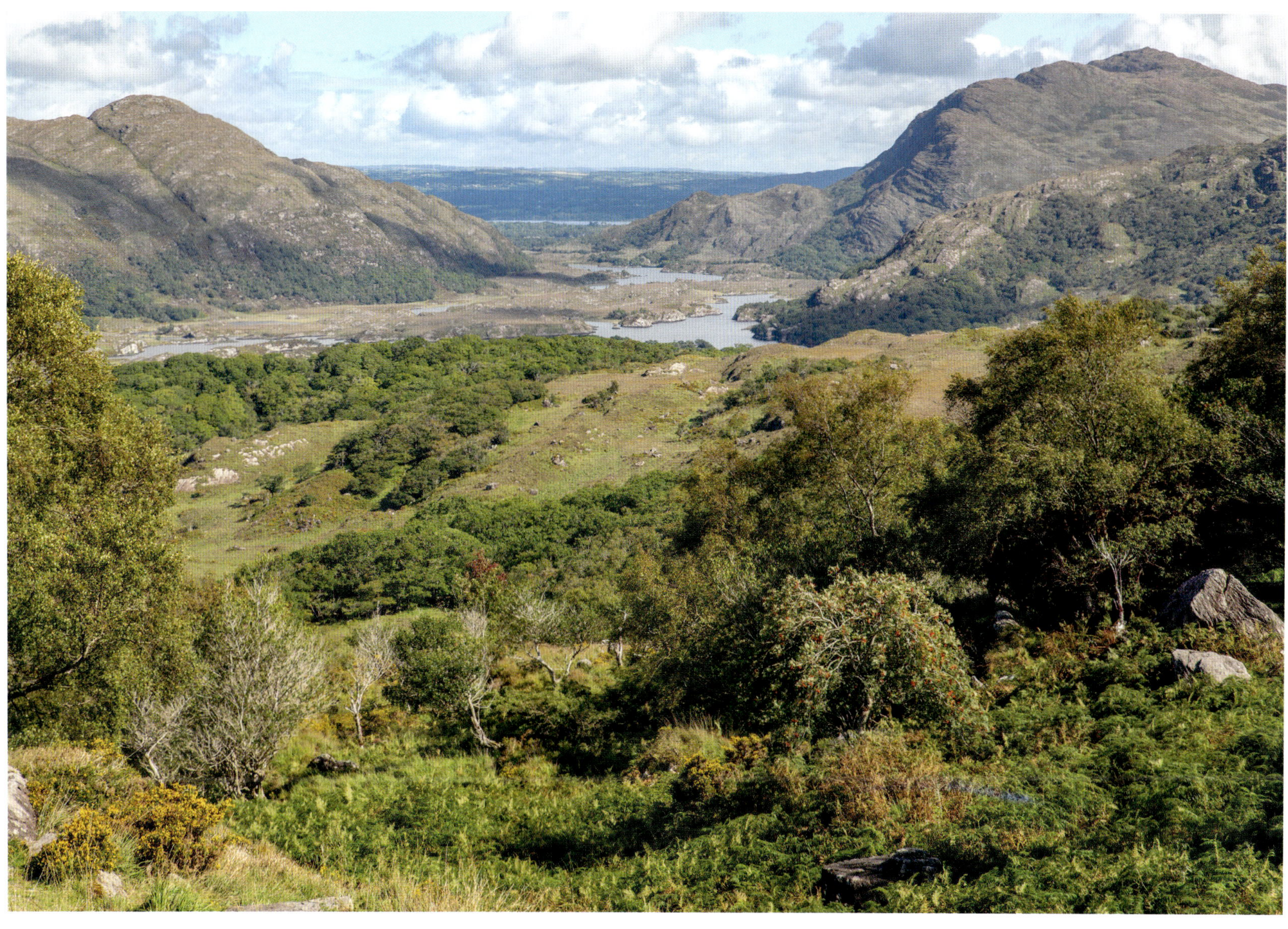

On the Ring of Kerry and in the heart of Killarney National Park is one of Ireland's best-known panoramas. Queen Victoria's ladies-in-waiting visited here during the royal tour of 1861. Apparently they were so smitten by the view that it was named after them. Even in its true colours today, you can clearly see what the ladies loved about it.

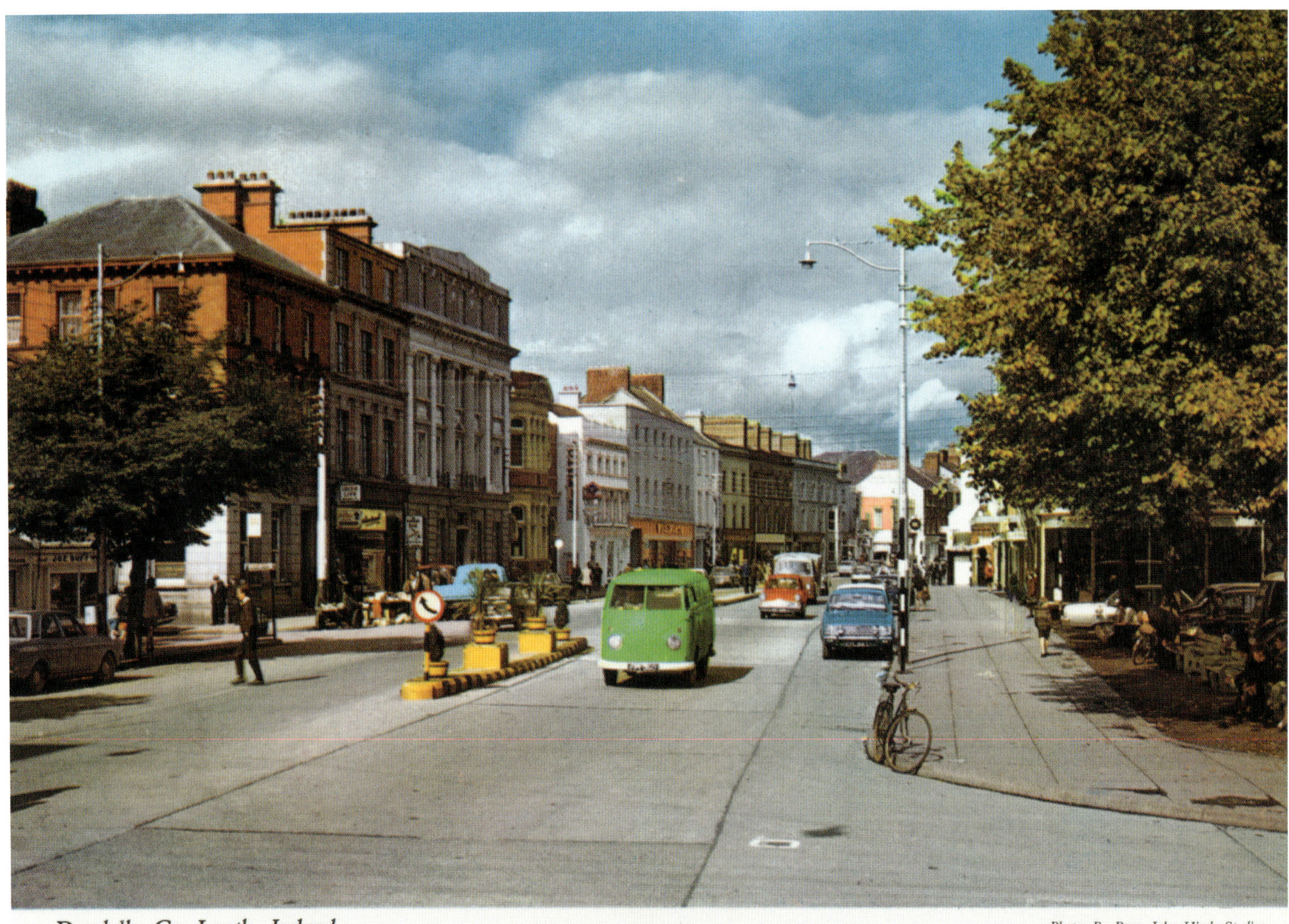

Dundalk, Co. Louth, Ireland. *Photo: R. Beer, John Hinde Studios.*

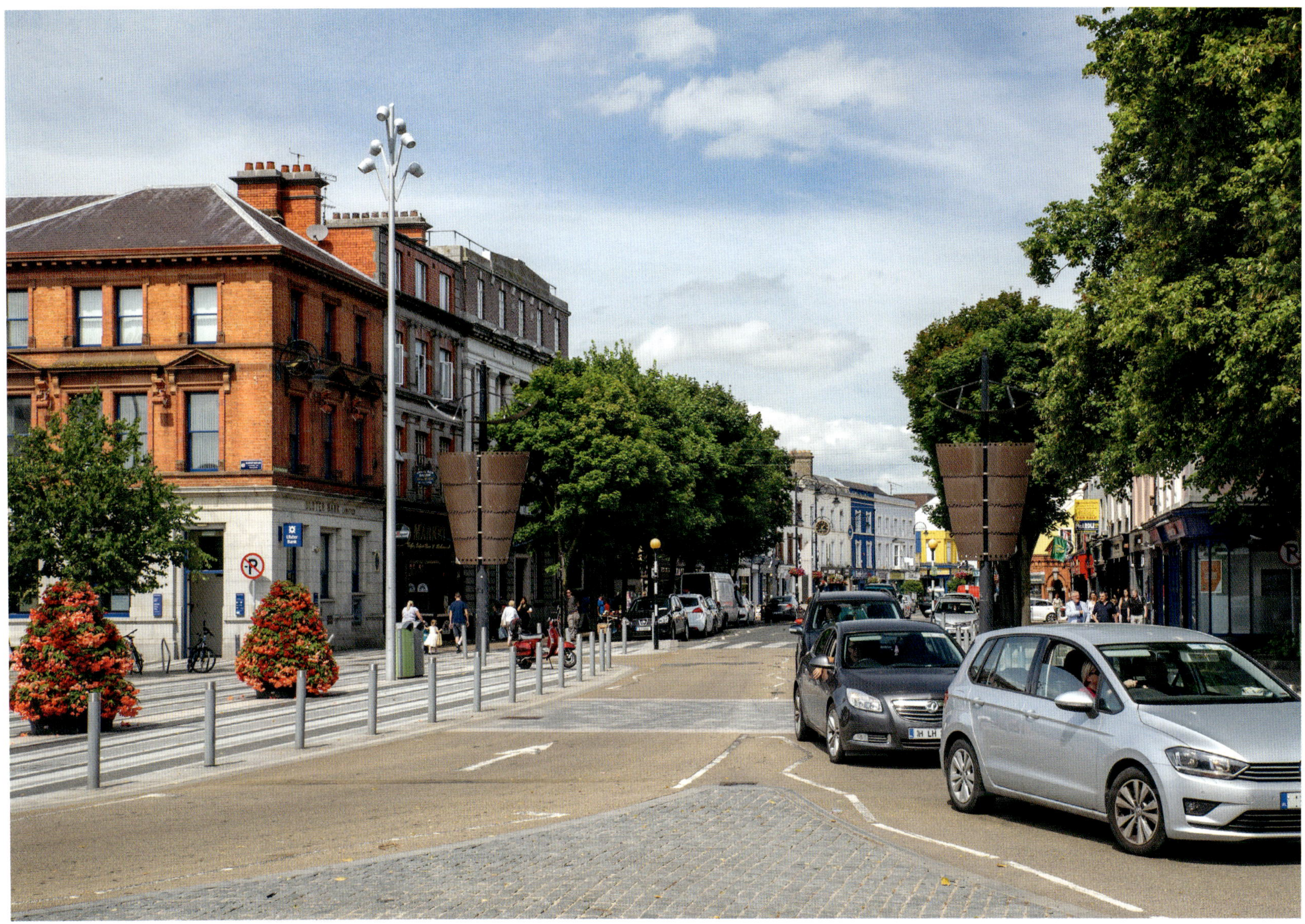

Dundalk benefits from being close to the border with Northern Ireland, and equidistant from Dublin and Belfast.

'I gave birth to brave Cú Chulainn', reads the town crest. It refers to the mythical warrior Cú Chulainn, also known as the Hound of Ulster, a local lad and ancient Gaelic hero gifted with superhuman strength, speed and skill.

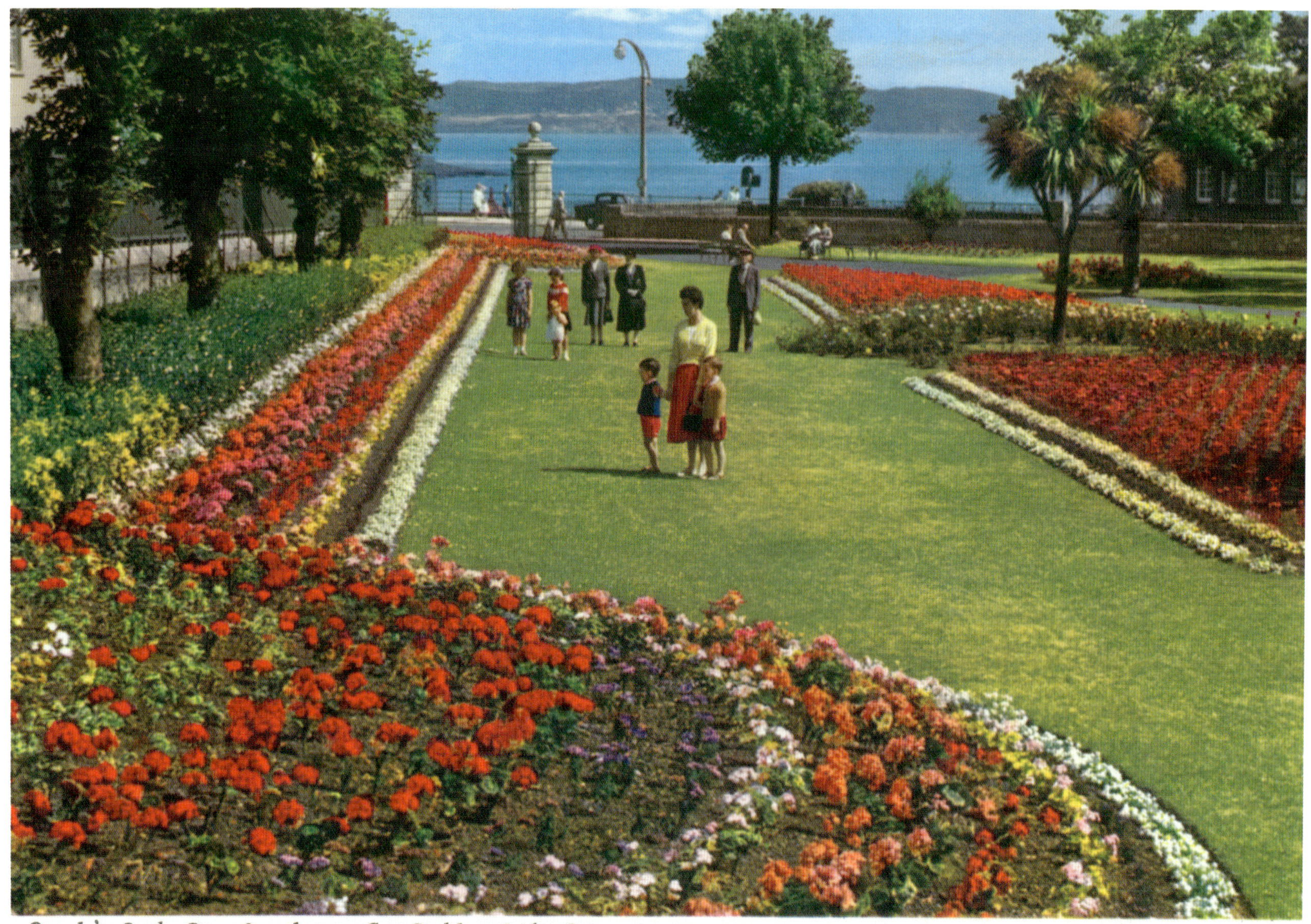

People's Park, Dun Laoghaire, Co. Dublin, Ireland.

Colour Photo by John Hinde, F.R.P.S.

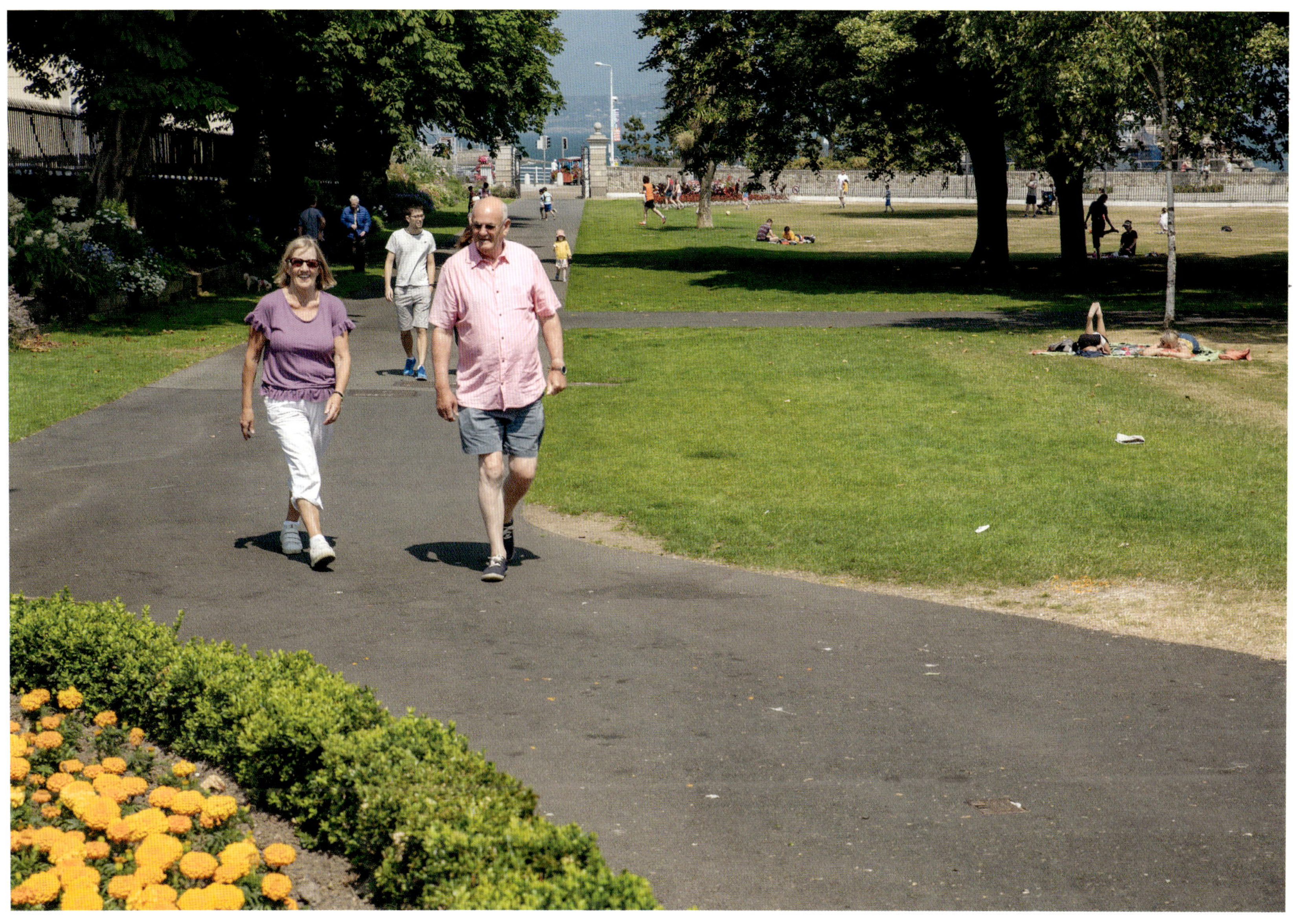

The People's Park is a Victorian-style park that opened in 1890, when Dún Laoghaire was known as Kingstown. It features a fine array of heritage buildings and structures, including a tearoom, gate lodge, bandstand and fountains. However, the orderly blooming ranks of startling colour are notably absent in my version.

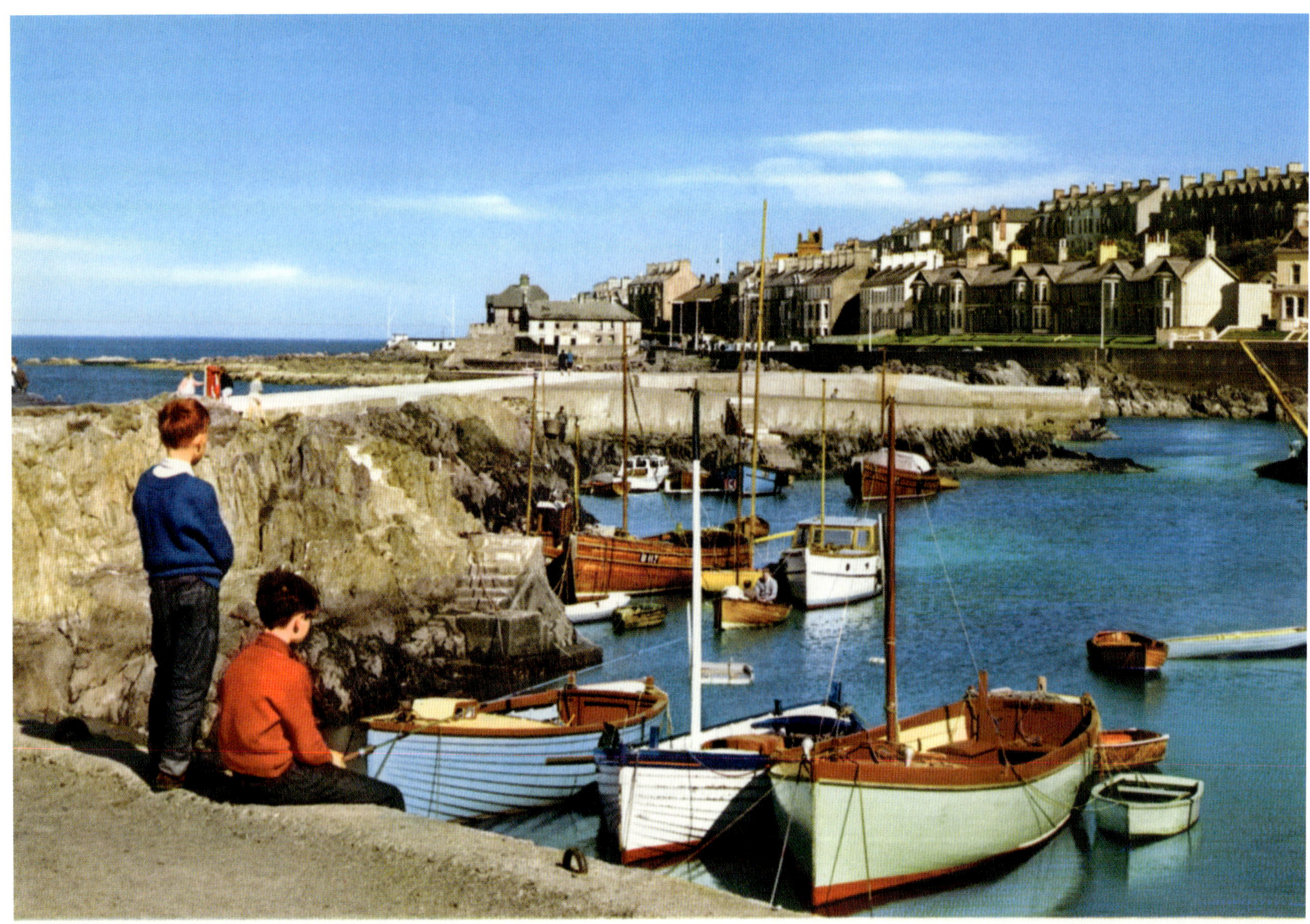

The "Long Hole", Bangor, Co. Down, N.I.

Photo : E. Nägele, John Hinde Studios.

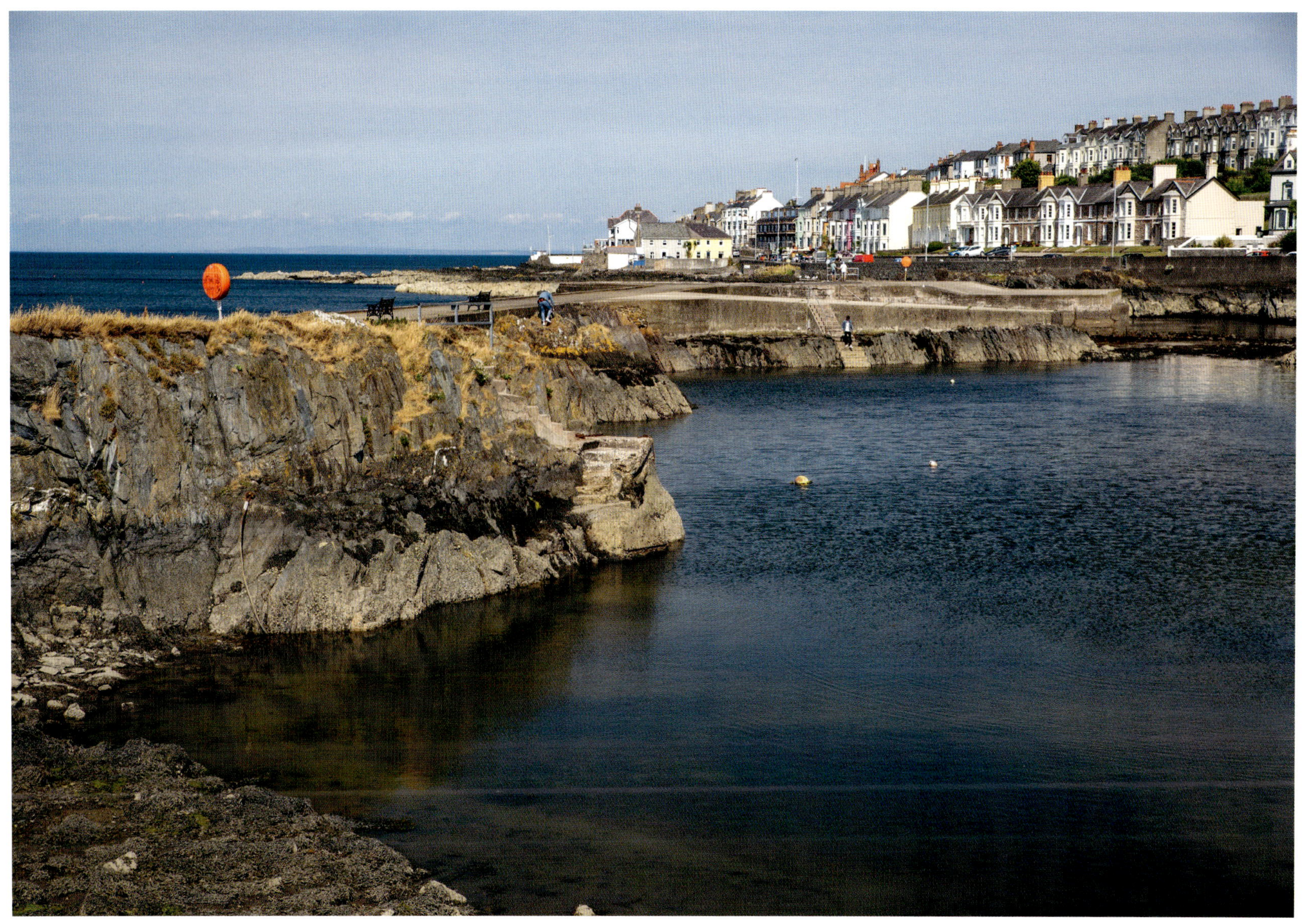

With the houses of Seacliff Road in the background, the Long Hole, created from a 19th-century stone quarry, was once filled with fishing and pleasure boats but today is silted up and largely disused. Now the little harbour ripples gently in the sun, dreaming of those colour-saturated days.

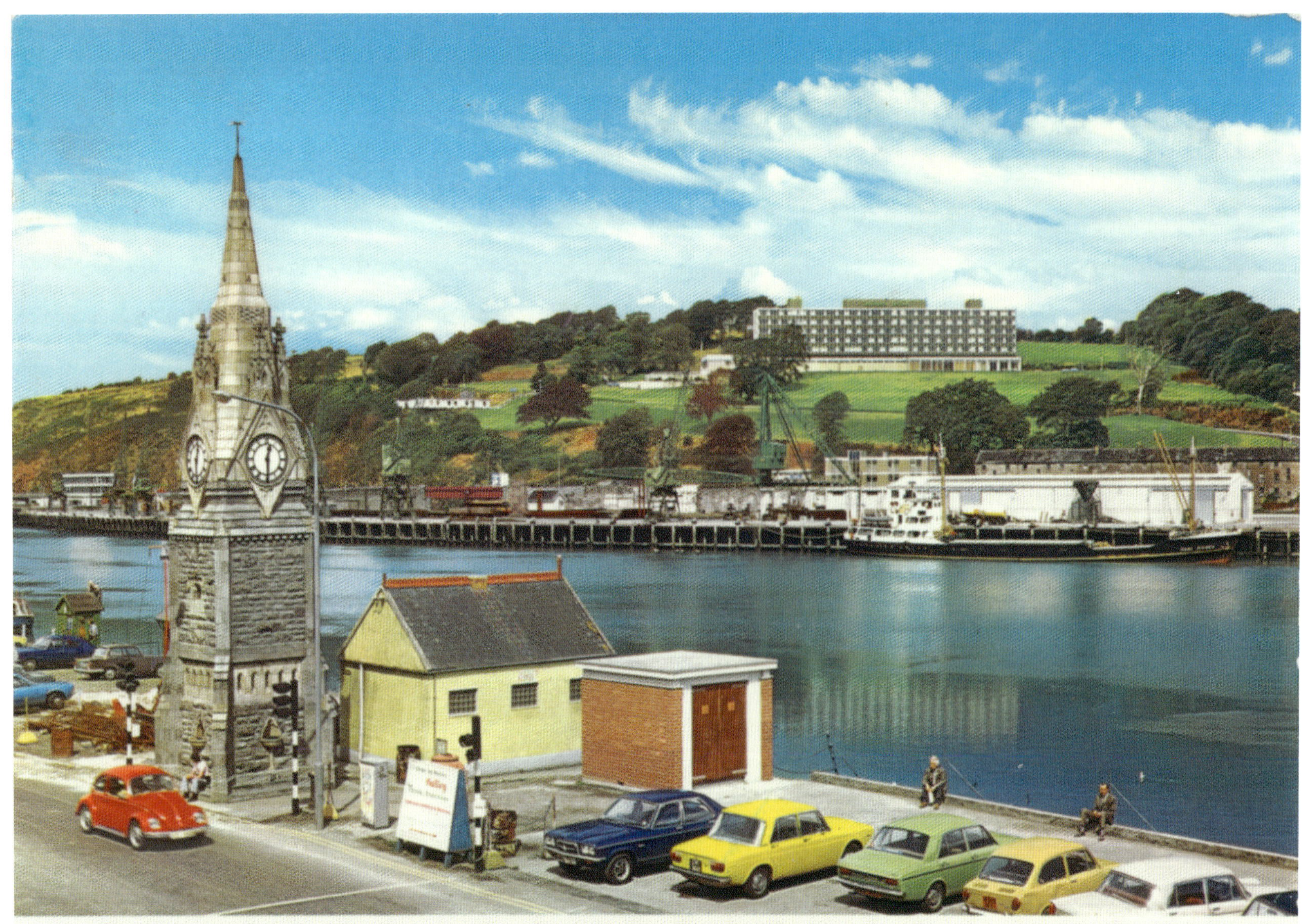

The Clock Tower and River Suir, showing Ardree Hotel, Waterford City, Ireland. *Photo: P. O'Toole, John Hinde Studios.*

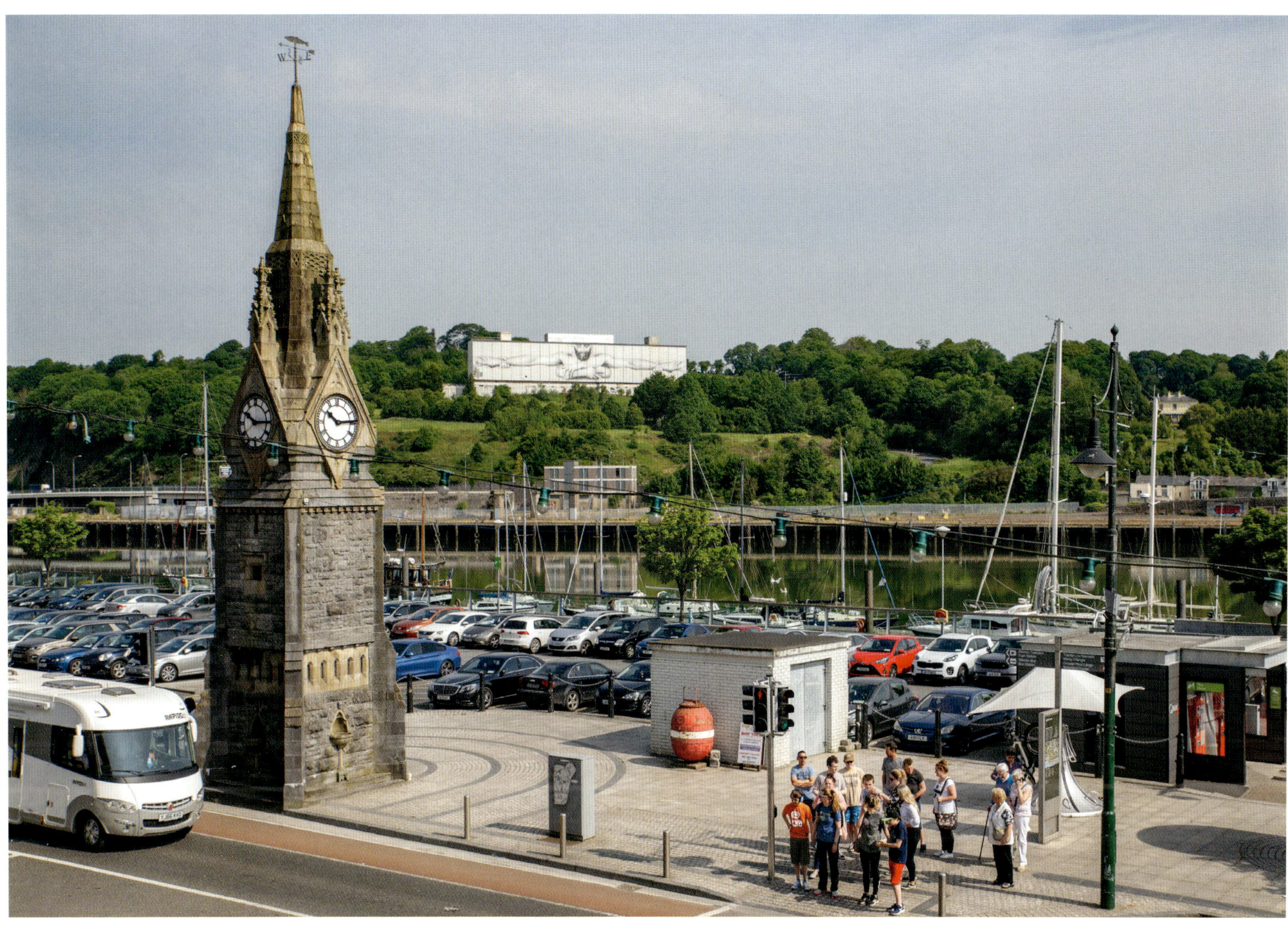

The clock tower was built in 1863, when Waterford was Ireland's busiest industrial port. I had to take this photograph at a different angle than I would have liked. I first tried Kelly's department store, but his second-floor windows were bolted shut. Thankfully, the bankers at AIB next door offered me the next best vantage point. The tower still stands foursquare, presiding now over a sea of cars.

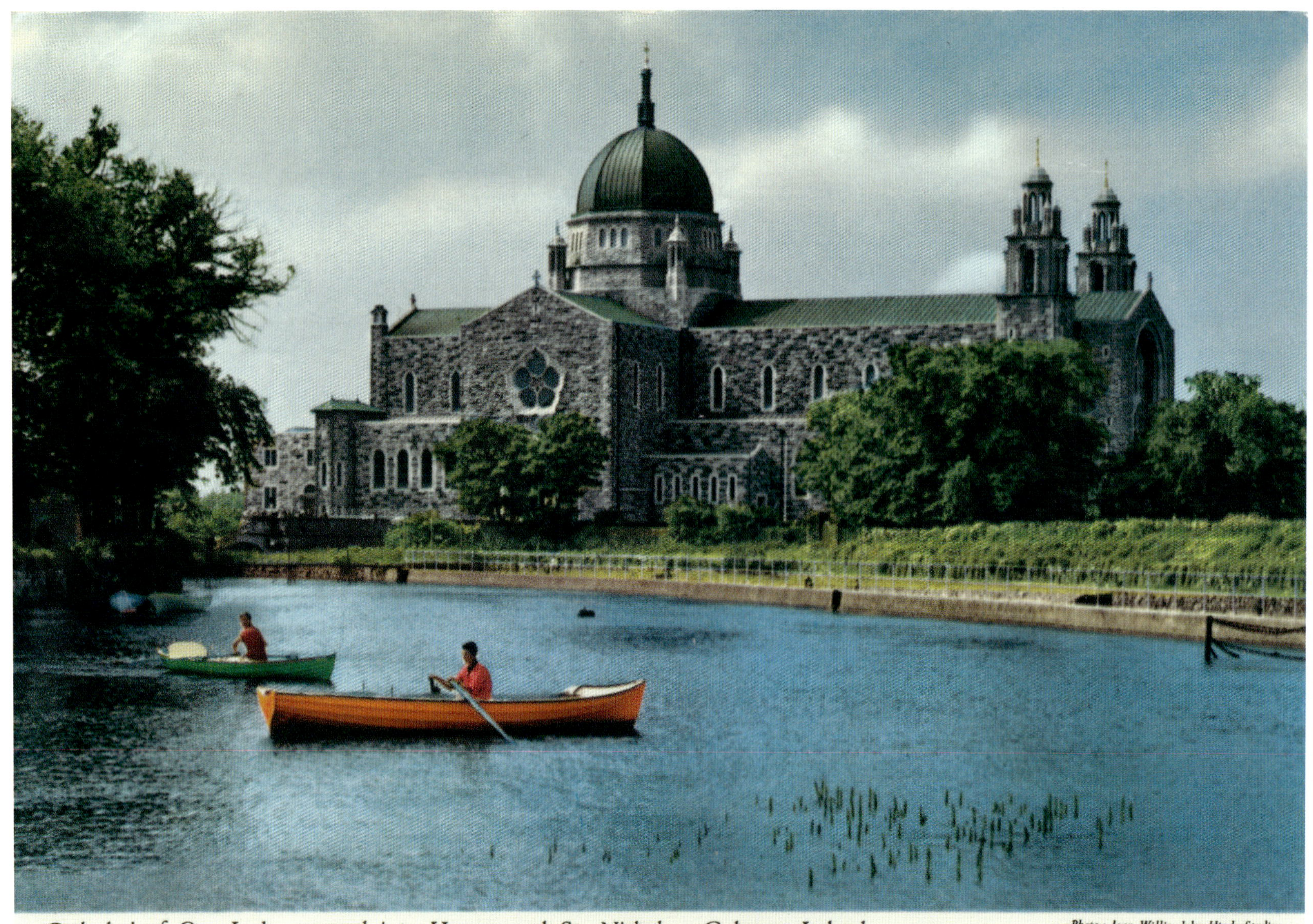

Cathedral of Our Lady assumed into Heaven and St. Nicholas, Galway, Ireland. *Photo: Joan Willis, John Hinde Studios.*

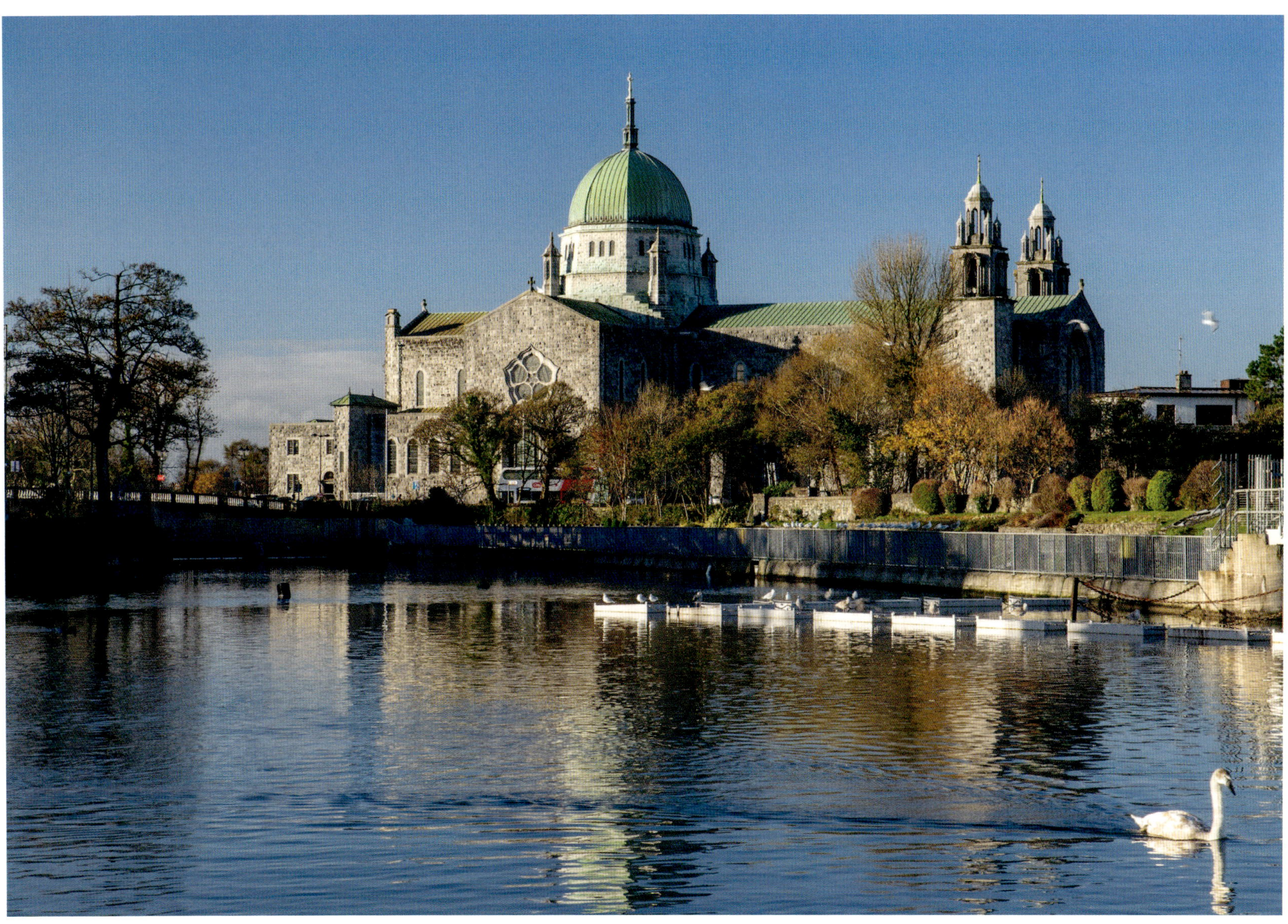

This postcard's caption measures the magnificence here: '*Dedicated in 1965, Galway's new cathedral, designed by John J. Robinson, is largely built from local limestone and Connemara marble. Its dome rises to 126 feet and the church seats 2,000. The Stations of the Cross are in Portland stone, designed by Gabrielle Hayes.*'

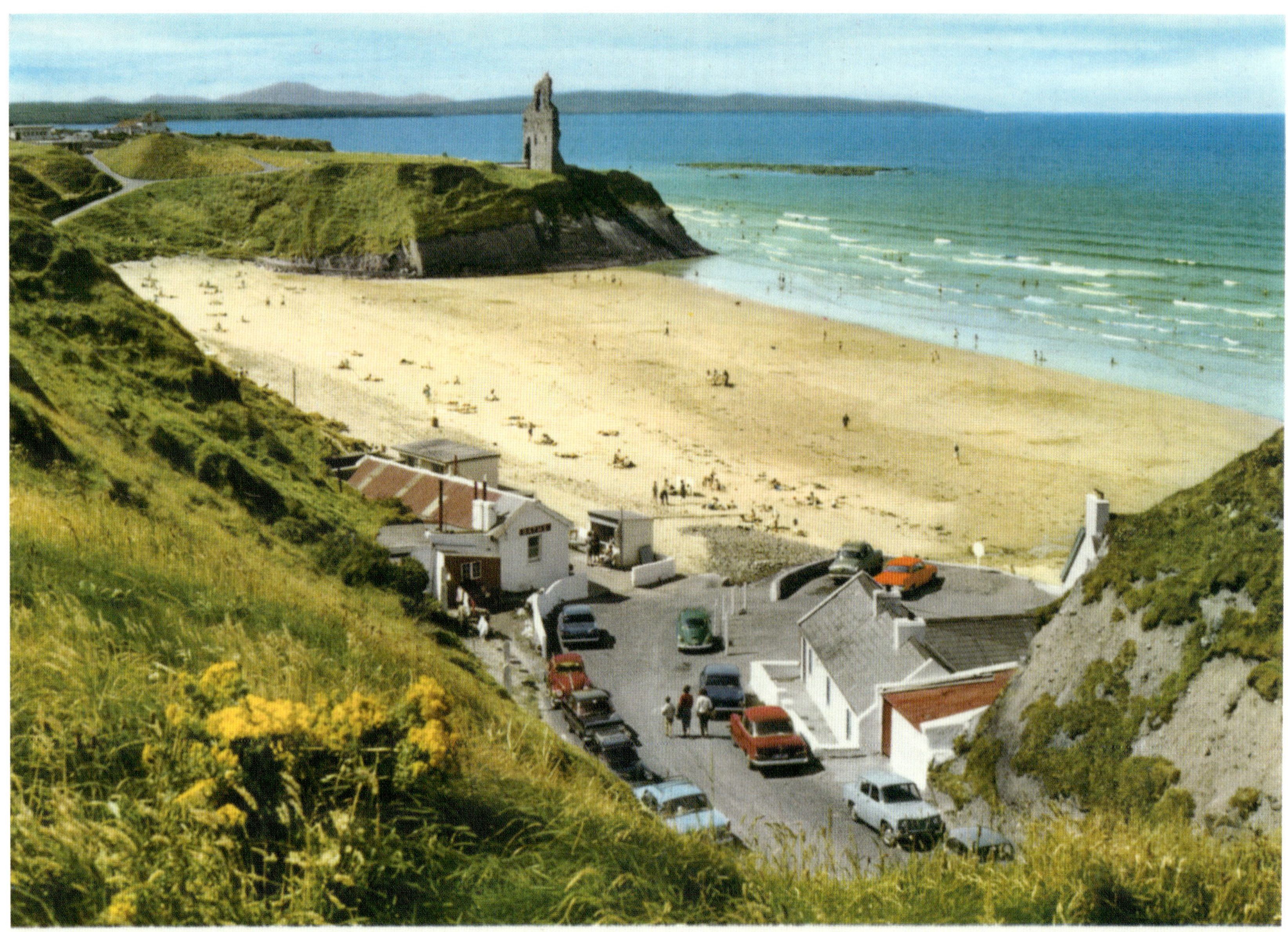

The Beach at Ballybunion, Co. Kerry, Ireland.

Photo: Joan Willis, John Hinde Studios.

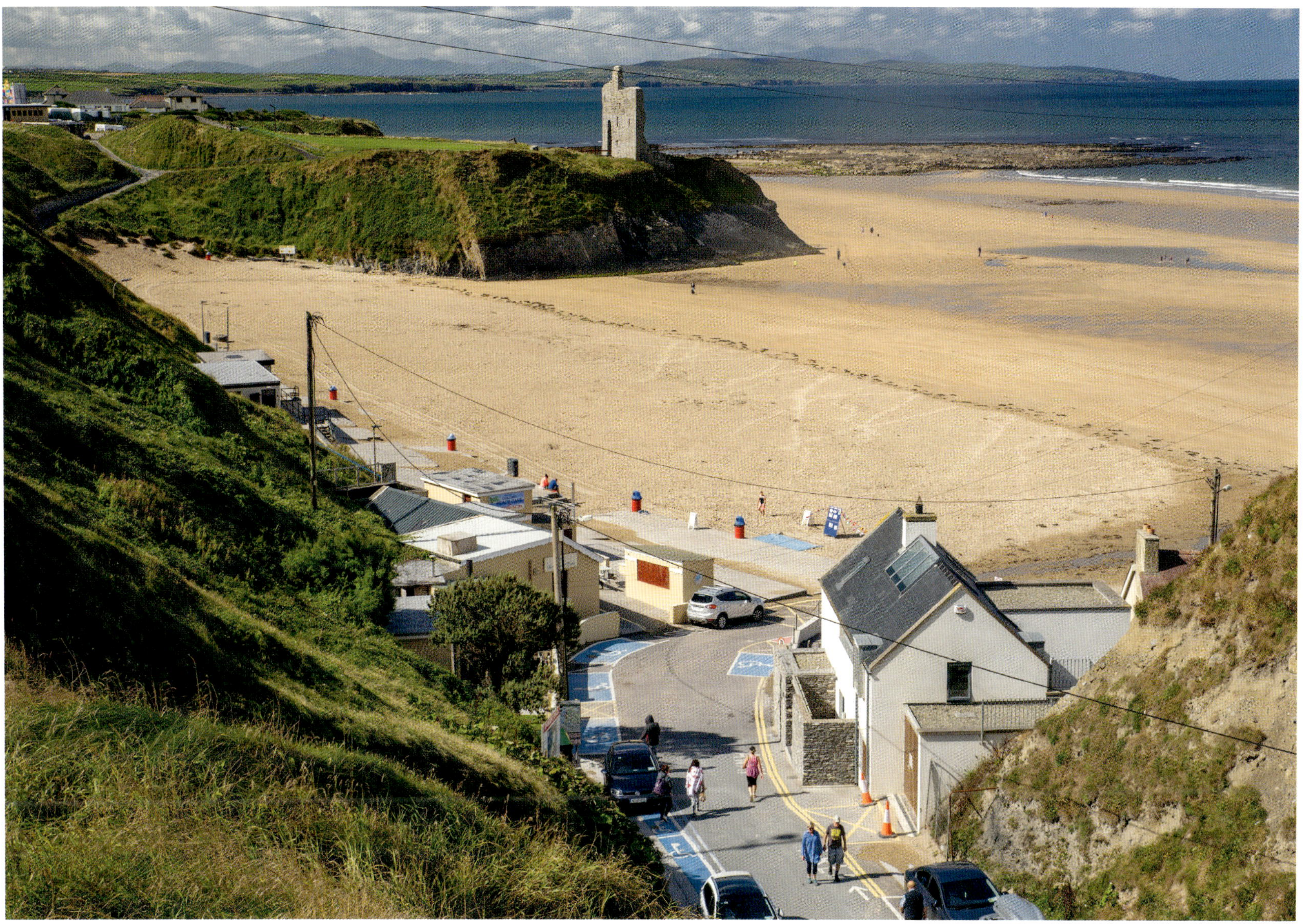

This beach to the right of the castle is known as 'Ladies' Beach'; the one to the left is the 'Men's Beach' because, back in the day, men used to bathe apart from women and children. Thankfully, this practice has not been observed for decades.

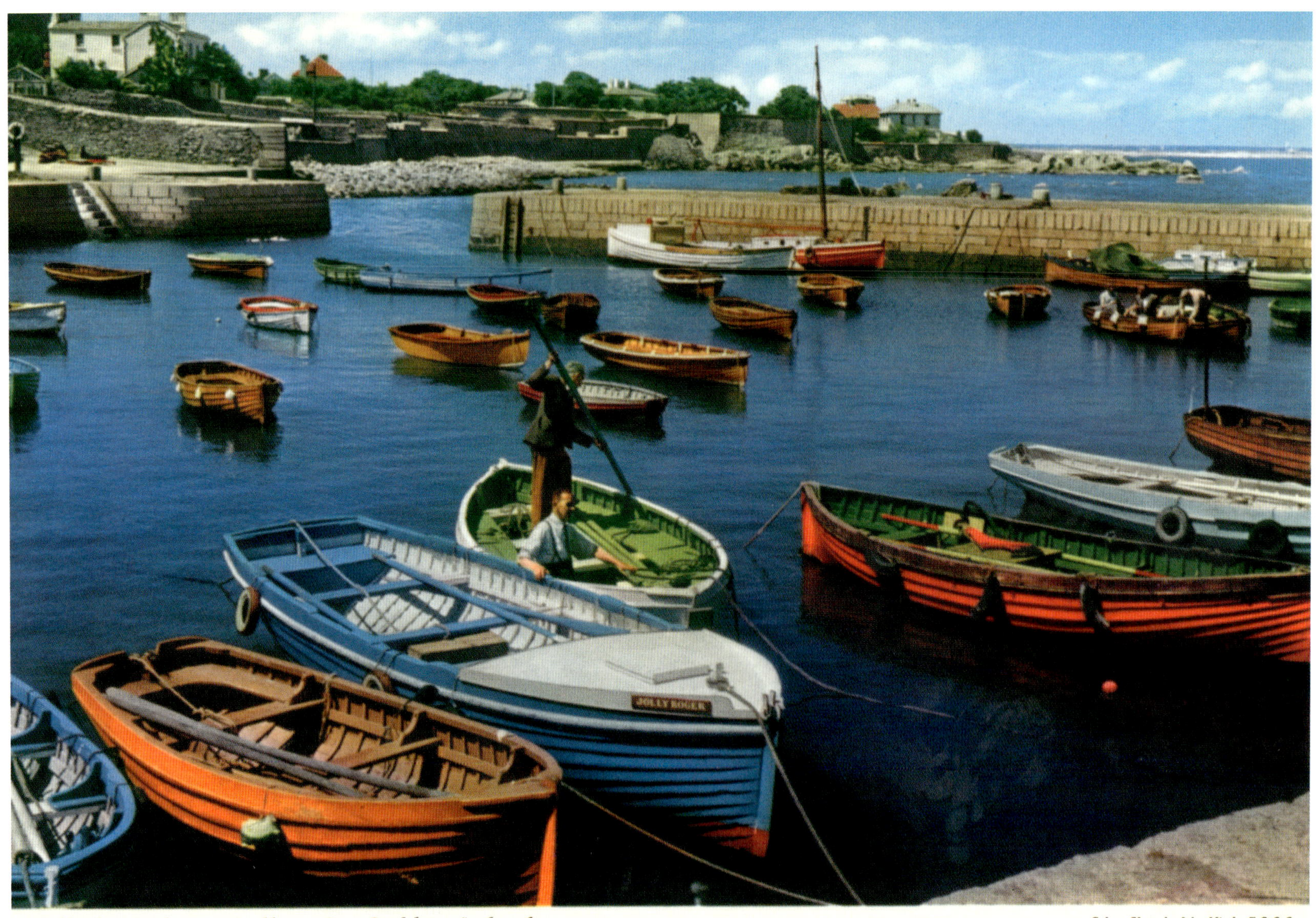

Bulloch Harbour, Dalkey, Co. Dublin, Ireland.

Colour Photo by John Hinde, F.R.P.S.

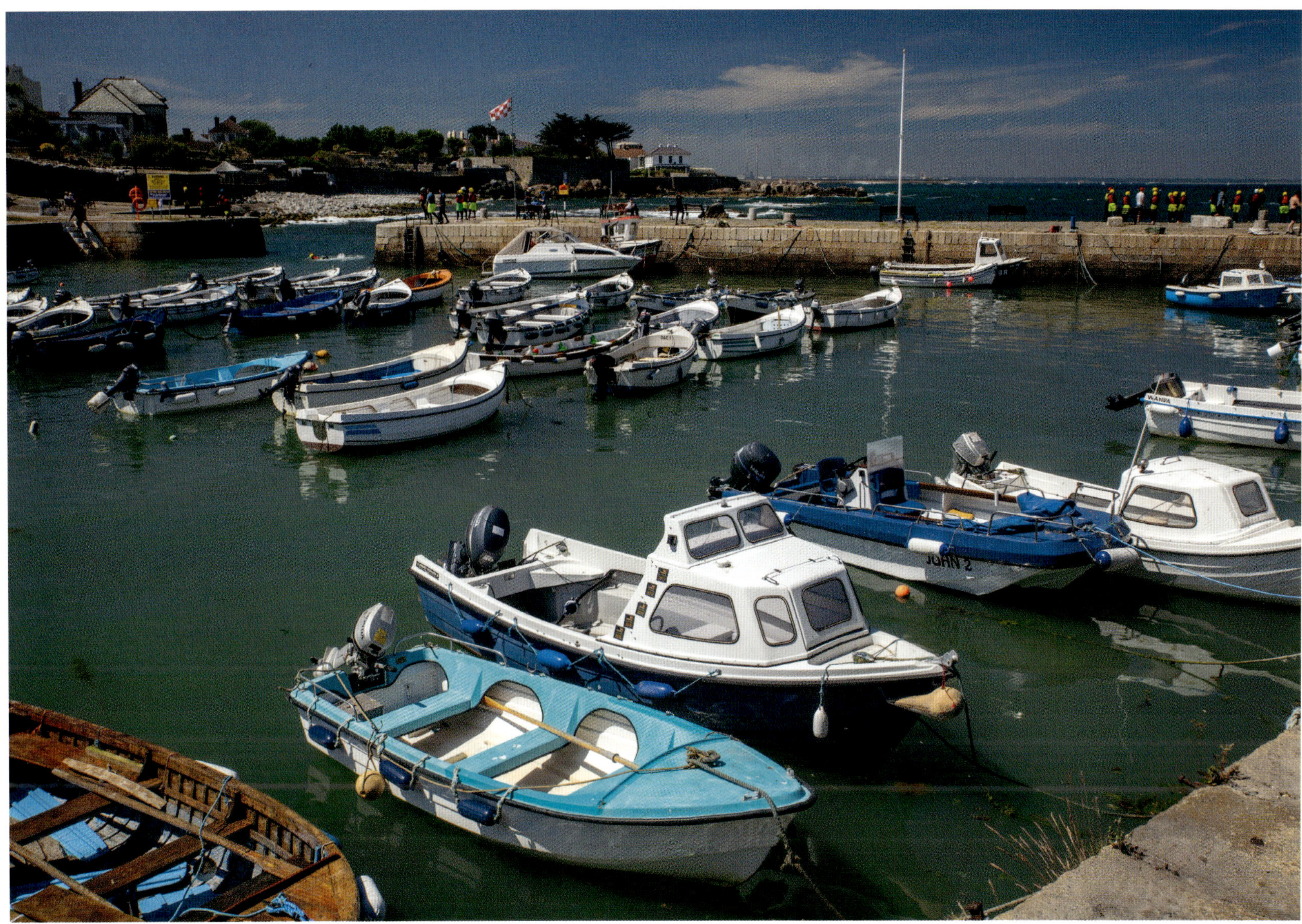

In 1956, John Hinde and his wife Jutta moved into a house near Bulloch Harbour in Dalkey, known as 'The Studio'. At the time, Hinde did not realise that, 72 years earlier, his mother was born at a house in Dalkey, less than a mile from his studio. Over the next two decades, this Englishman captured some of the most iconic images of Ireland.

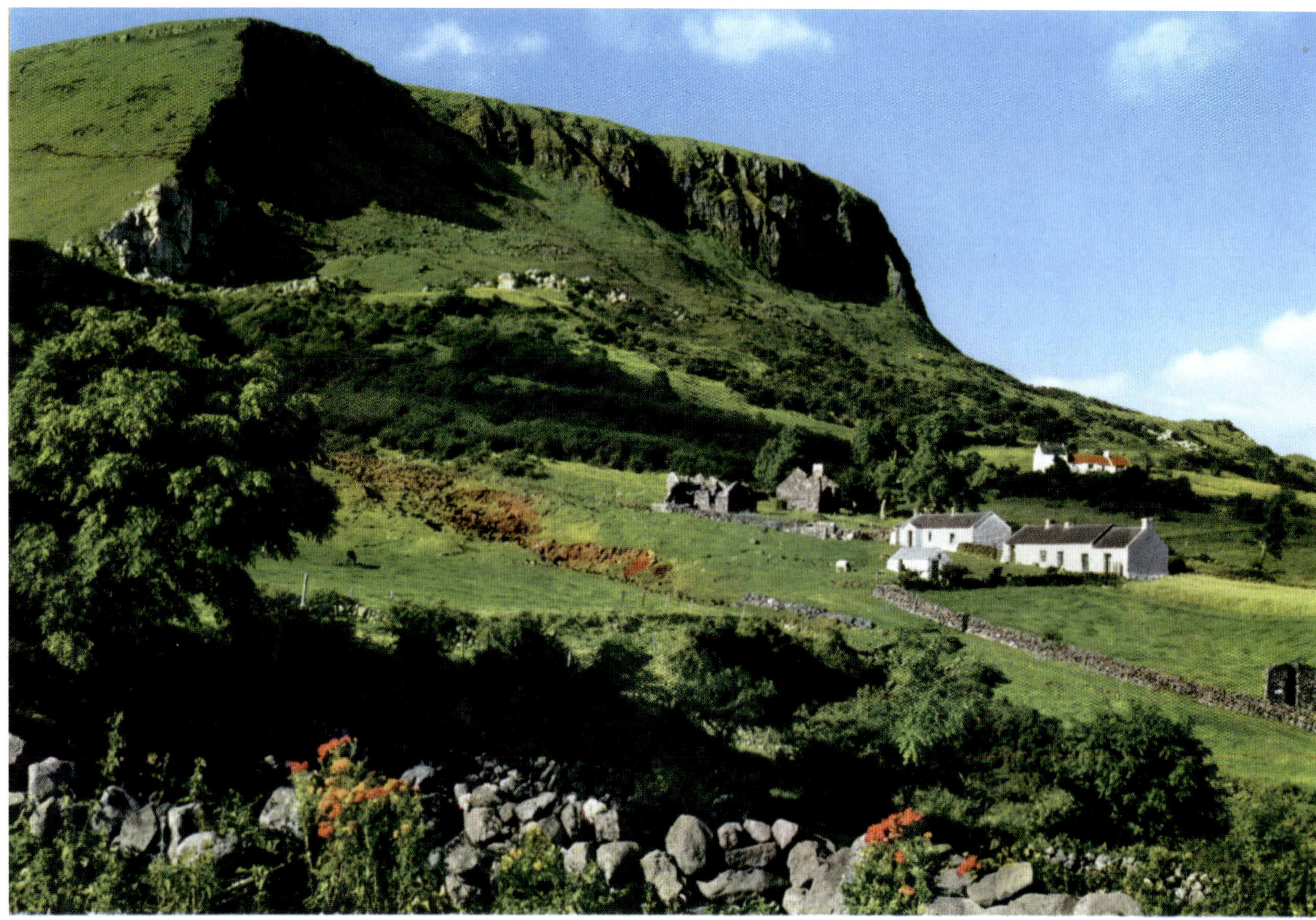

Farm in the Antrim Glens, N.I. *Photo: E. Nägele, John Hinde Studios.*

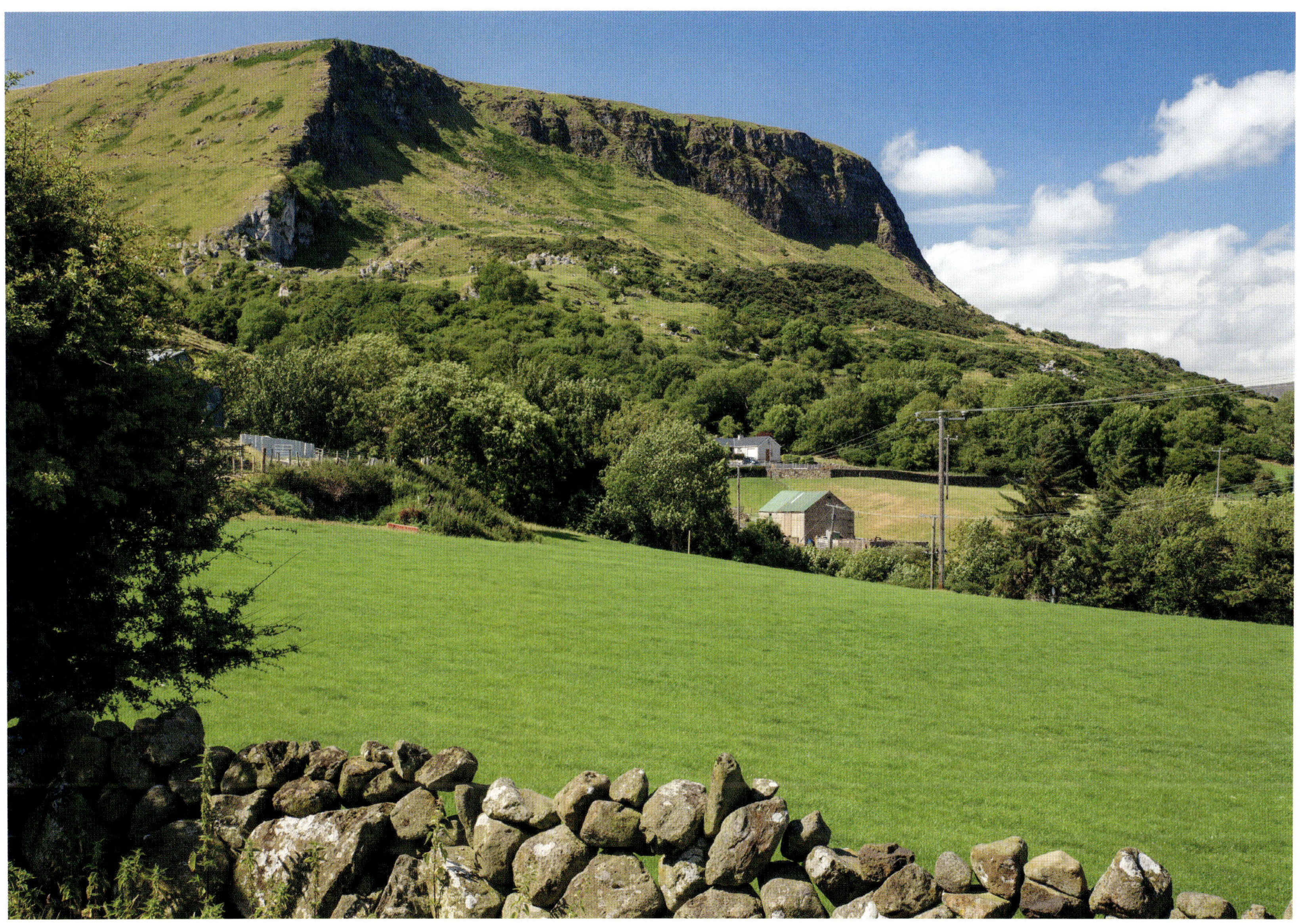

Just off the coastal road in Co. Antrim are the ruins of Ardclinis Church and its small graveyard, near where this postcard was taken. I took this photo near a solitary 'fairy tree', where fairies or the 'wee folk' are said to gather. And as everyone knows, if you cut down a fairy tree, bad luck will befall you. Wouldn't dream of it!

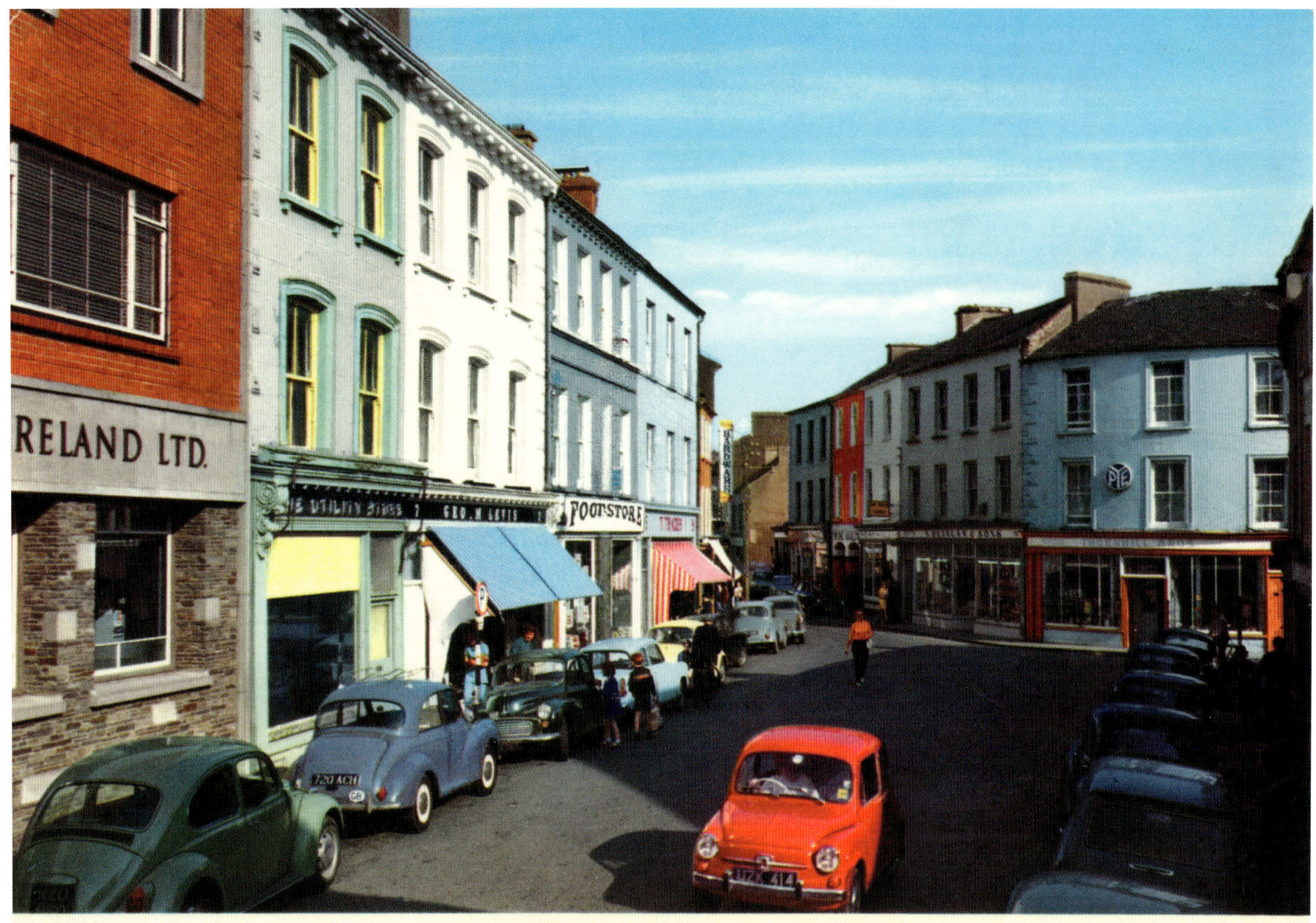

Skibbereen, Co. Cork, Ireland.

Photo: D. Noble, John Hinde Studios.

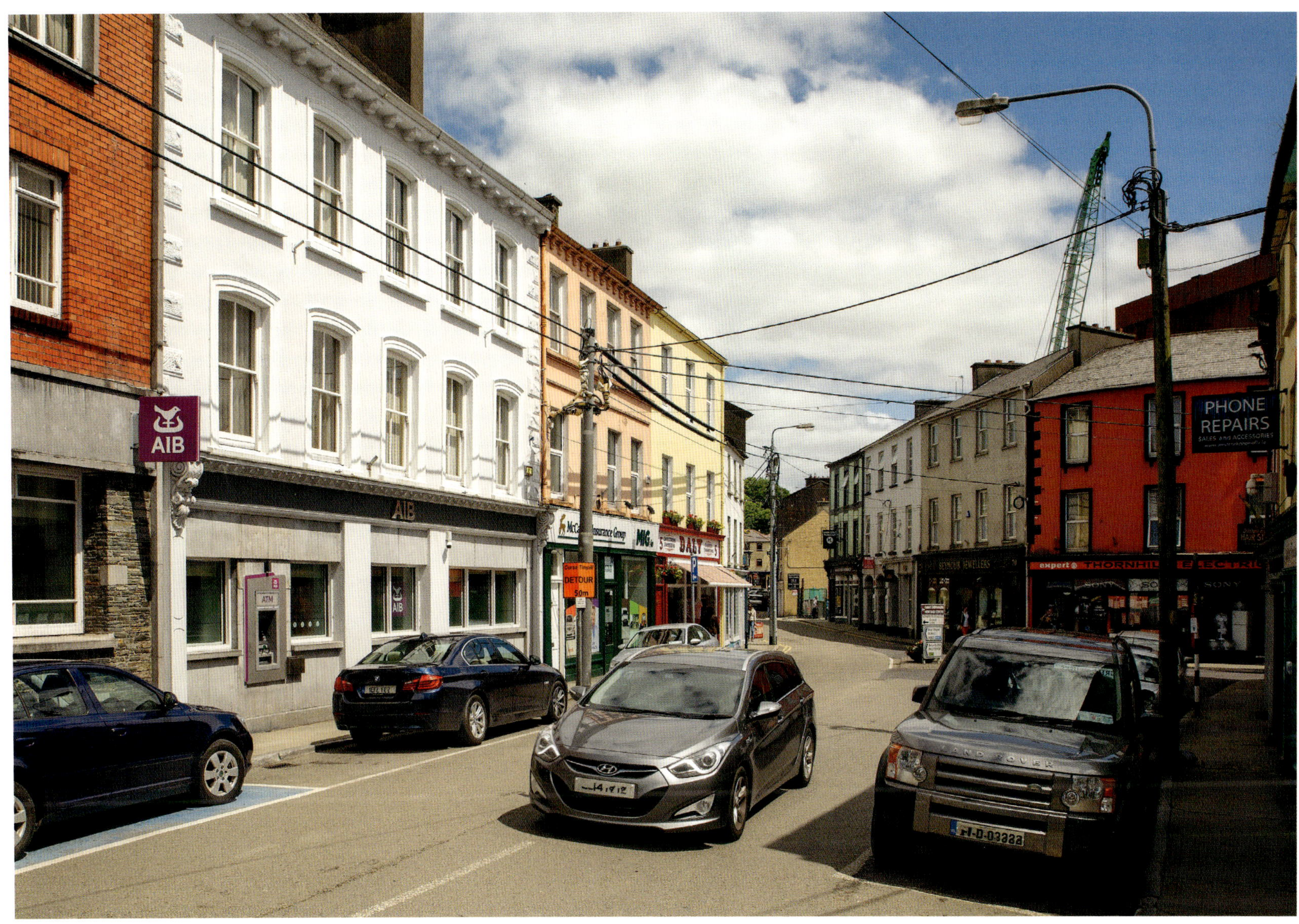

O son, I loved my native land with energy and pride
'Til a blight came o'er my crops, my sheep and cattle died
My rent and taxes were too high, I could not them redeem
And that's the cruel reason that I left old Skibbereen.
'Dear Old Skibbereen'

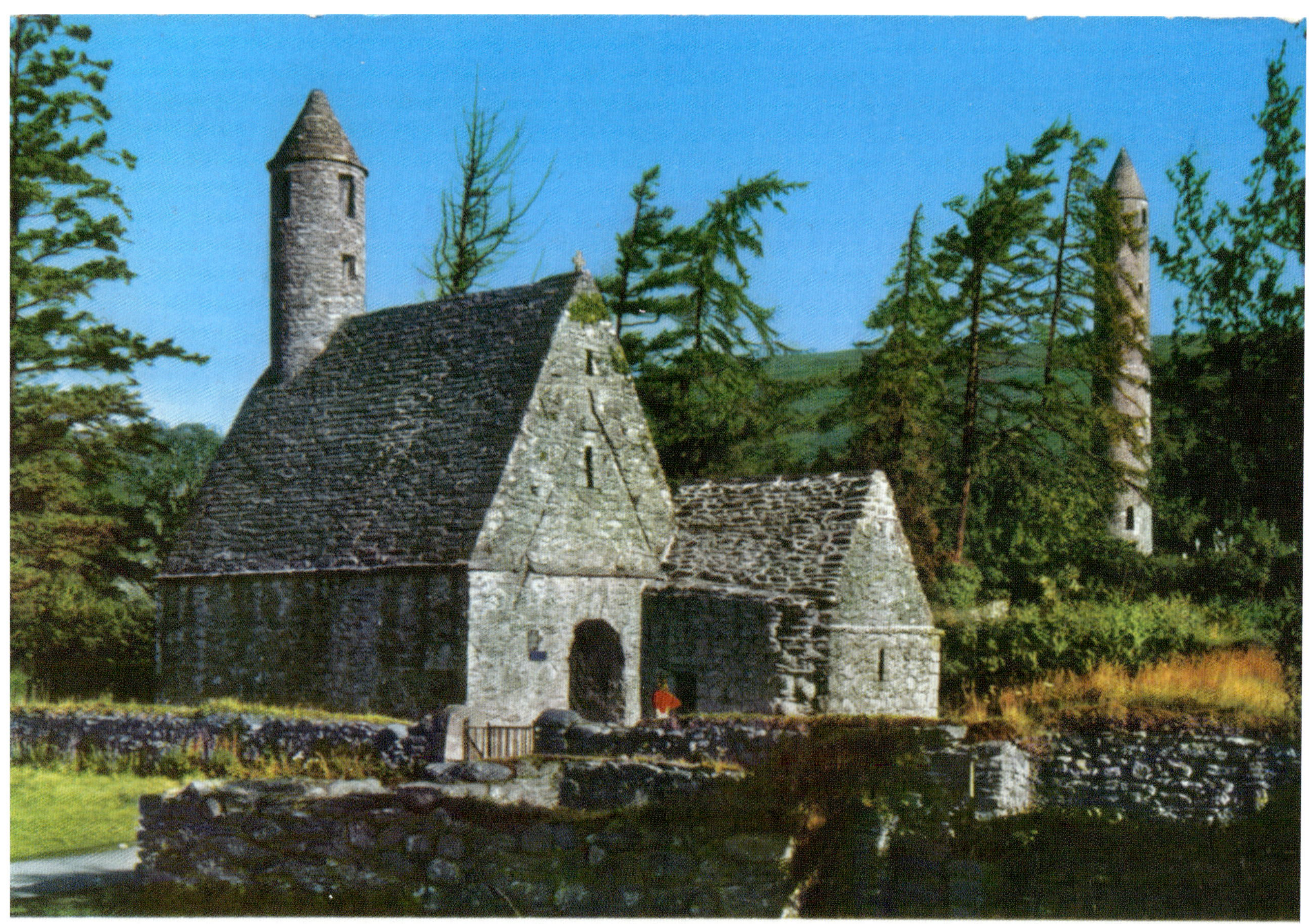

St. Kevin's Kitchen, and Round Tower, Glendaloch, Co. Wicklow, Ireland.

Colour Photo by John Hinde, F.R.P.S.

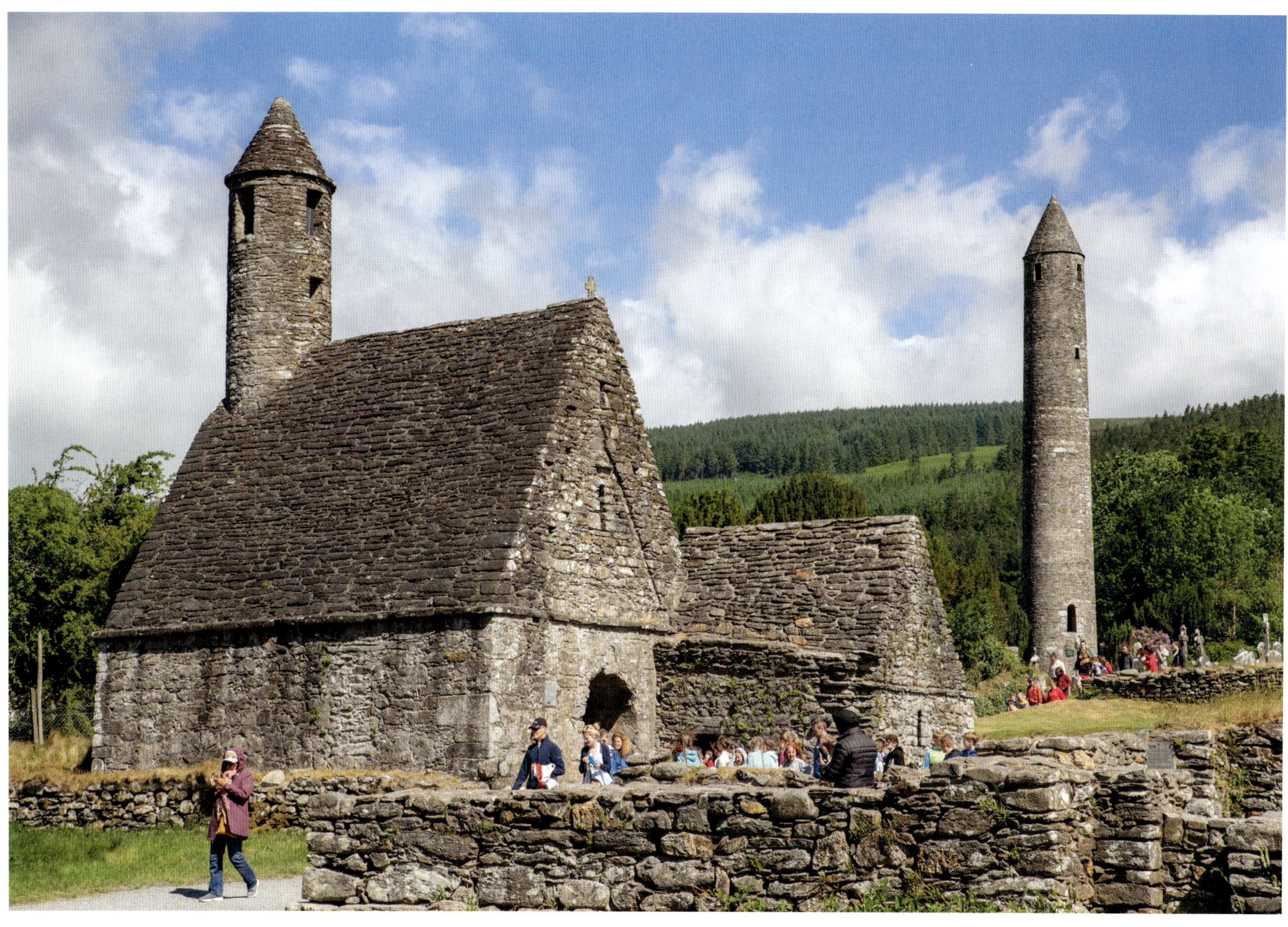

The 12th-century St Kevin's Church is better known as St Kevin's Kitchen, because people mistakenly believed that the bell tower was a kitchen chimney. Built by the monks of St Kevin's monastery nearly 1,000 years ago, this round tower is considered one of the finest remaining in Ireland.

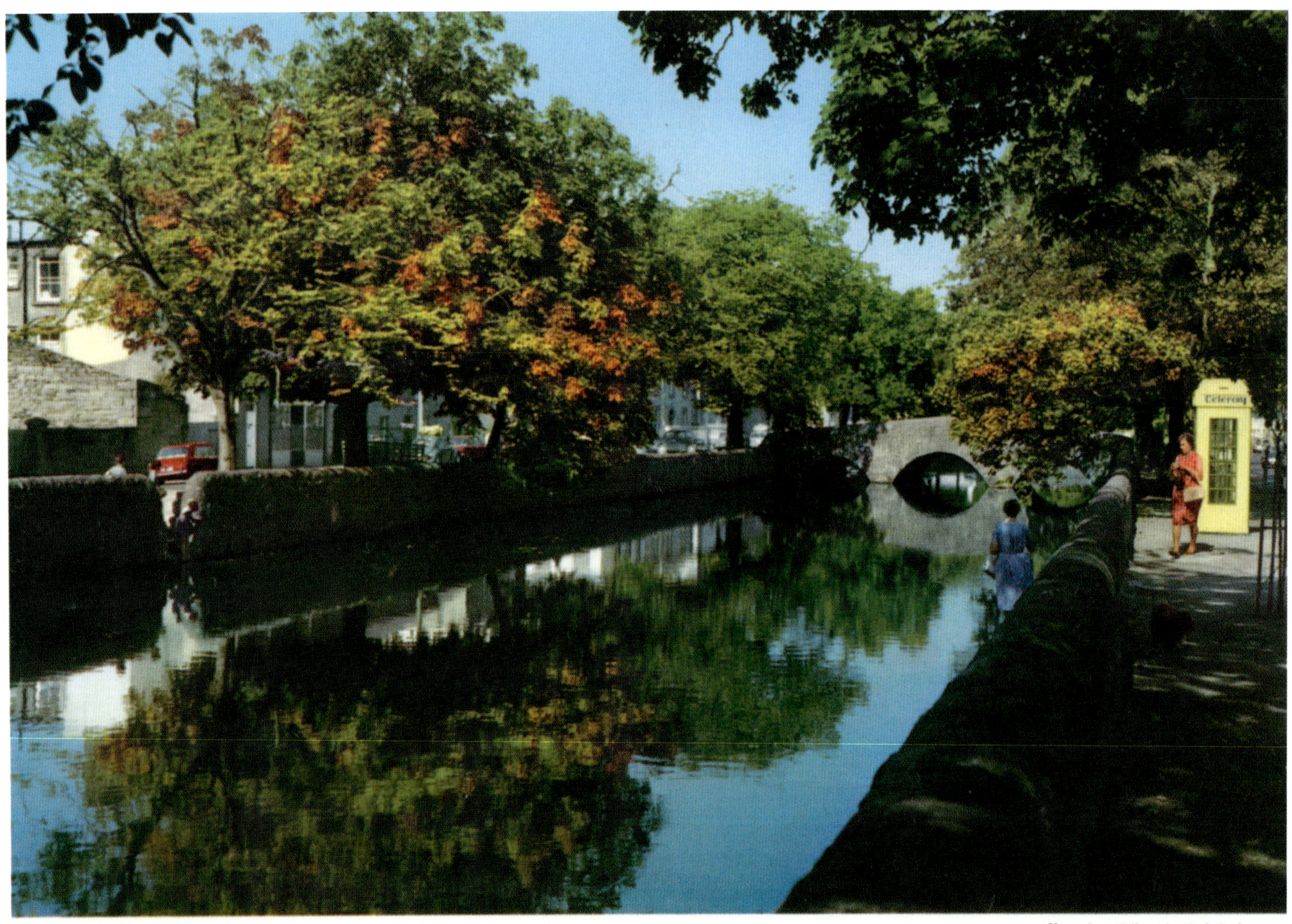

The Mall, Westport, Co. Mayo, Ireland.

Photo: Joan Willis, John Hinde Studios.

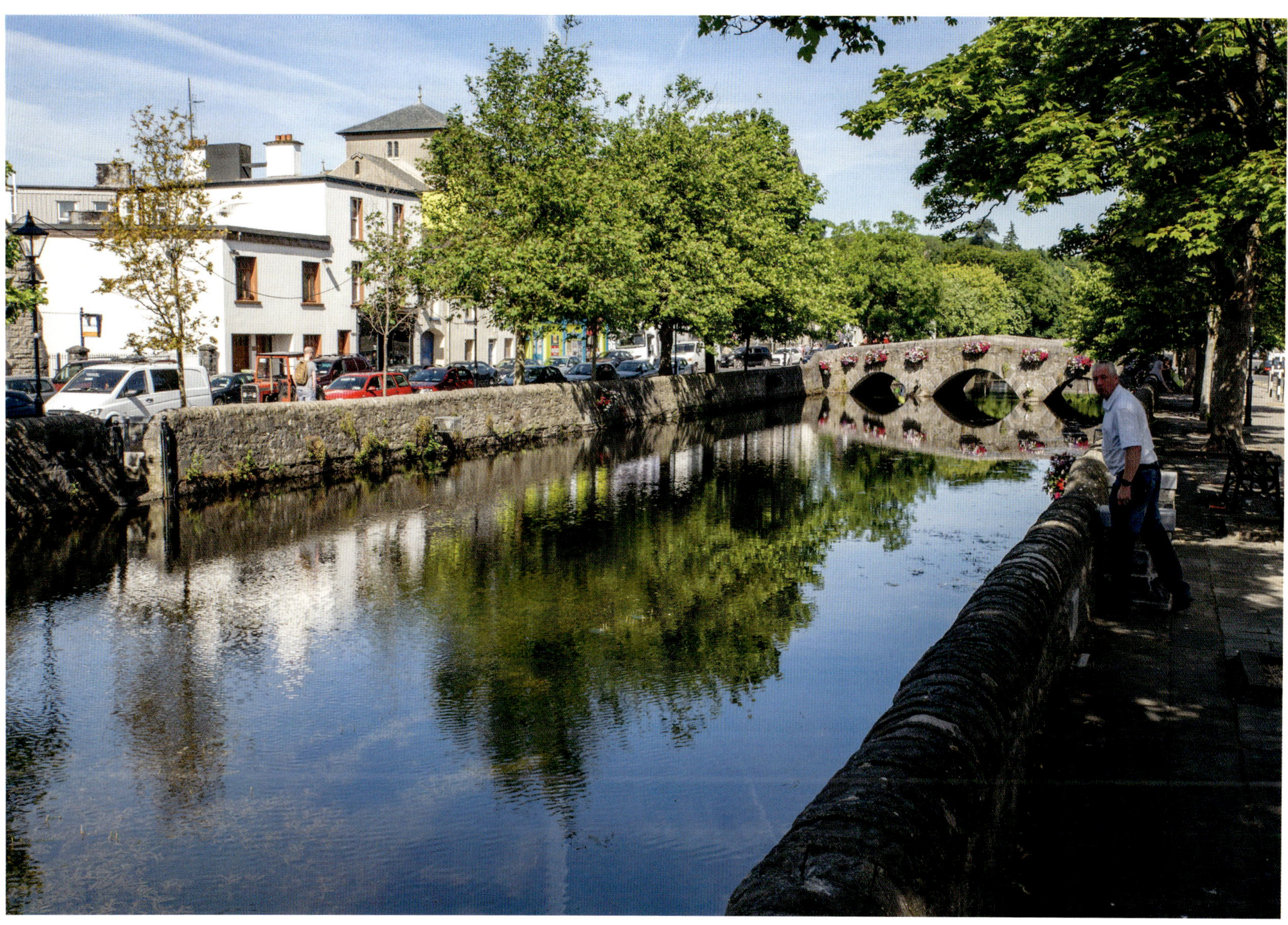

They are now calling Westport the 'Riviera of the Wild Atlantic Way'. When I first came here with my father in 1969, we'd be happy enough just strolling along the Mall after tea.

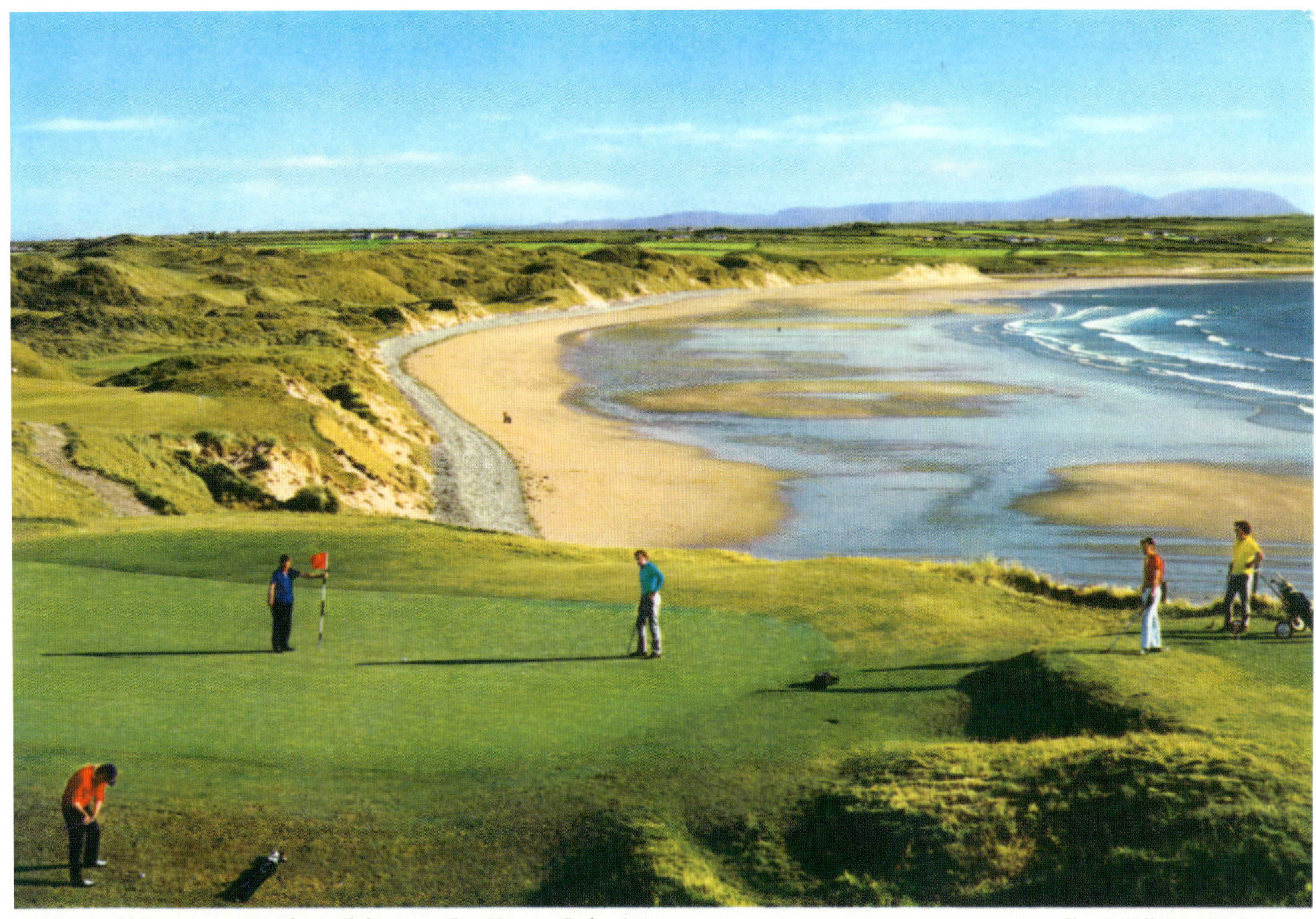

The Golf Course and Beach, Ballybunion, Co. Kerry , Ireland. *Photo: D. Noble, John Hinde Studios.*

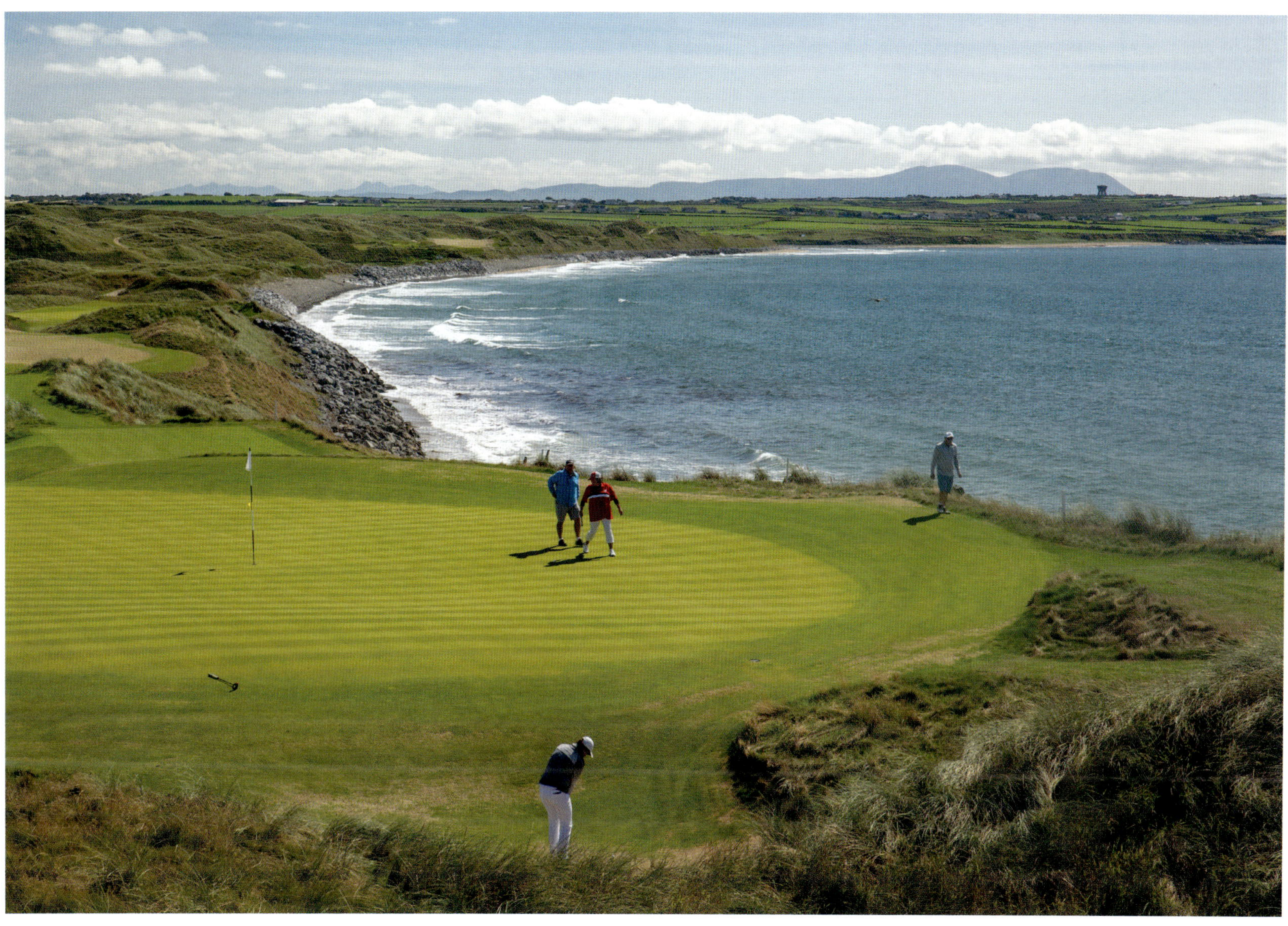

Founded in 1893, Ballybunion Golf Club is located on the north-west coast of Co. Kerry on a beautiful stretch of sand dunes overlooking the Atlantic. The Old Course, ranked as one of the world's top ten golf courses, features a graveyard by the first tee.

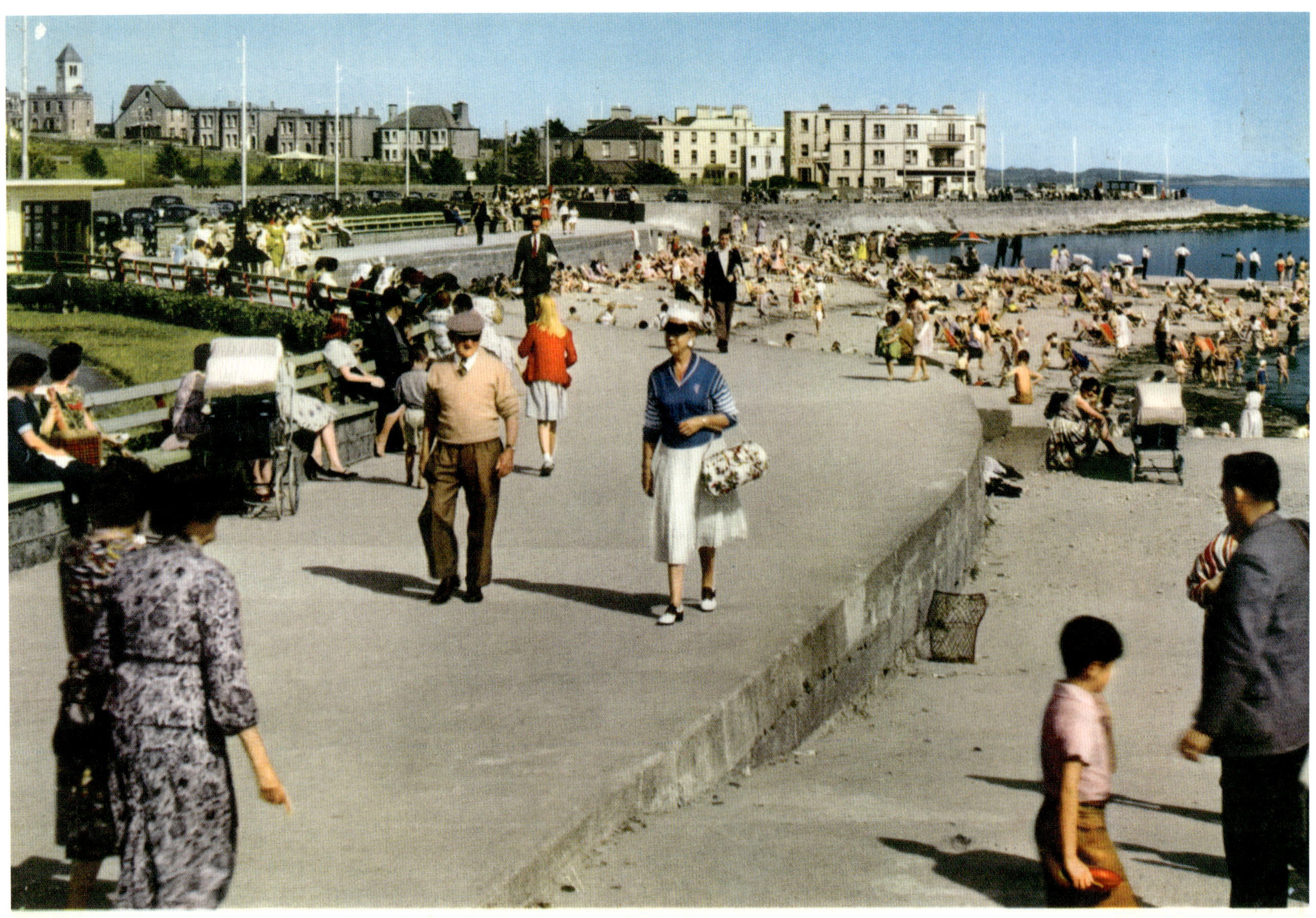

Promenade, Salthill, Galway Bay, Ireland.

Colour Photo by John Hinde, F.R.P.S.

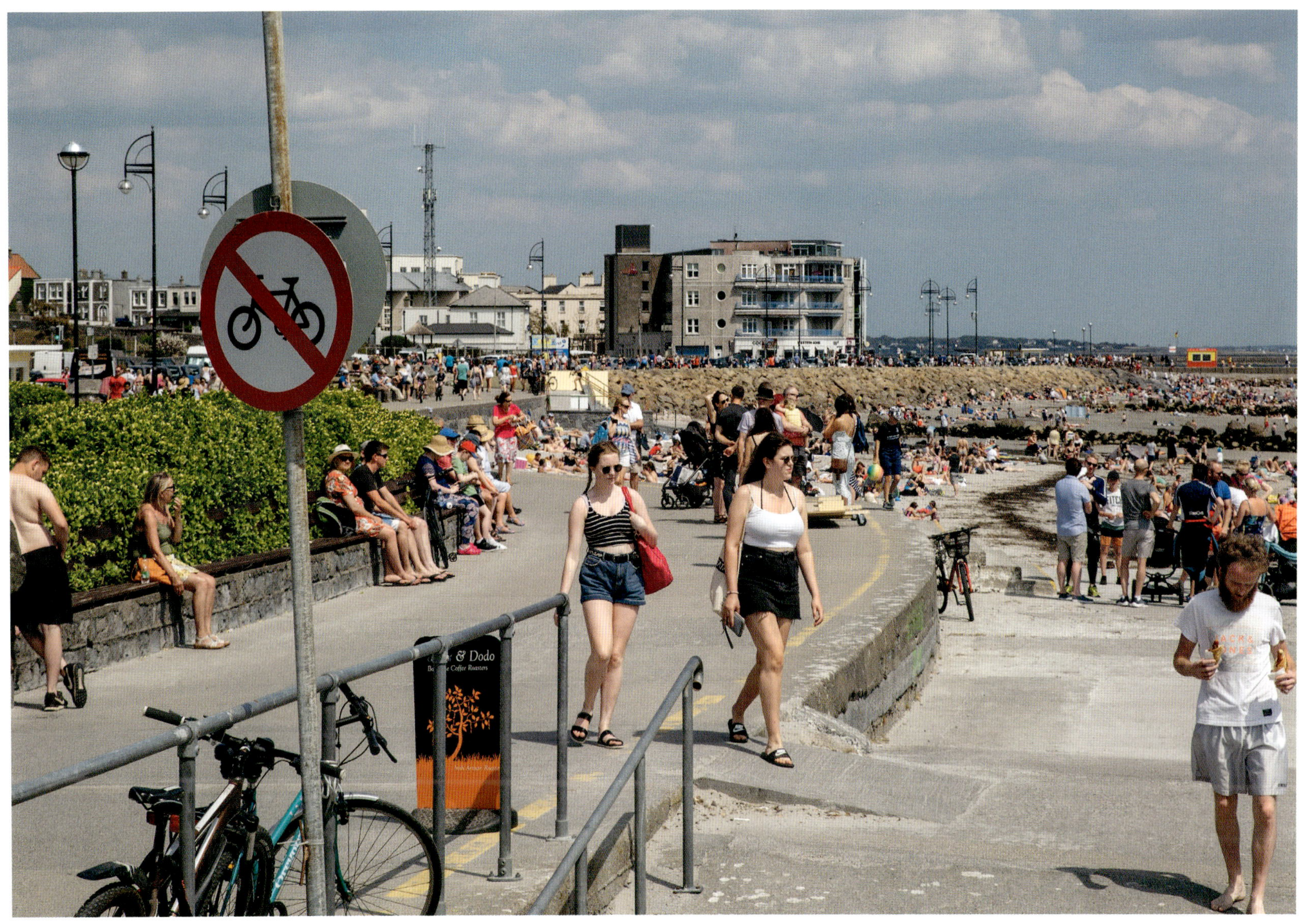

Salthill Beach is located just two kilometres from Galway city centre and is really several small beaches separated by rocky outcrops. People still love to walk, swim and relax here today. I wonder what John Hinde would think of today's view. It's a very different version of pink and white.

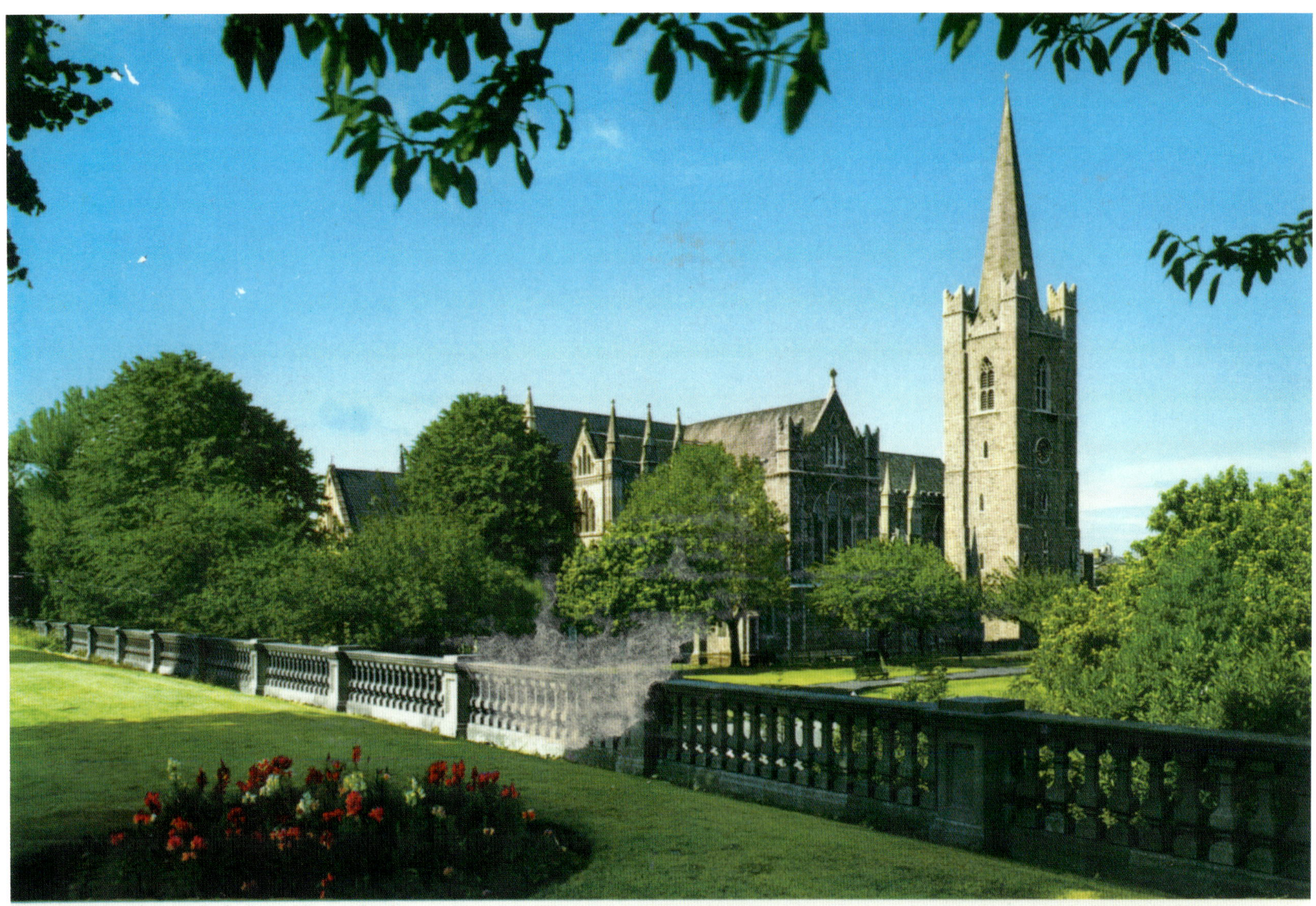

St. Patrick's Cathedral, Dublin, Ireland. *Photo: P. O'Toole, John Hinde Studios.*

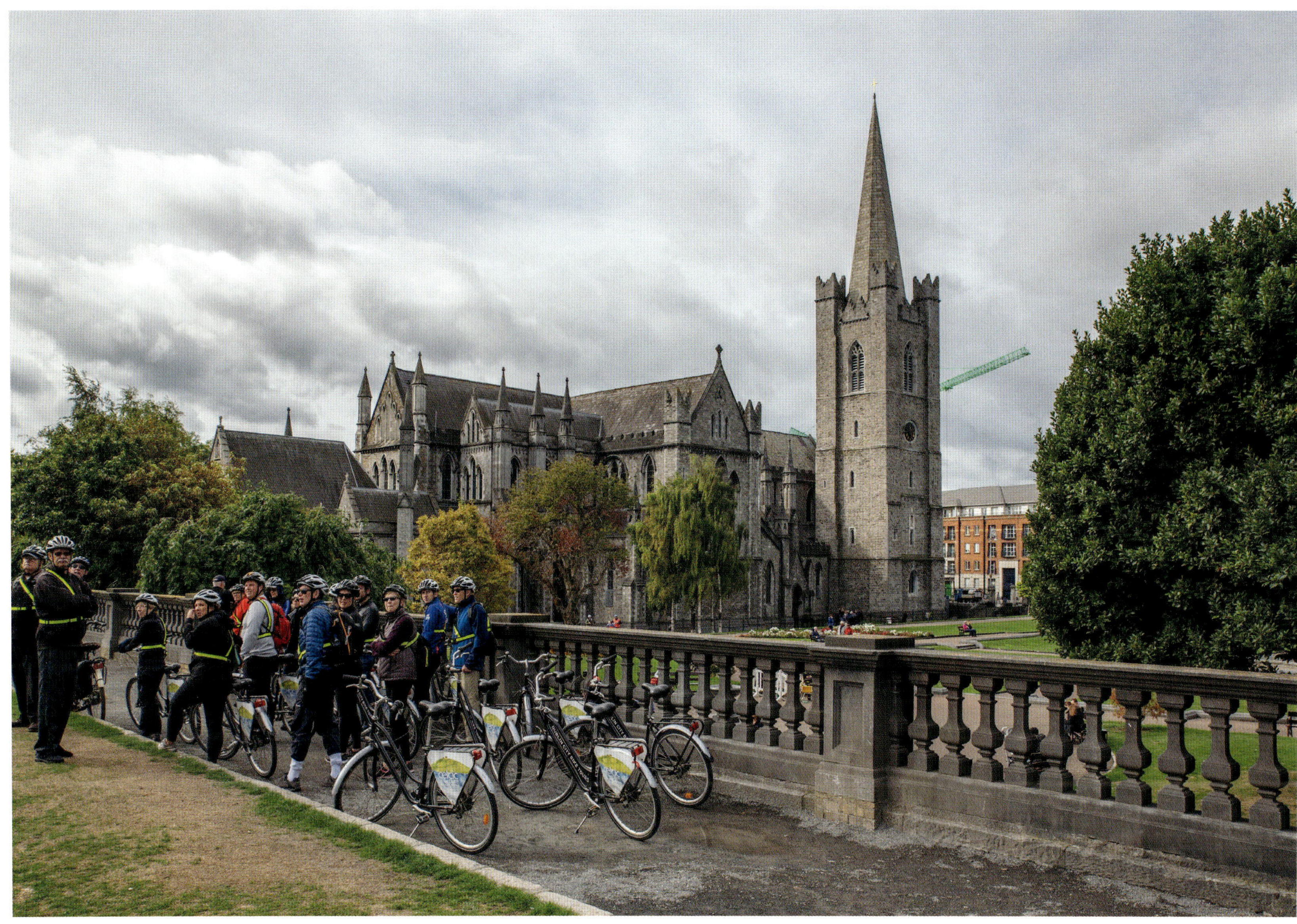

Besides this Dublin city bike group and their 'easy-paced, eco-friendly' tours, not much has changed in this view of St Patrick's Cathedral. Hinde's postcards played a key role in promoting Irish tourism in the 1960s and '70s. Today, Instagram and Facebook continue this work.

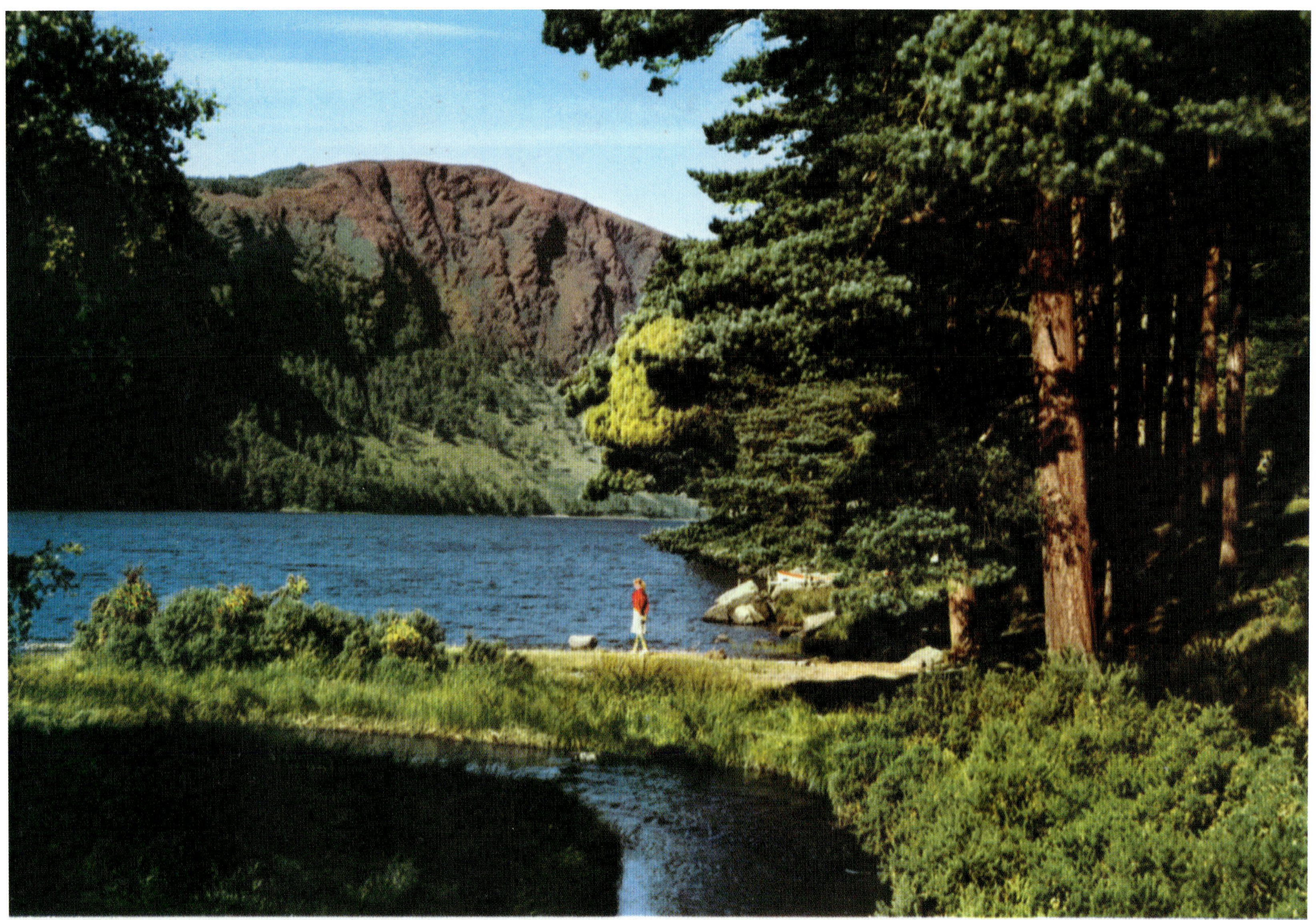

The Upper Lake, Glendalough, Co. Wicklow, Ireland.

Colour Photo by John Hinde, F.R.P.S.

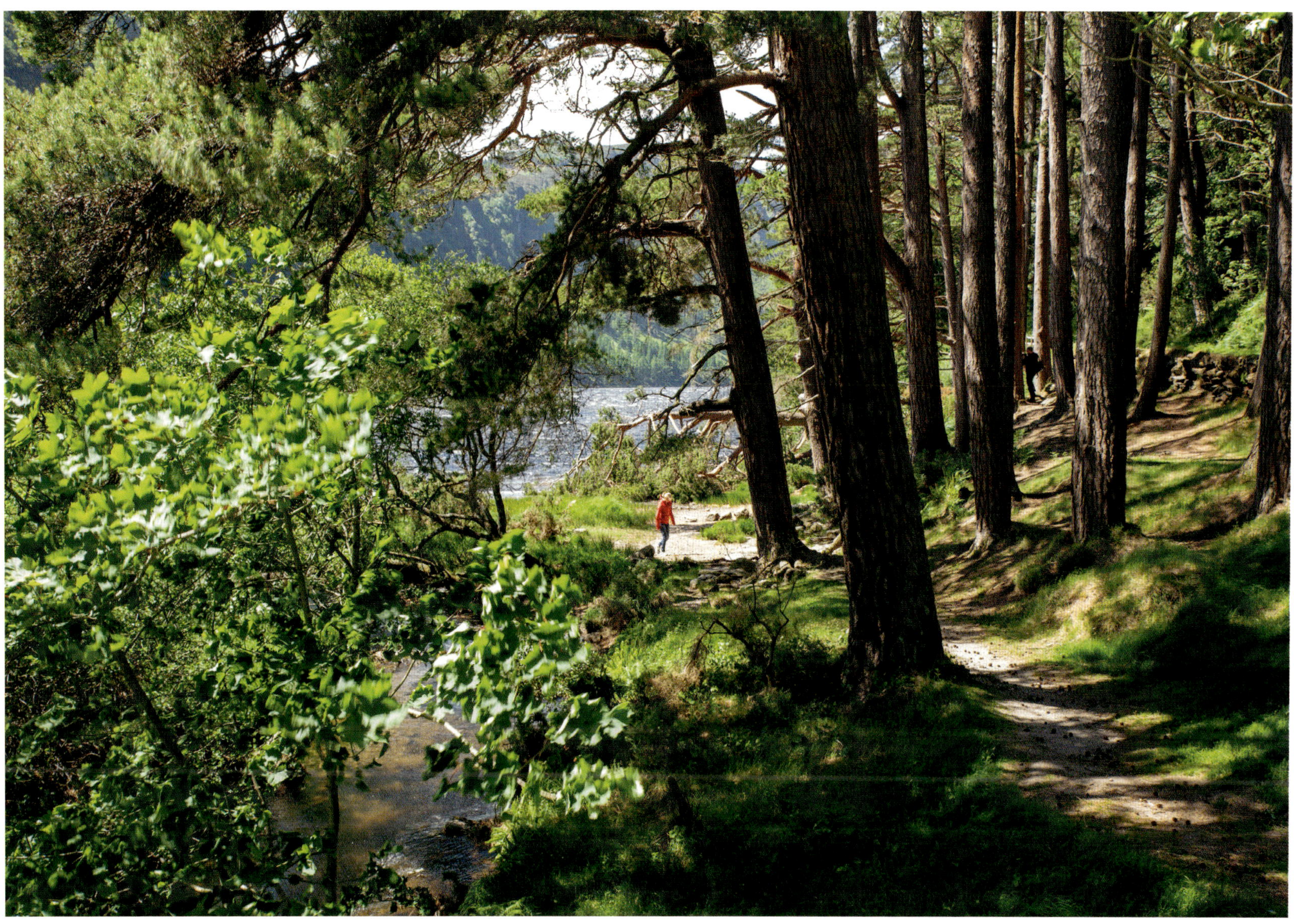

Today, shot through sun-dapple and branch-tangle, the 'Glen of the Two Lakes' still holds the austere beauty of glacial mountain reflected in water. At the far end of this valley is 'Van Diemen's Land'. The now disused mining works has yielded traces of the rare mineral pyromorphite.

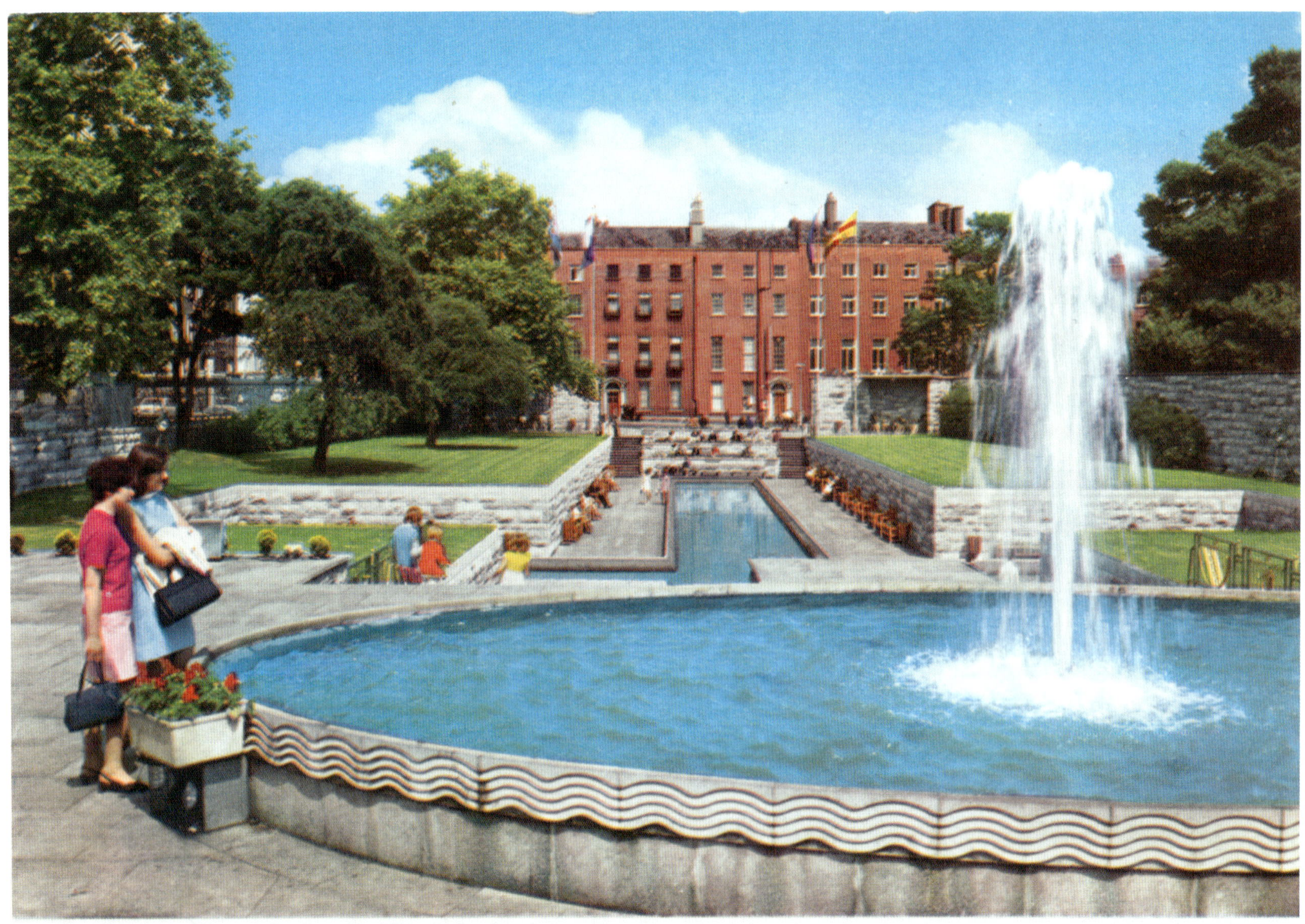

The Garden of Remembrance, Dublin, Ireland.

Photo: R. Beer, John Hinde Studios.

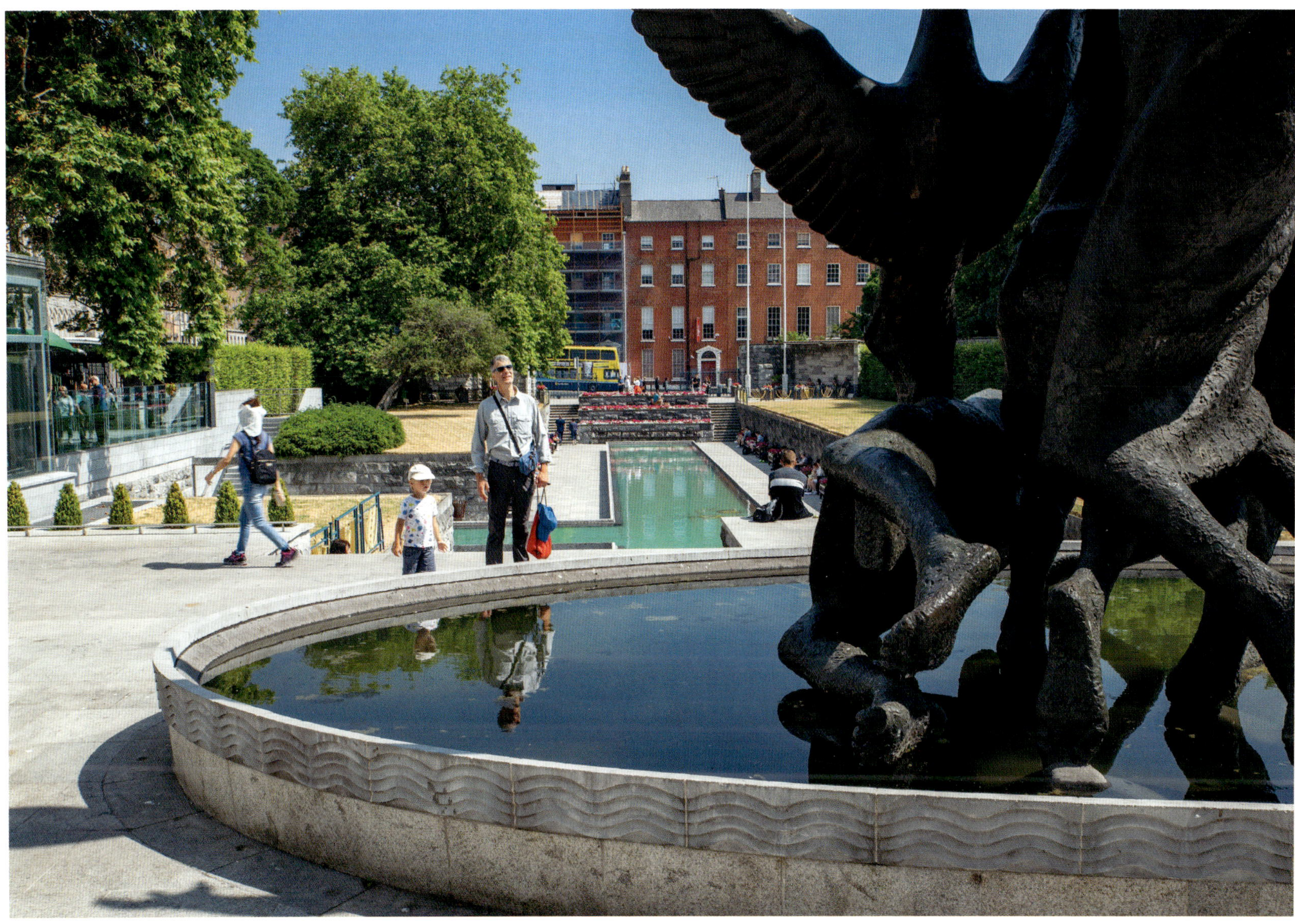

The Garden of Remembrance was opened in 1966, the 50th anniversary of the 1916 Easter Rising and around the time this postcard was created. The statue of the Children of Lir by Oisín Kelly, symbolising rebirth and resurrection, replaced the fountain in 1971.

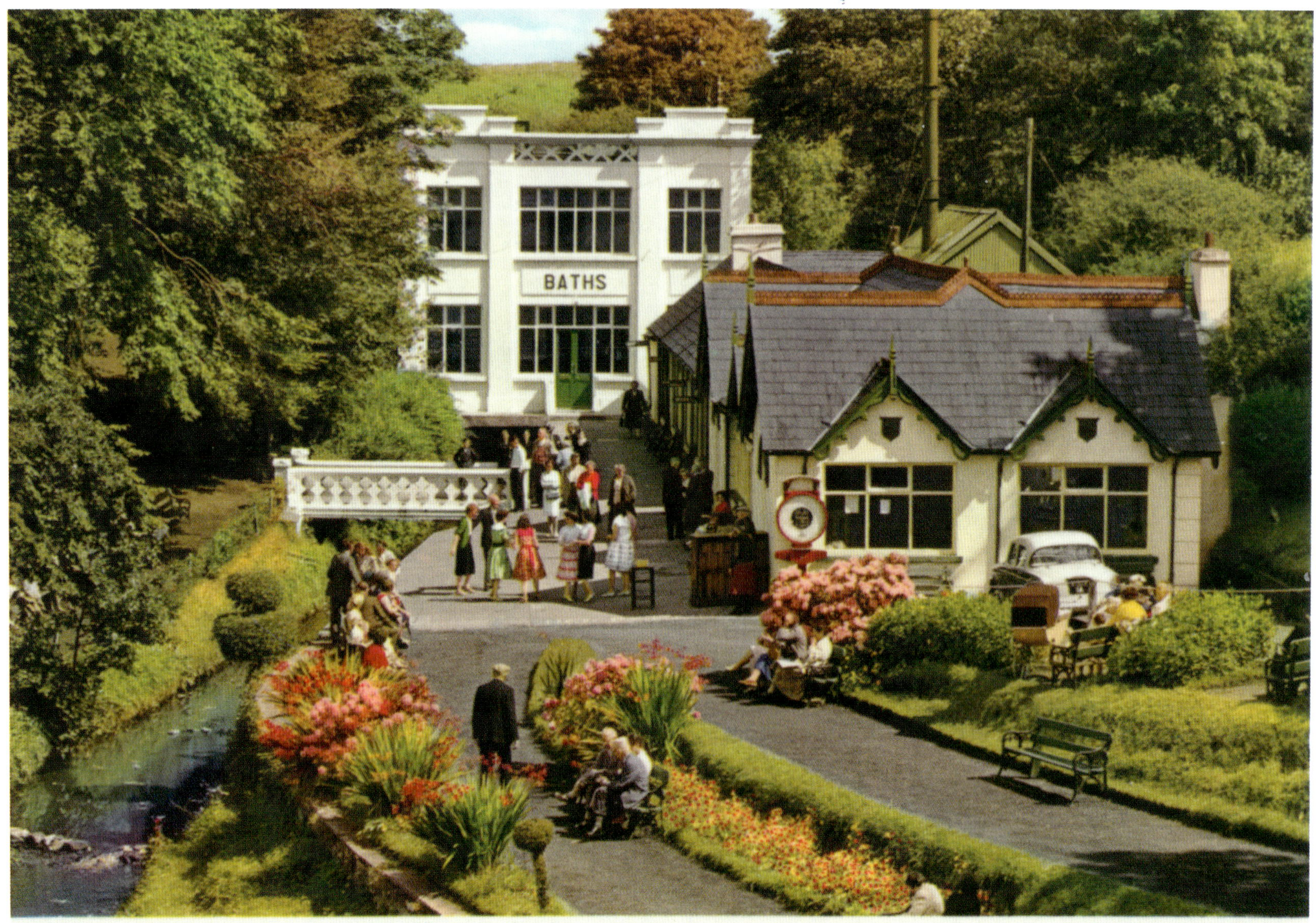

The Spa Wells, Lisdoonvarna, Co. Clare, Ireland.

Colour Photo by John Hinde, F.R.P.S.

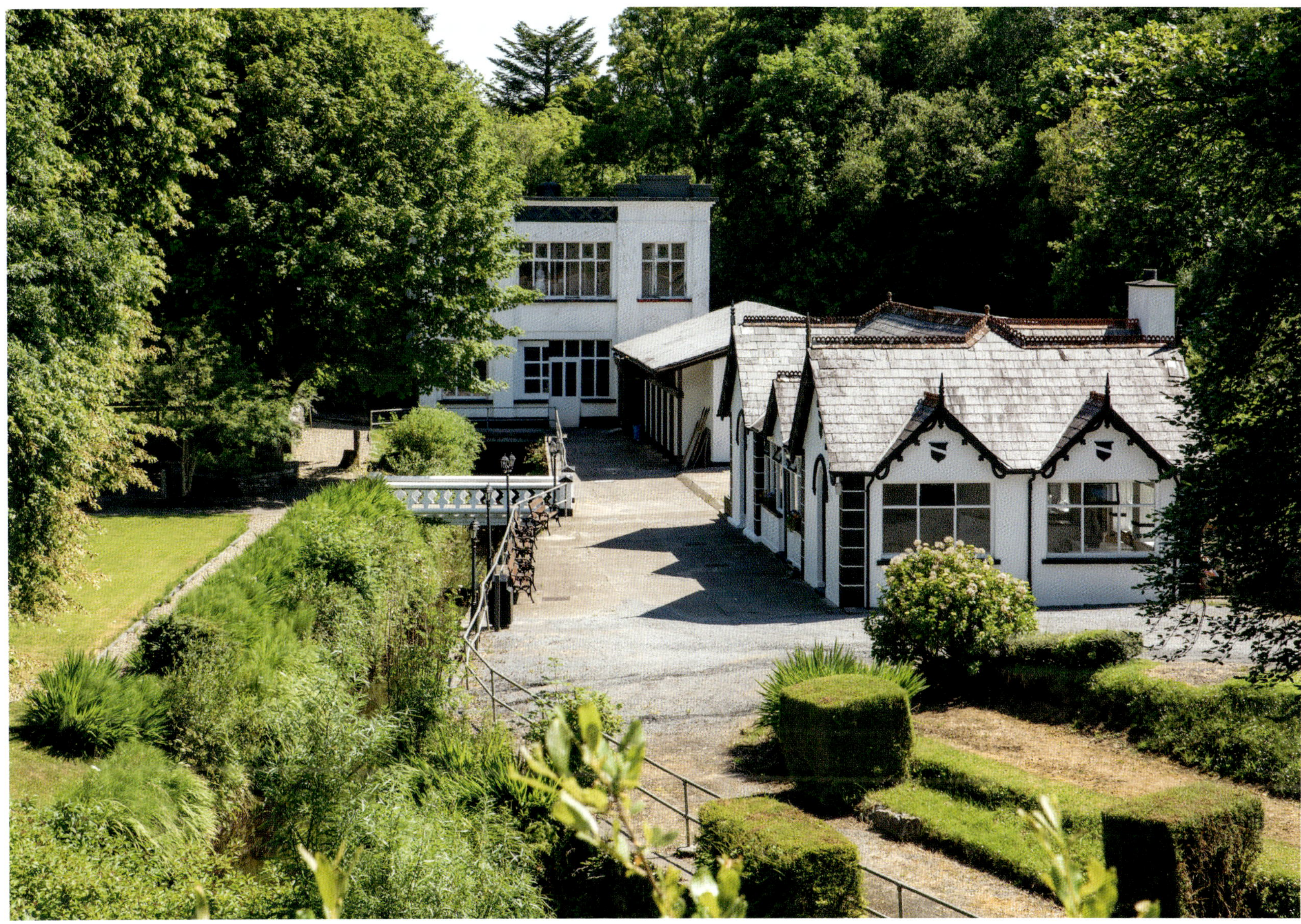

Lisdoonvarna is the only natural spa town in Ireland; the healing effects of its waters were first noted by writers as early as 1740. Traditionally, come September, bachelor farmers would combine holidays here with their search for a soulmate. These days, its world-famous annual matchmaking festival welcomes up to 60,000 people, all looking for true romance at 'Europe's biggest singles festival'.

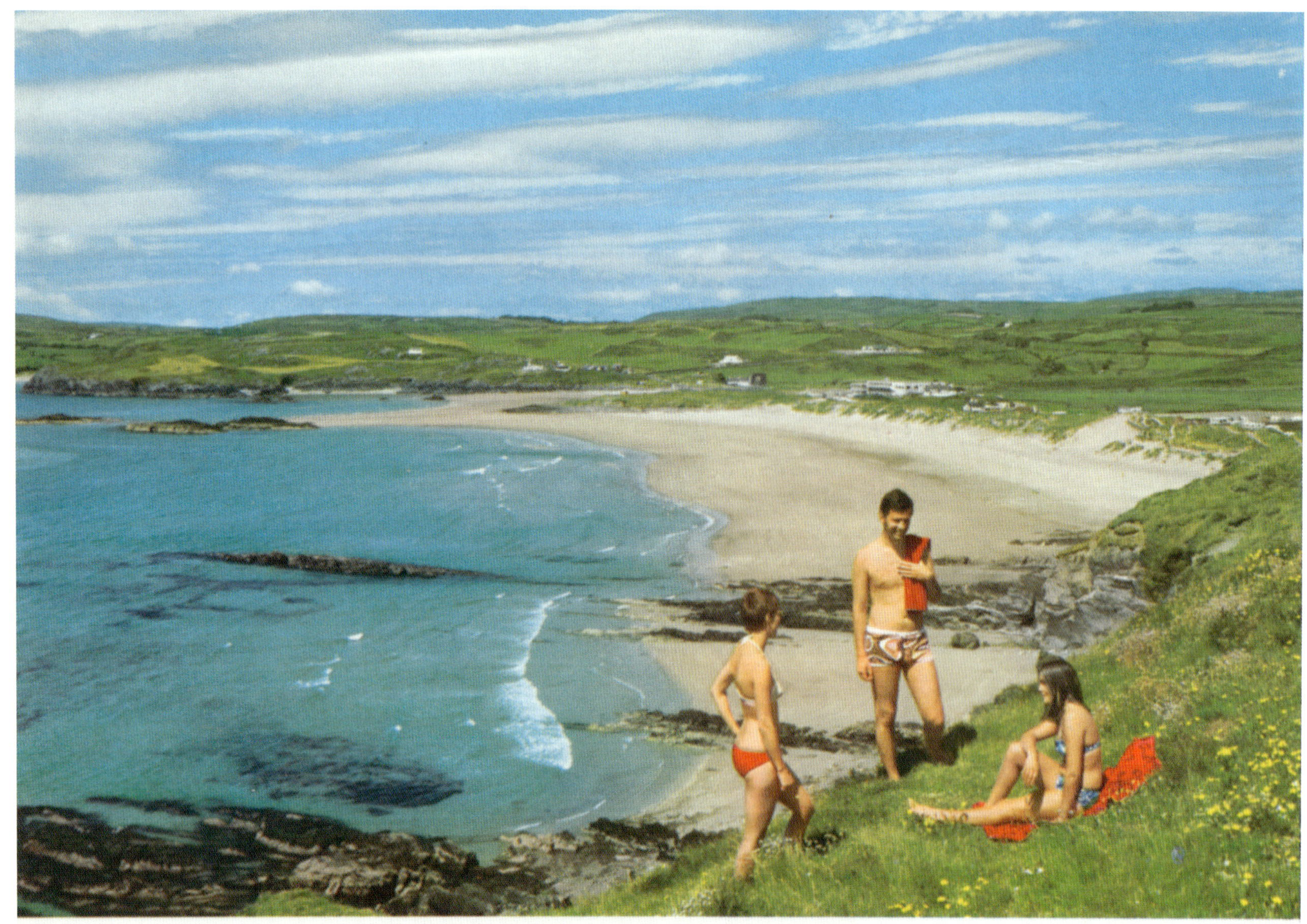

Owenahincha Strand, Rosscarbery, Co. Cork, Ireland. *Photo: D. Noble, John Hinde Studios.*

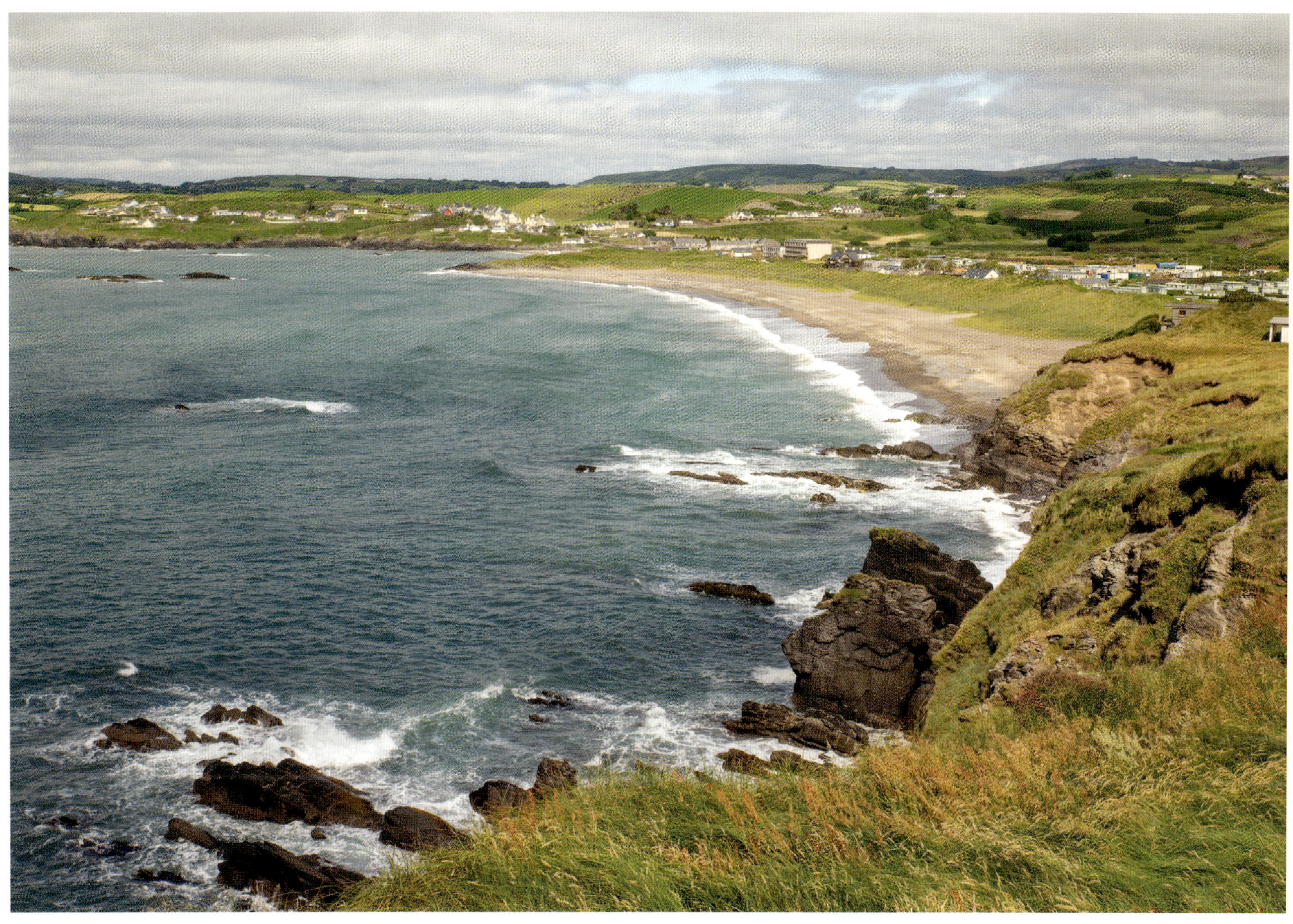

Sadly, I couldn't find anyone insane enough to pose for me in swimming attire on the blustery day I was here. However, as I was setting up, a cyclist rode by and shouted out, 'If you could remove that caravan park as you enter town, you'd have a much better photograph and we'd have a much better town.'

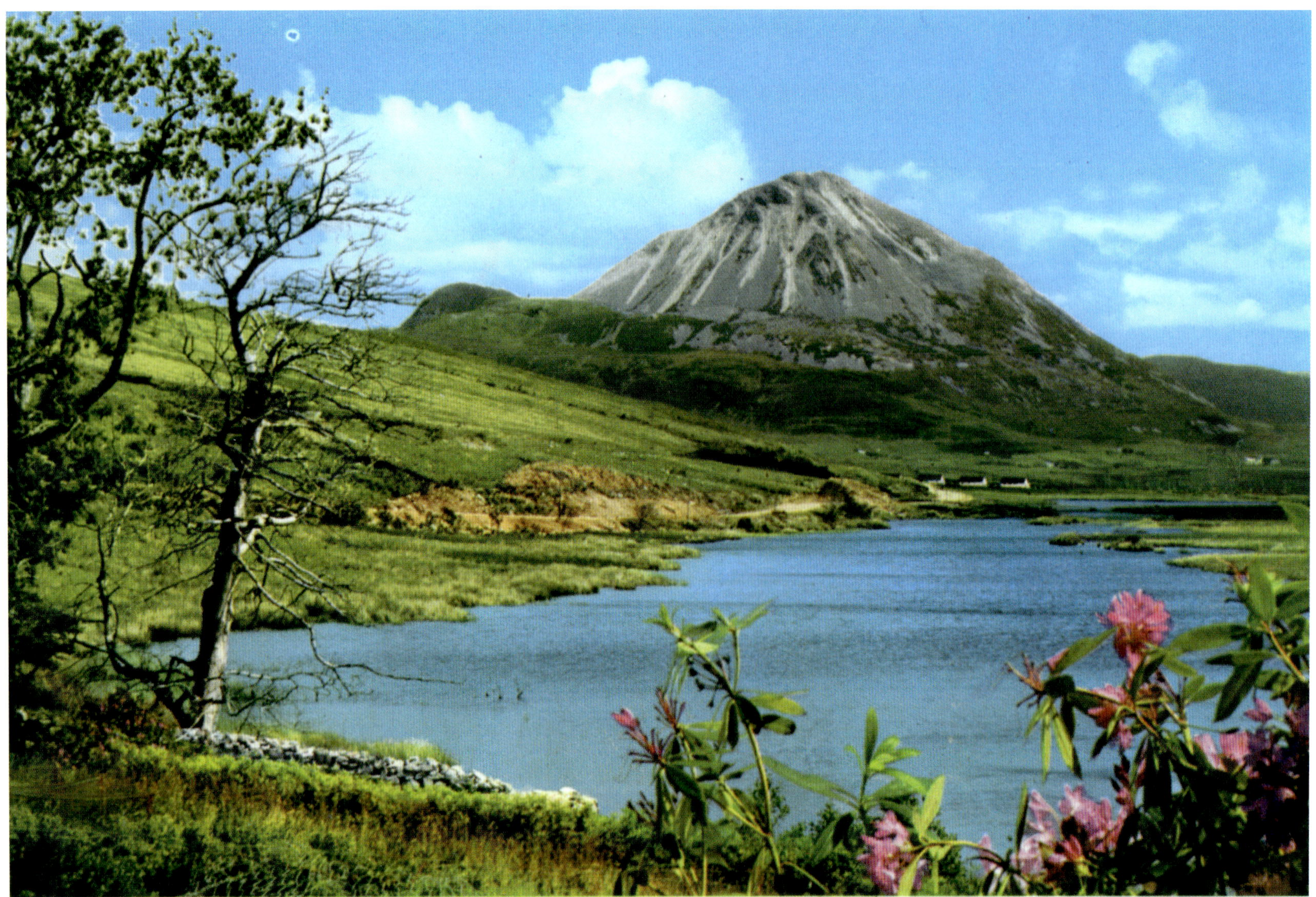

Errigal Mountain from Gweedore, Co. Donegal, Ireland.

Colour Photo by John Hinde, F.R.P.S.

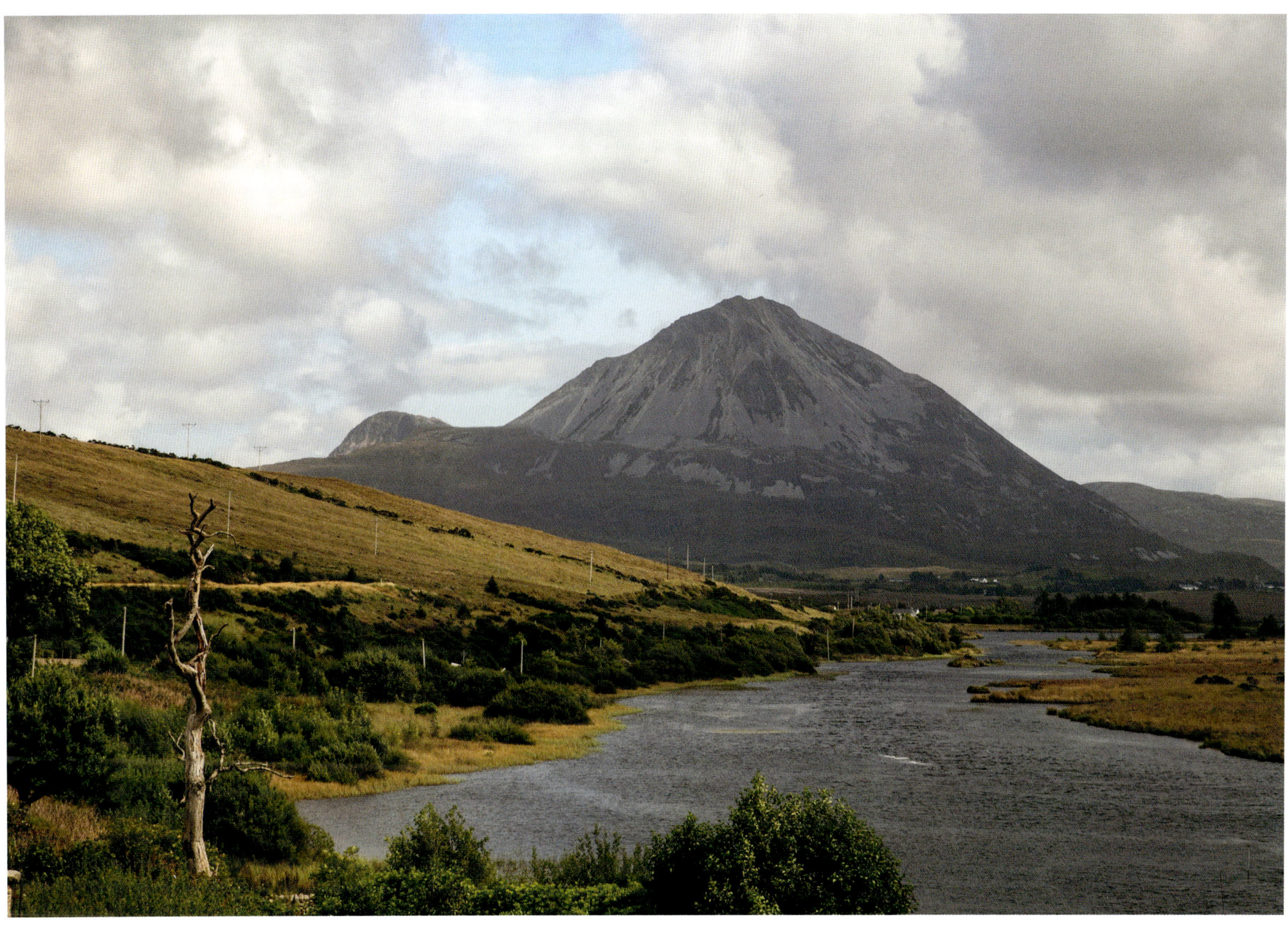

With its glowing rose-toned hues of quartzite, I can see why Mount Errigal has long been considered the most iconic mountain in Ireland. The 751-meter mountain near Gweedore might look like a volcano, but to soothe any alarm, it's actually formed from metamorphic rock.

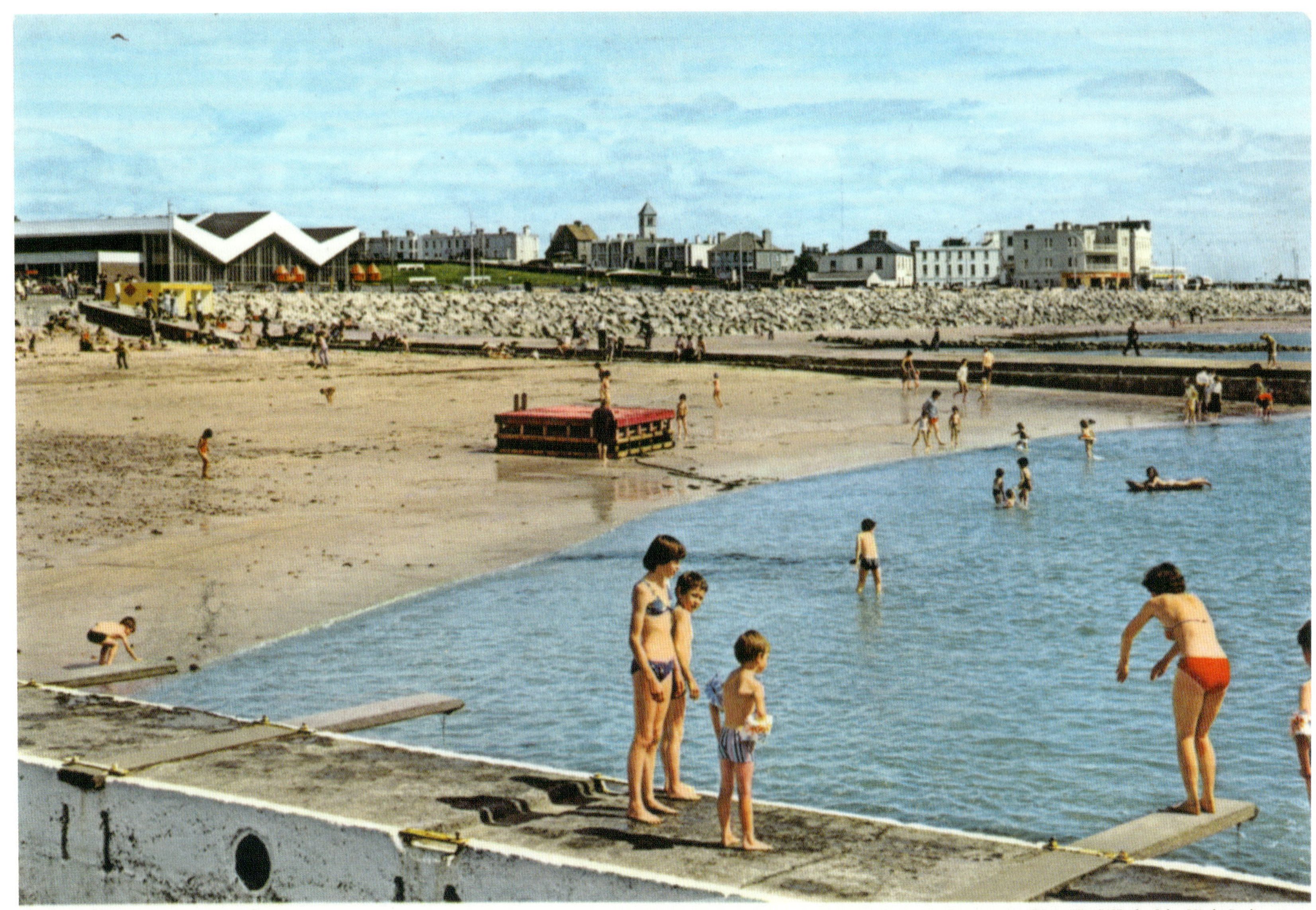

Salthill, Co. Galway, Ireland.

Photo: P. O'Toole, John Hinde Studios.

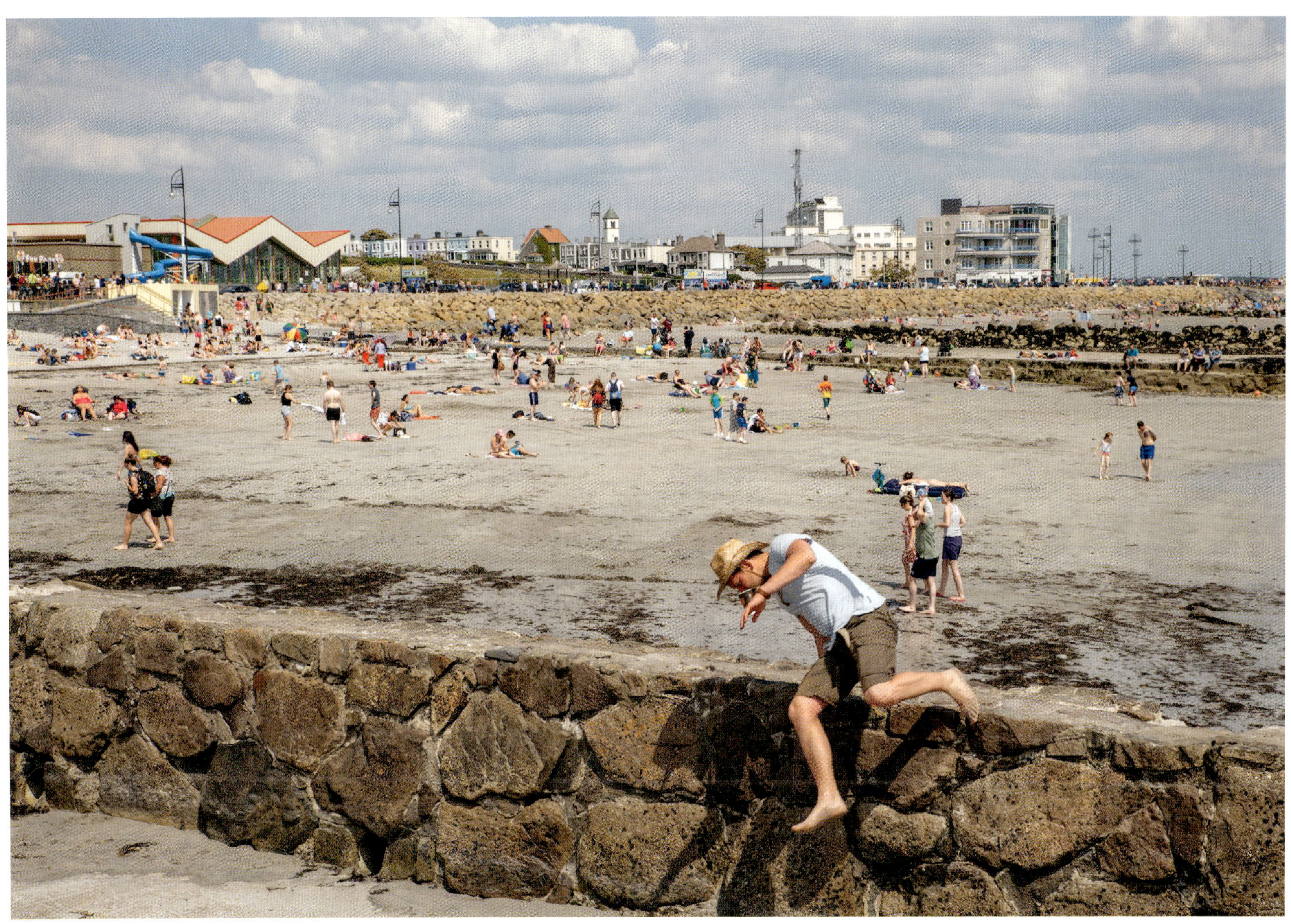

Taking a leap with a coffee-to-go, this lad probably didn't know that, 50 summers ago, other youngsters were also diving from this same spot. Interesting that the angular roof of the pavilion is no 21st-century addition but a bold architectural flourish from the brave new world of the past.

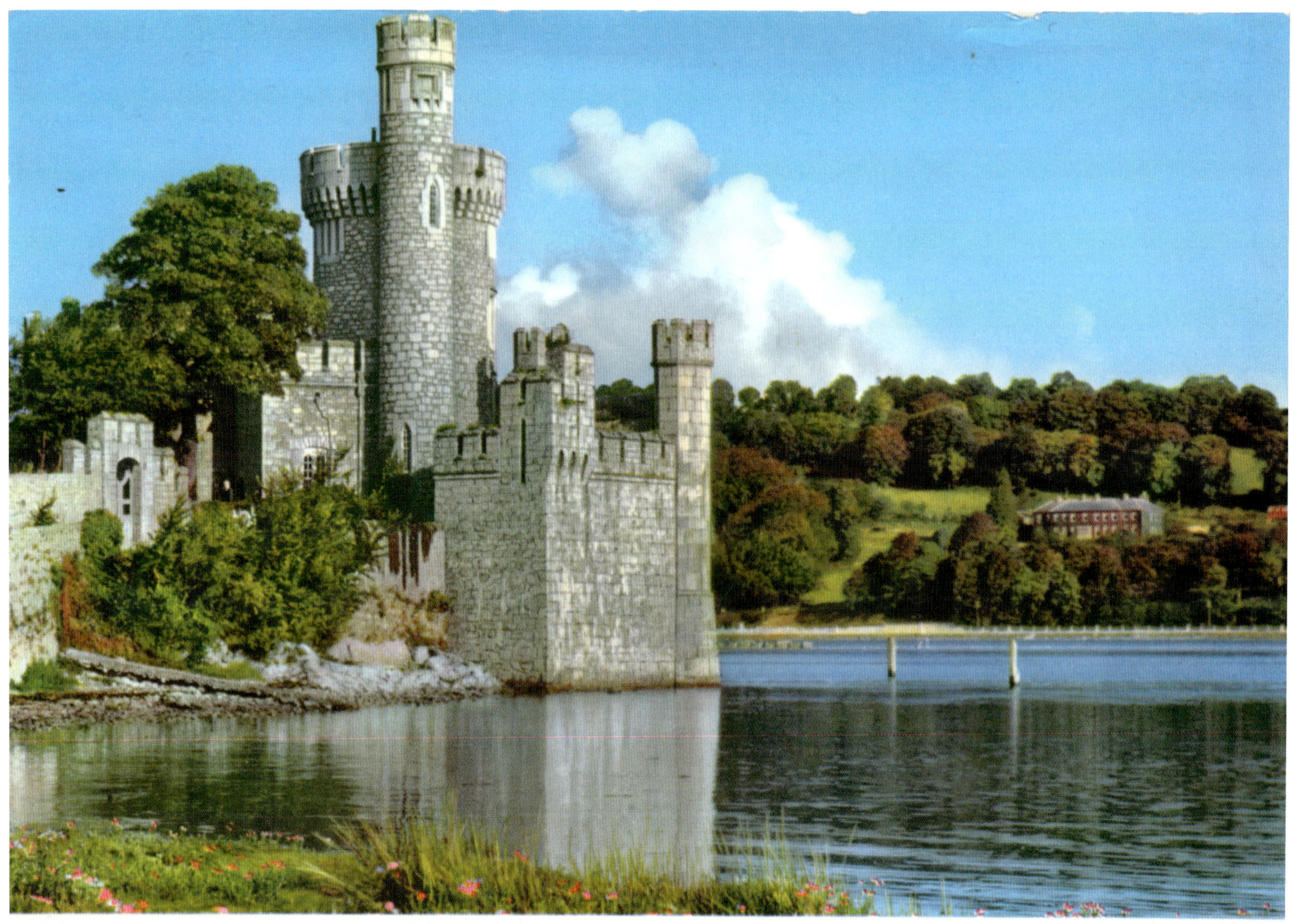

Blackrock Castle on The River Lee, Approaching Cork City, Ireland.

Colour Photo by John Hinde, F.R.P.S.

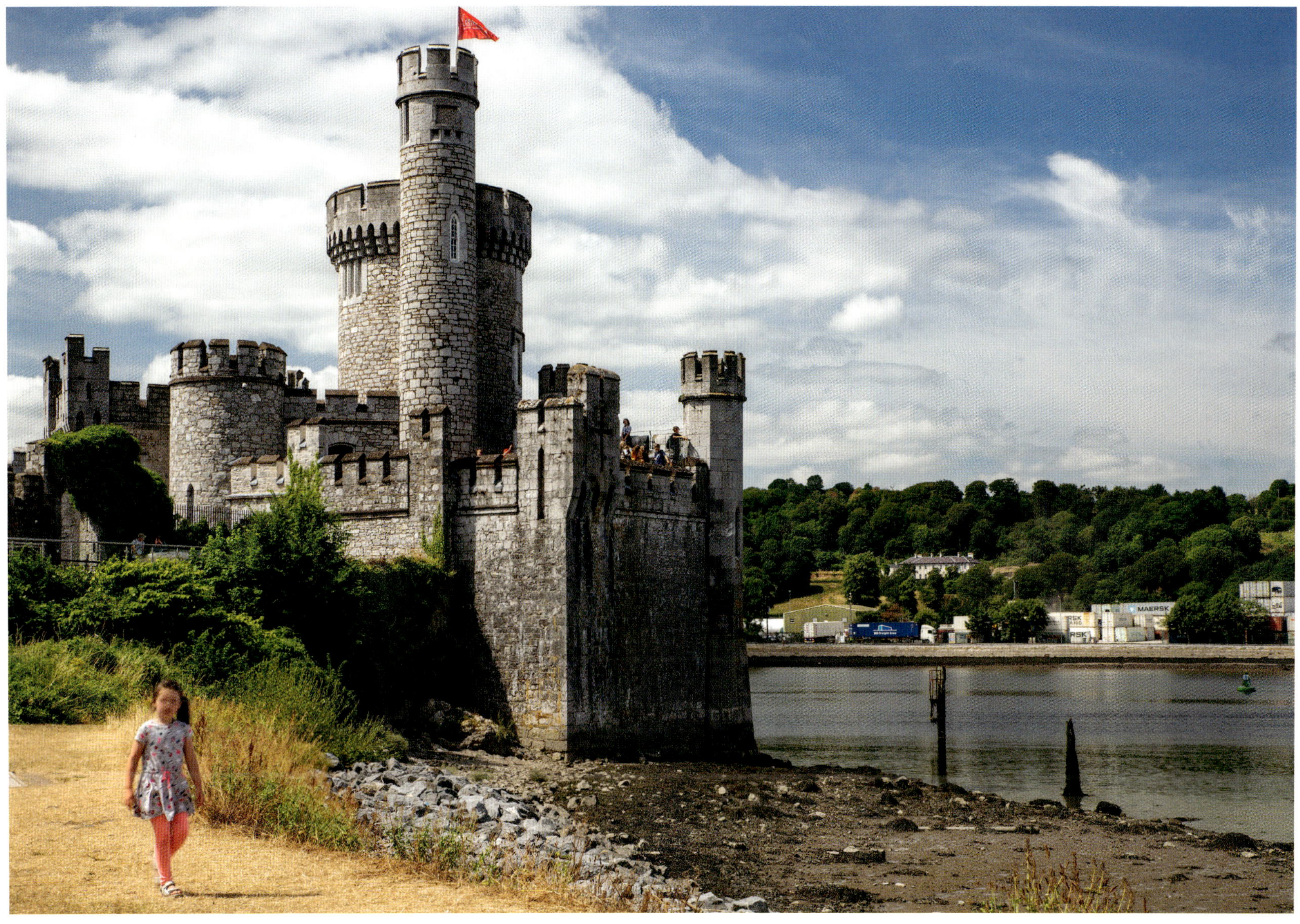

Blackrock Castle is a 16th-century fortification built on the river Lee as a watch tower and fort to protect the entrance to Cork city against pirates and other invaders. Today, the castle is the CIT Blackrock Castle Observatory, an award-winning interactive astronomy exhibition that highlights scientific discoveries. The day I was here, it was teeming with stargazing students from all over the planet.

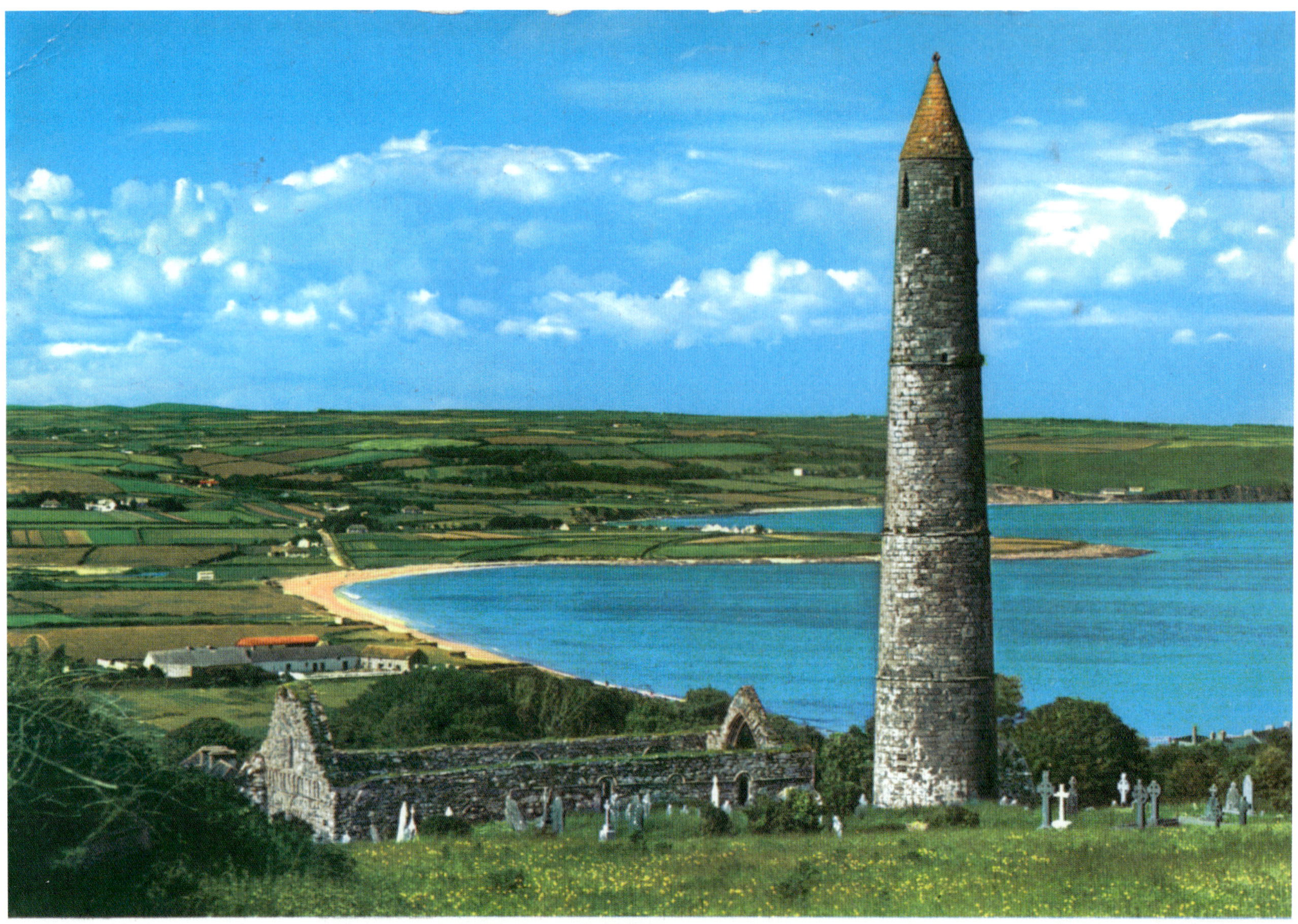

The Round Tower (9th Century), Ardmore, Co. Waterford, Ireland.

Colour Photo by John Hinde, F.R.P.S.

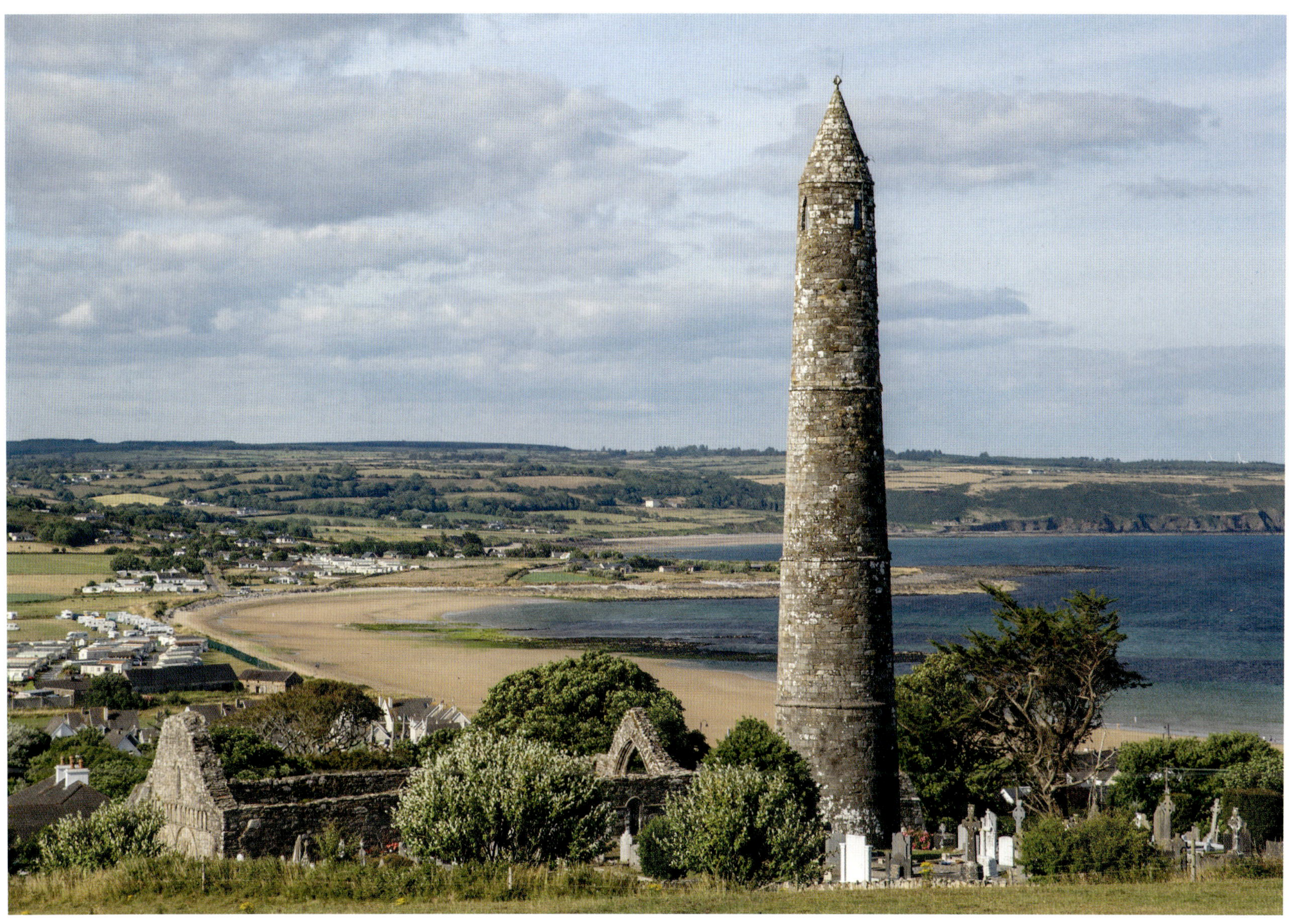

Ardmore, or 'Aird Mhór' in Irish, means 'the great height', and that it has, in the form of its renowned 12th-century round tower. At 30 meters, it is one of Ireland's finest. St Declan founded the ecclesiastical centre here in the seventh century, the oldest Christian settlement in Ireland. Truly, a pinnacle of achievement.

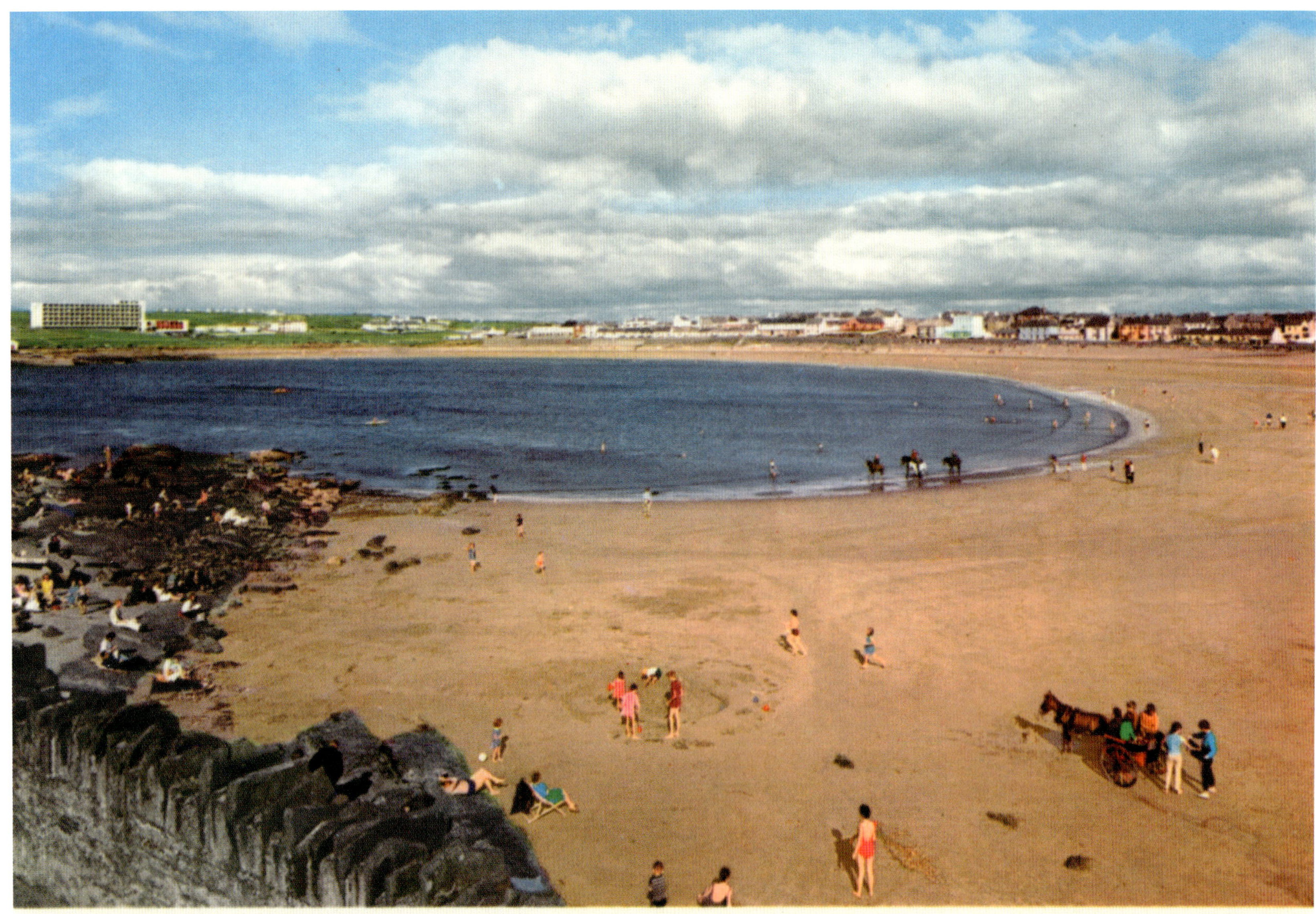

The Beach, Kilkee, Co. Clare, Ireland

Photo: D. Noble, John Hinde Studios.

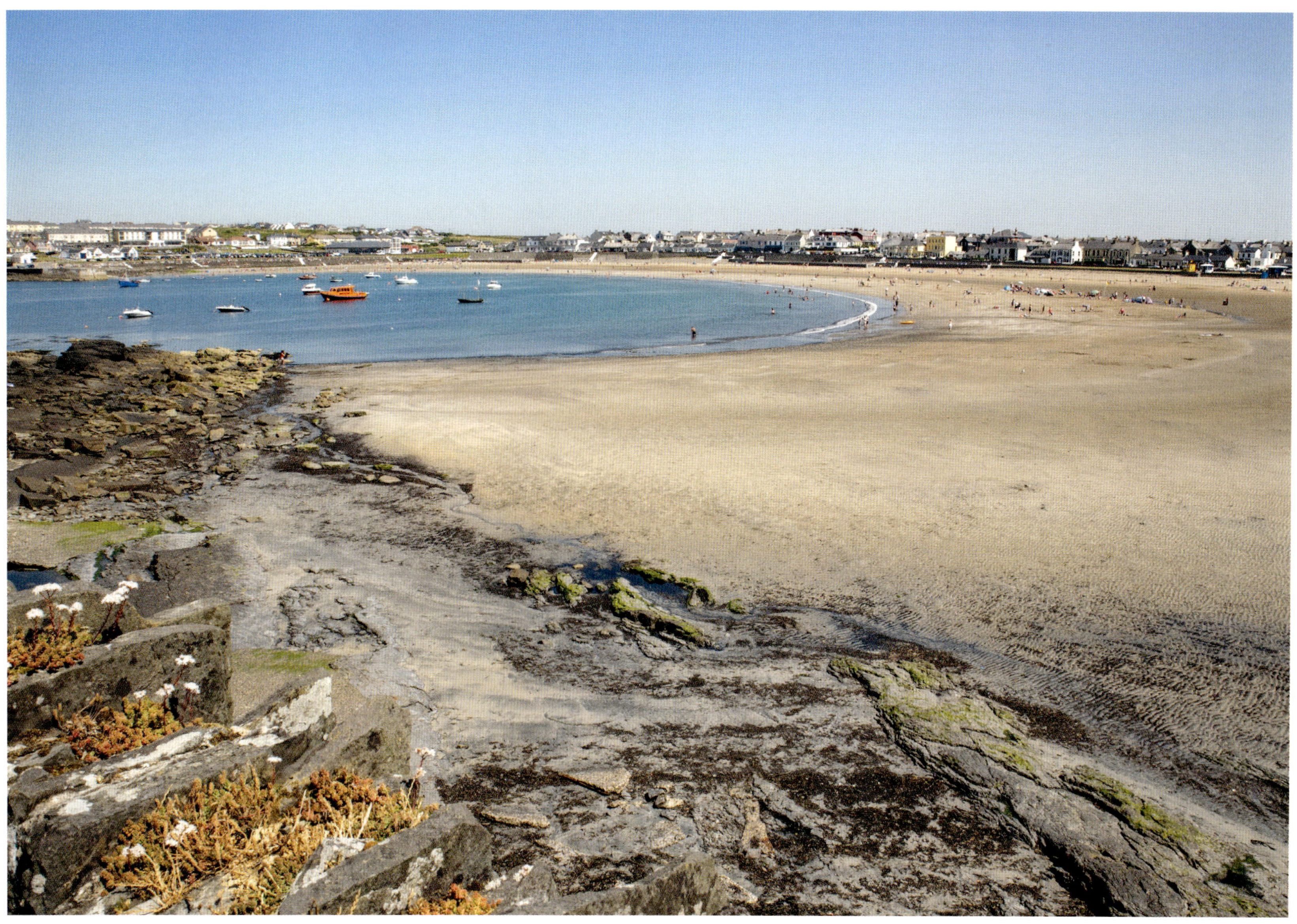

Along the Wild Atlantic Way, nestled in the horseshoe curves of Moore Bay, is charming Kilkee. Well-to-do 19th-century visitors basked in the town's benevolent climate and popular bathing areas, protected from the Atlantic by the rugged embrace of the Duggerna Reef. I can report that it retains its old-world ambience.

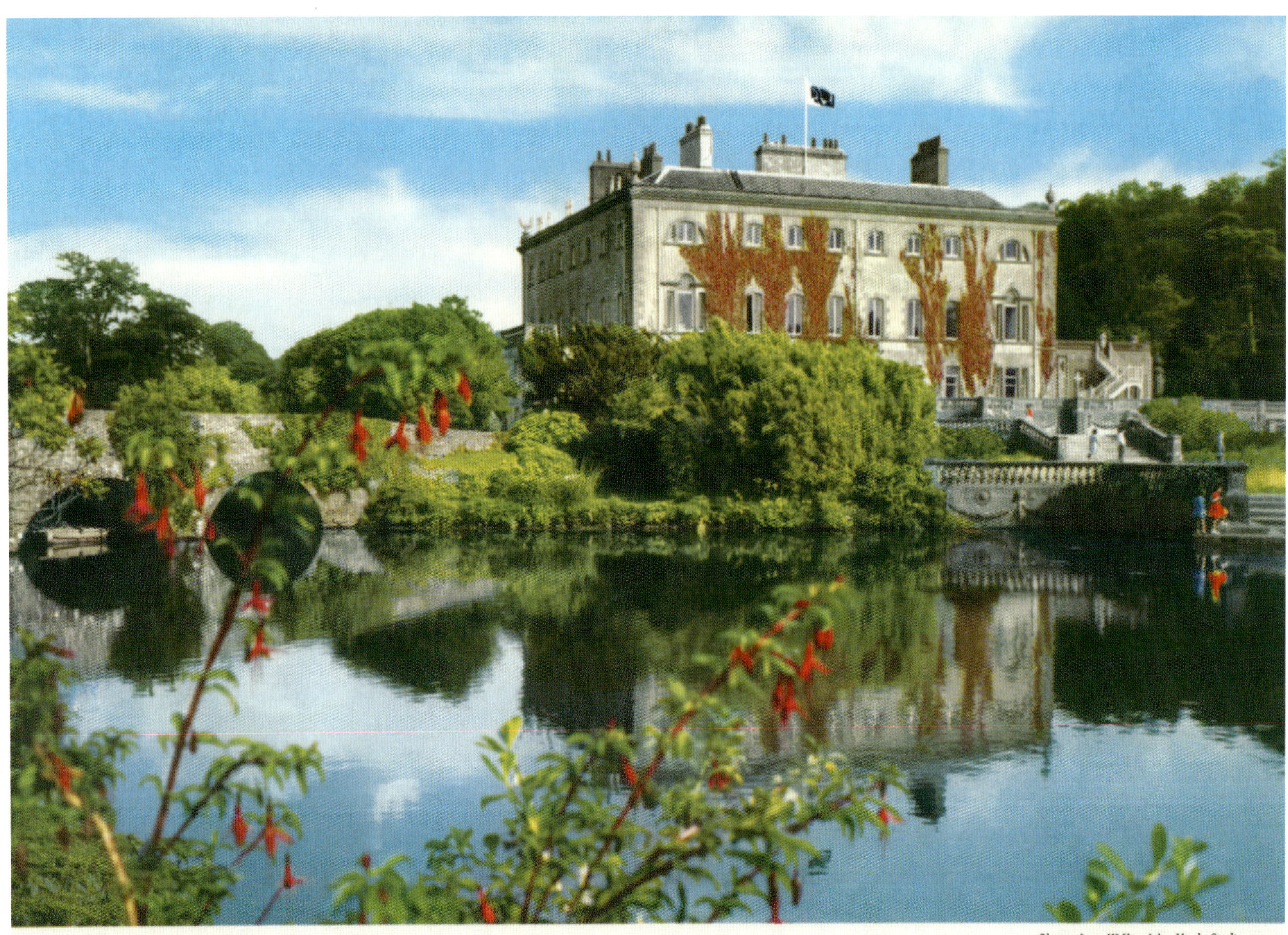

Westport House, Co. Mayo, Ireland. Photo: Joan Willis, John Hinde Studios.

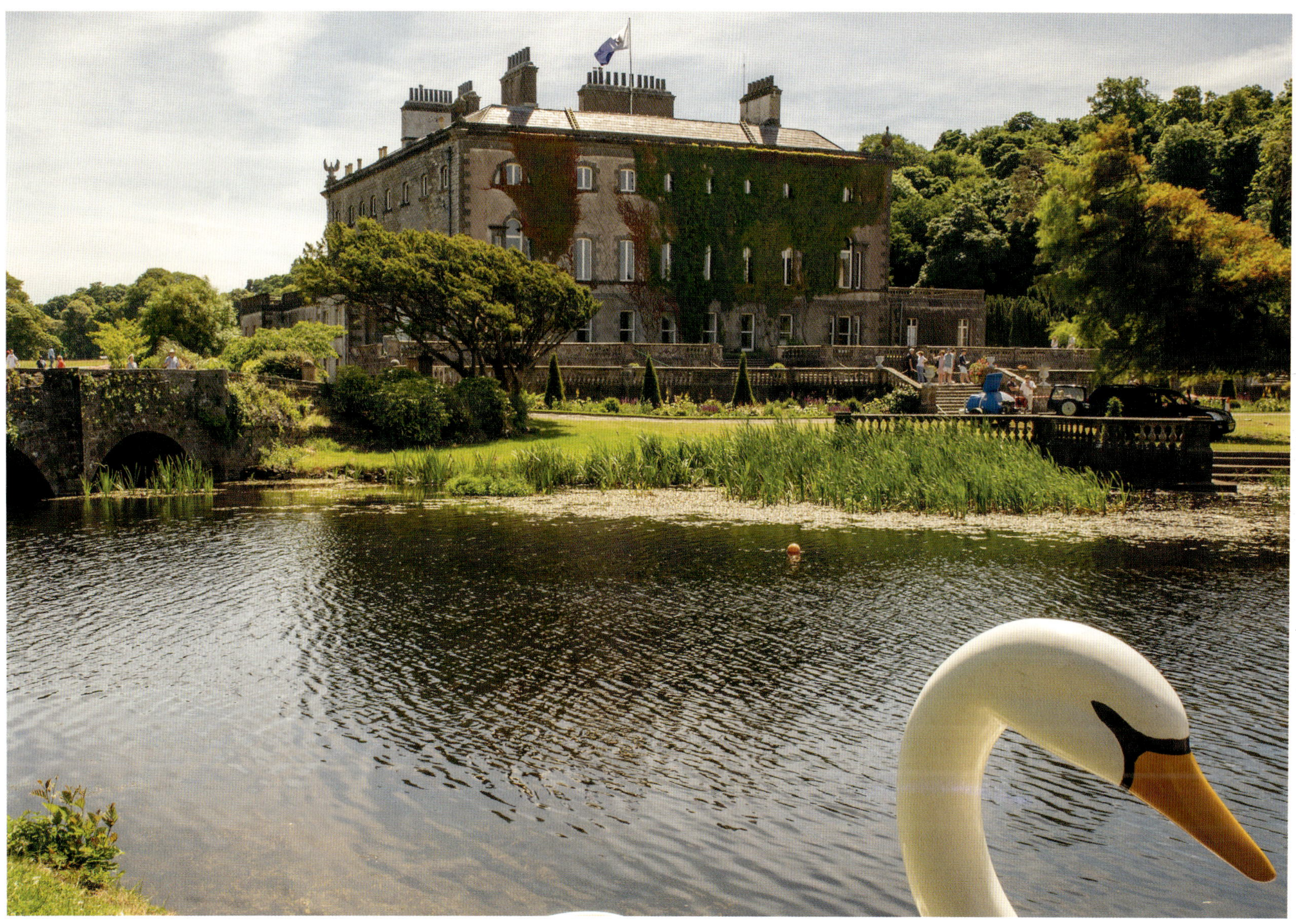

Before Westport House was built in the 18th century, it was a stronghold of 16th-century 'Pirate Queen' Grace O'Malley and, until very recently, was still owned by her descendants. Now there's a pirate adventure park and bouncy castle. That queenly swan gliding past? It's a pedal boat, of course.

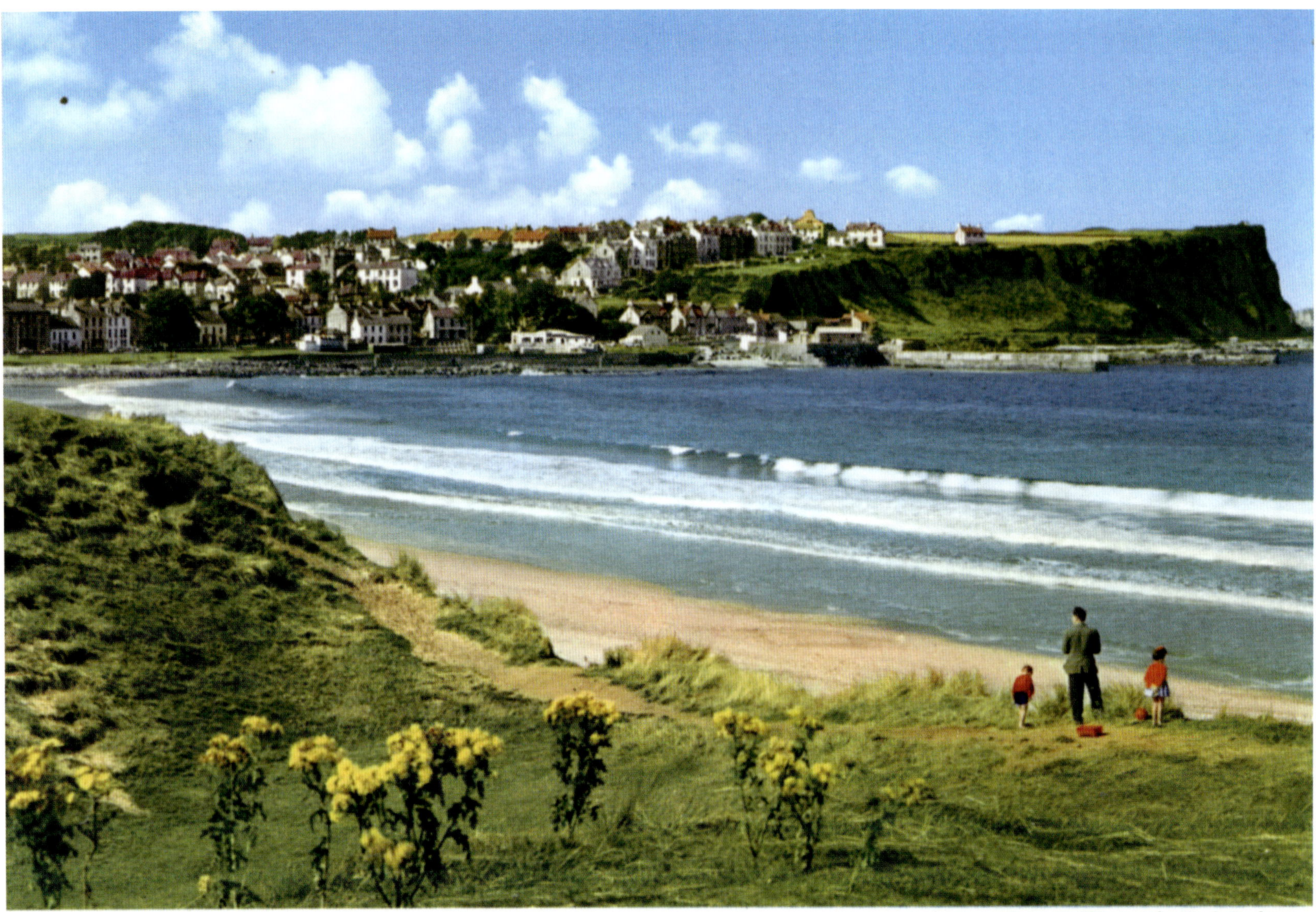

Ballycastle and Strand, Co. Antrim, N.I.

Photo : E. Nägele, John Hinde Studios.

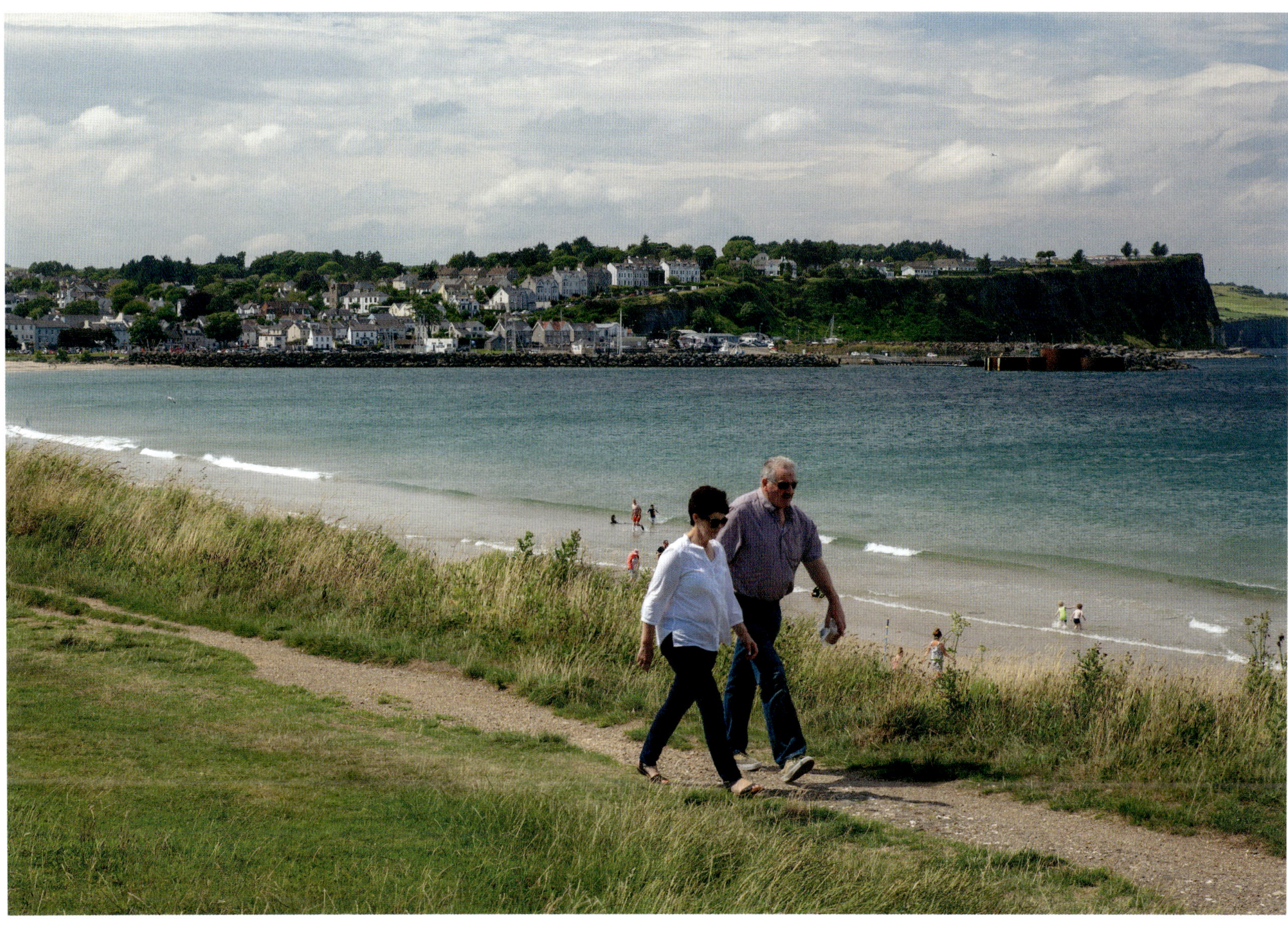

To take this photo I had to stand on the tee box of the eighth hole at Ballycastle Golf Club. This charming harbour town marks the eastern end of the Causeway coast. Stride out along the strand – this bracing walk offers exhilarating views of Ballycastle, Rathlin Island, Fairhead and Scotland.

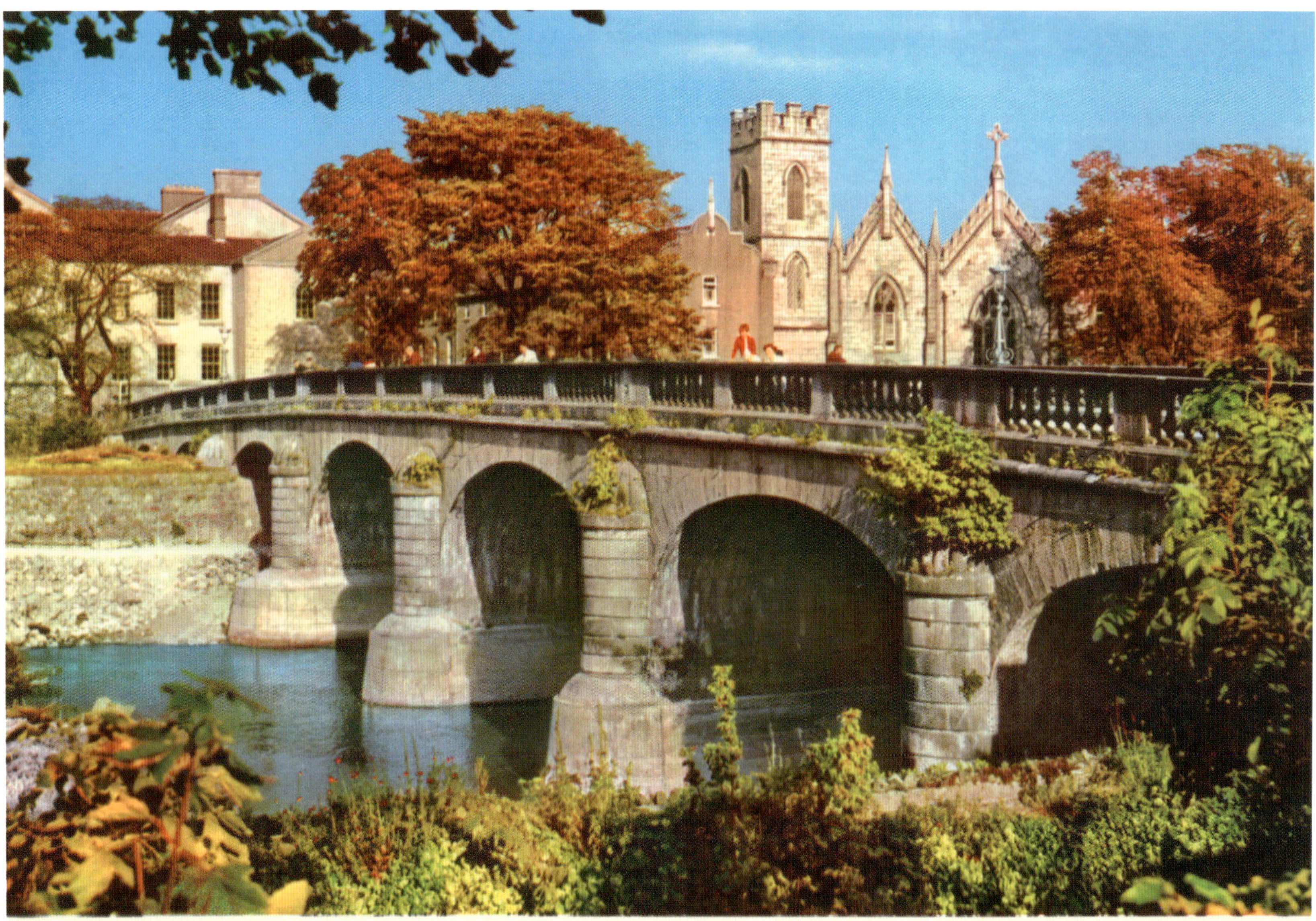

The Salmon Weir Bridge, Galway City, Ireland.

Colour Photo by John Hinde, F.R.P.S.

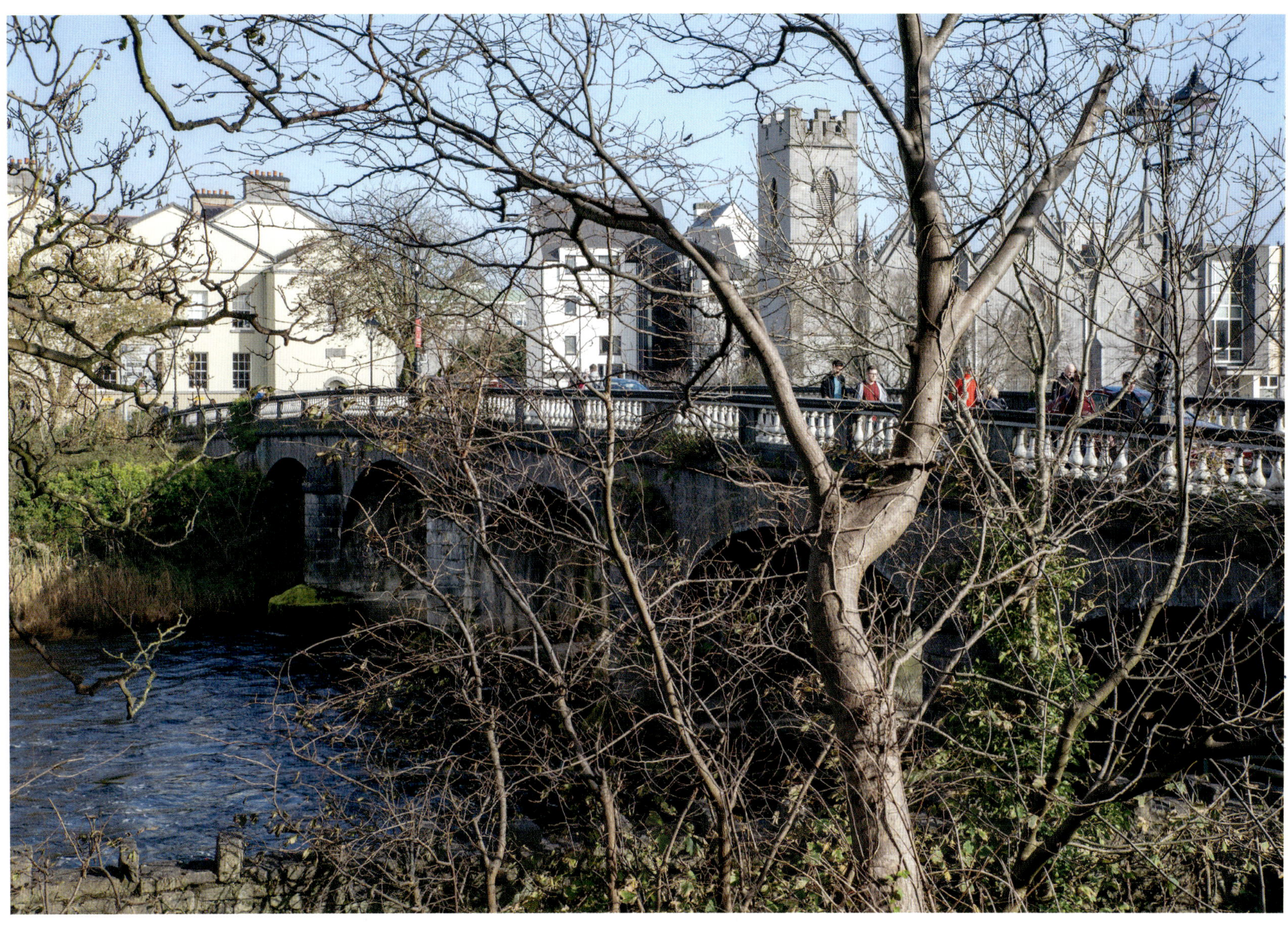

Now 200 years old, this busy little bridge brings scores of pedestrians and cars across the river Corrib to Galway Cathedral and NUI Galway. The river Corrib, which runs through Galway city, is swarming with fish in season.

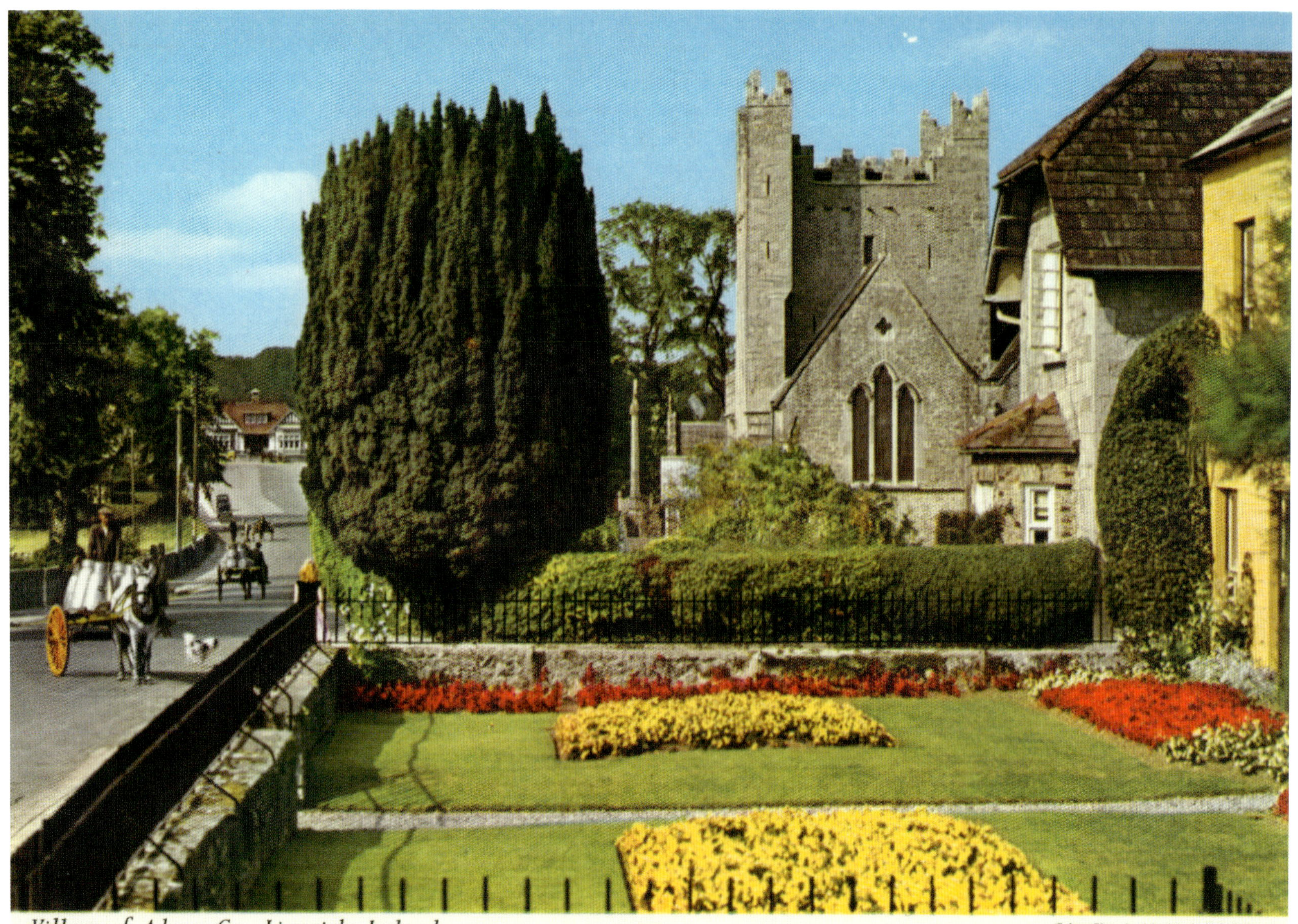
Village of Adare, Co. Limerick, Ireland.
Colour Photo by John Hinde, F.R.P.S.

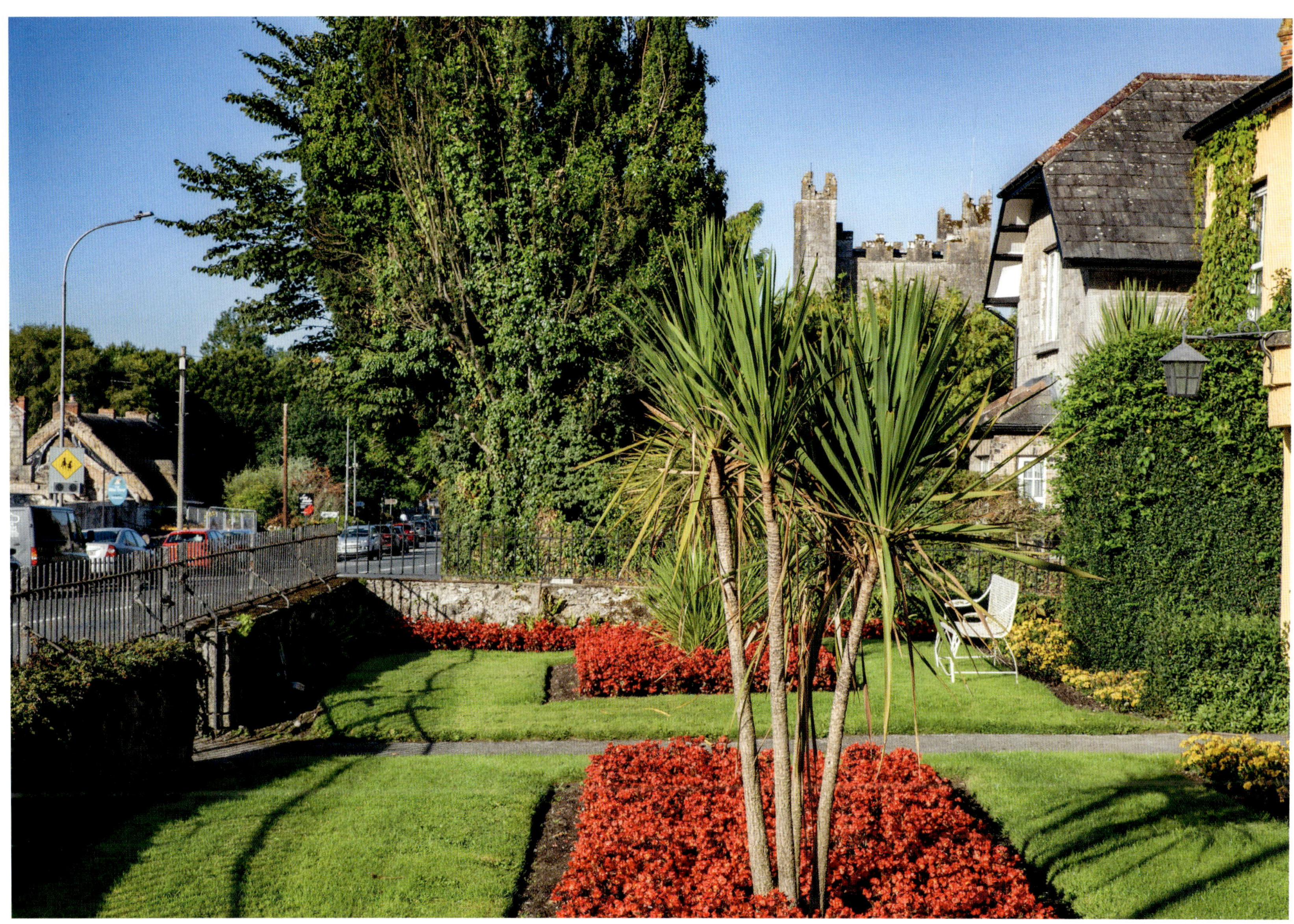

With scarlet flowerbeds that would have made John Hinde happy, this photo was taken on the doorstep of the Dunraven Arms. My father and I stayed and ate here often in the 1970s. I remember Adare as a quaint village of thatched cottages and lichened medieval churches. Today, it is full of craft shops, fine restaurants – and golf enthusiasts.

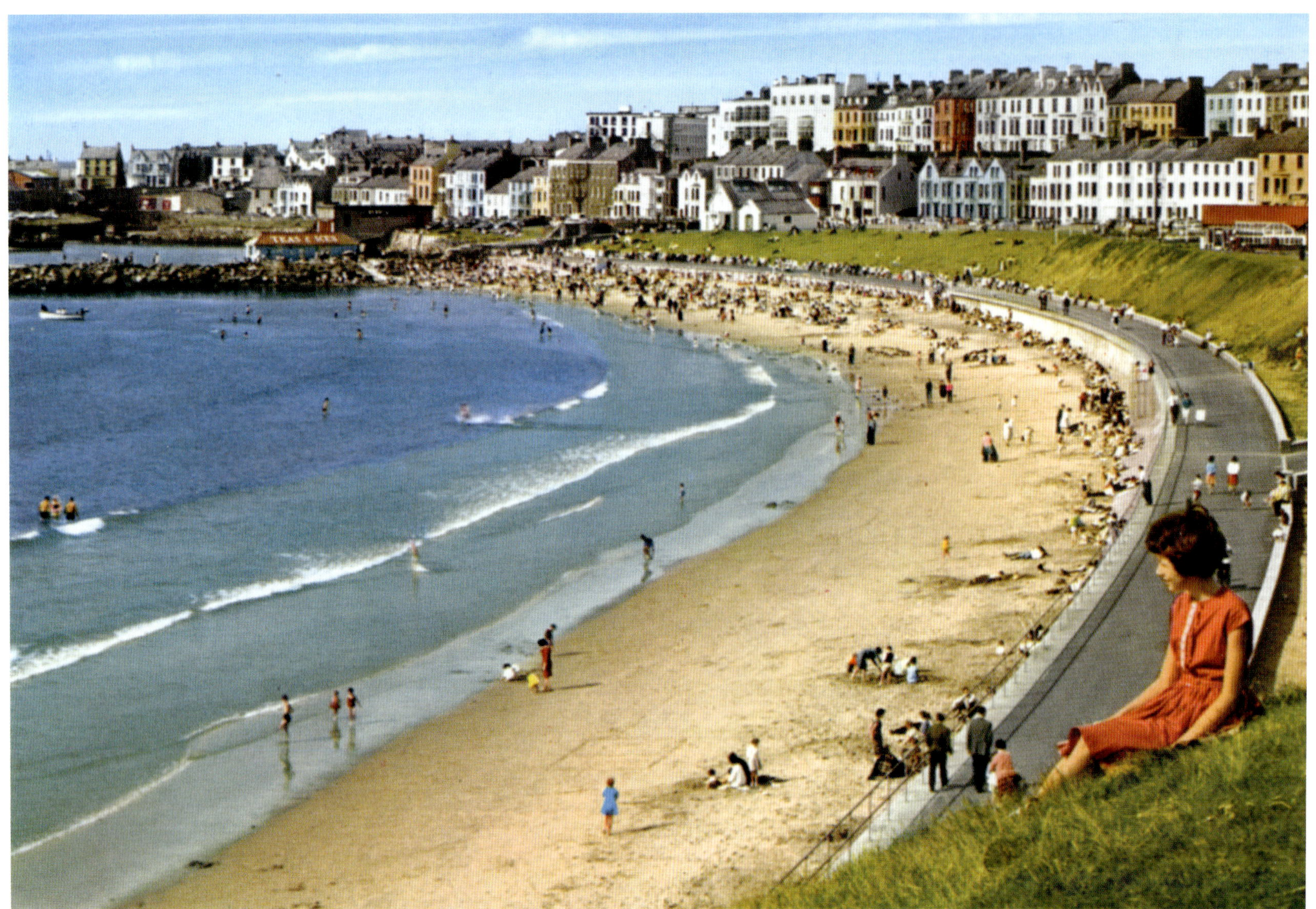

West Strand, Portrush, Co. Antrim, N.I. *Photo : E. Nägele, John Hinde Studios.*

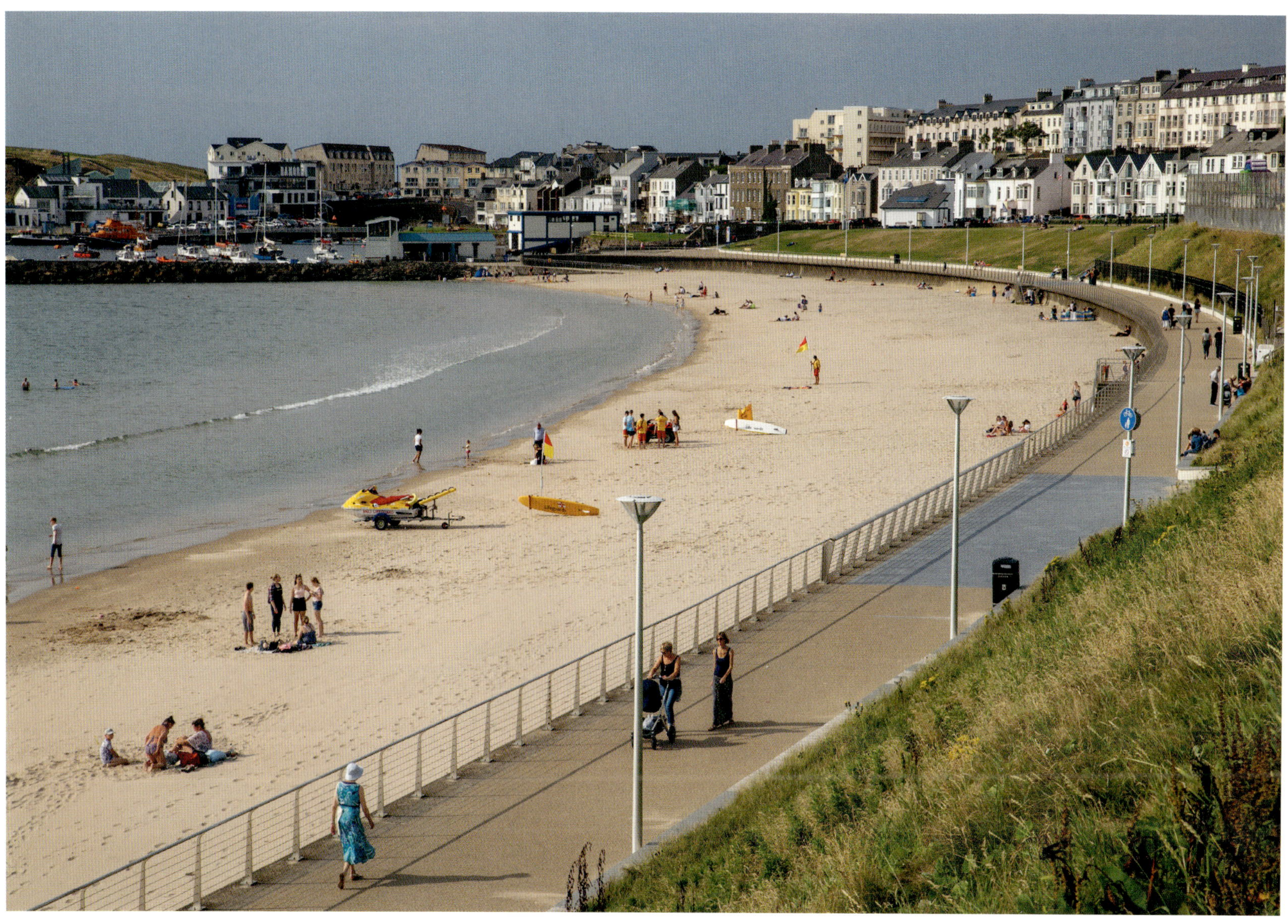

Fashionable since Victorian times, Portrush is a seaside town that grew from a small fishing village into a very popular holiday destination, known for its beautiful Blue Flag beaches. In the postcard, you can see the energetic sightseer in a scarlet dress, who managed to get into many of John Hinde's shots.

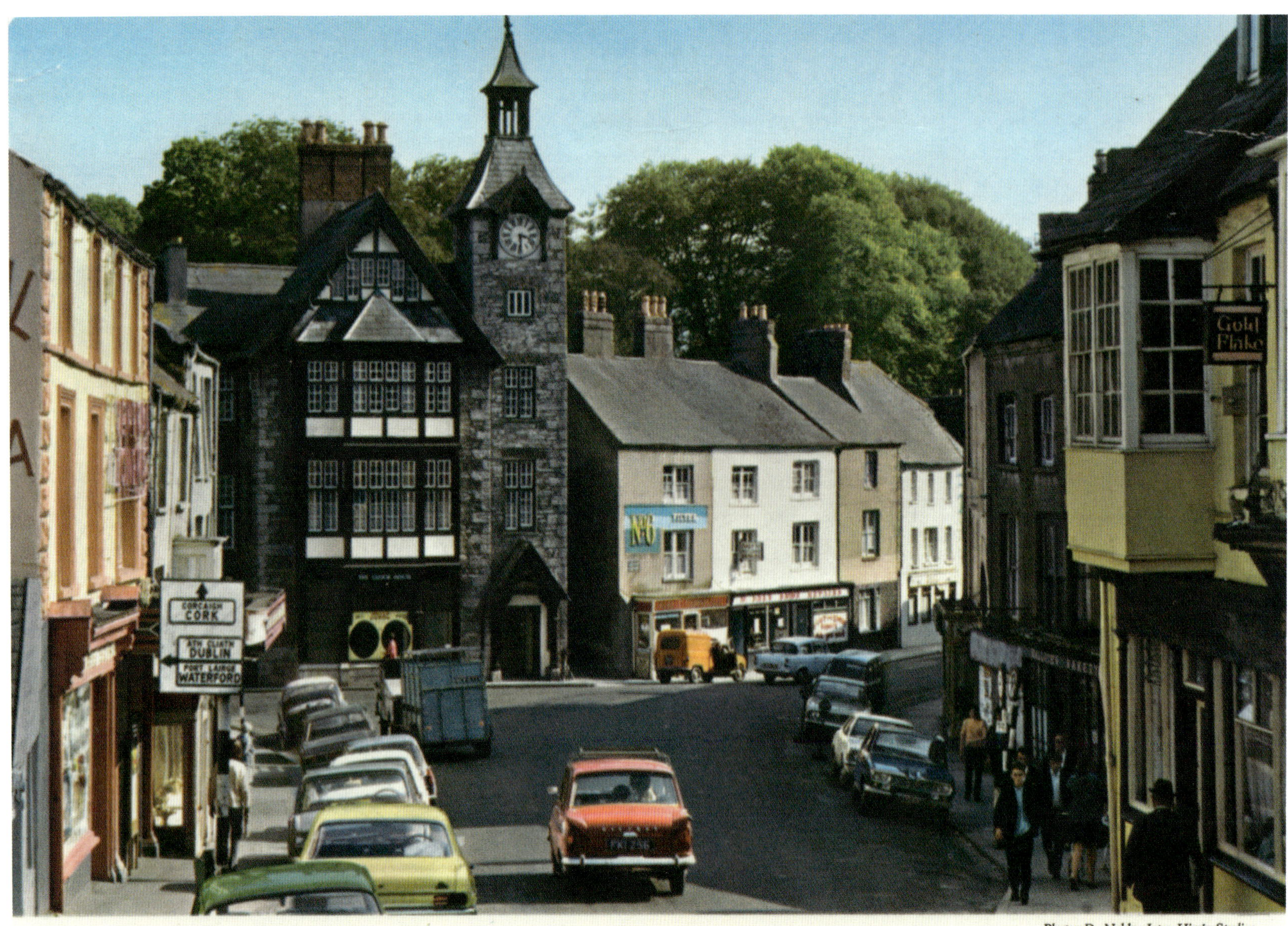

Mallow, Co. Cork, Ireland.

Photo: D. Noble, John Hinde Studios.

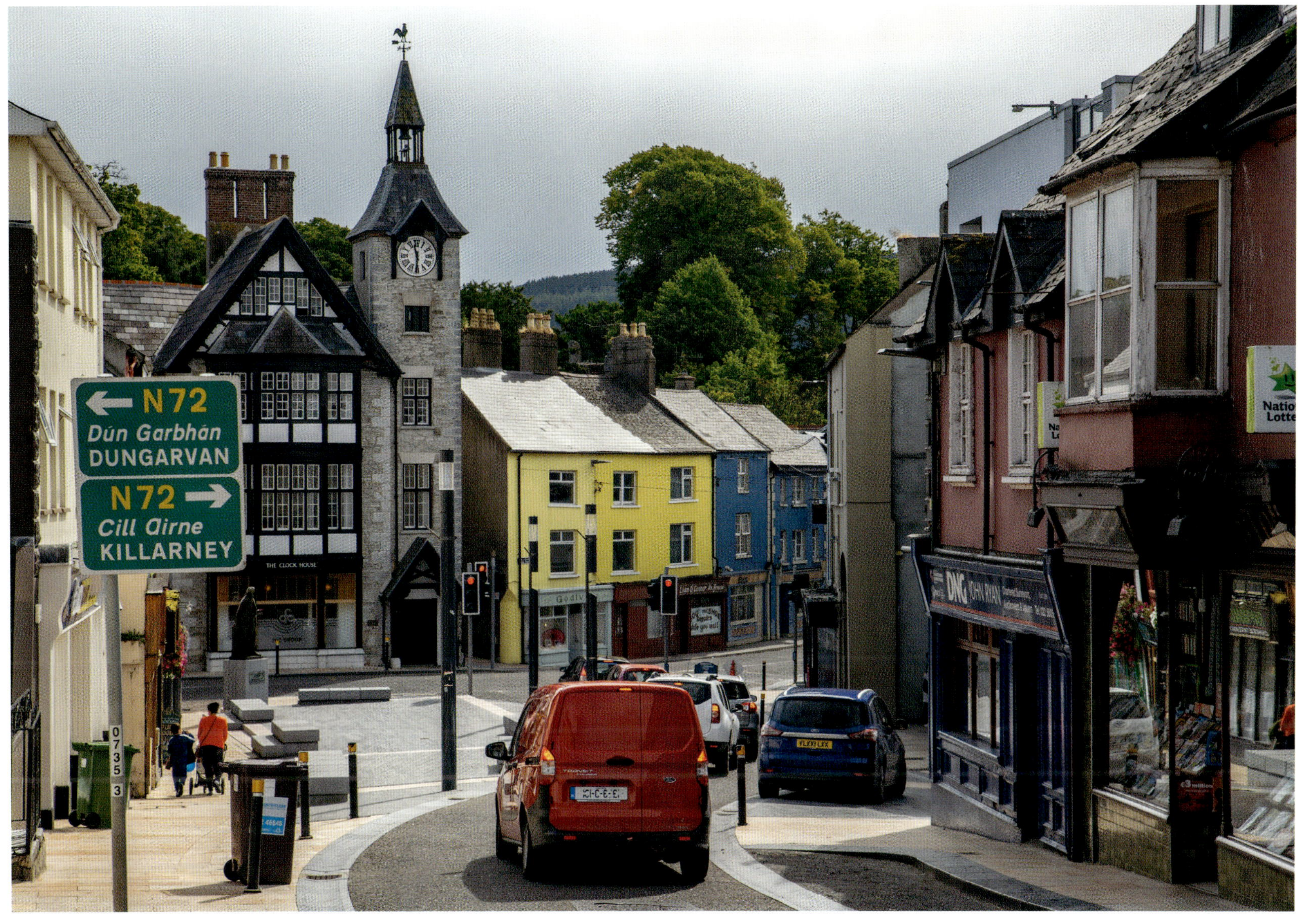

I remember in 1983, a Mexican pilot was forced to make an emergency landing at Mallow racecourse. Captain Ruben Ocana and his crew then had to stay at the Central Hotel in Mallow for 39 days, until a proper runway was laid to get his Gulfstream airborne again. Needless to say, Captain Ocana became a local celebrity and is still revered today.

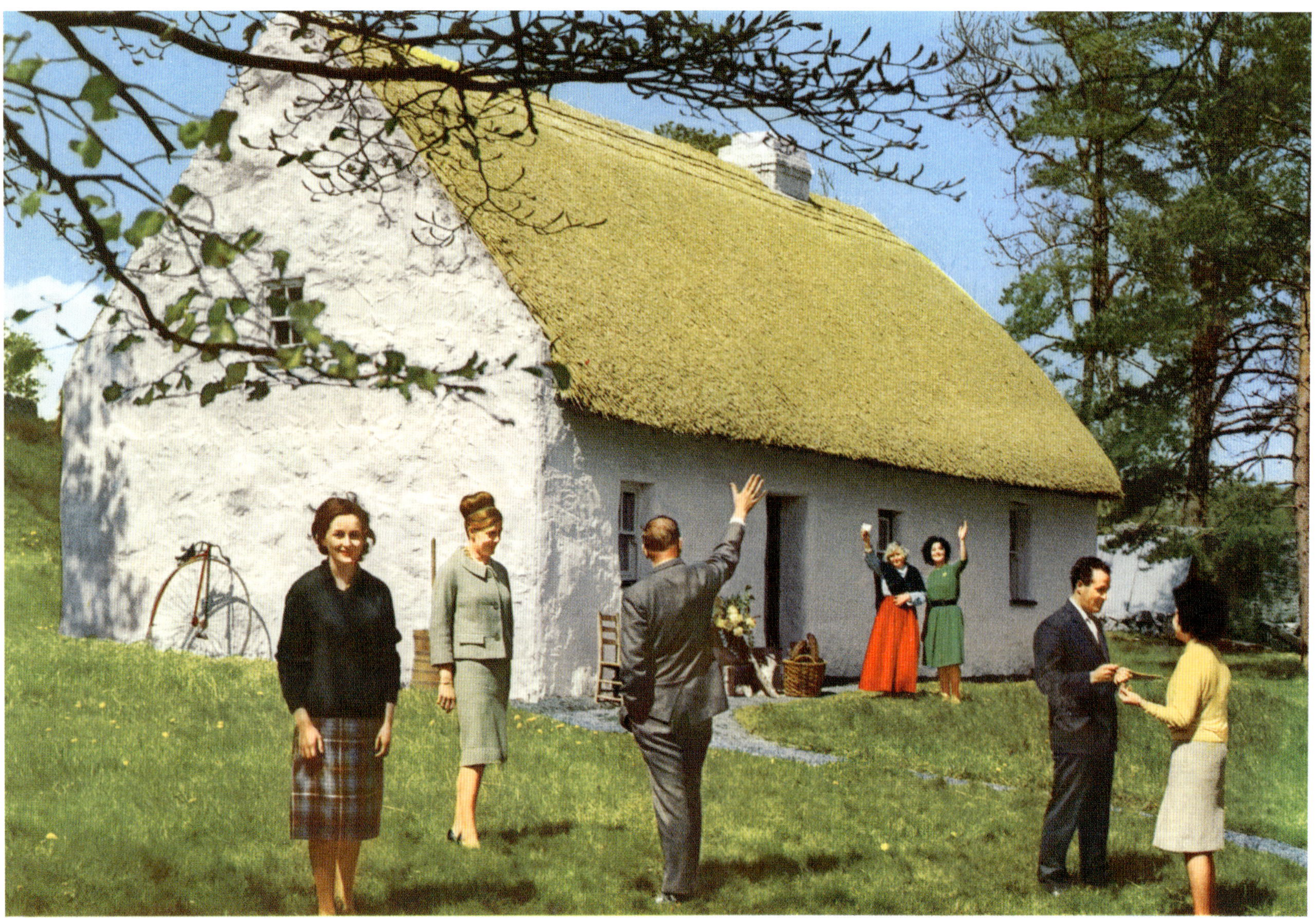

Irish Thatched Cottage, Bunratty, Co. Clare, Ireland.

Photo: E. Ludwig, John Hinde Studios.

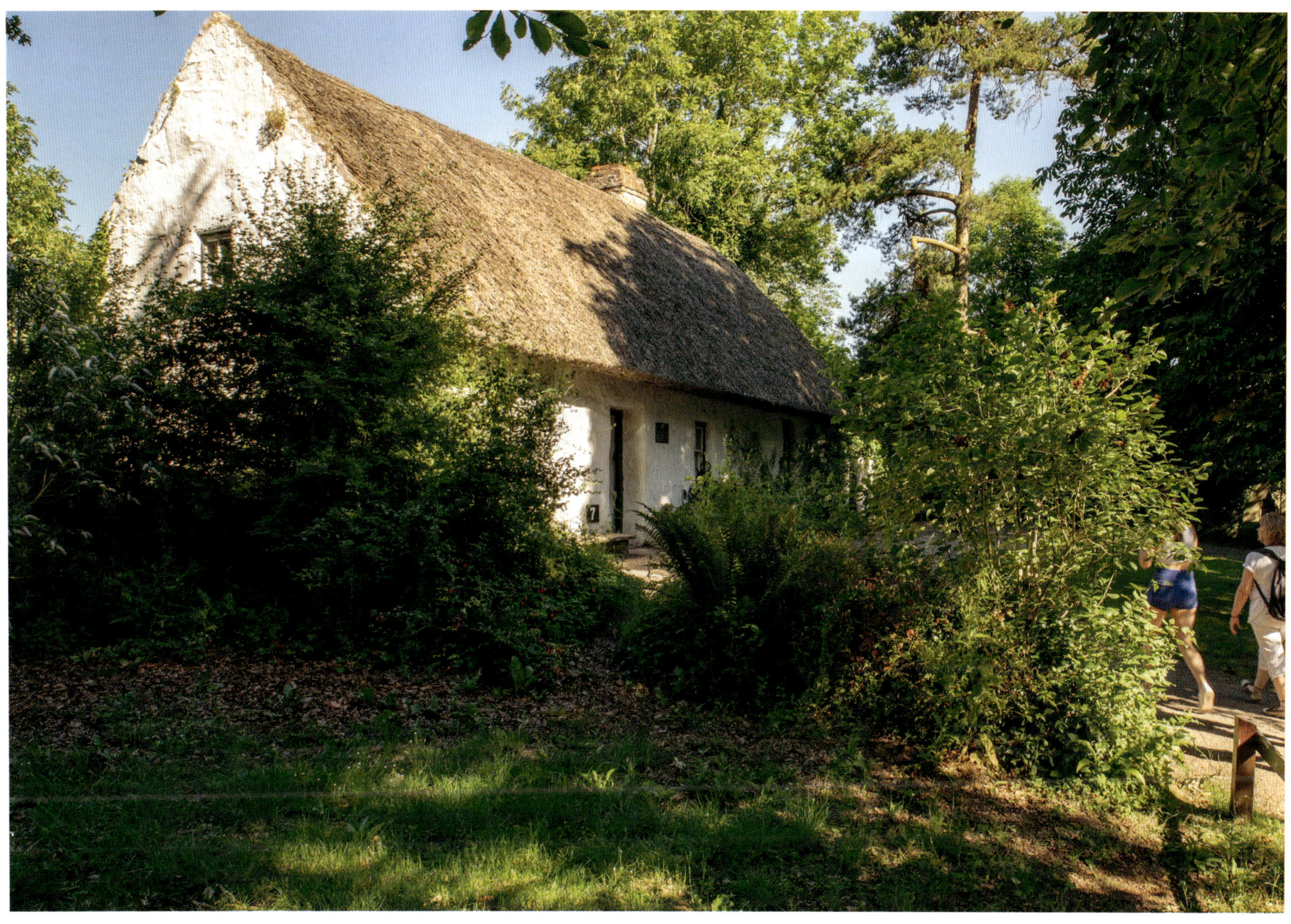

Since it opened in 1964, the 26-acre Bunratty Folk Park has offered visitors a living reconstruction of rural Irish homes and settings from over a century ago. I first came here in 1972, yet I'm still spellbound. It all seems changeless, except for the leisurewear.

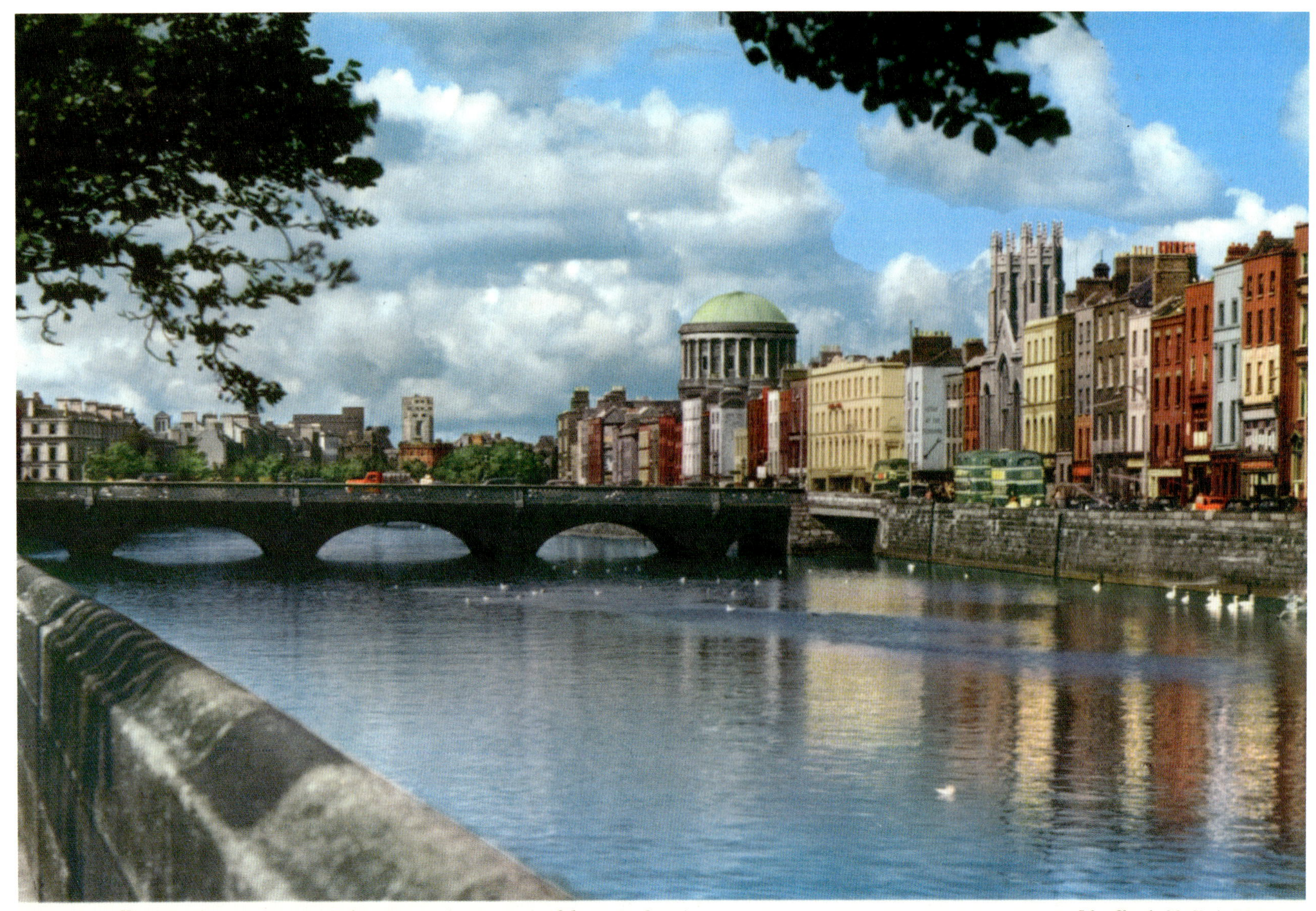

River Liffey, looking towards the Four Courts, Dublin, Ireland.

Colour Photo by John Hinde, F.R.P.S.

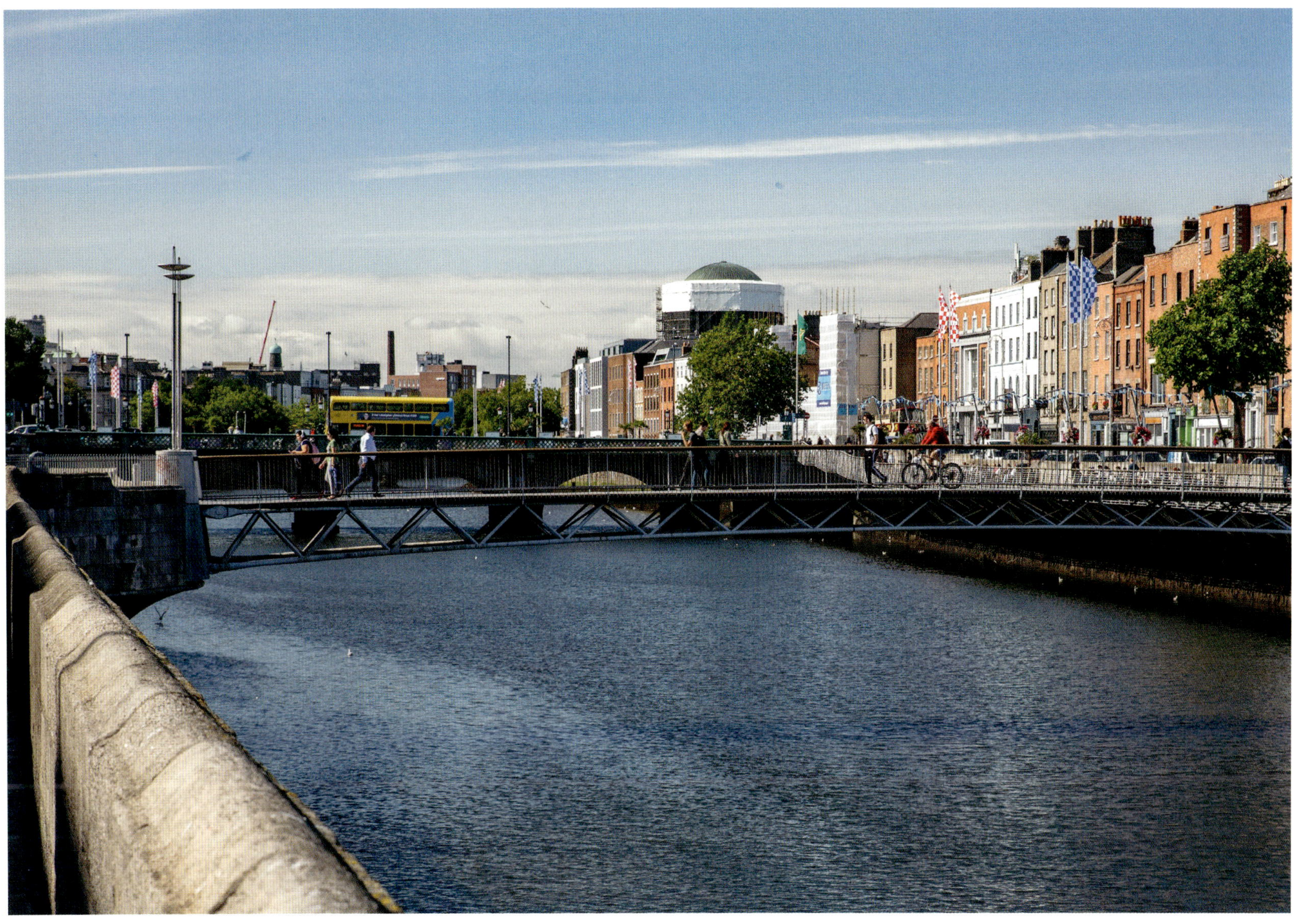

The Four Courts – housing the Supreme Court, Court of Appeal, High Court and Dublin Circuit Court – still dominates the river Liffey landscape. Its dome is one of the most recognisable landmarks in Dublin. Quite right, as the old adage states, that justice must also be seen to be done.

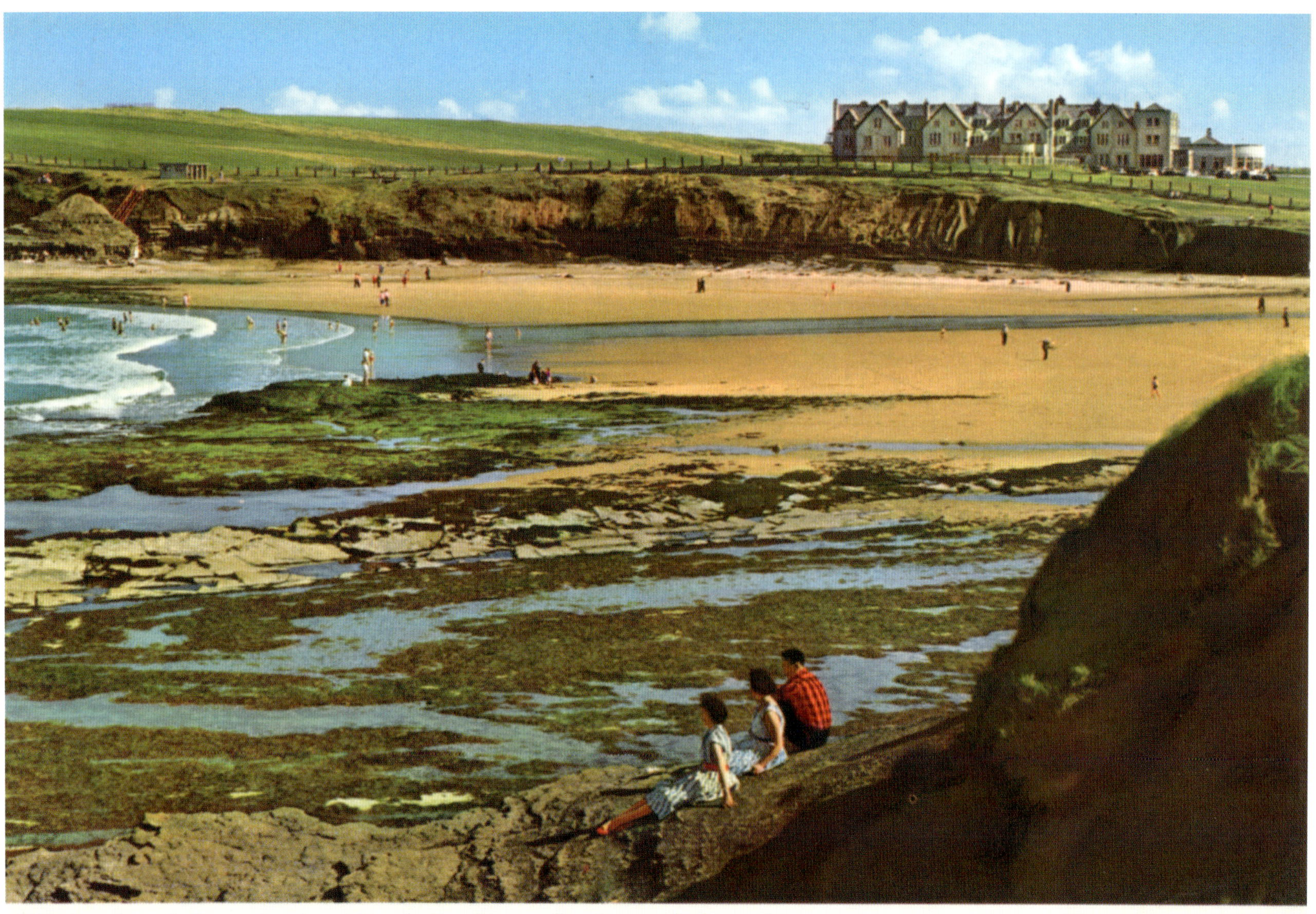

The Beach and Great Southern Hotel, Bundoran, Co. Donegal, Ireland. Colour Photo by John Hinde, F.R.P.S.

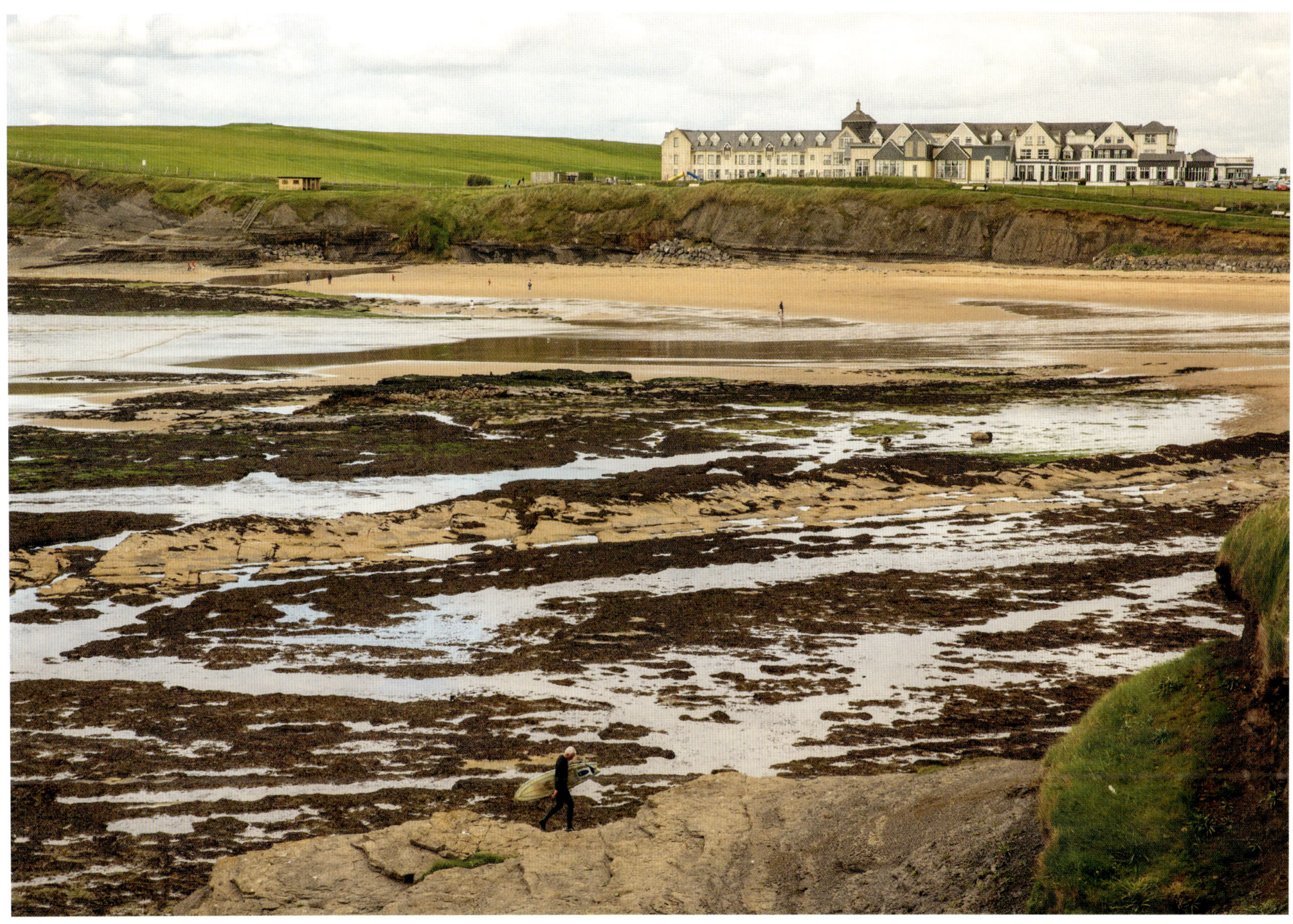

Today, Bundoran is a world-renowned surfing spot. One of its best-known landmarks is the Great Northern Hotel, constructed by the Great Northern Railway Company following the opening of the railway link to Belfast and on to Dublin in the 1860s. This was the heyday of Bundoran, which became one of Ireland's most popular seaside resorts.

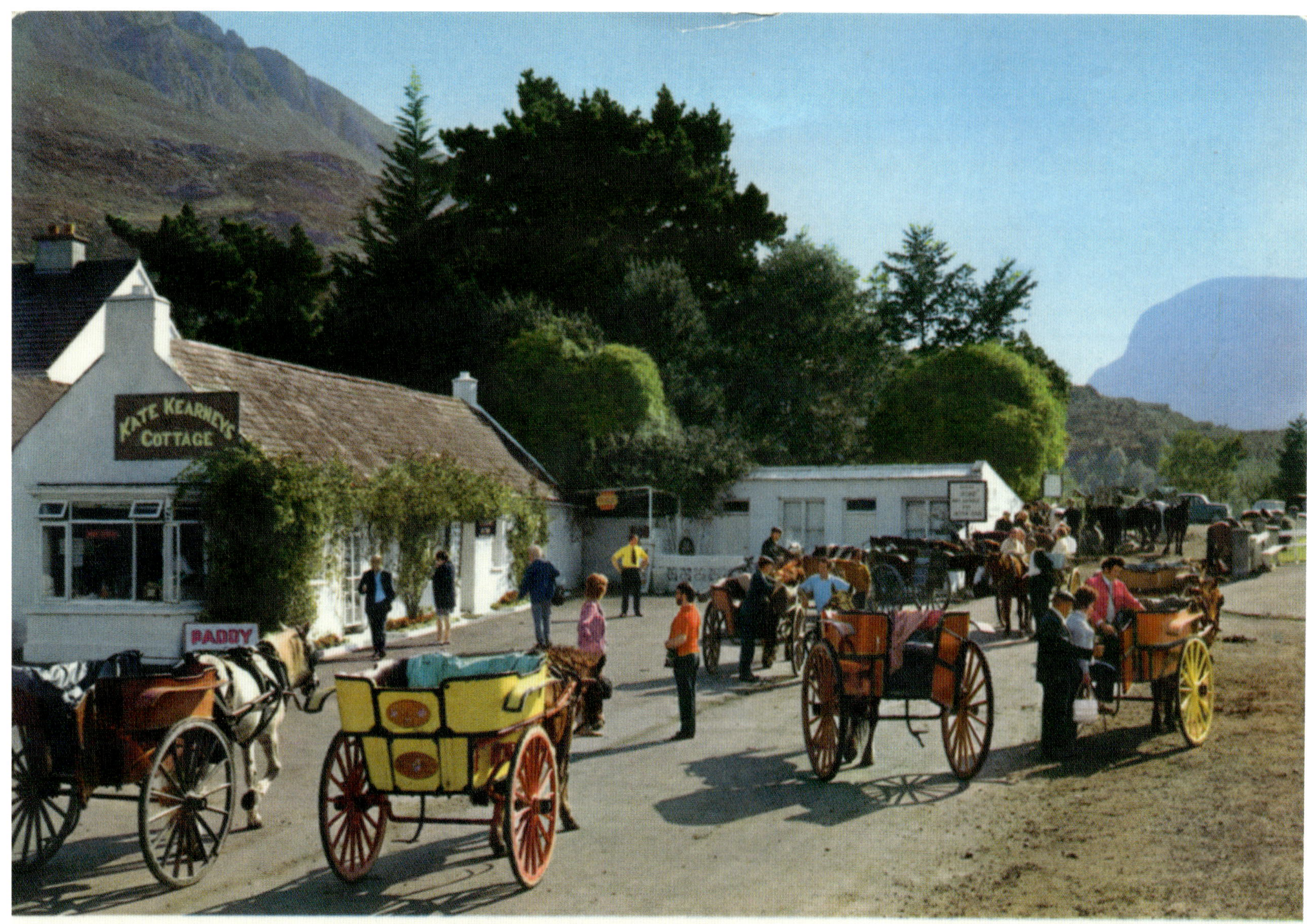

Kate Kearney's Cottage, entrance to Gap of Dunloe, Killarney, Co. Kerry, Ireland.

Photo: D. Noble, John Hinde Studios.

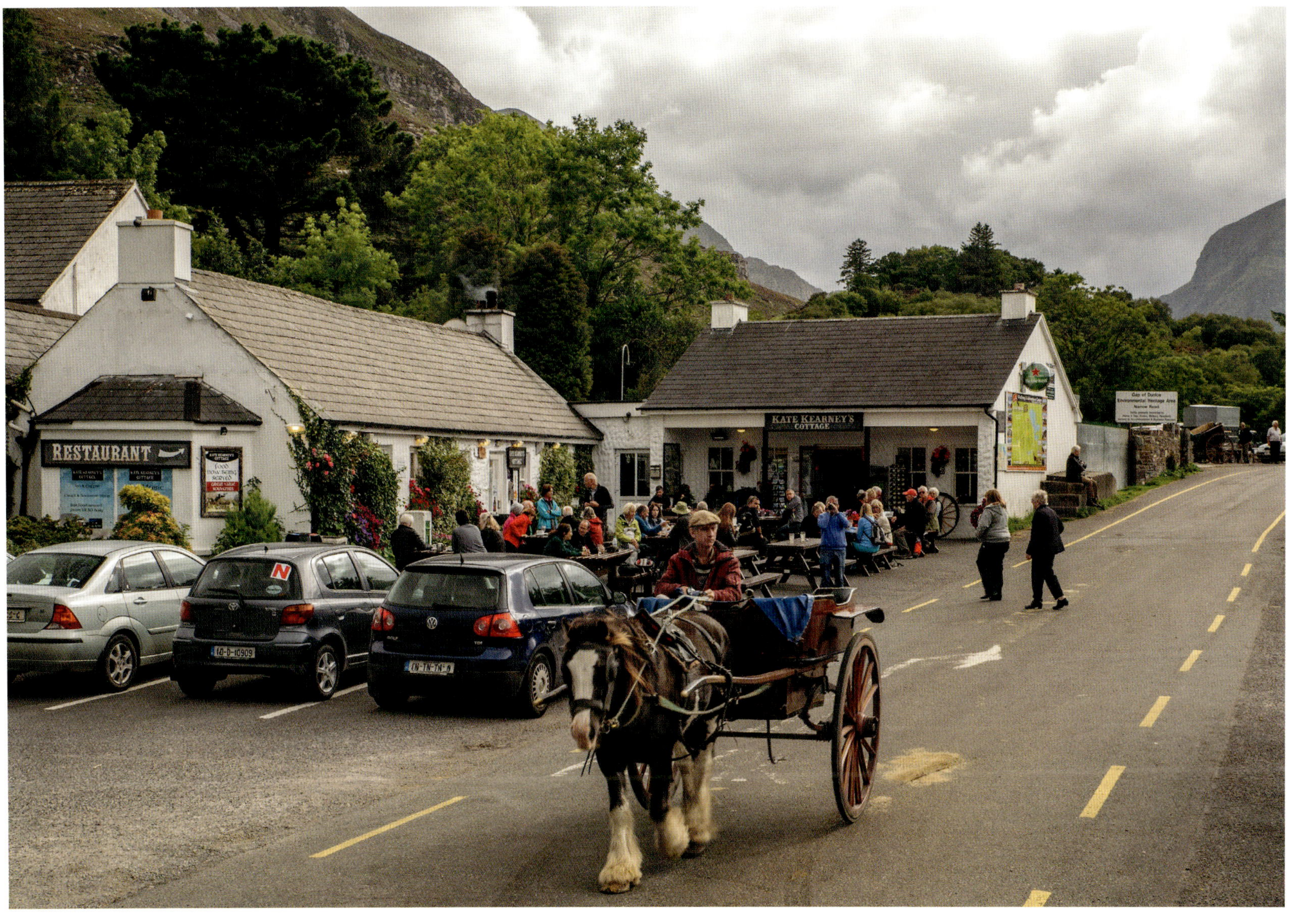

'Four wheels' and 'horsepower' meant something different back then. Today, visitors enter the Gap from Killarney through a very large carpark humming with coaches and rental cars. Booming out from Kate Kearney's, you can hear 'The Rare Ould Times', as American tourists contentedly sip their cappuccinos and half-pints of Guinness.

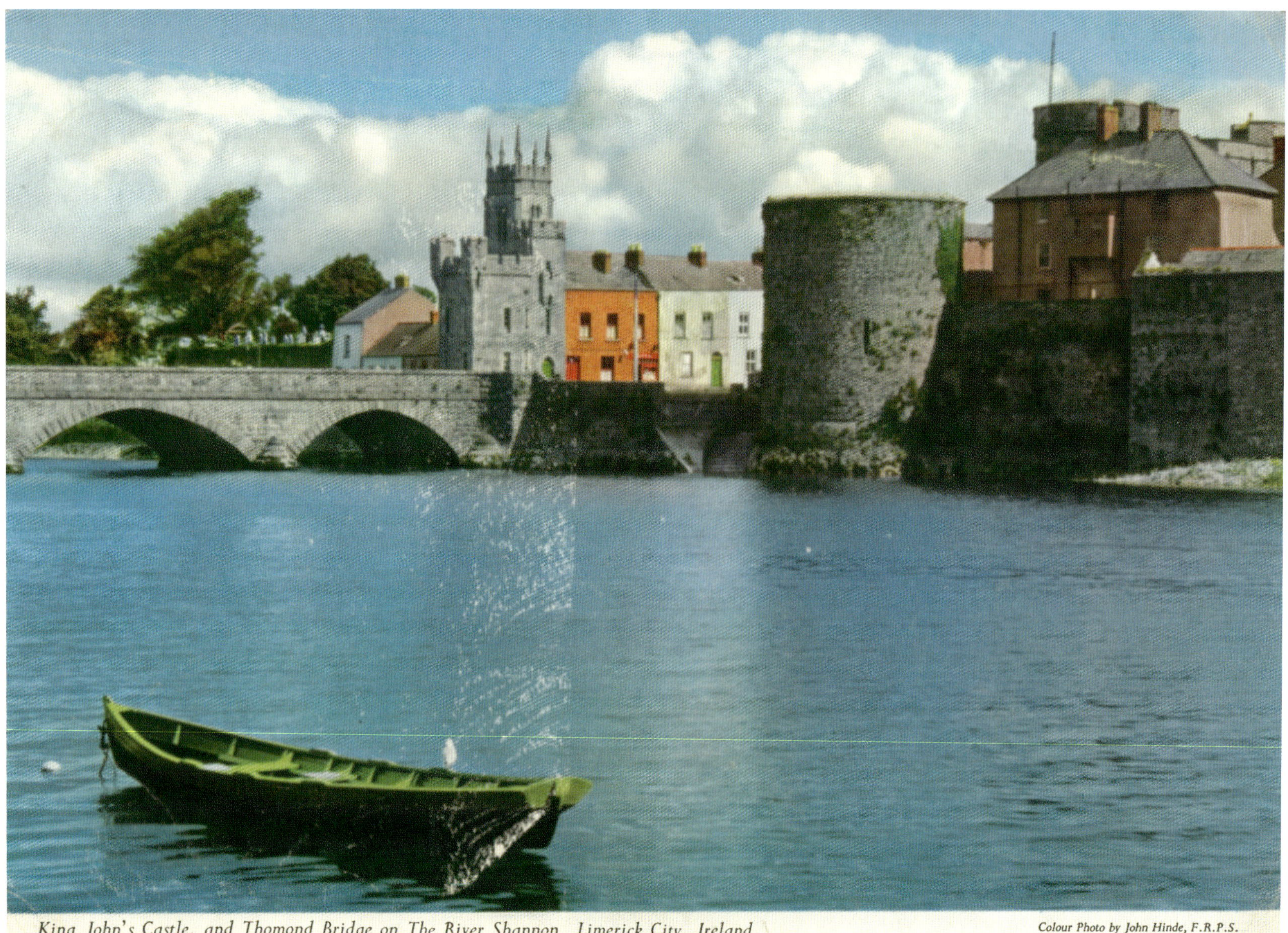
King John's Castle, and Thomond Bridge on The River Shannon, Limerick City, Ireland.
Colour Photo by John Hinde, F.R.P.S.

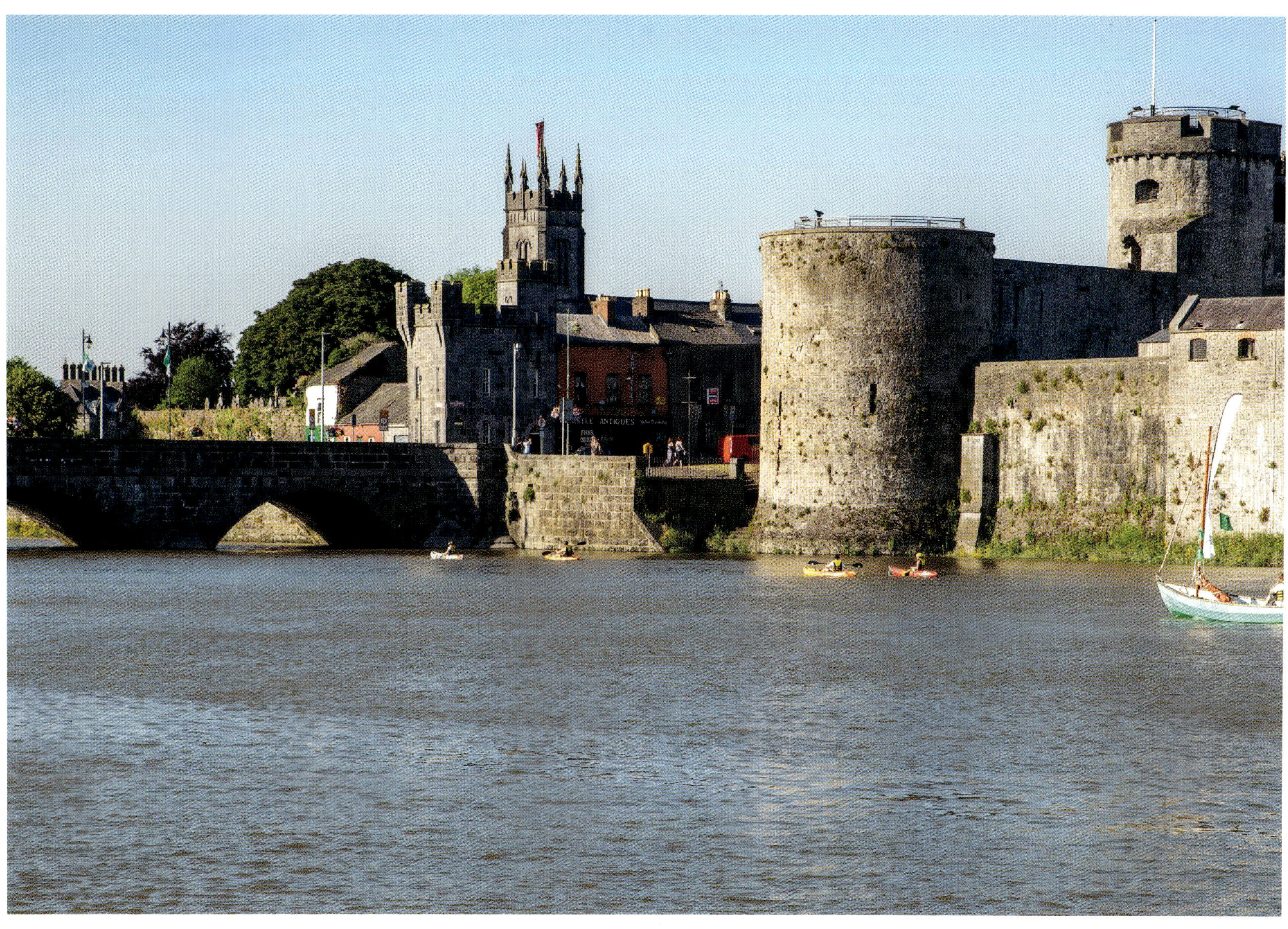

The epic poem 'The Drunken Thady and the Bishop's Lady' by Michael Hogan is about the Bishop of Limerick's wife, who was murdered in the palace next to the castle. Each night, her ghost would roam the streets of Limerick, picking fights with any poor soul she met. One night she happened on a drunken thief known as Thady and pushed him off the Thomond Bridge into the Shannon. As he was drowning, Thady repented all his sins and his life was spared. He was Drunken Thady no more.

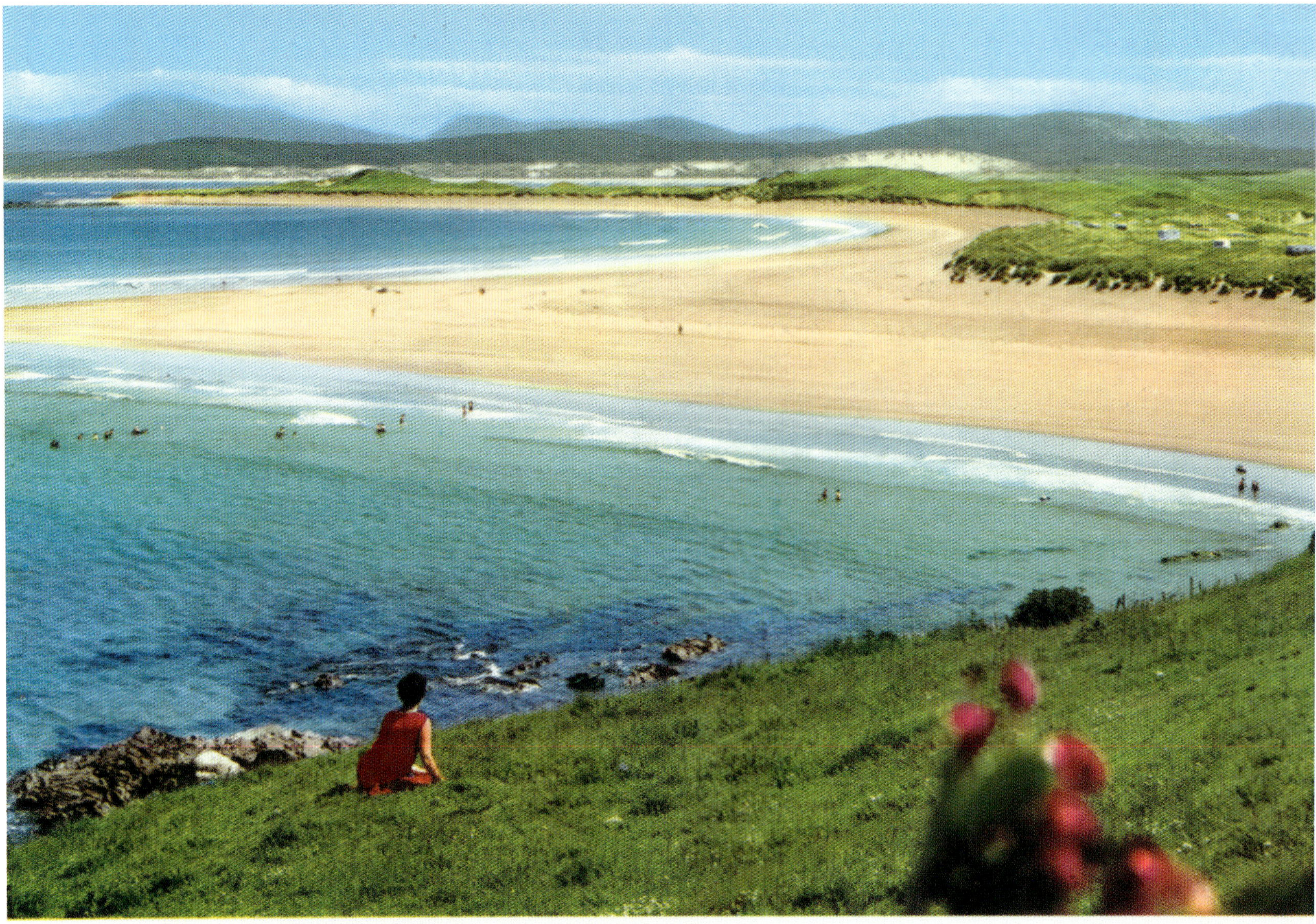

The Strand, Narin, Co. Donegal, Ireland.

Photo: Joan Willis, John Hinde Studios.

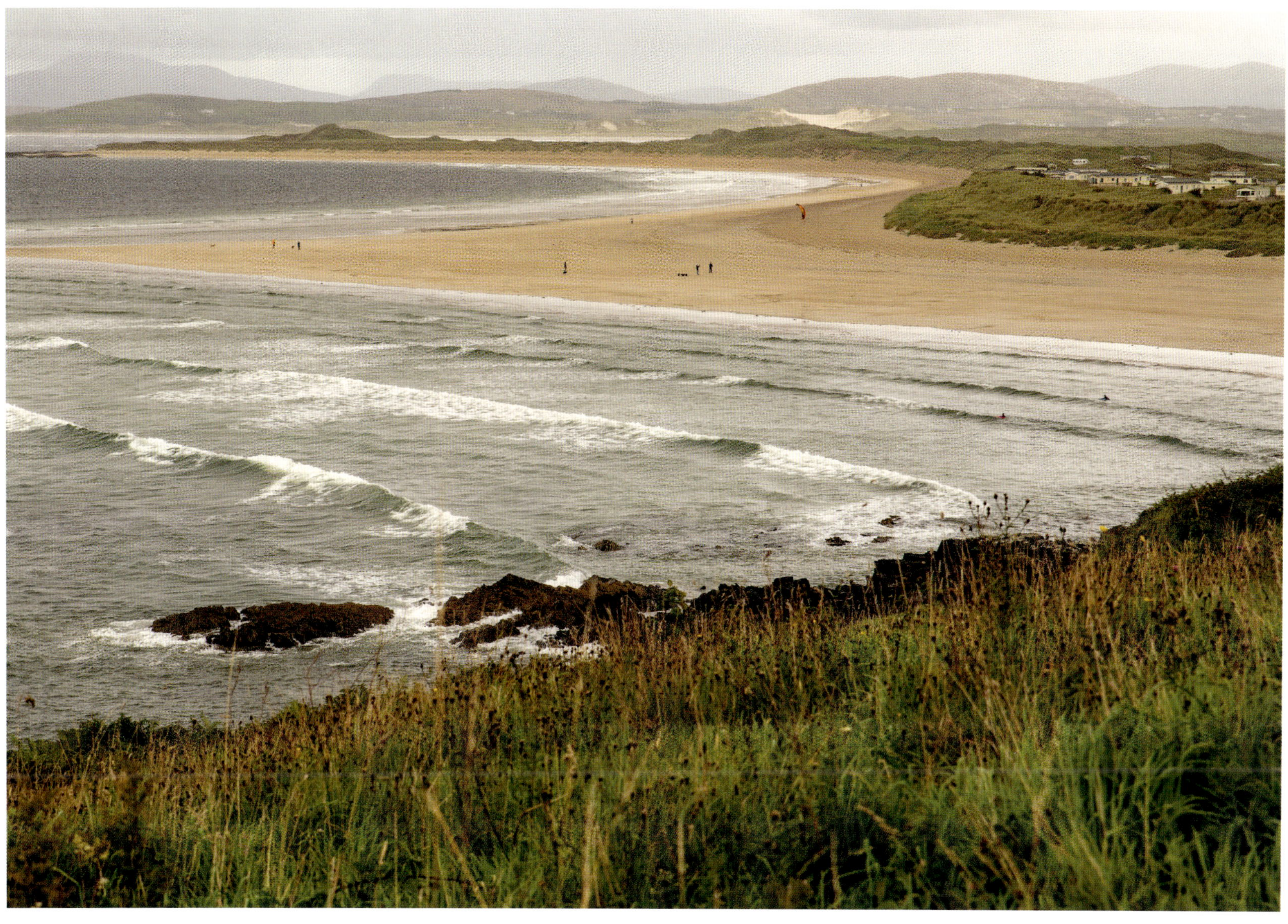

Narin is a Blue Flag beach set in a cove and, with the welcome protection of Dunmore Head, is relatively sheltered. Taking this photograph was rather difficult as I was forced to fight howling winds and driving rain. Nothing the warm and cosy Annora pub and café just down the road couldn't cure, though.

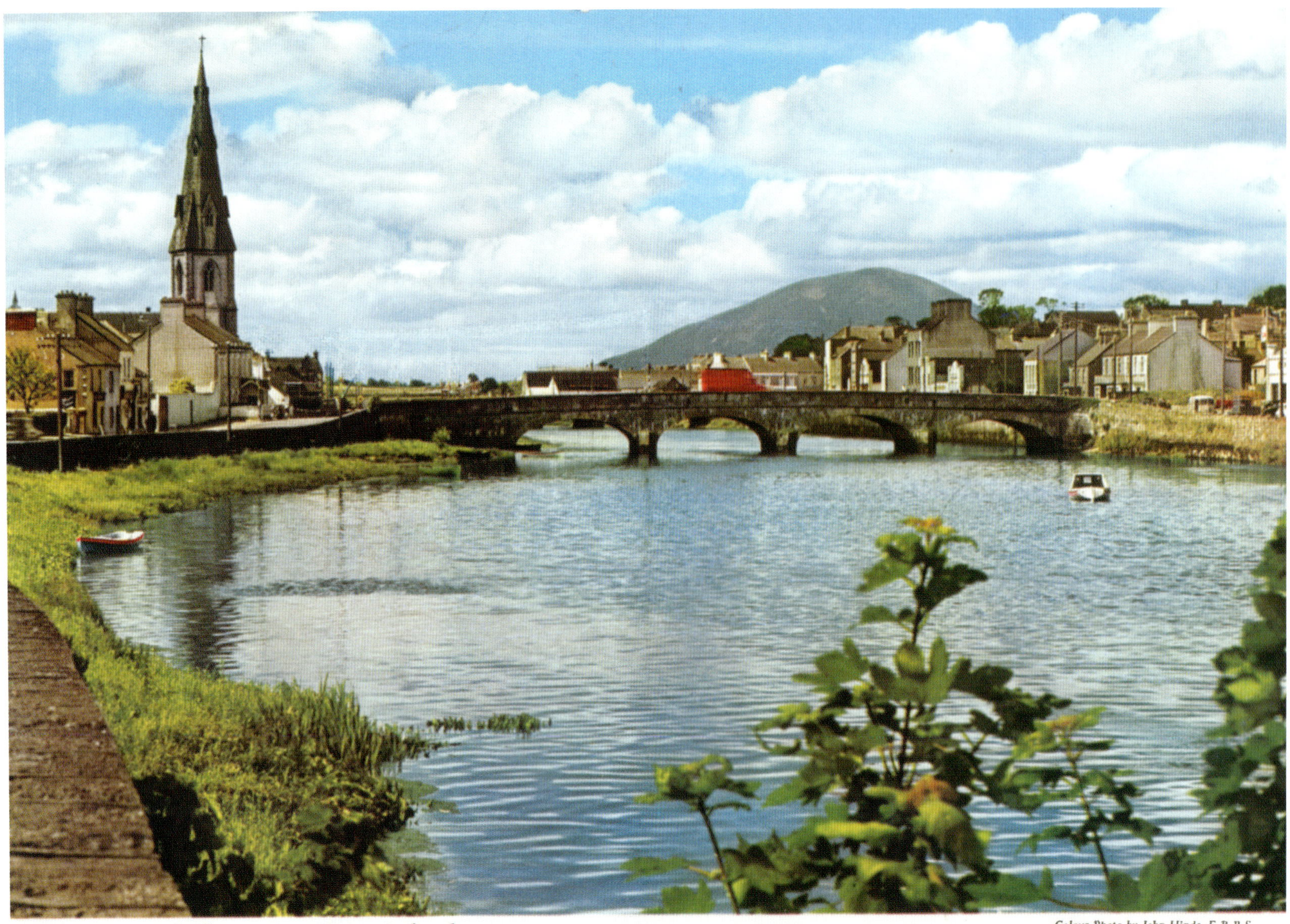

River Moy at Ballina, Co. Mayo, Ireland.

Colour Photo by John Hinde, F.R.P.S.

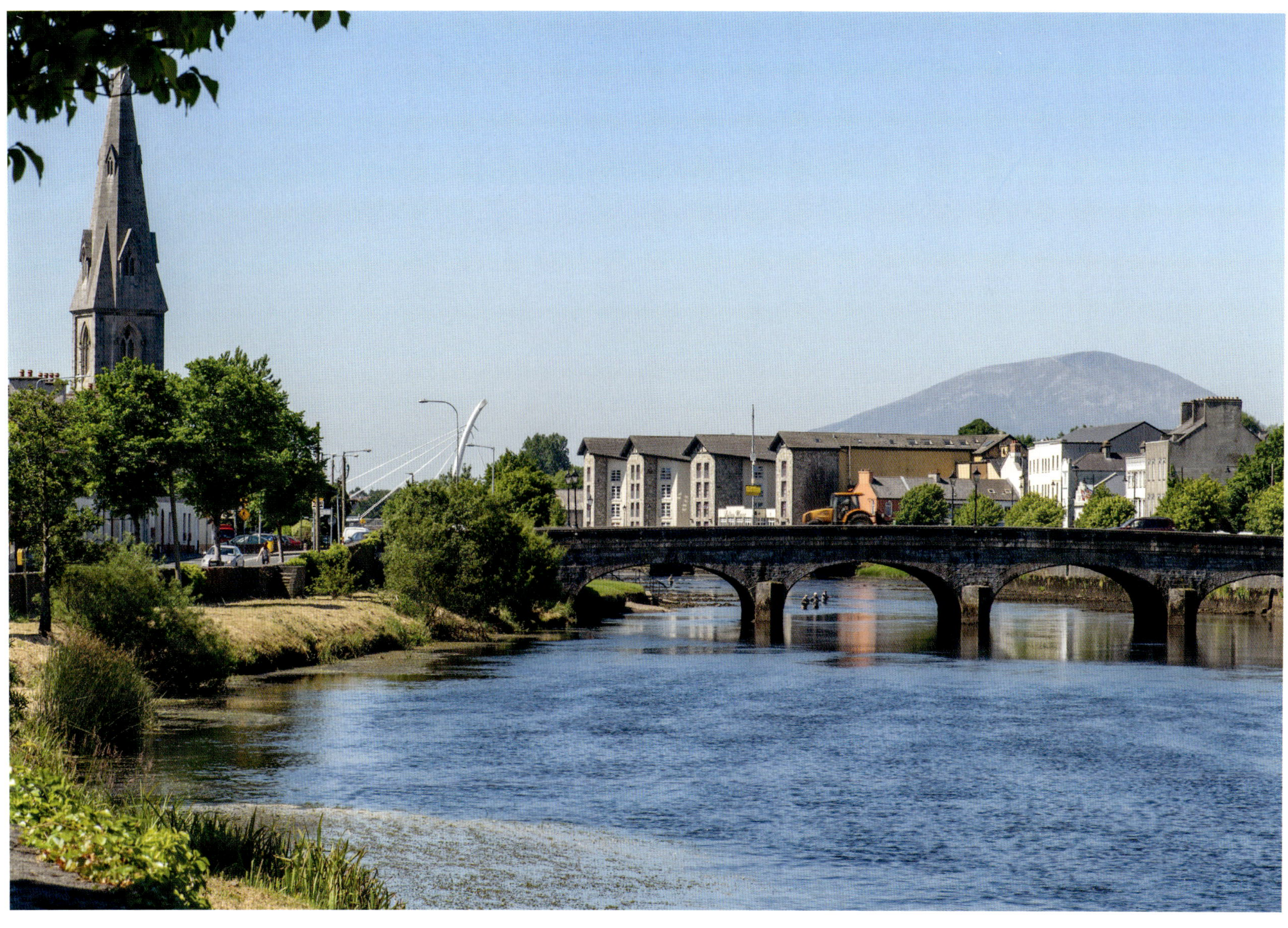

Ballina, Mayo's largest town and home to the river Moy, is internationally known as an exceptional site for salmon fishing. The famous Ridge Pool, a salmon angler's paradise, is located in the heart of the town. Ballina is also the home of the former President of Ireland, Mary Robinson.

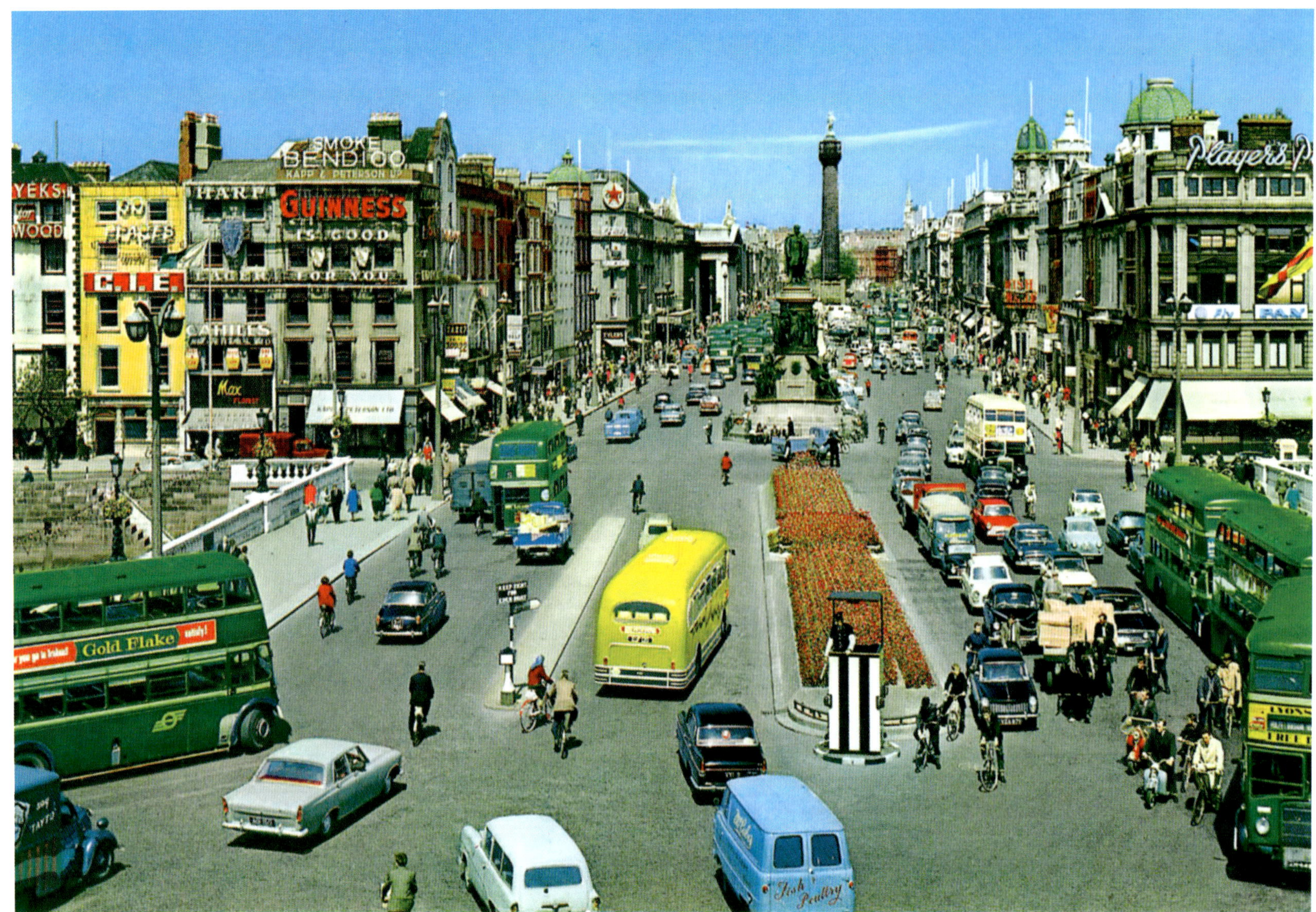

O'Connell Street and Bridge, showing Nelson's Pillar, Dublin, Ireland.

Photo: E. Ludwig, John Hinde Studios.

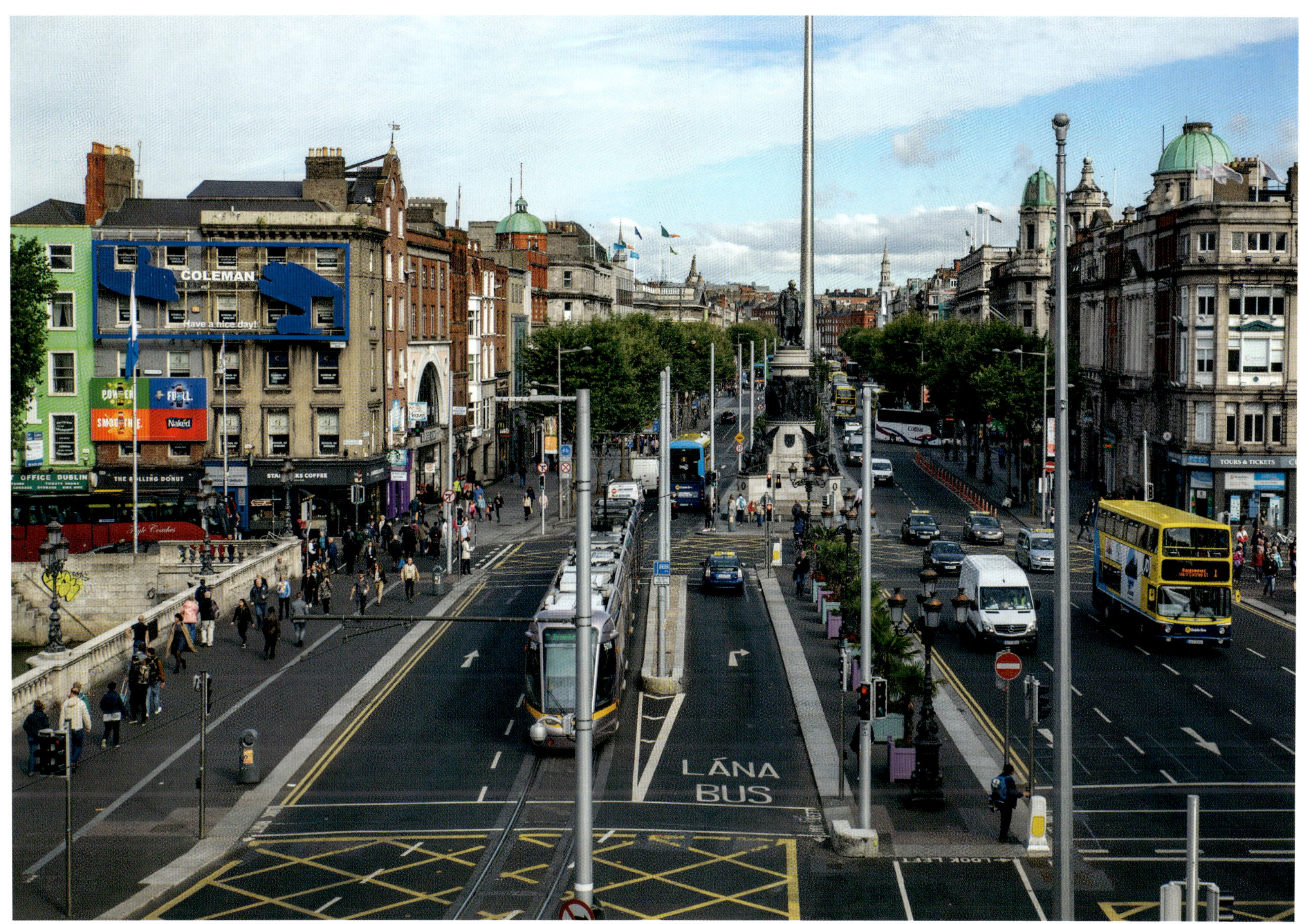

If you'd like to give blood at the blood clinic at Lafayette House on D'Olier Street, you'll be able to enjoy this spectacular view looking up O'Connell Street.

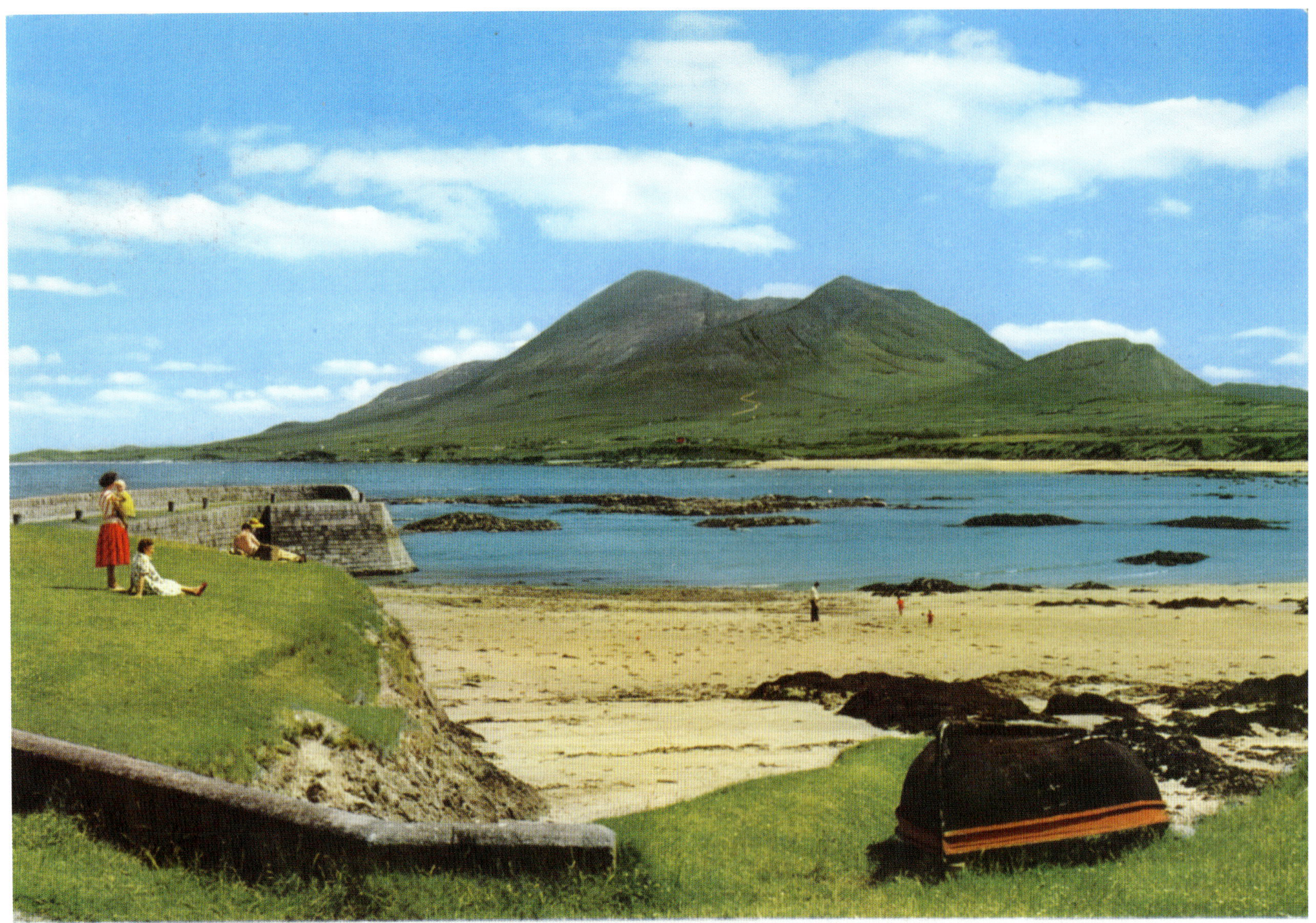

Croagh Patrick and the Beach, Old Head, Louisburgh, Co. Mayo, Ireland.

Colour Photo by John Hinde, F.R.P.S.

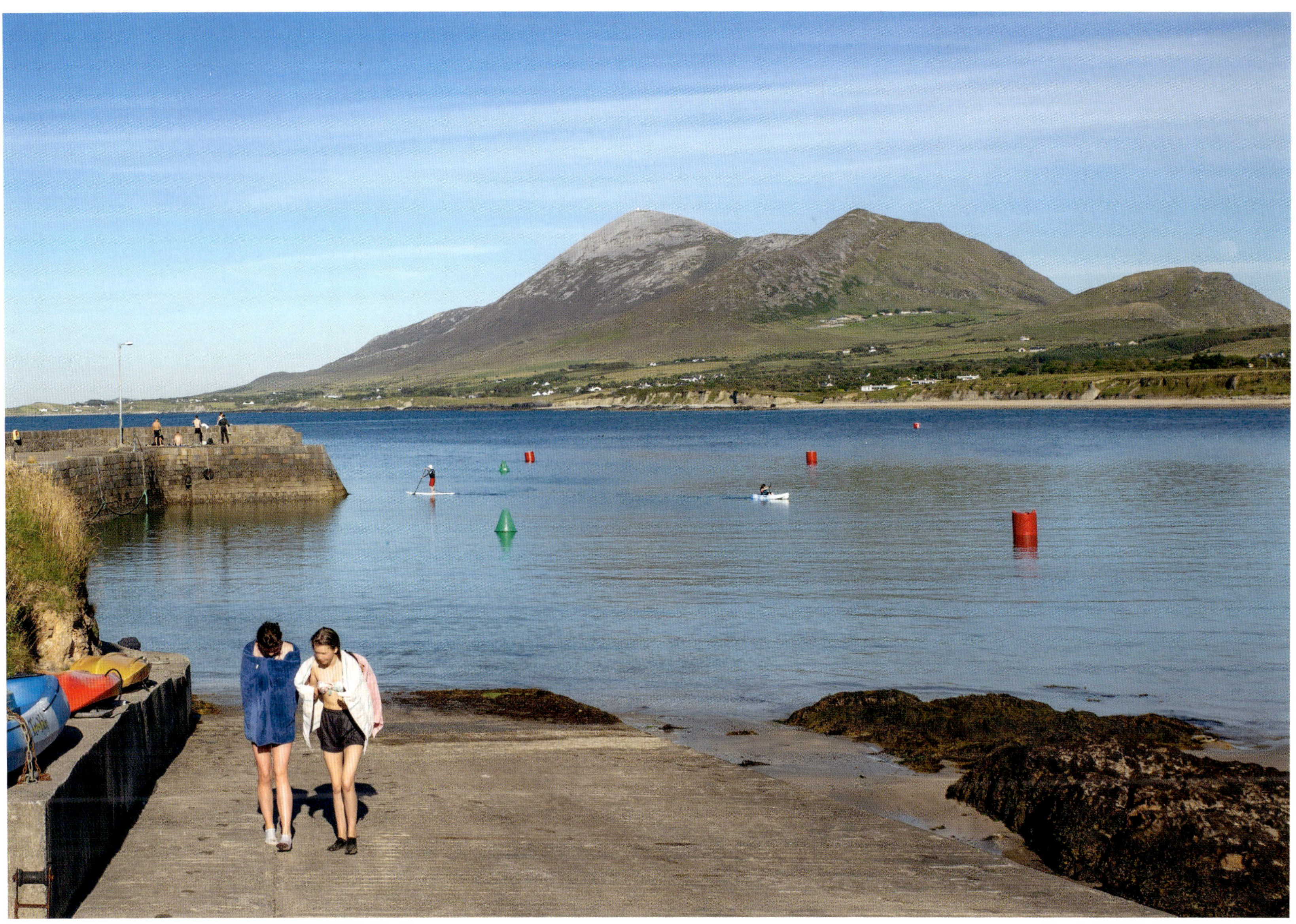

With a great view of Croagh Patrick, Old Head is a Blue Flag beach just east of Louisburgh village. The seafront has a small harbour, an attractive and popular sandy beach and a woodland walk. What do you get the beauty spot that has everything? Maybe some startlingly green mountains.

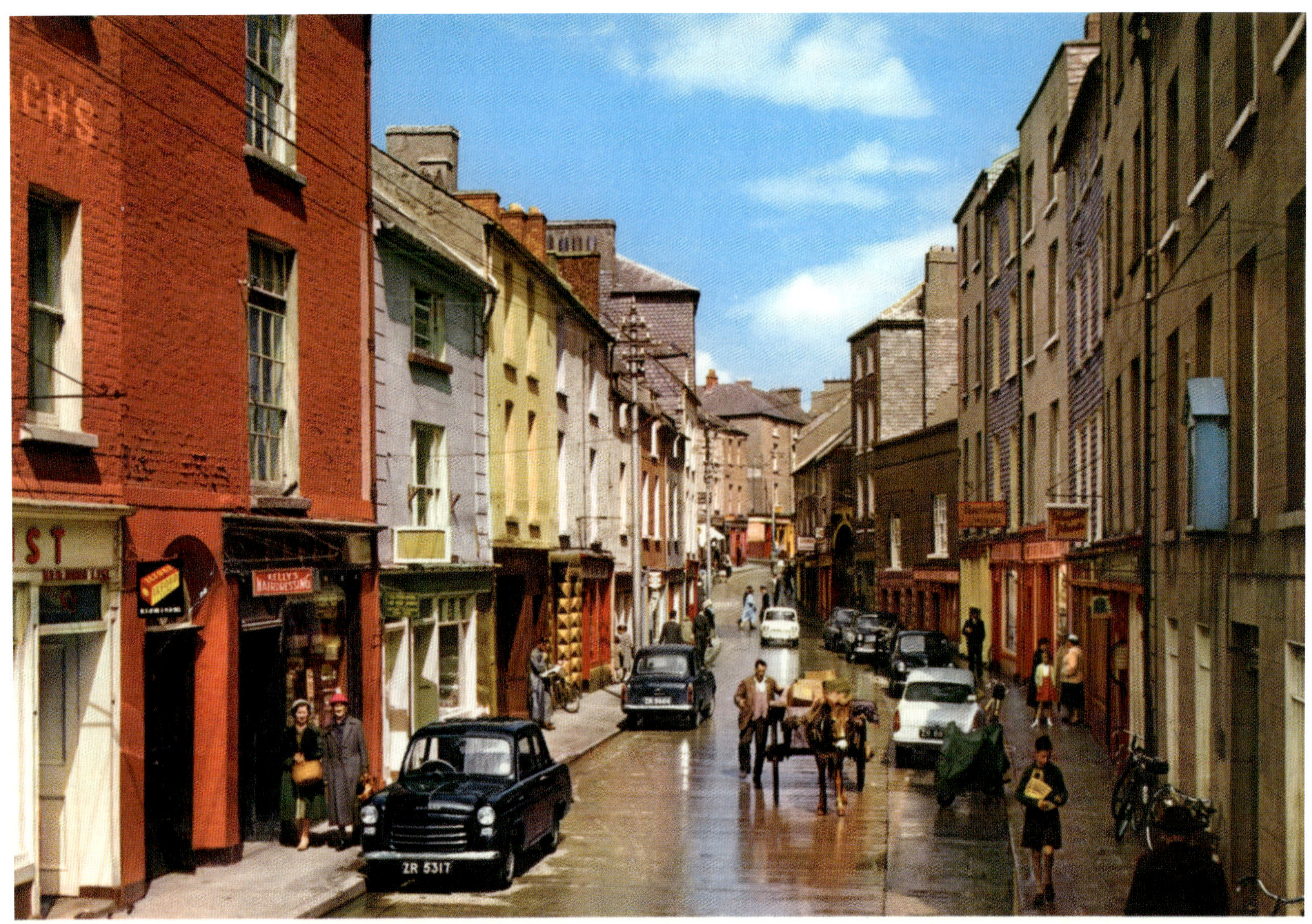

A Narrow Street in Wexford Town, Ireland.

Colour Photo by John Hinde, F.R.P.S.

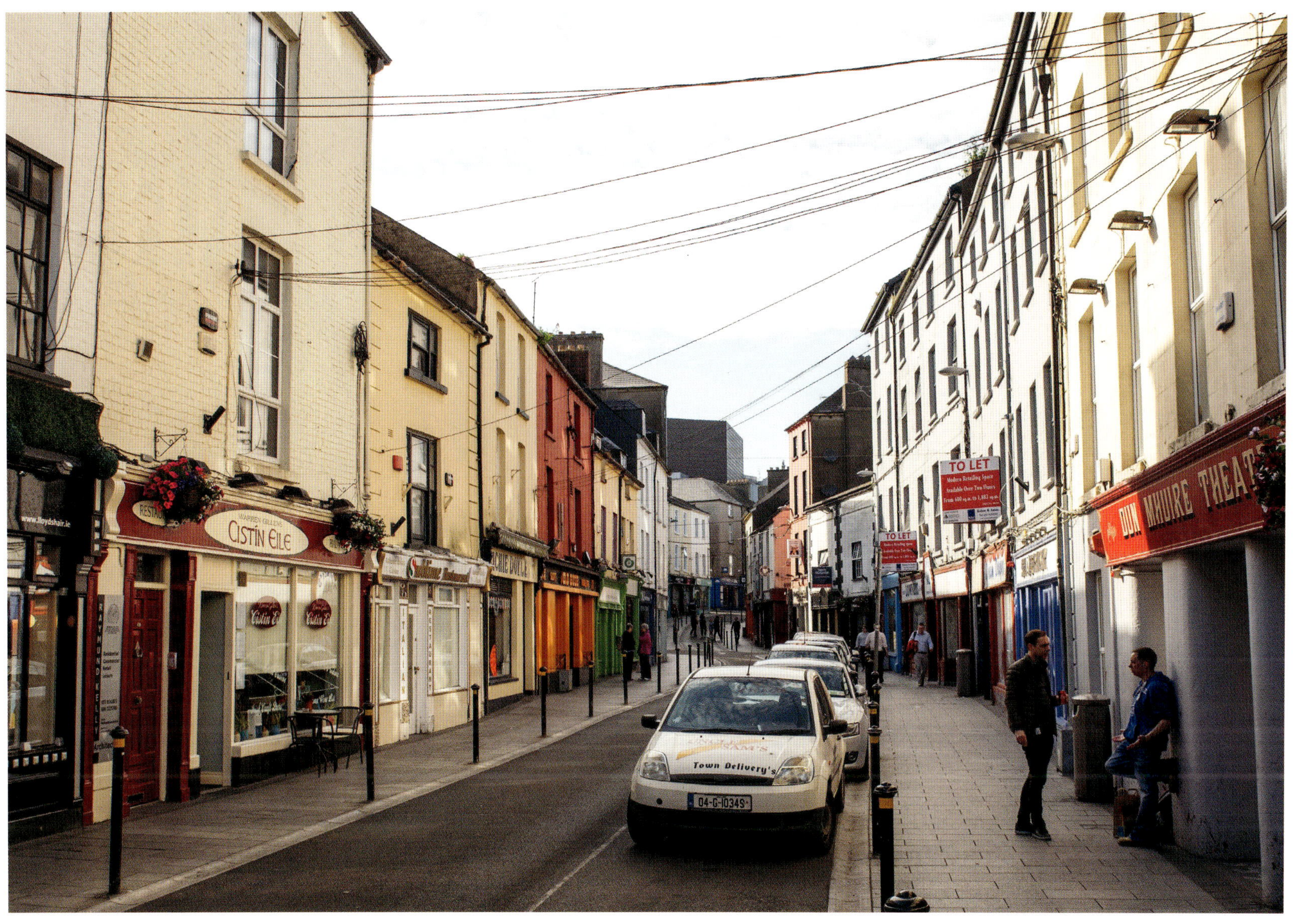

Wexford town was founded by the Vikings in the ninth century. Narrow South Main Street, in the town centre, still retains its commercial colour and diversity. Zigzagging through medieval lanes, I saw a happy jumble of upmarket shops and traditional pubs, nestled between deserted buildings and futuristic architecture.

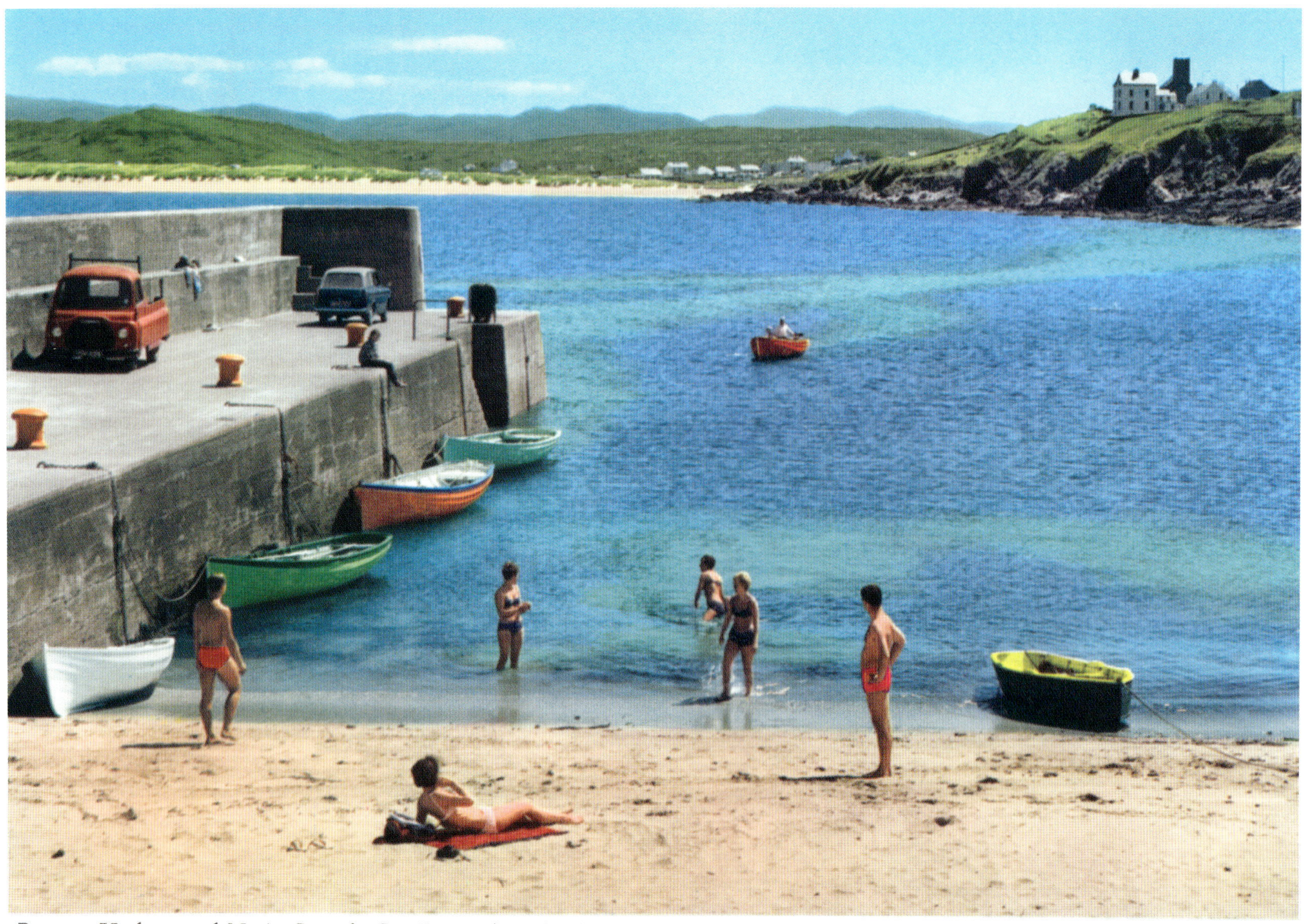

Portnoo Harbour and Narin Strand, Co. Donegal, Ireland.

Photo: Joan Willis, John Hinde Studios.

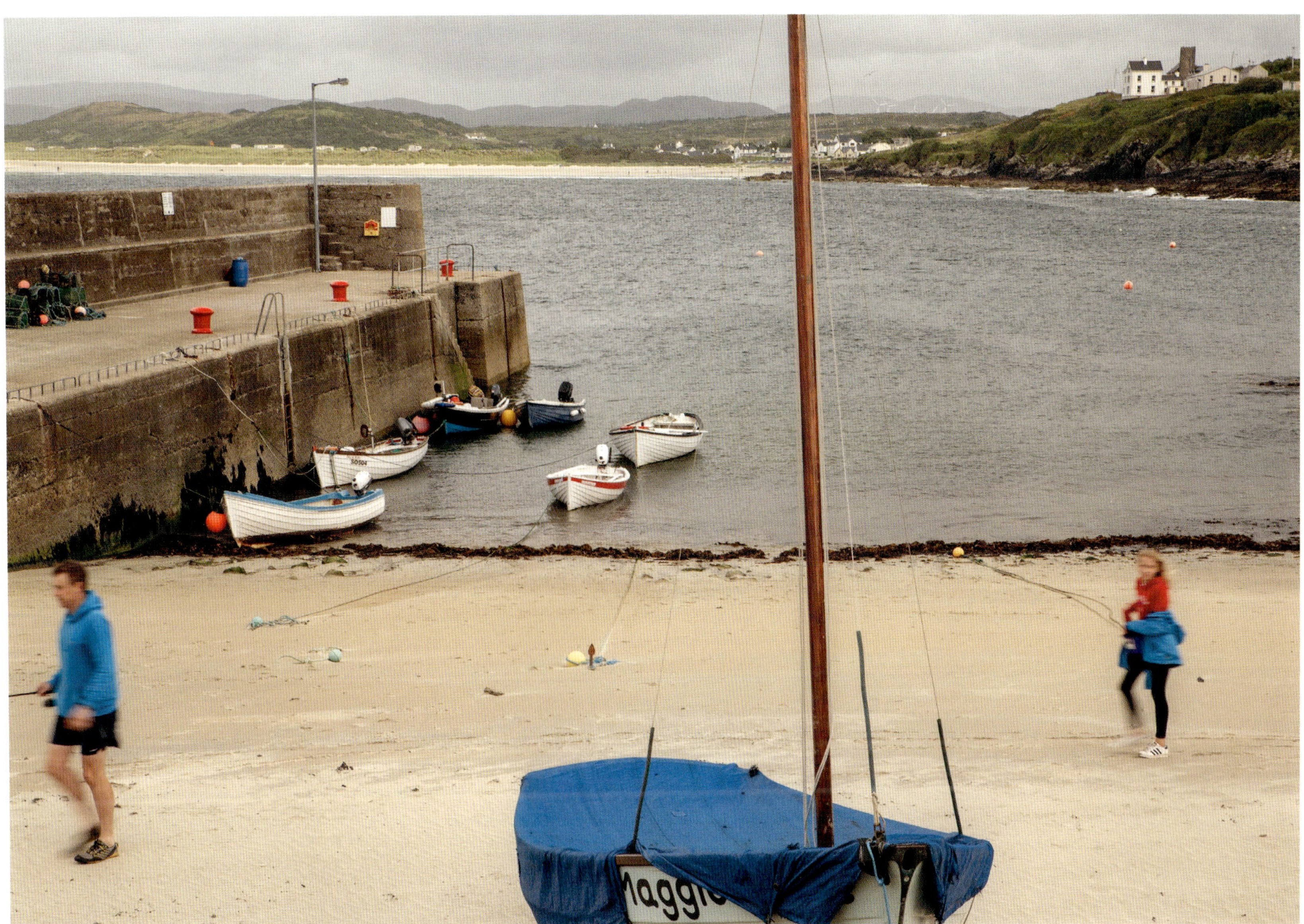

This pier was built in 1904, when herring fishing was the main source of income in the area. Today, Portnoo and its sister village of Narin are small, attractive holiday resorts on the northern shore of the Dawros peninsula, a few miles along the coast from Glenties.

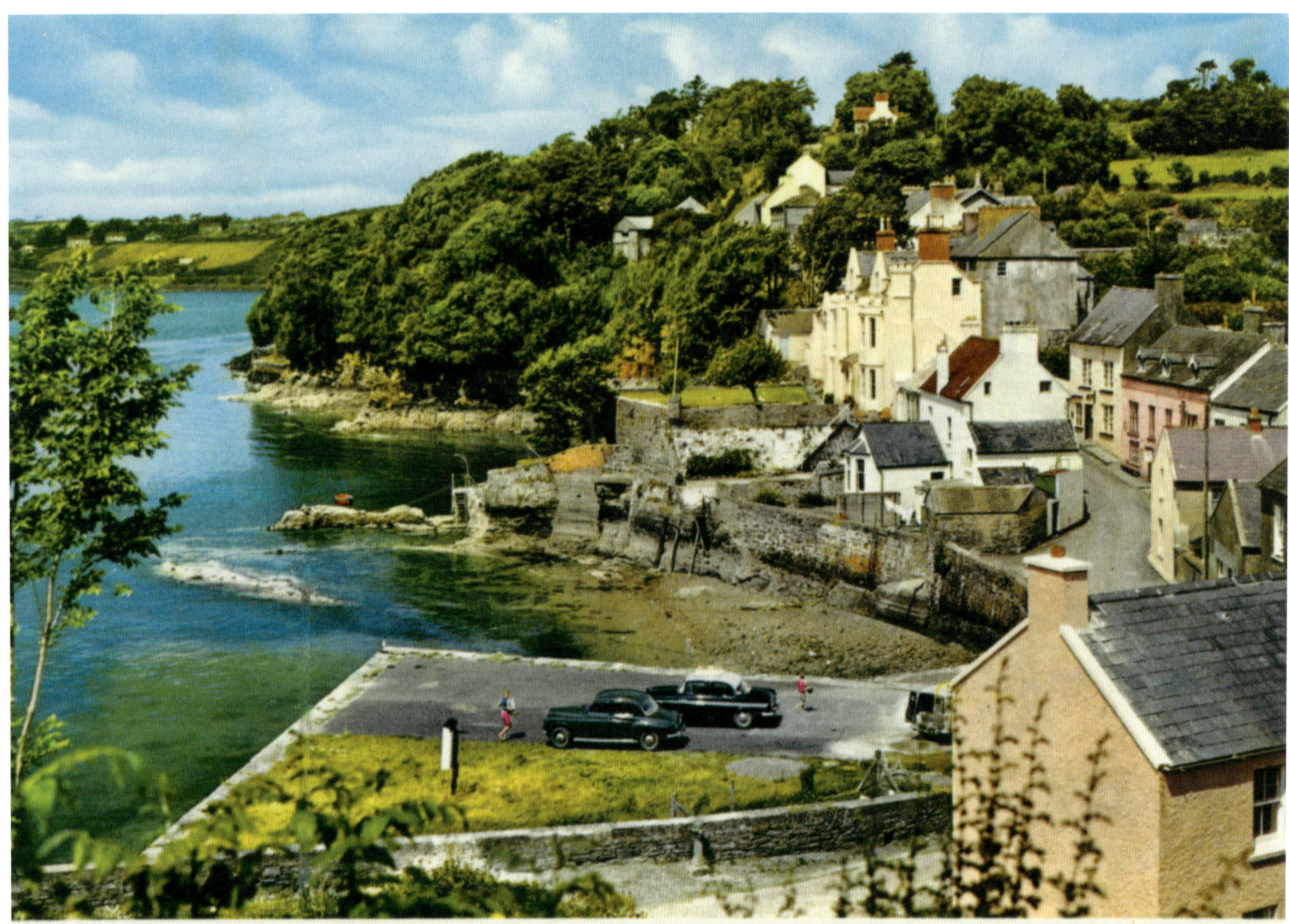

Summer Cove near Kinsale, Co. Cork, Ireland. Colour Photo by John Hinde, F.R.P.S.

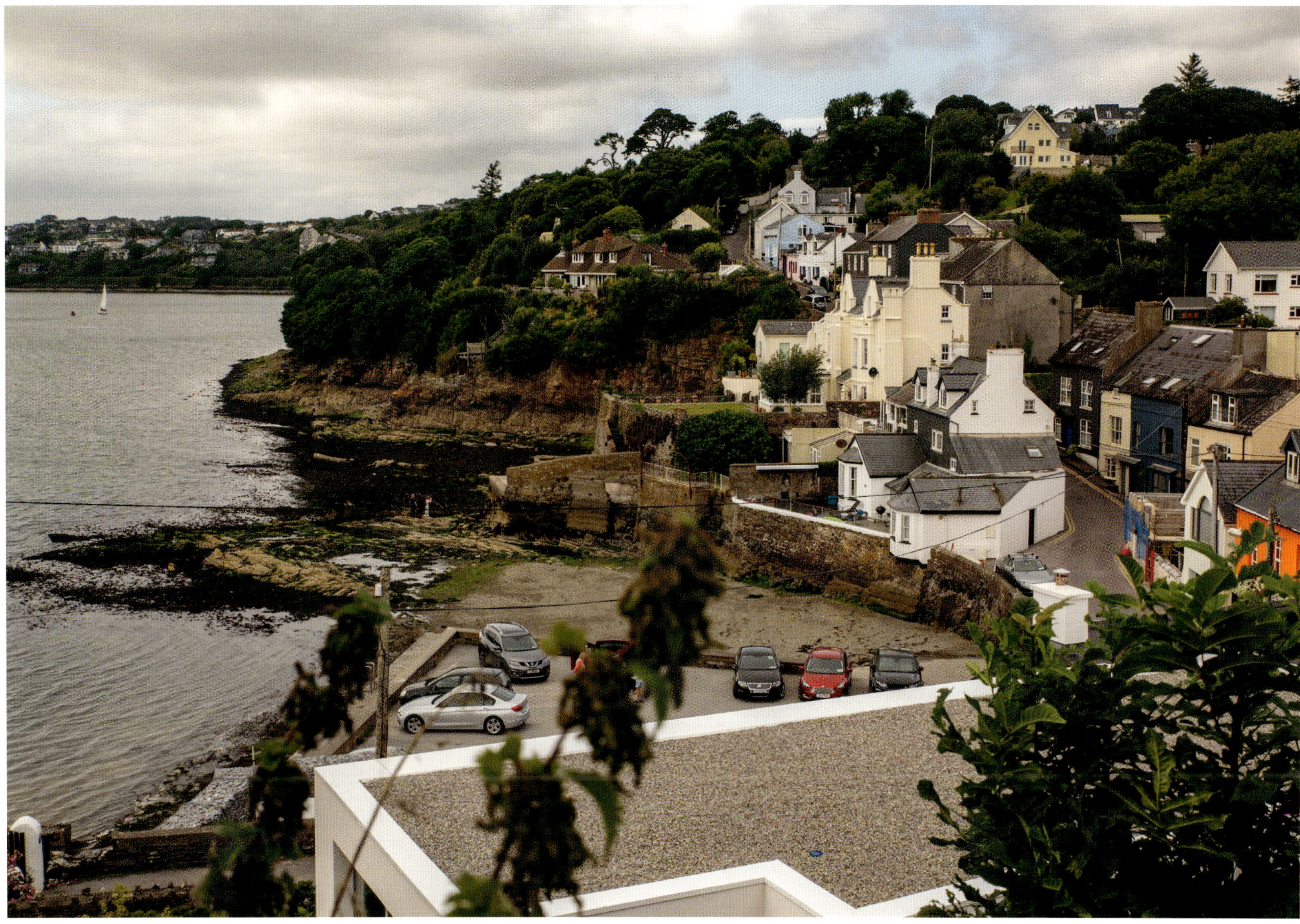

Summercove village, just five minutes from Kinsale, is popular with tourists and locals alike. The Bulman pub, located in the centre, is one of Ireland's best-known bars and restaurants. To snap this shot, behind the Anchor Lodge B&B, I had to sit in a field of stinging nettles, and lived with the results for some days.

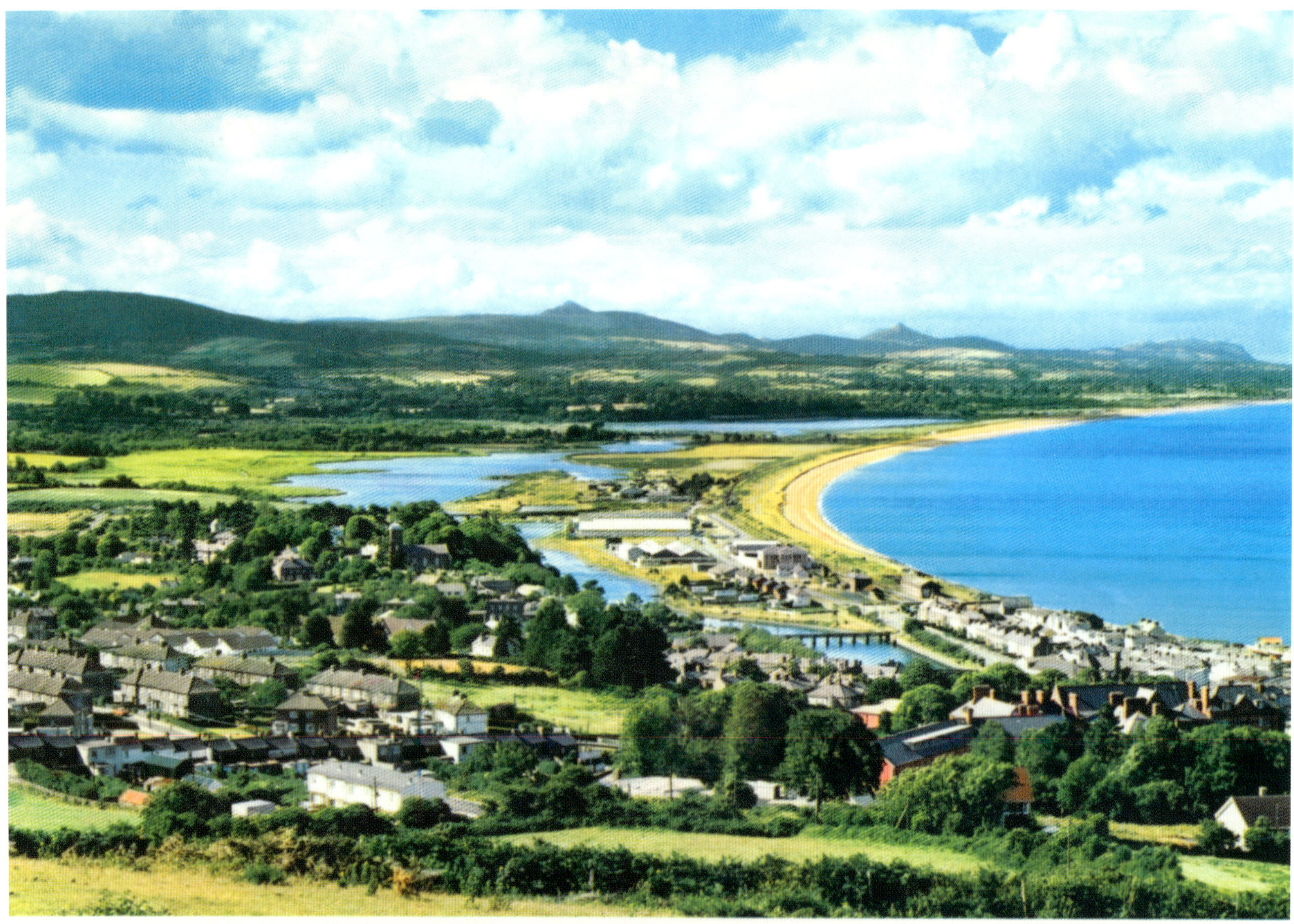

Wicklow Town and Bay, Co. Wicklow, Ireland. *Photo: P. O'Toole, John Hinde Studios.*

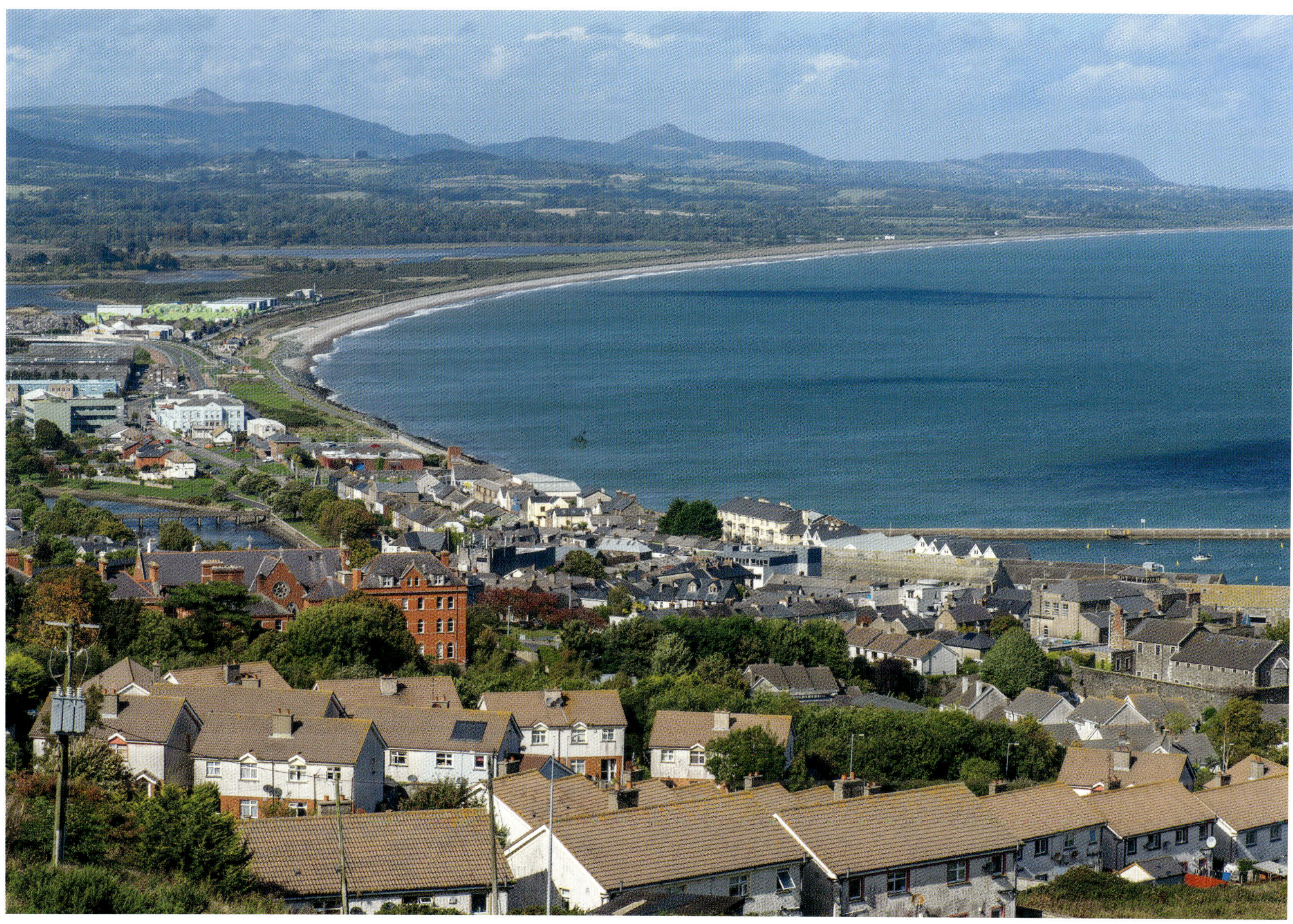

Founded by Viking adventurers in the eighth century, the county town of Wicklow has certainly continued to grow and thrive. Local hero Robert Charles Halpin, one of the world's finest mariners, reinforced this seafaring tradition in the 19th century. North along the coast, a magnificent wetland reserve graces a region of outstanding natural heritage.

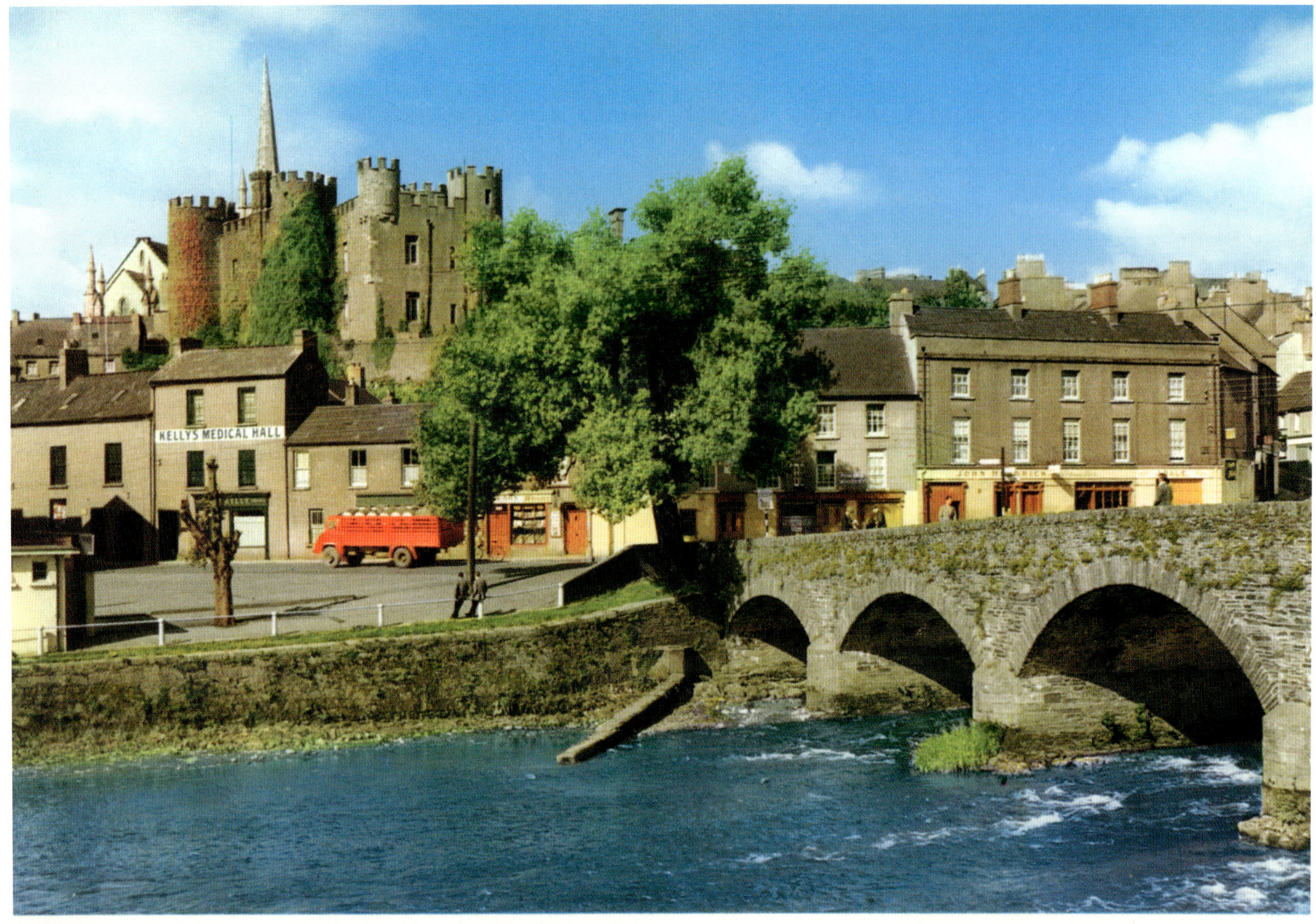

The Castle and River Slaney, Enniscorthy, Co. Wexford, Ireland.

Colour Photo by John Hinde, F.R.P.S.

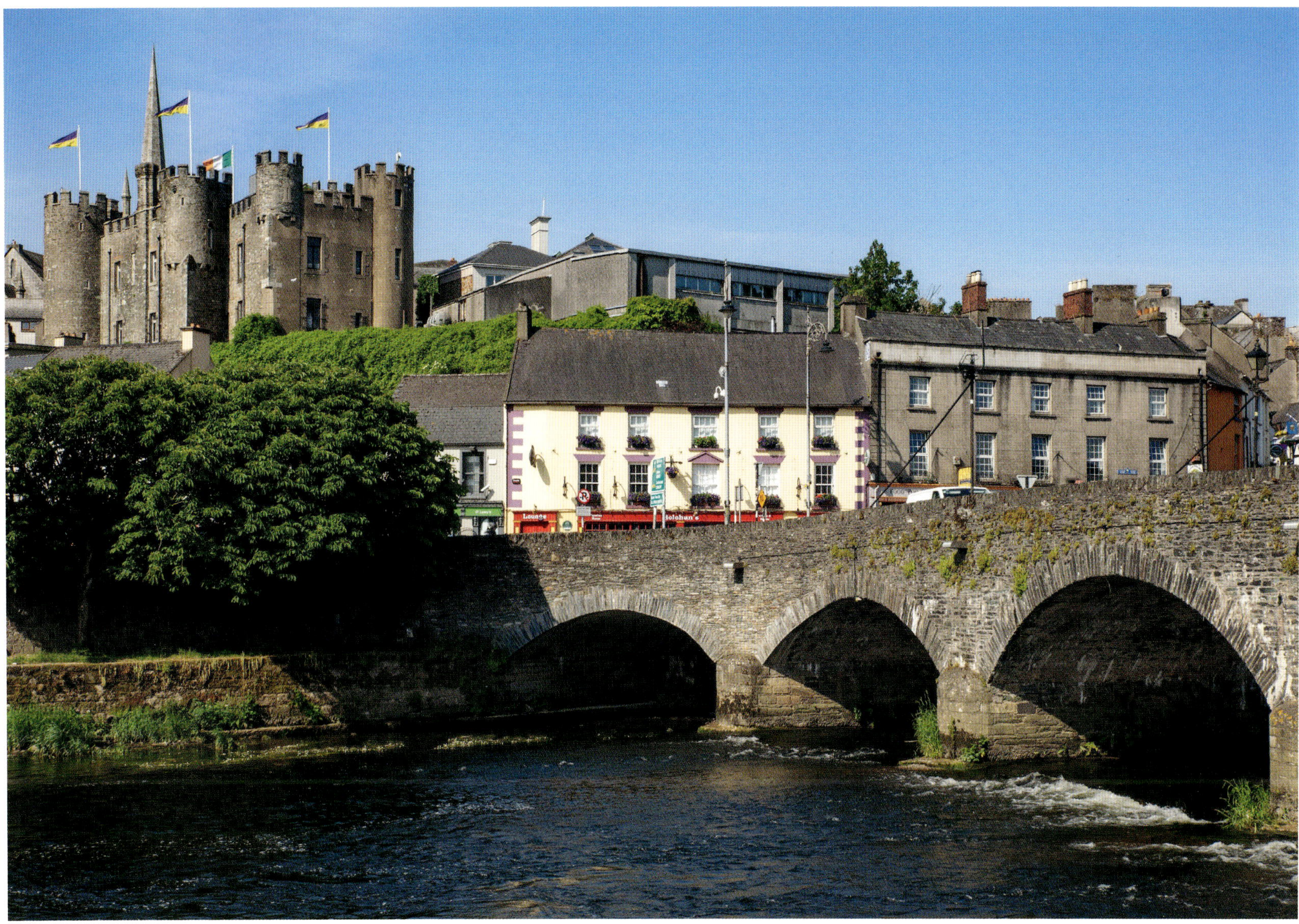

There is a reference to Enniscorthy as 'the finest place in the world' in James Joyce's *Ulysses*, though he mistakenly places it in Co. Wicklow, not Wexford. In this 'land that time forgot', the 13th-century Norman castle still broods over this busy town, home in turn to Norman knights, English armies, Irish rebels and prisoners, and local merchant families.

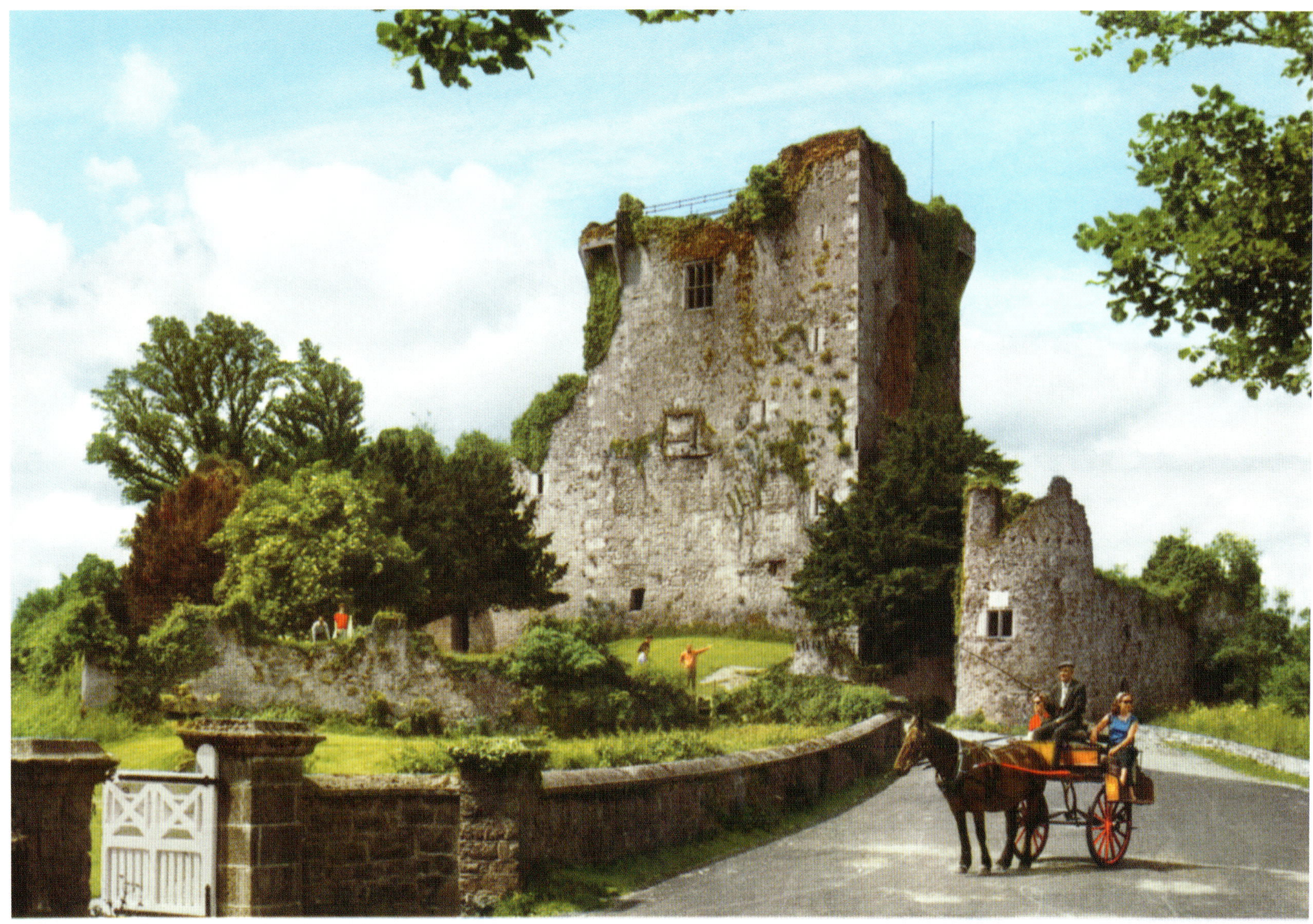

Jaunting Car at Ross Castle, Killarney, Co. Kerry, Ireland.

Photo: Joan Willis, John Hinde Studios.

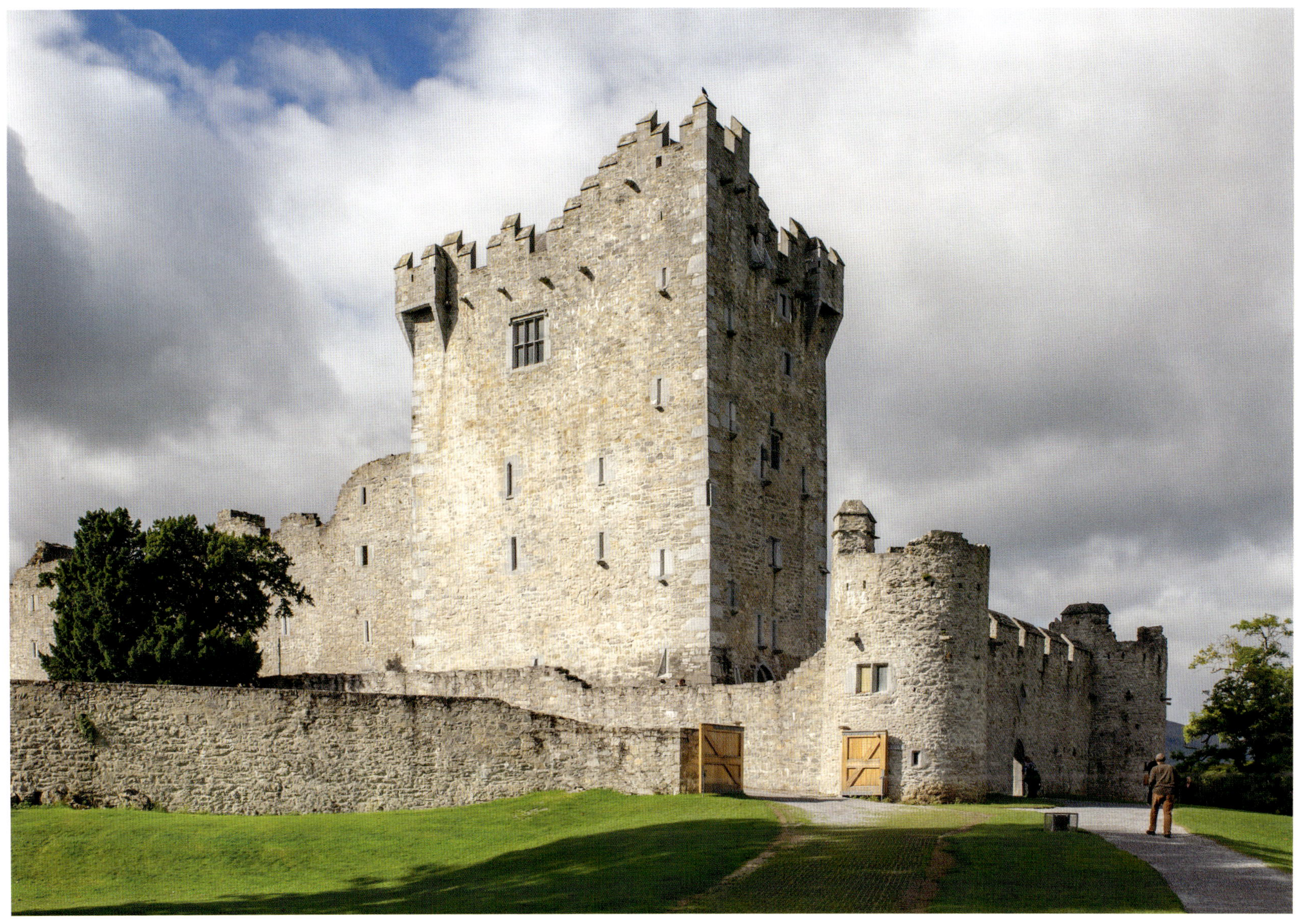

Ross Castle was built in the late 15th century by the clan O'Donoghues Mor. A mighty stronghold for a powerful chieftain, the castle was authentically restored in the 1990s. Legend has it that O'Donoghue jumped from a high window here and disappeared into the lake below, from where he continues to keep a close eye on the family home.

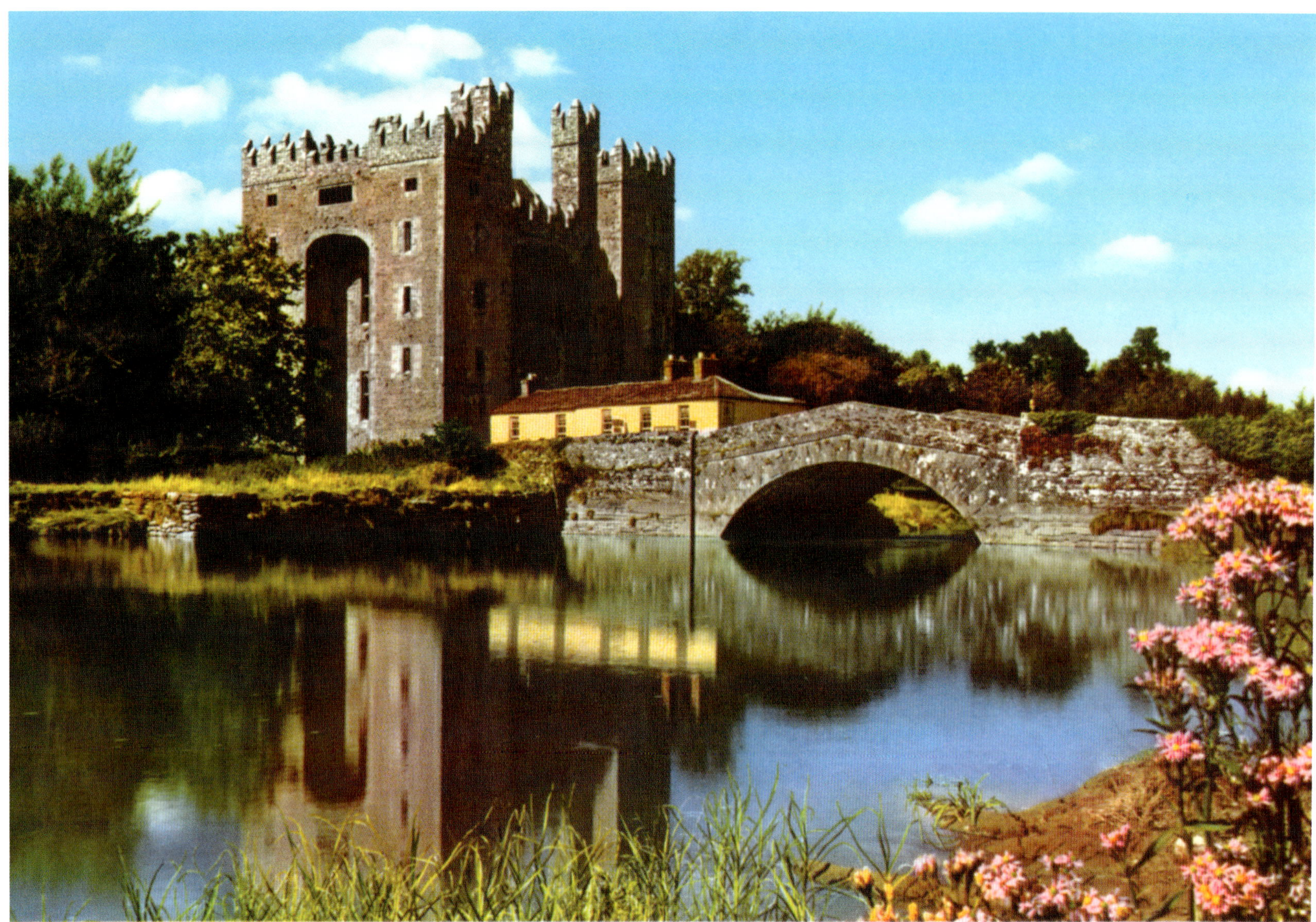

Bunratty Castle, situated between Limerick and Shannon Airport, Co. Clare, Ireland. Colour Photo by John Hinde, F.R.P.S.

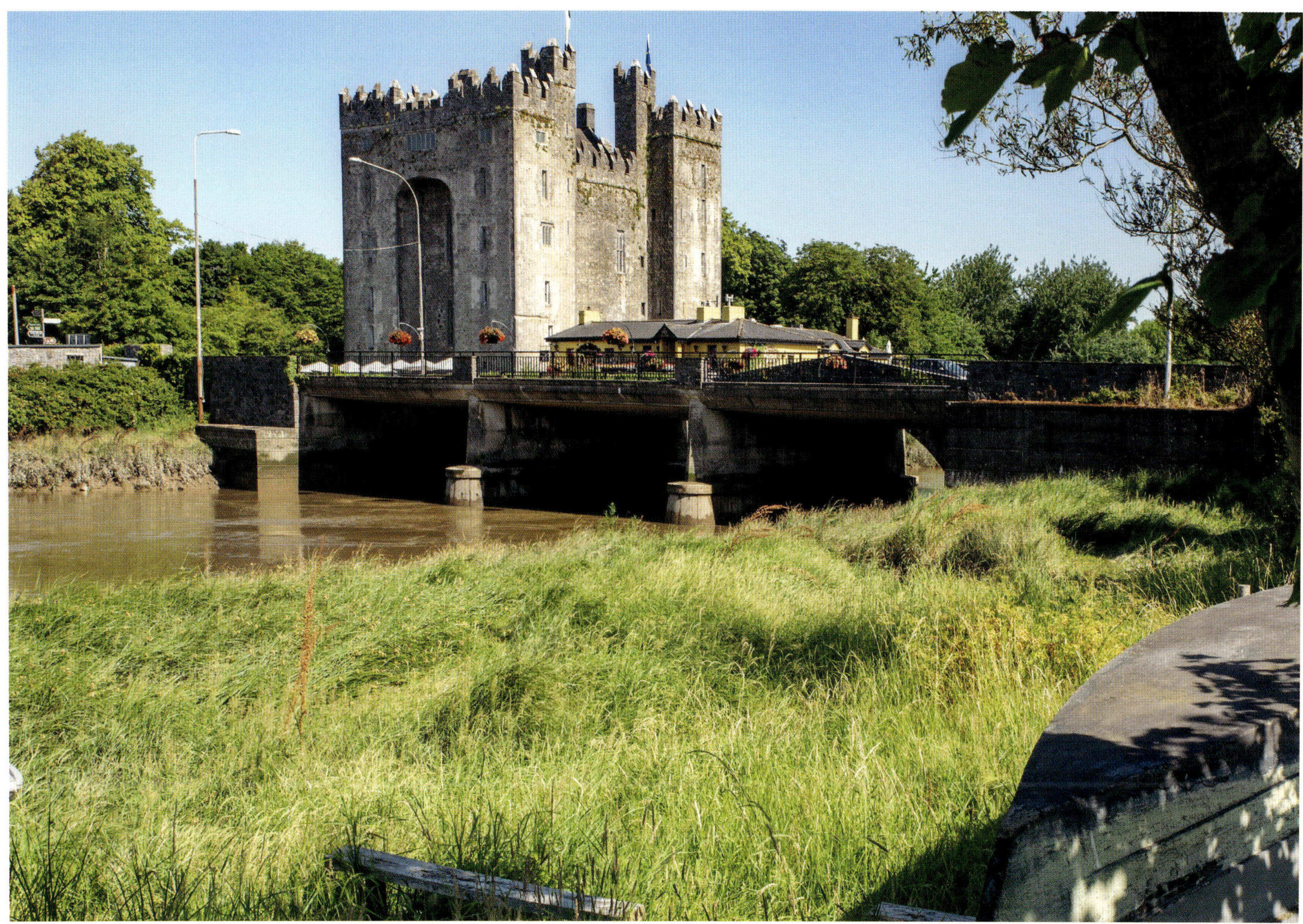

I have many treasured memories of Bunratty Castle and the famous Durty Nelly's pub on the banks of the Ralty river. Travelling with my father, we would usually arrive via Shannon Airport and celebrate our first night in Ireland here. We often attended the medieval banquet at Bunratty and then finished up at Durty Nelly's for a nightcap and a singalong.

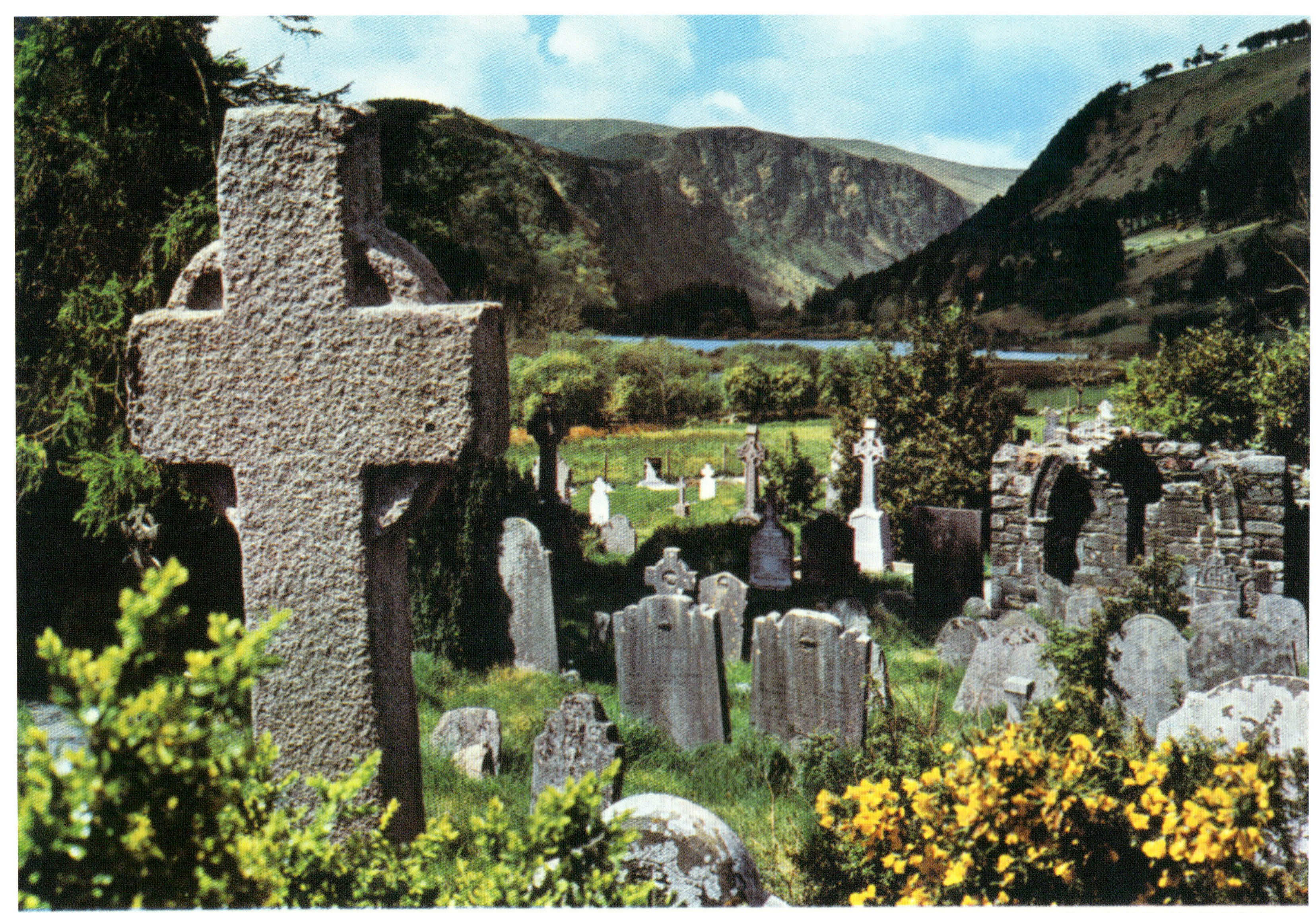

St. Kevin's Cross, Glendalough, Co. Wicklow.

Photo: D. Noble, John Hinde Studios.

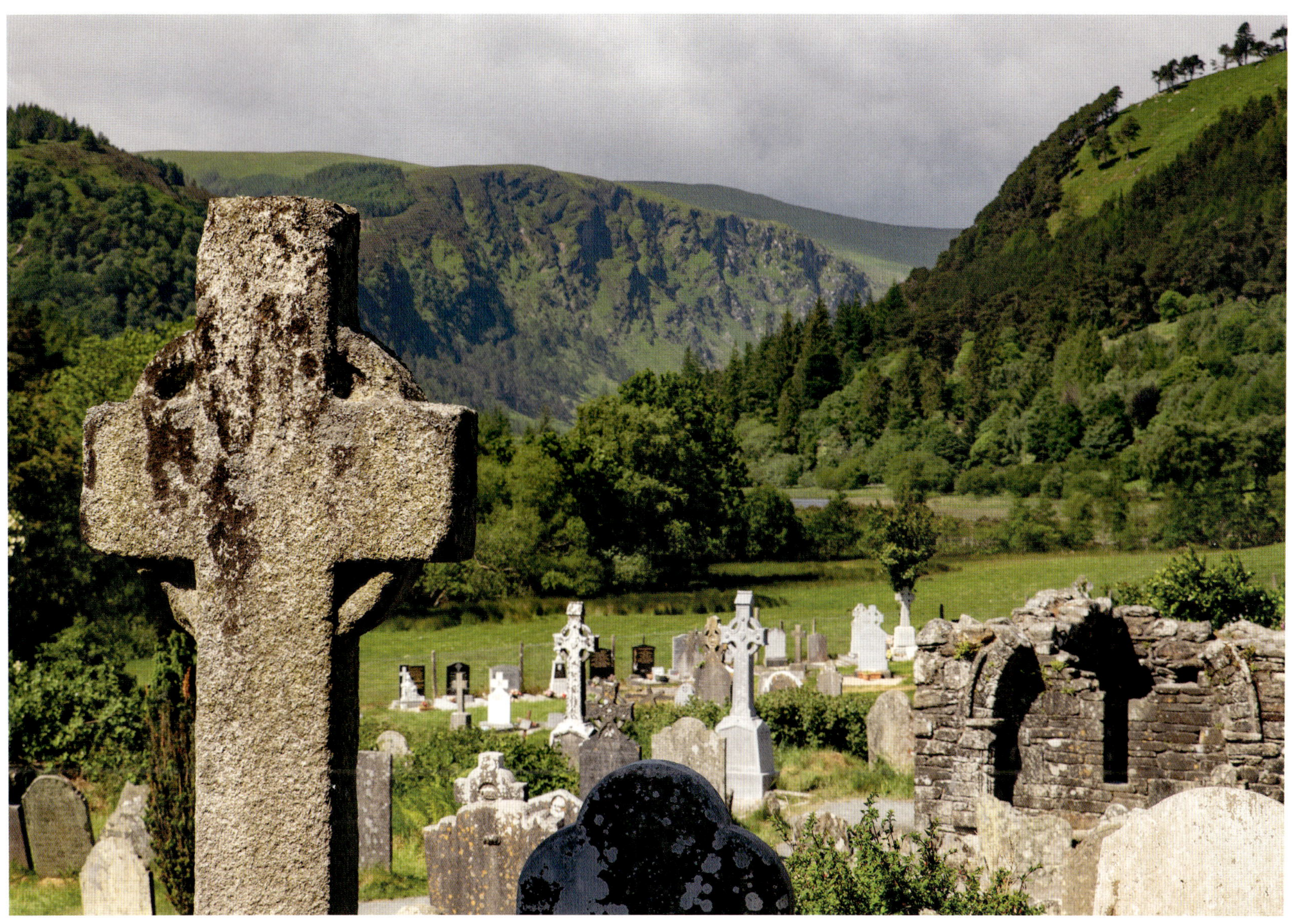

The legend of St Kevin's Cross claims that if you can wrap your arms around the entire width of the cross's body and close the circle by touching your fingertips, you will have your wish granted. When I was there, an Irish tourist cried out, 'I wish I was slimmer', as he hopelessly tried to drape his arms around the cross.

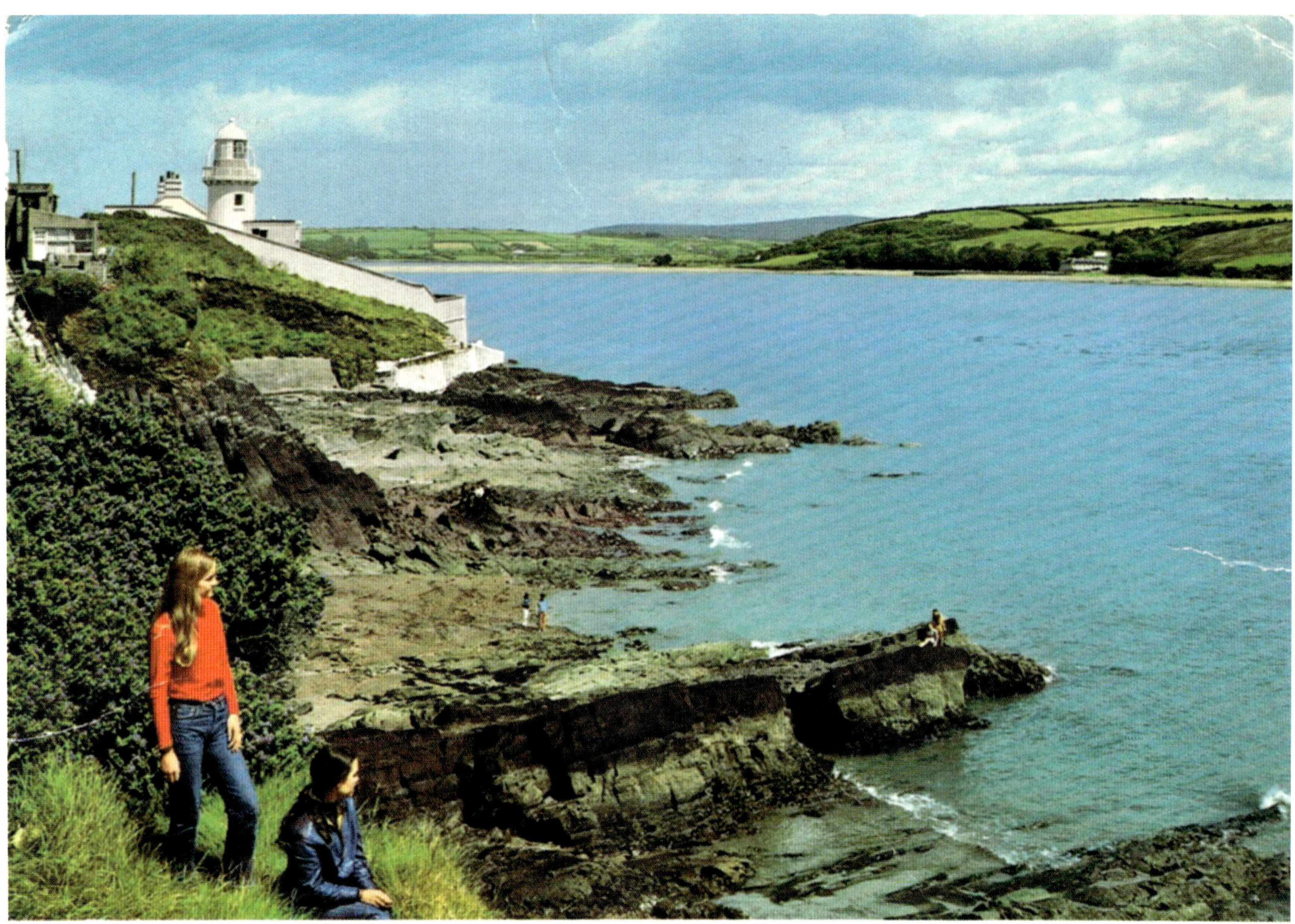

The Lighthouse, Youghal, Co. Cork, Ireland.

Photo: D. Noble, John Hinde Studios.

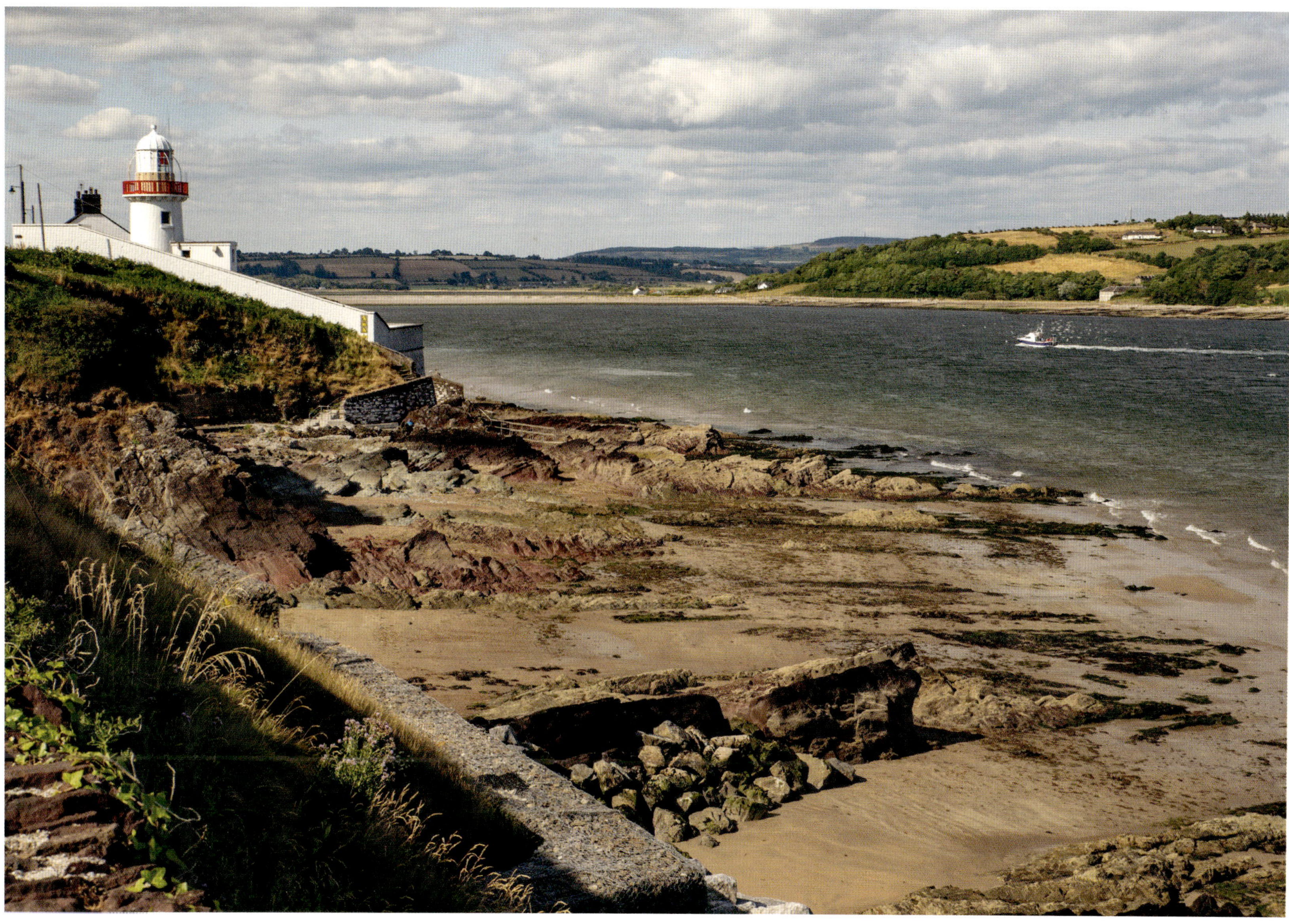

This shot was taken next to Moll Goggin's Corner, so named because a young Moll Goggin lost her love to the sea when his ship sank. She often kept watch here, waiting for his return, even after all hope had been lost. A sad tale, and a reminder that even the picturesque has its darker side.

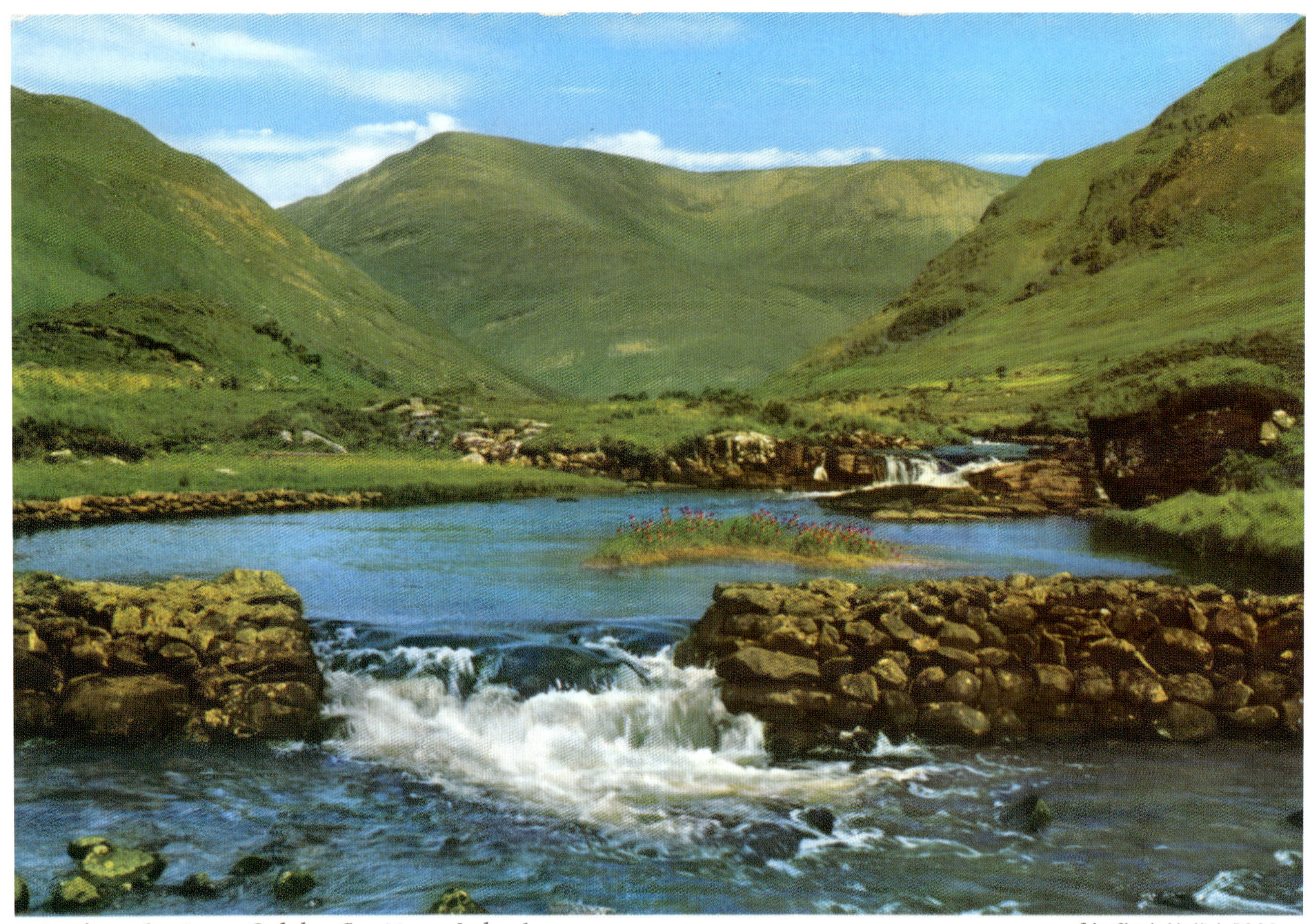

Bundorragha River, Delphi, Co. Mayo, Ireland.

Colour Photo by John Hinde, F.R.P.S.

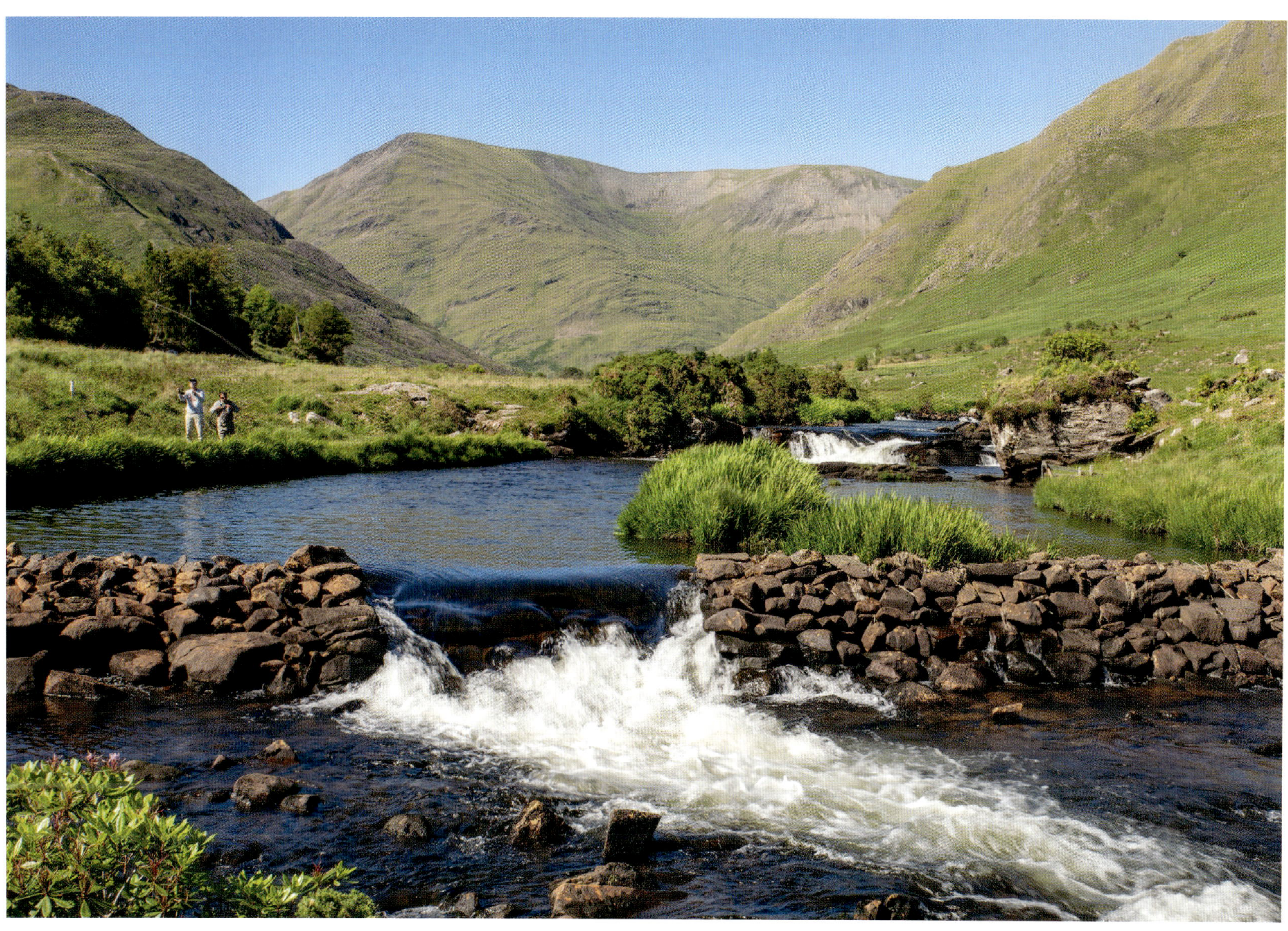

Completely isolated from the modern world, the Bundorragha river is only a few kilometres long and a haven for fly fishermen. Looking at these images side by side, I'm reminded that nature sculpts Irish scenery at the pace of eternal time, not of our fast-paced time.

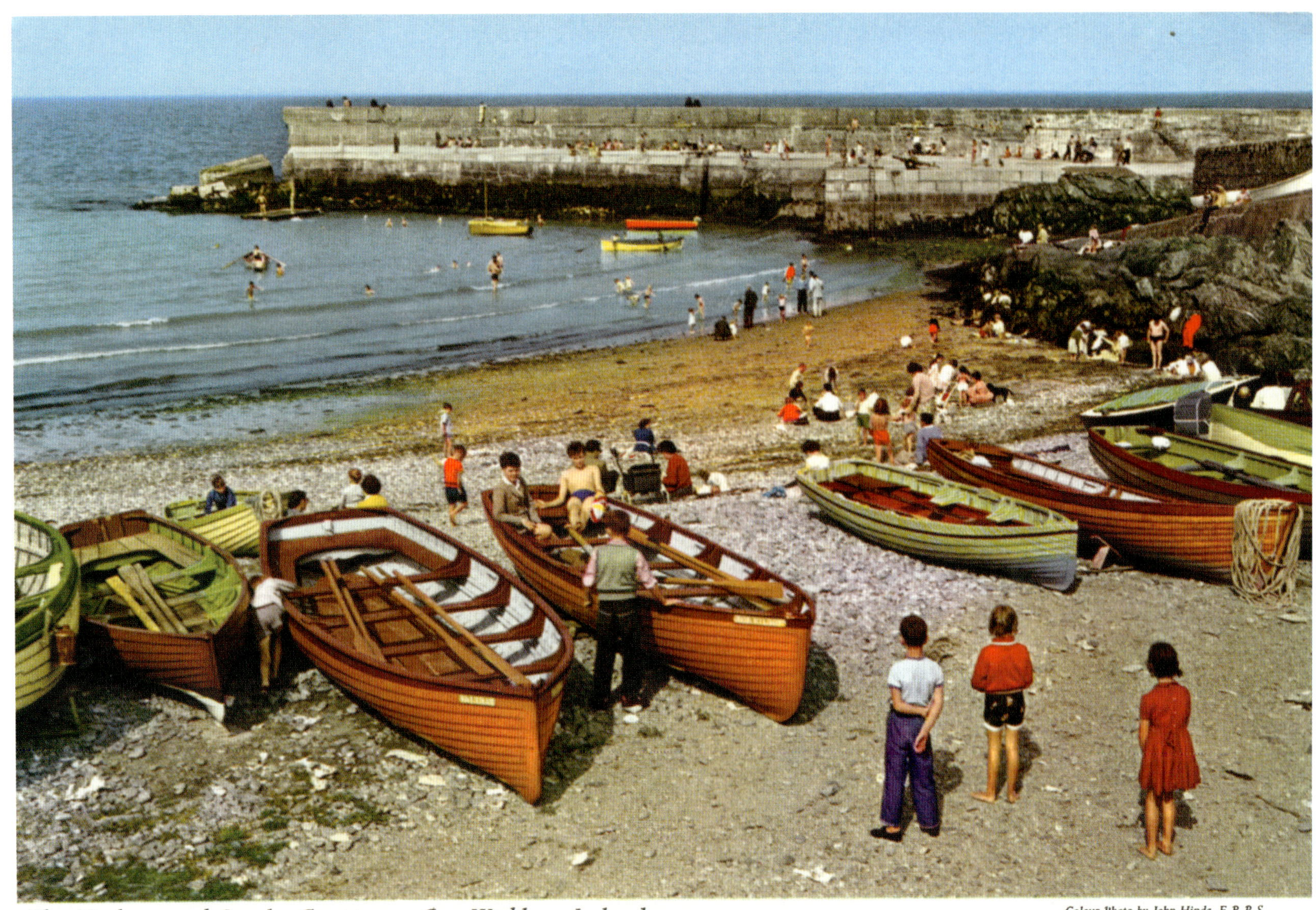

The Harbour and Beach, Greystones, Co. Wicklow, Ireland.

Colour Photo by John Hinde, F.R.P.S.

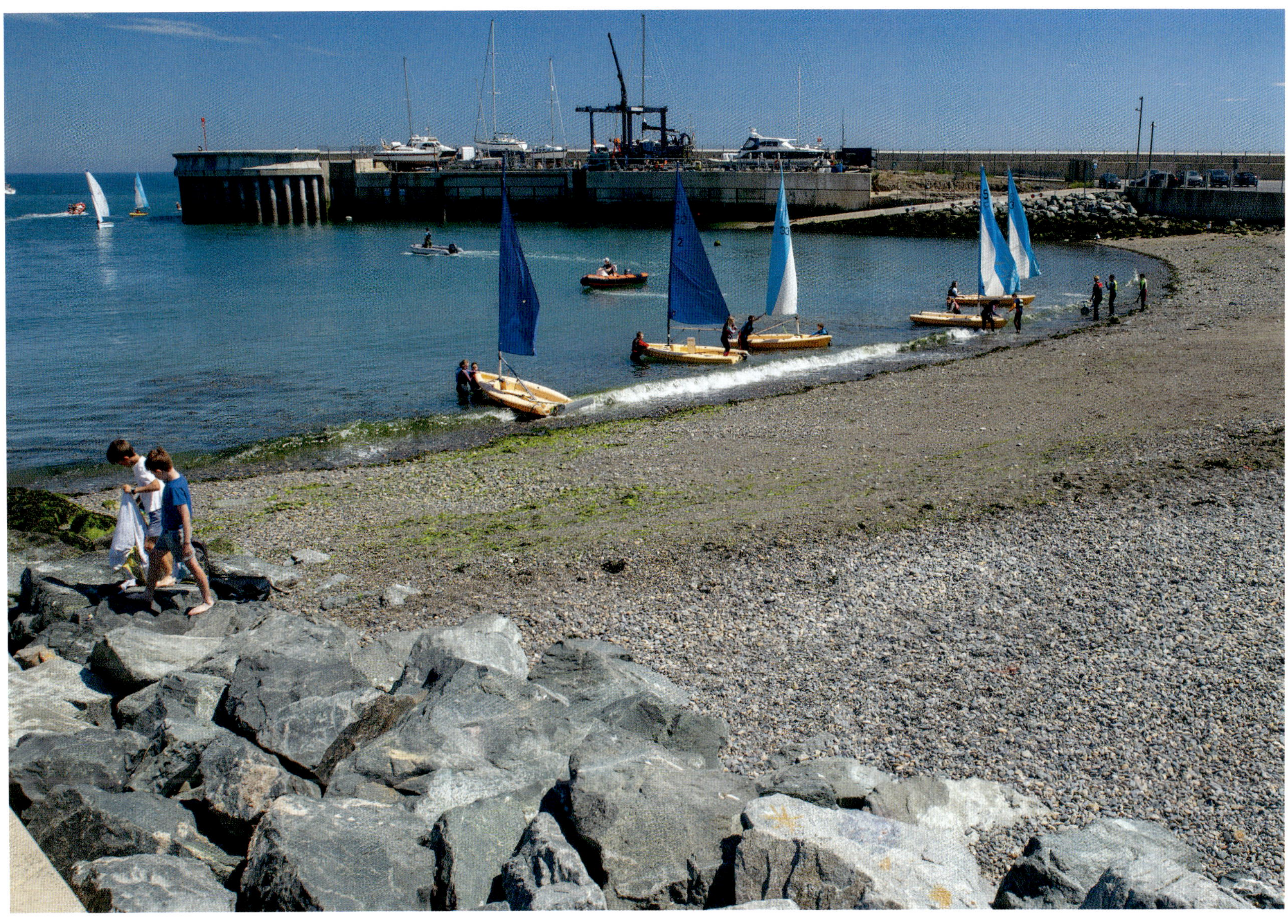

John Hinde's postcard describes Greystones as, '*Retaining in part the atmosphere of the former quiet fishing village*'. Today, things are certainly changing. A new marina and harbour was built and opened in 2013, followed by a residential development featuring architect-designed homes and apartments. Still, the grey stones are there, right enough.

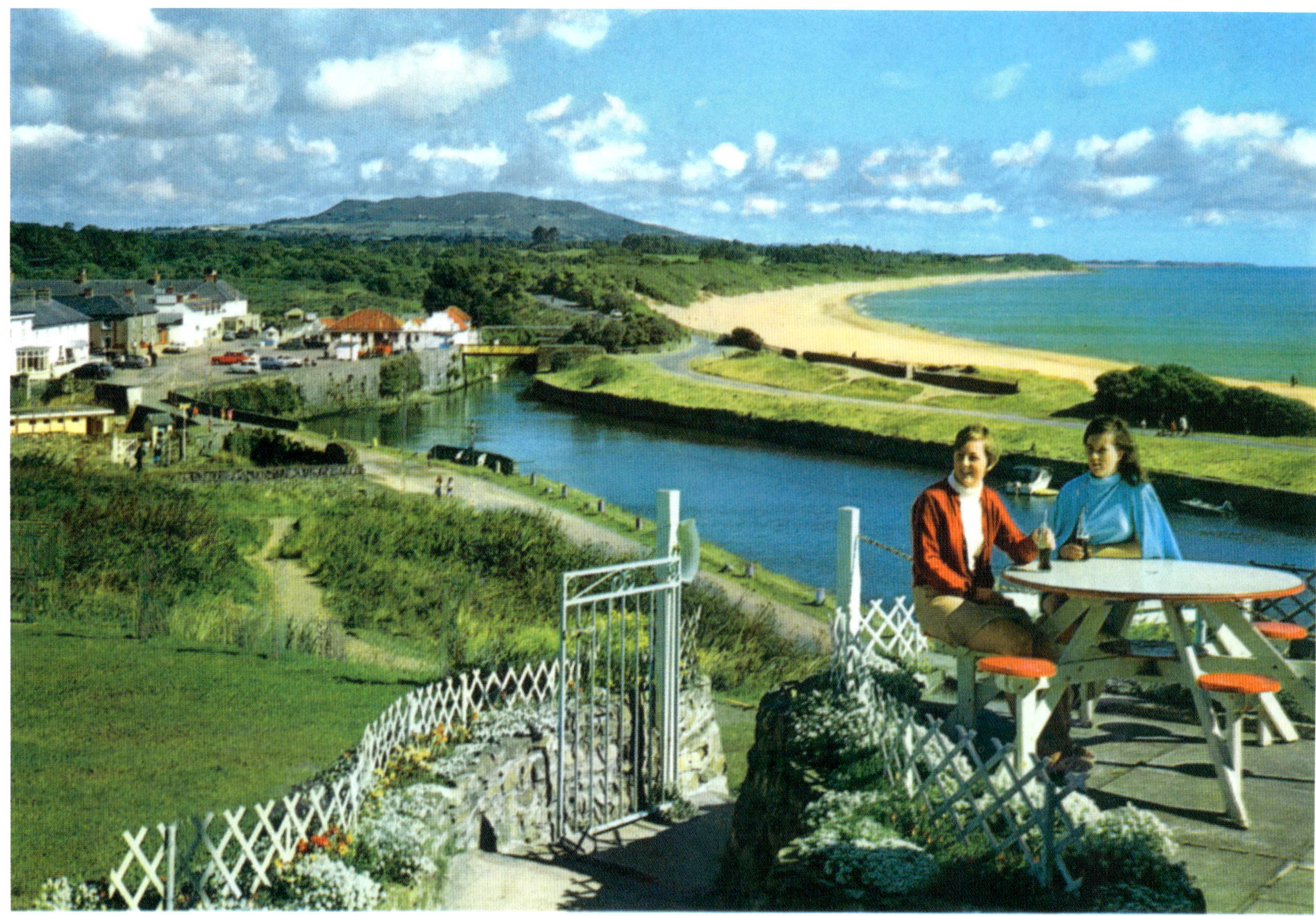

Courtown Harbour and Beach, Co. Wexford, Ireland.

Photo: R. Beer, John Hinde Studios.

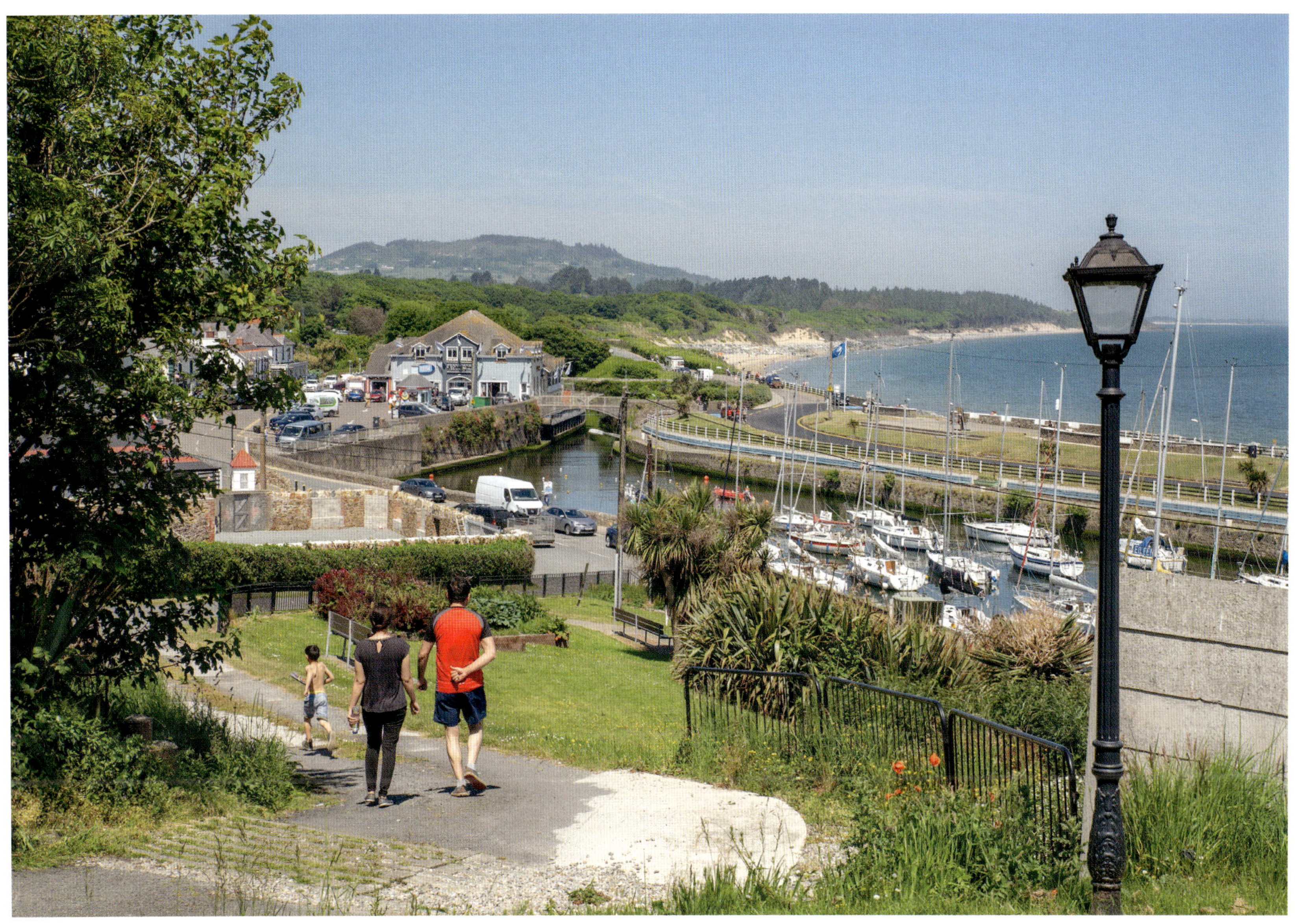

I arrived here on a hot June day. I asked a woman sitting on the bench in the park below if she knew the location of the photo.

'I know exactly where that was taken,' she responded, and then escorted me up the small knoll to the very spot. 'I remember it well', she told me with a smile. 'It was here we could get a Coca-Cola from a lady who ran a small shop. Life was so much simpler then.'

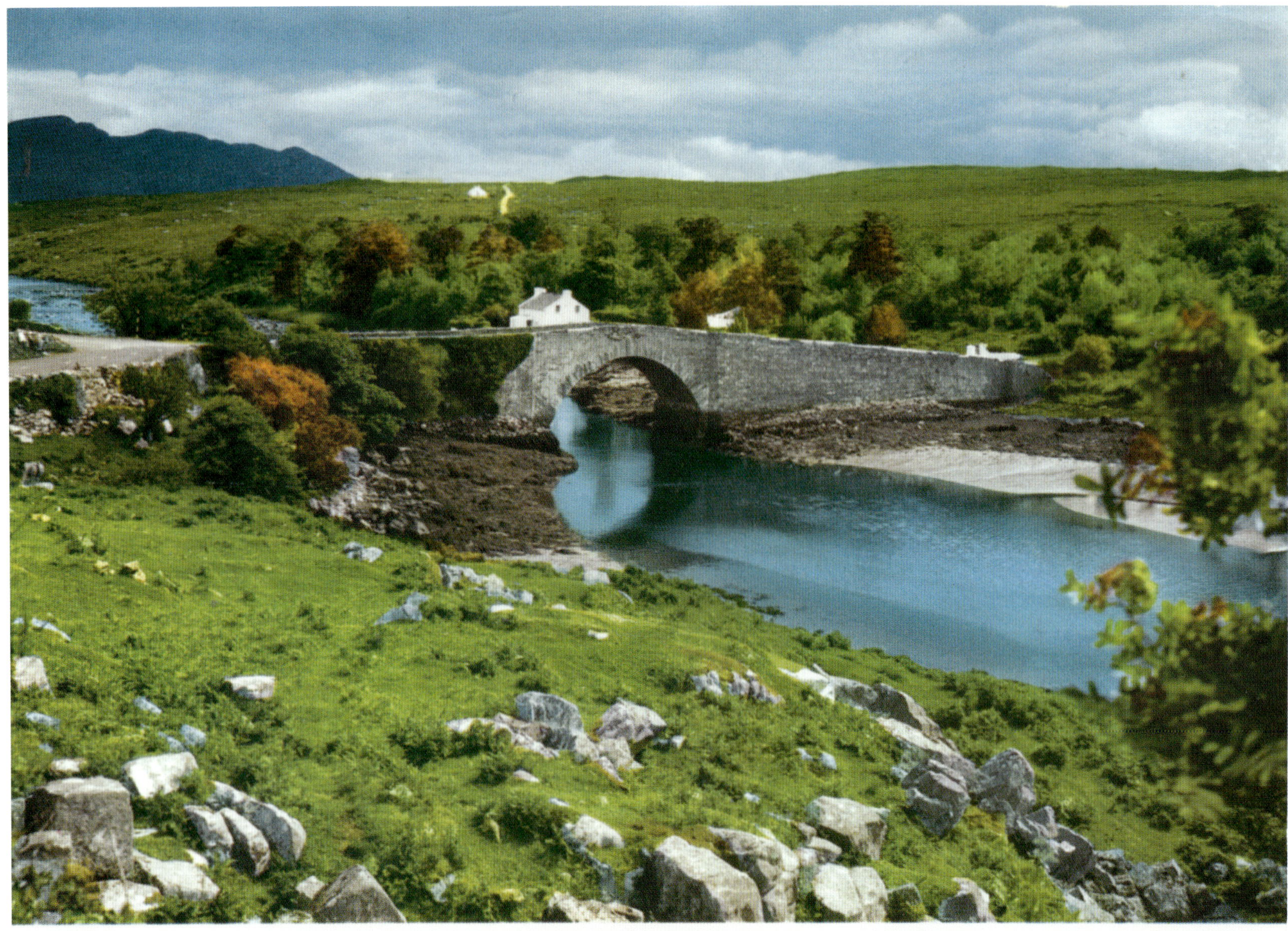

Lackagh Bridge, between Carrigart and Creeslough, Co. Donegal, Ireland.

Photo: Joan Willis, John Hinde Studios.

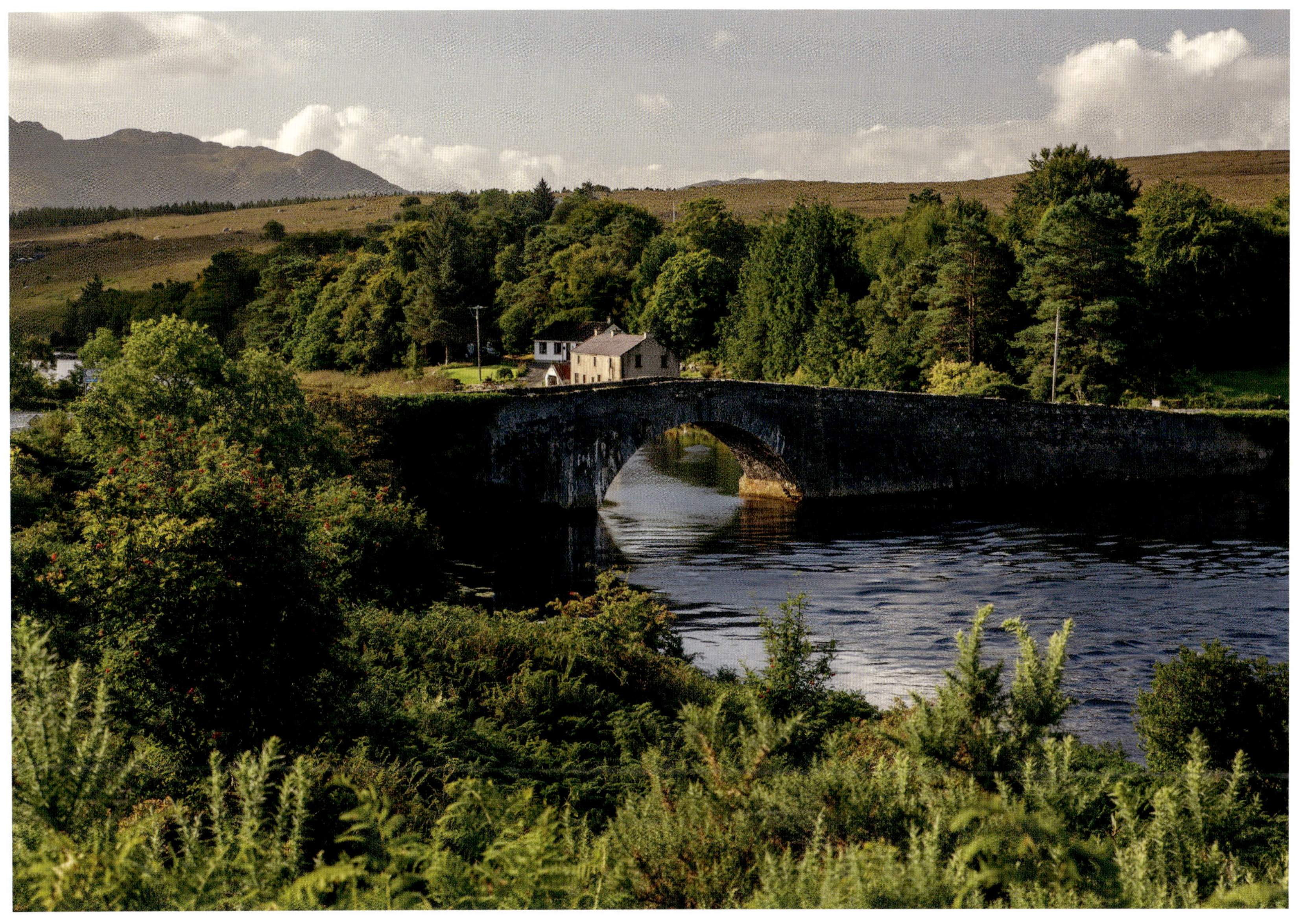

The Lackagh Bridge, at Drumlackagh, between Carrigart and Creeslough, in Co. Donegal, was built in 1750. The Lackagh river is known for its abundant stocks of salmon and sea trout, and who can blame them? It's clearly a beautiful place for floating, or flipping a fin.

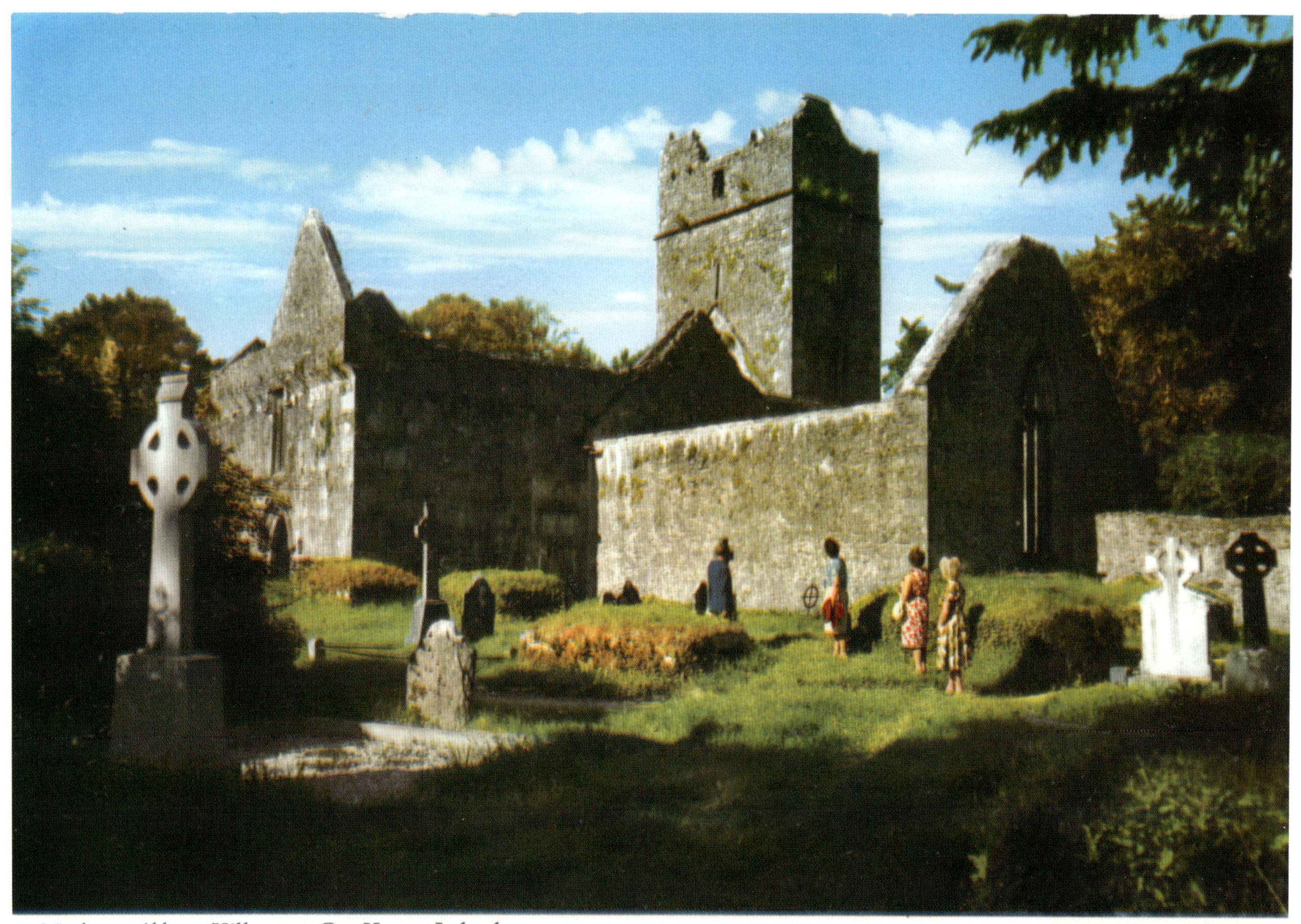

Muckross Abbey, Killarney, Co. Kerry, Ireland. Photo: Joan Willis, John Hinde Studios.

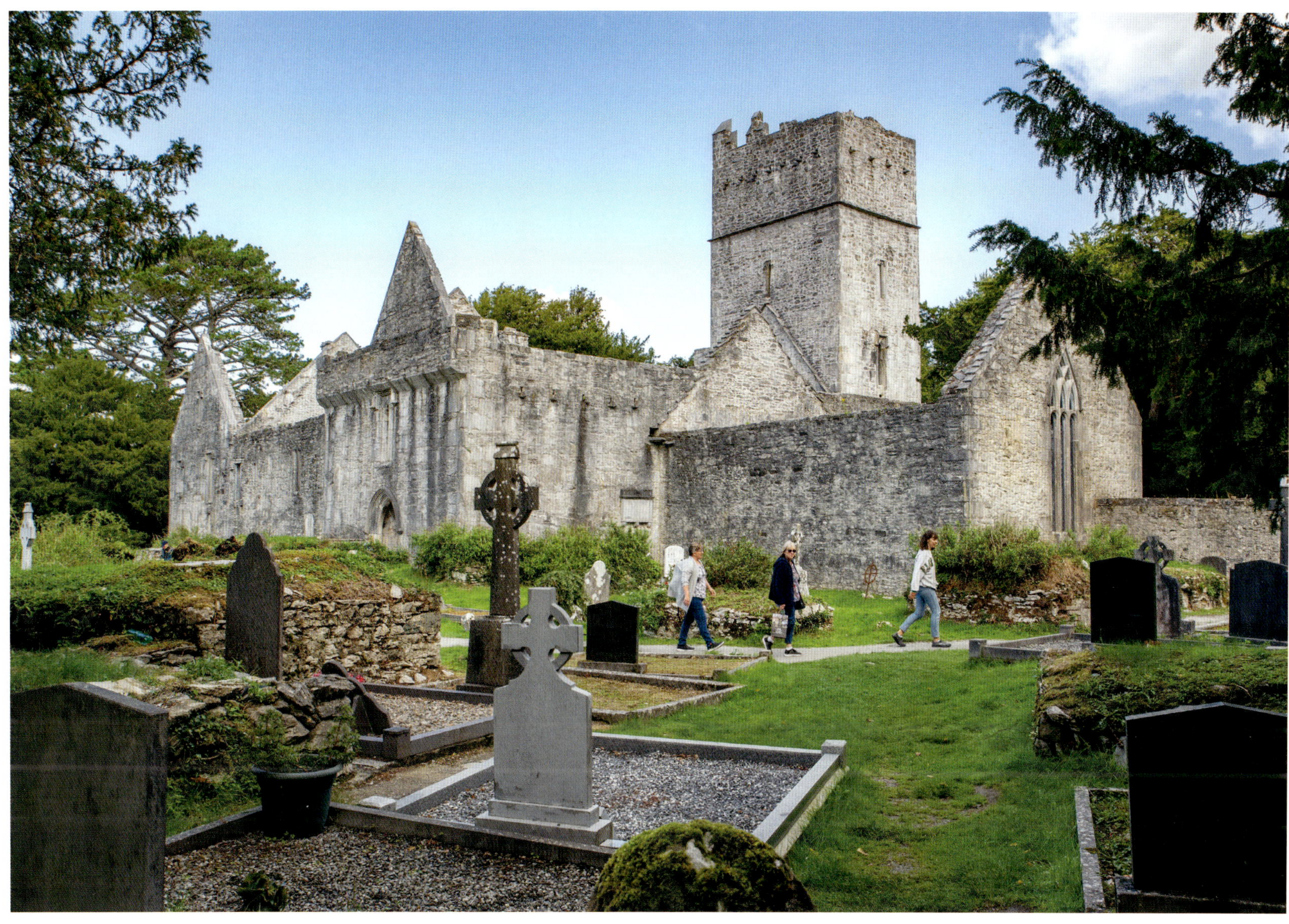

Winding through the piercing beauty of Killarney National Park, you come at last to Muckross Abbey, a 15th-century Franciscan friary, fiercely fought over and much restored. Set before its austere and antique walls, the abbey's graveyard is still in use today.

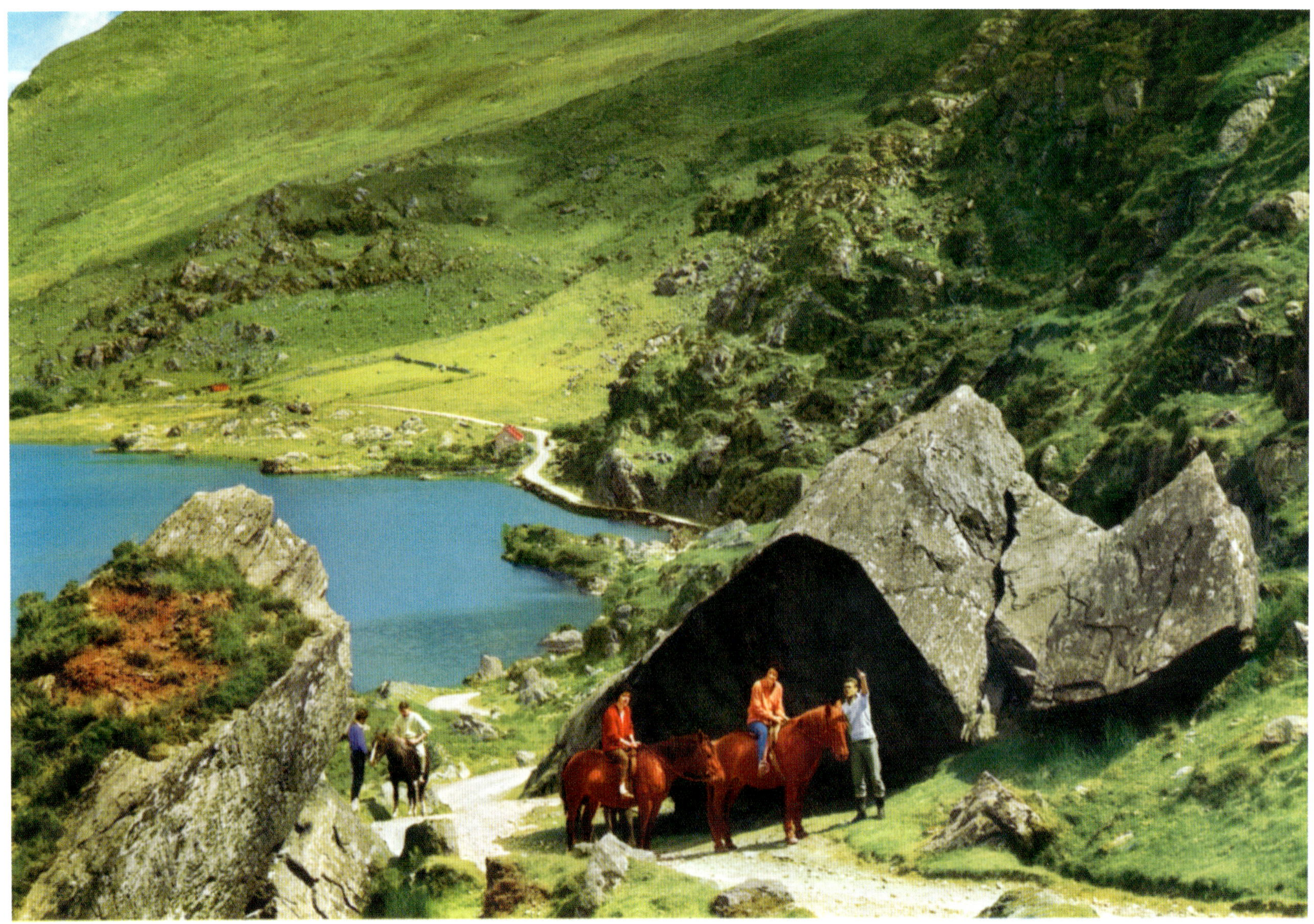

Pony Trekking in the Gap of Dunloe, Killarney, Co. Kerry, Ireland. *Photo: E. Nägele, John Hinde Studios.*

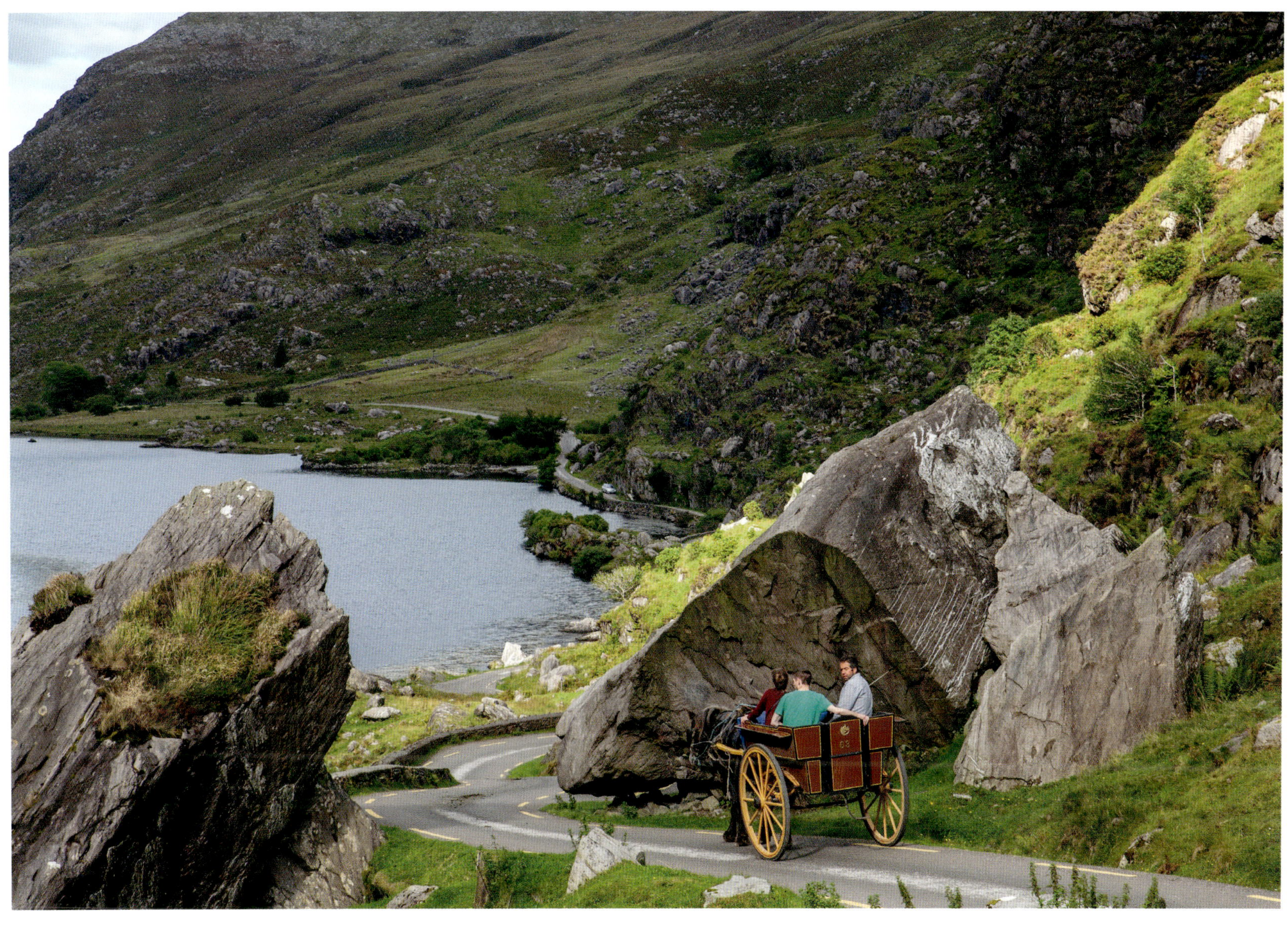

Local jaunting-cart drivers, or 'jarveys', are renowned for their wit and storytelling. So as he 'jaunts' you through the Gap of Dunloe, expect your jarvey to regale you with local history, stories of old times and Irish legends.

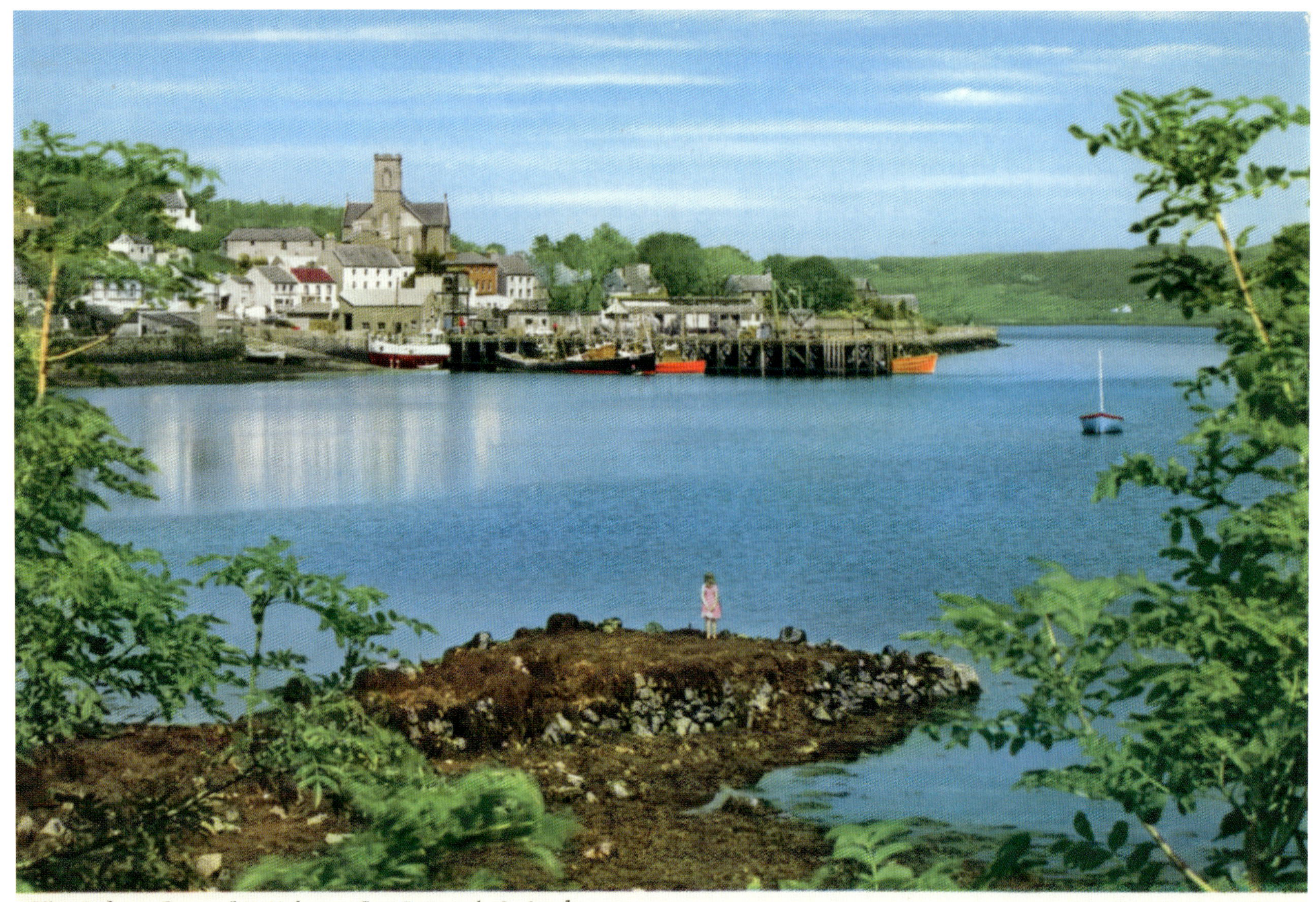

The Fishing Port of Killybegs, Co. Donegal, Ireland.

Colour Photo by John Hinde, F.R.P.S.

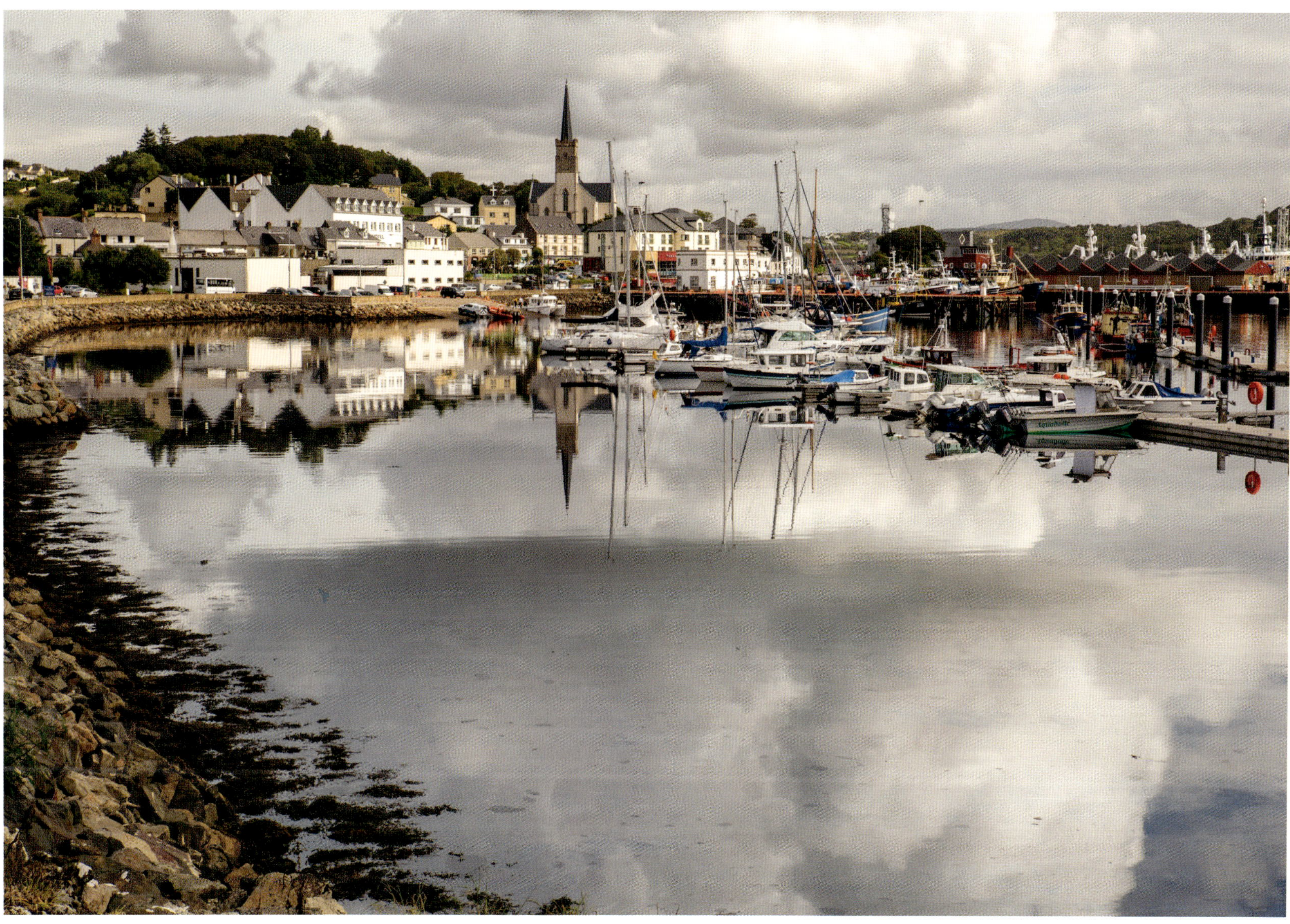

When I finally found this spot, I could not believe how it had changed from the postcard view. Killybegs is the largest fishing port on the island of Ireland. A new €50-million pier was completed in 2004. Note the new church spire added in 2012, 170 years after the church was built – possibly symbolic of the port's soaring aspirations.

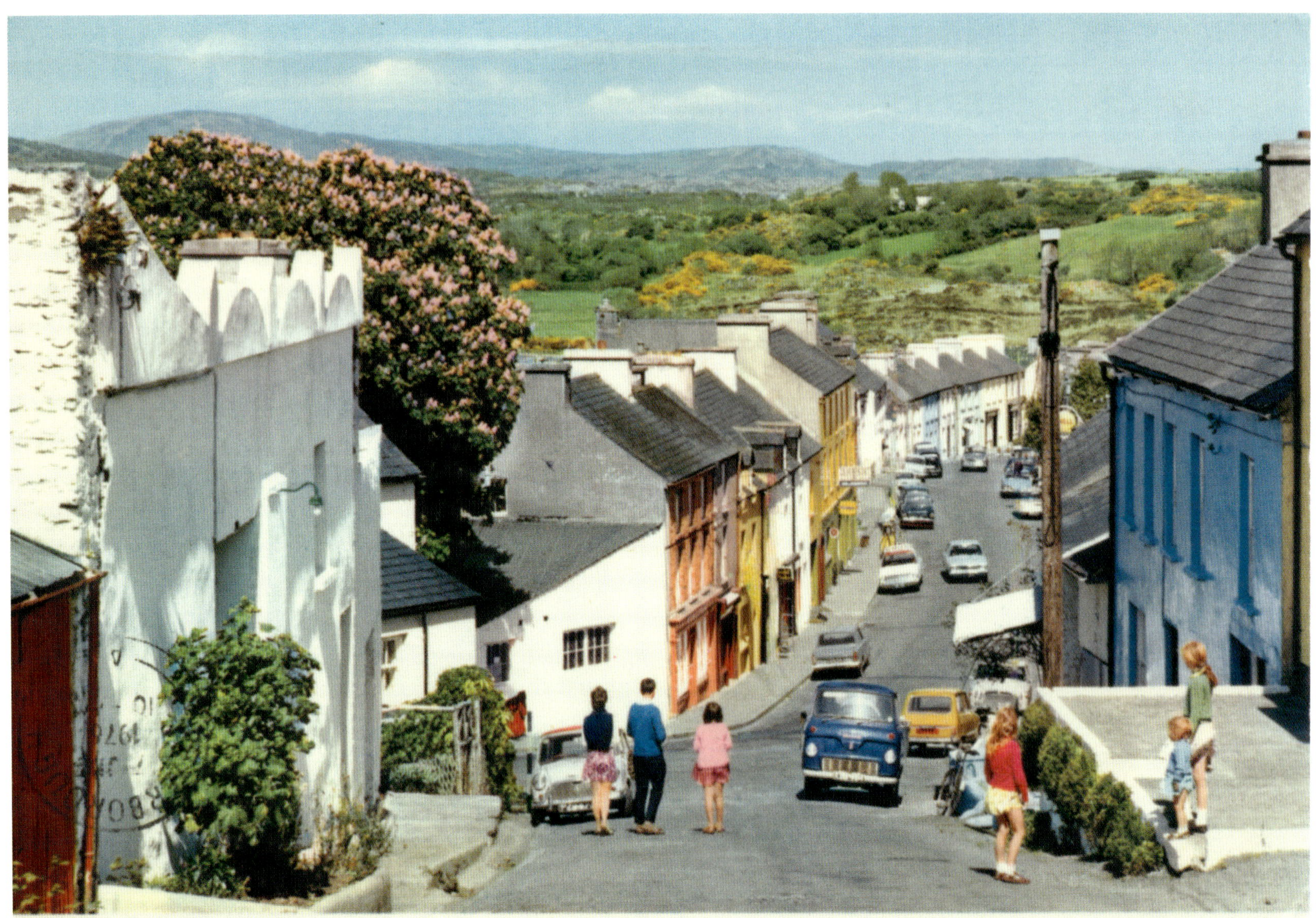

Ballydehob Village, West Cork, Ireland. *Photo: D. Noble, John Hinde Studios.*

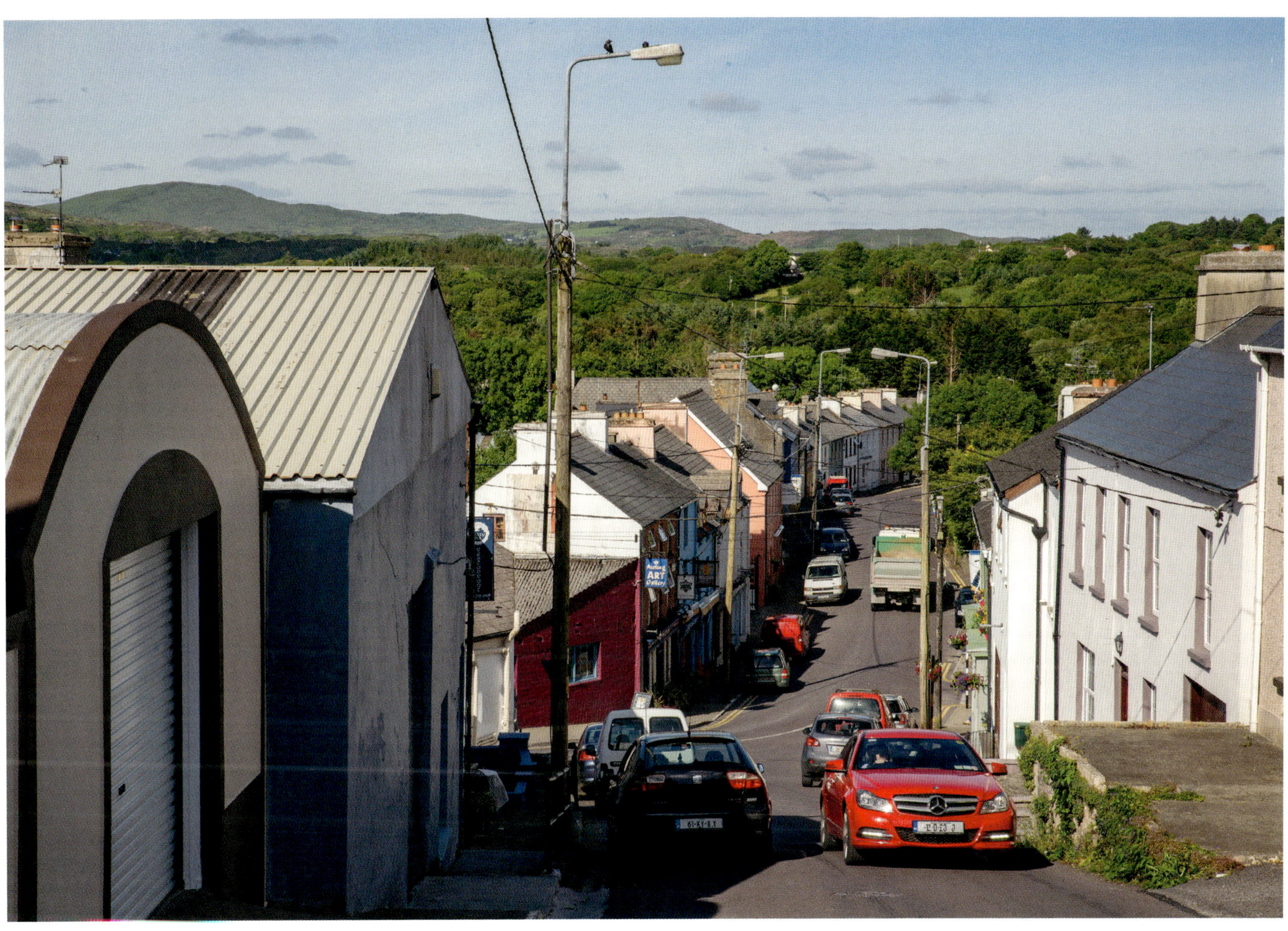

No kids or grown-ups on my visit, but the town itself is vibrant enough. Ballydehob now hosts many festivals, including four devoted to music – jazz, country, traditional and folk. There is even a yoga and threshing festival, though it is unclear to me if these activities occur concurrently.

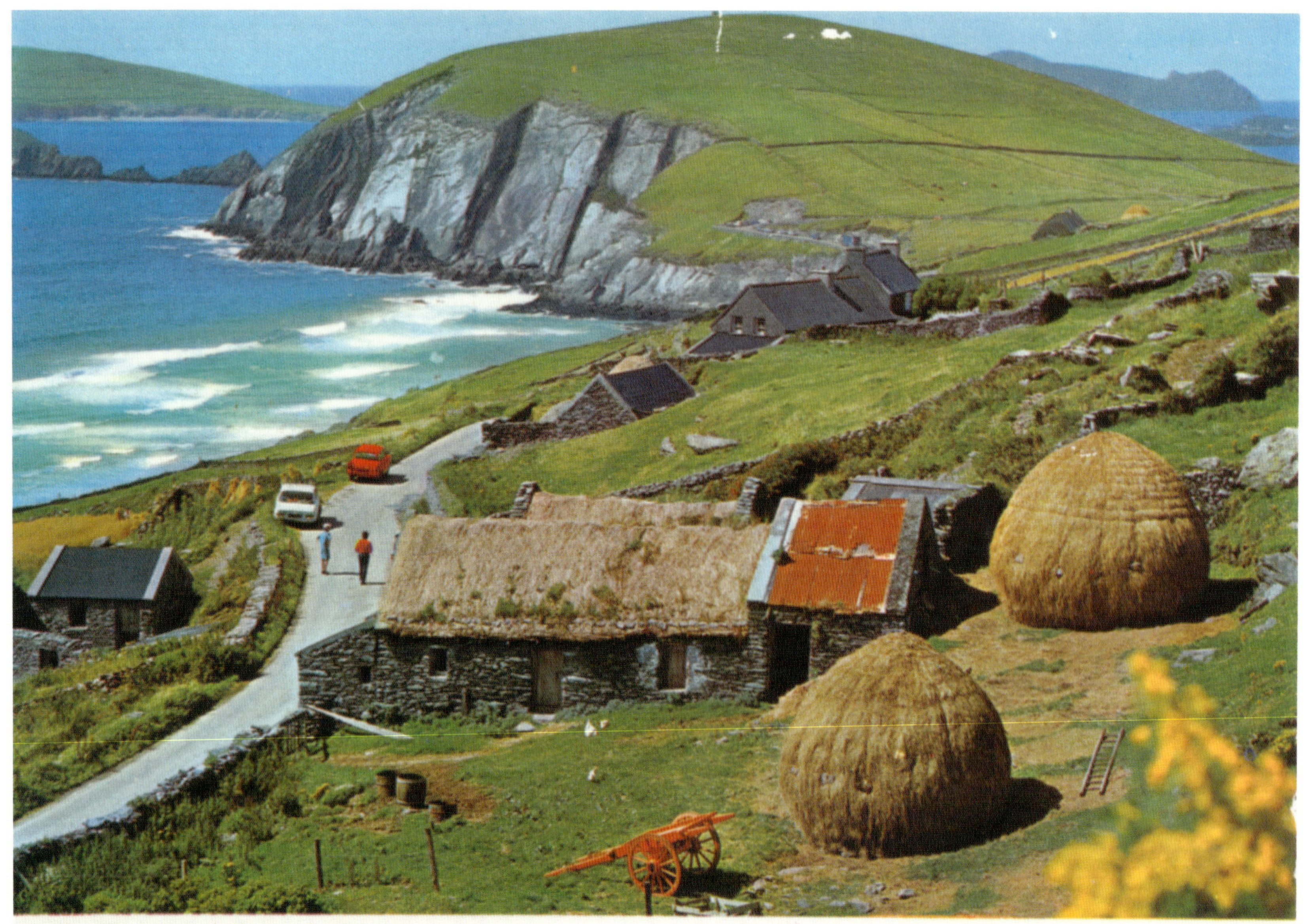

Slea Head, Dingle Peninsula, Co. Kerry, Ireland. *Photo: R. Beer, John Hinde Studios.*

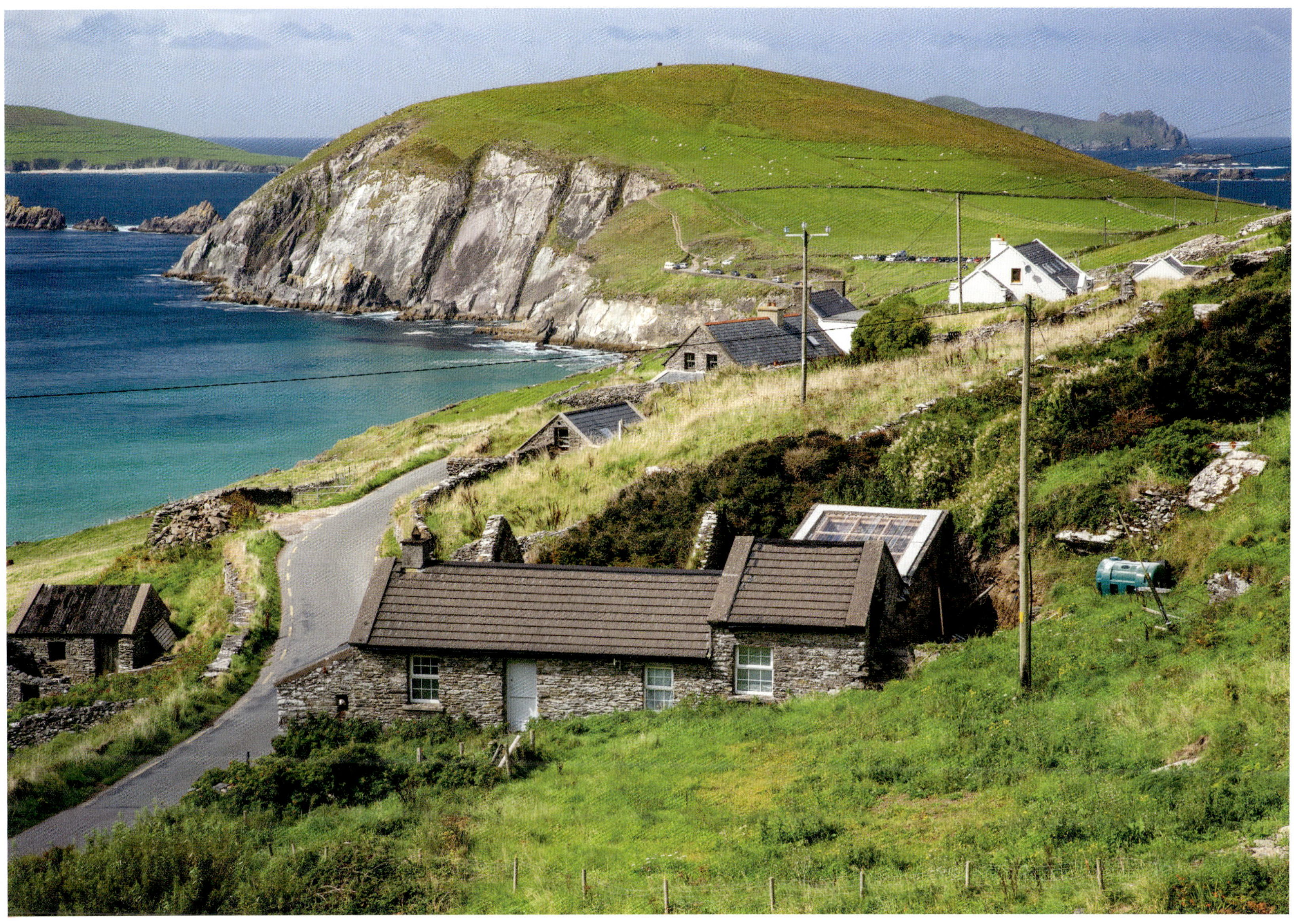

After I took this photograph, I walked up the road to the Teac Couminole café, a small café where Eileen and her mother made me the most delicious rhubarb pie.

'Be sure to take pictures of those ugly coaches coming up the road,' her mother said to me as I departed. 'They're destroying the place.'

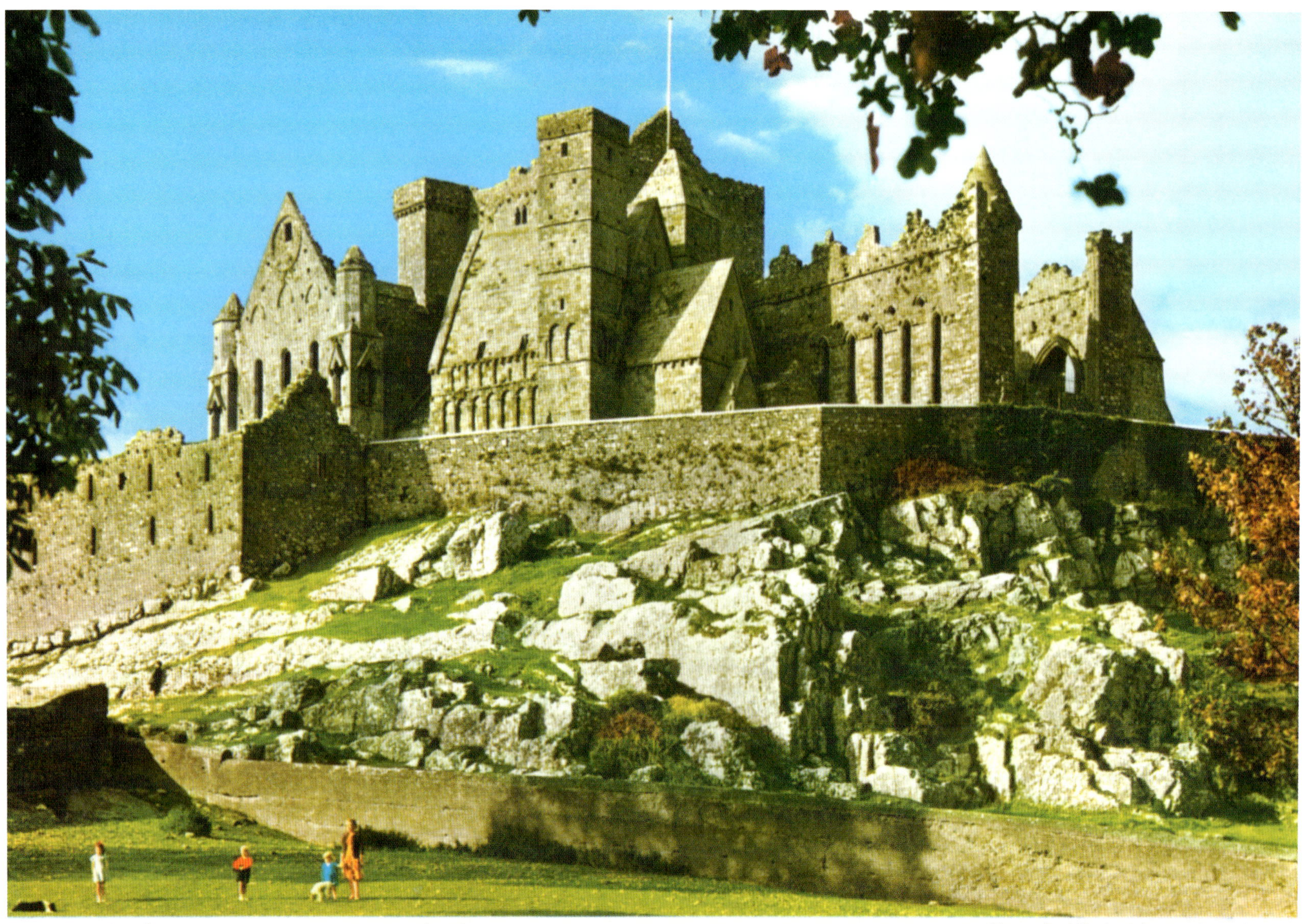

The Rock of Cashel, Co. Tipperary, Ireland. *Photo: E. Nägele, John Hinde Studios.*

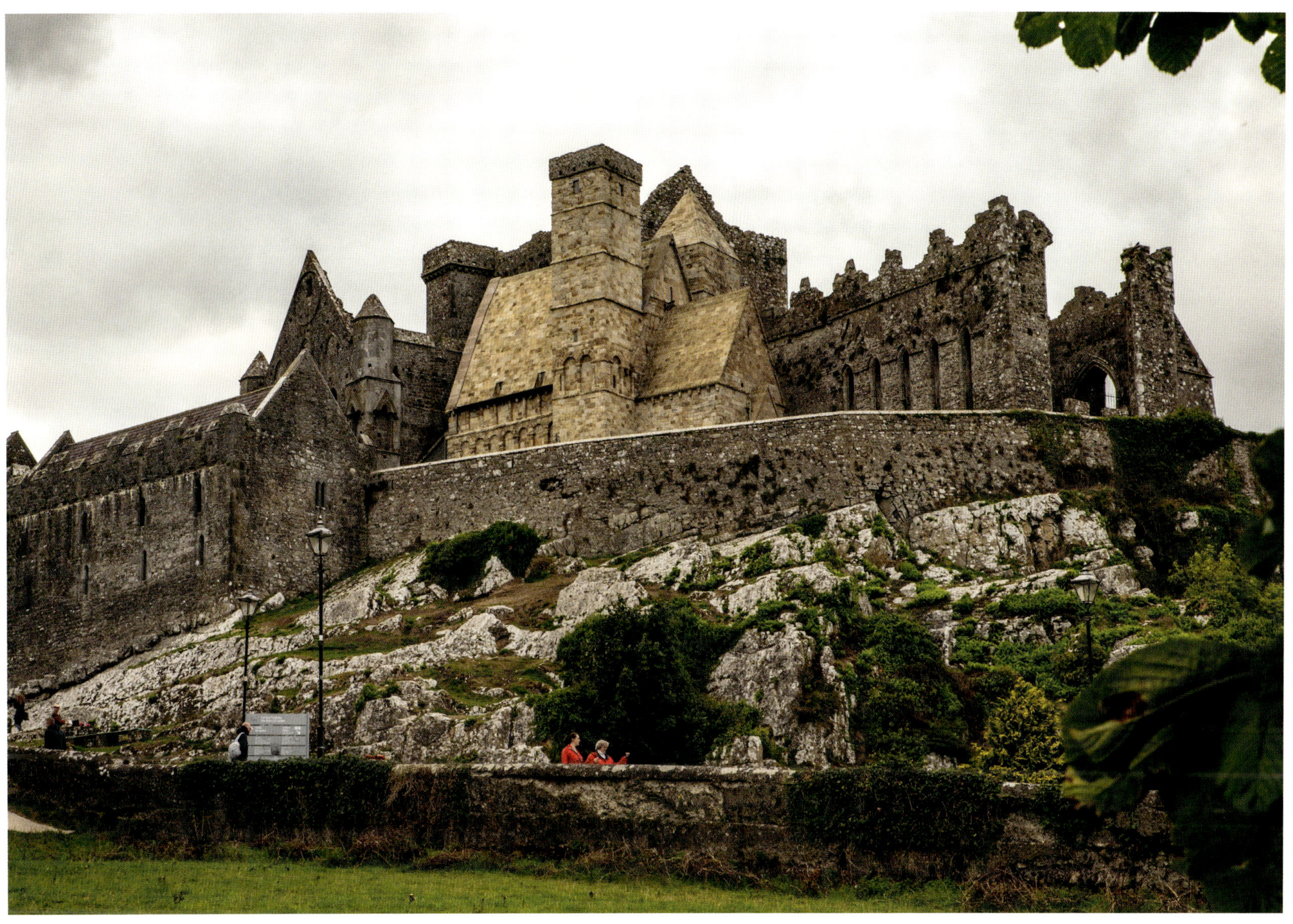

The Rock of Cashel is one of Ireland's iconic early medieval monuments. The round tower, the tallest and oldest building, dates from the 12th century. Centre stage, Cormac's Chapel was restored in 2018, its priceless wall paintings now preserved from the elements. The neat gardens seem a dramatic foil for the grim, strident beauty of the rock.

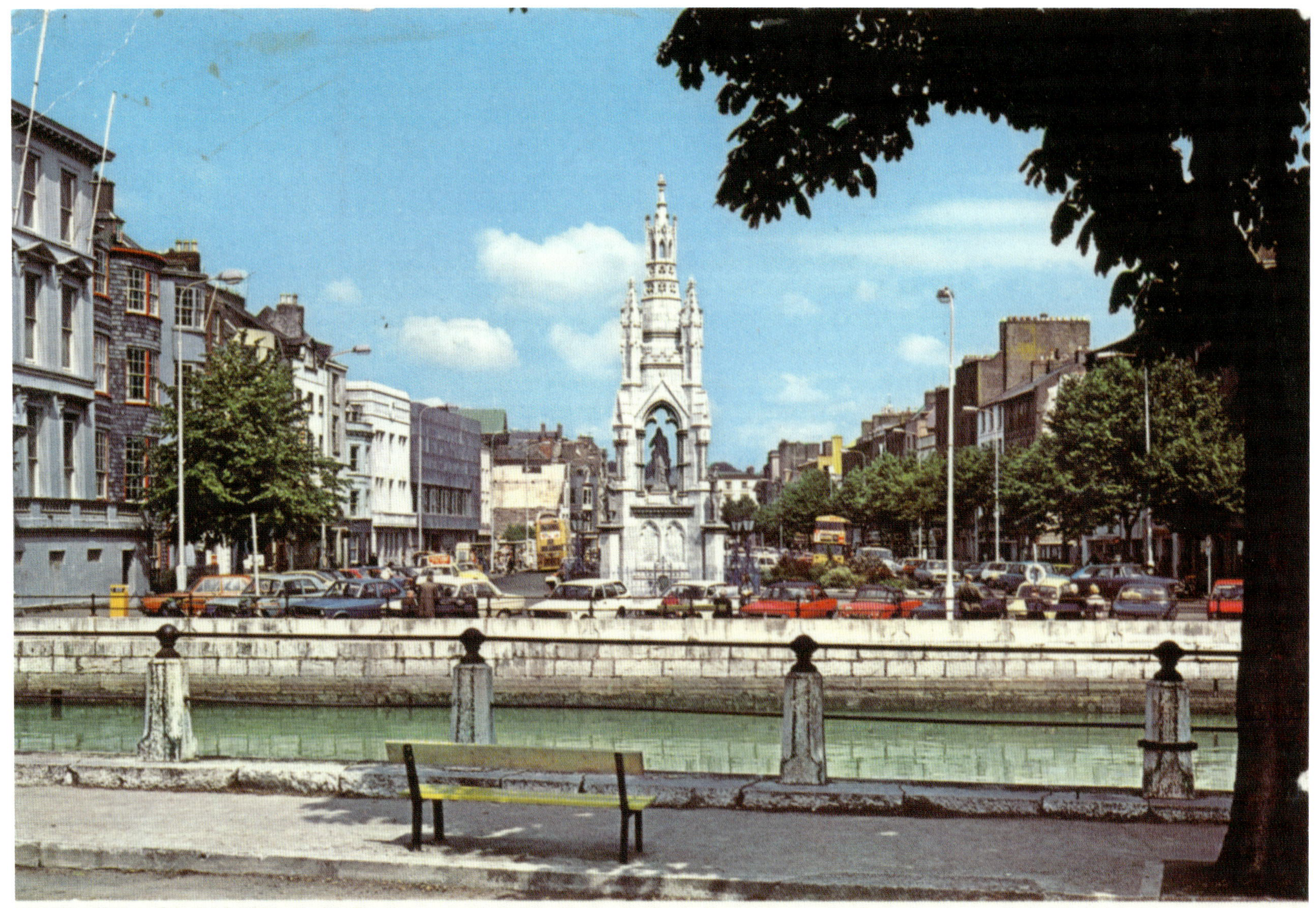

Grand Parade, Cork City, Ireland.

Photo: P. O'Toole, John Hinde Studios.

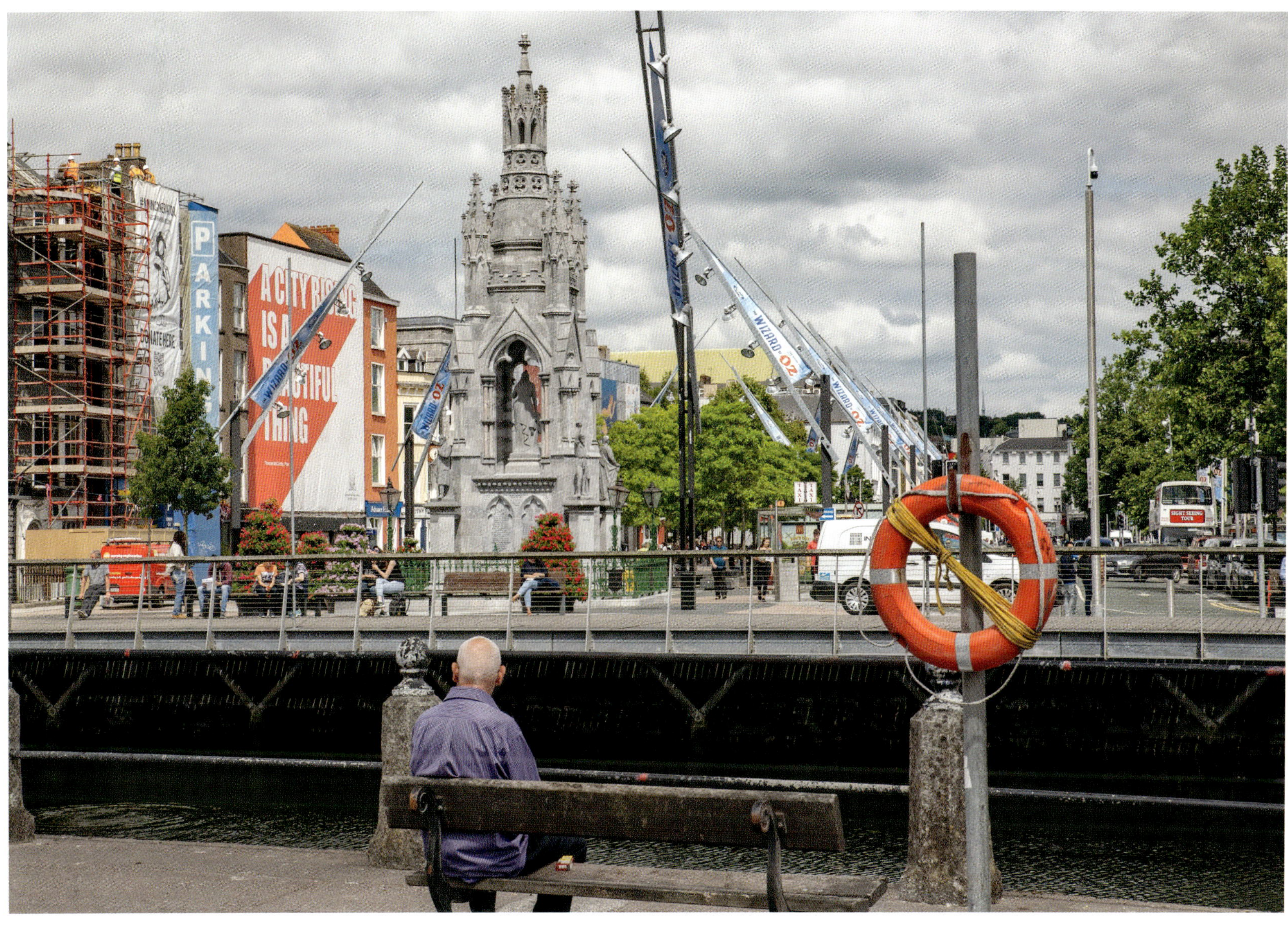

The Grand Parade is built over a channel of the river Lee and the widest street in Cork. From Sullivan's Quay, we are looking across the Lee at the National Monument, unveiled in 1906 and commemorating the rebellions of 1798, 1803, 1848 and 1867. A fiery people it seems, the denizens of Cork.

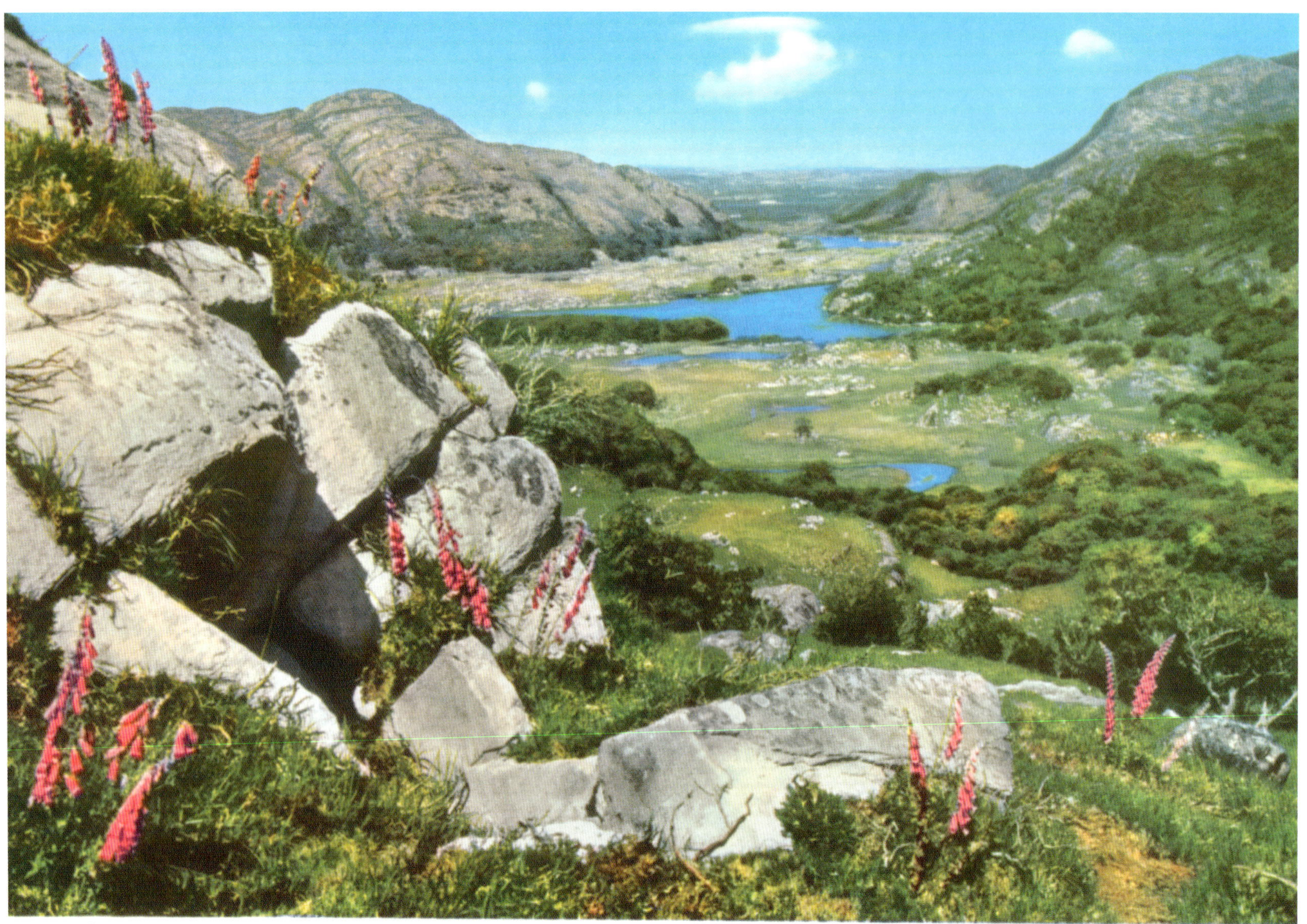

Ladies' View, Killarney, Ireland.

Colour Photo by John Hinde, F.R.P.S.

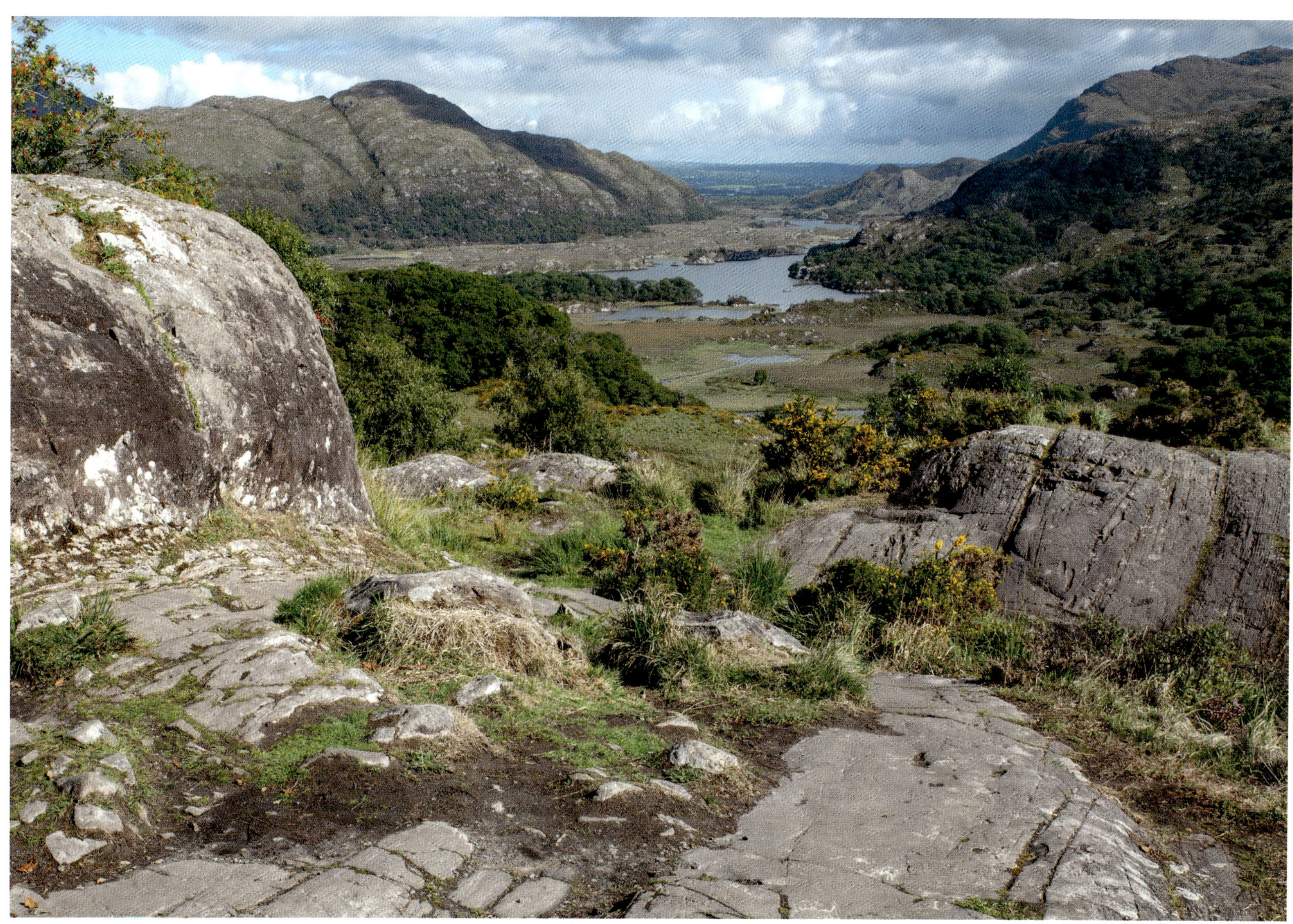

Ladies' View has been a major stopping point for tourists of both sexes for many years. Today, it's a selfie hotspot.

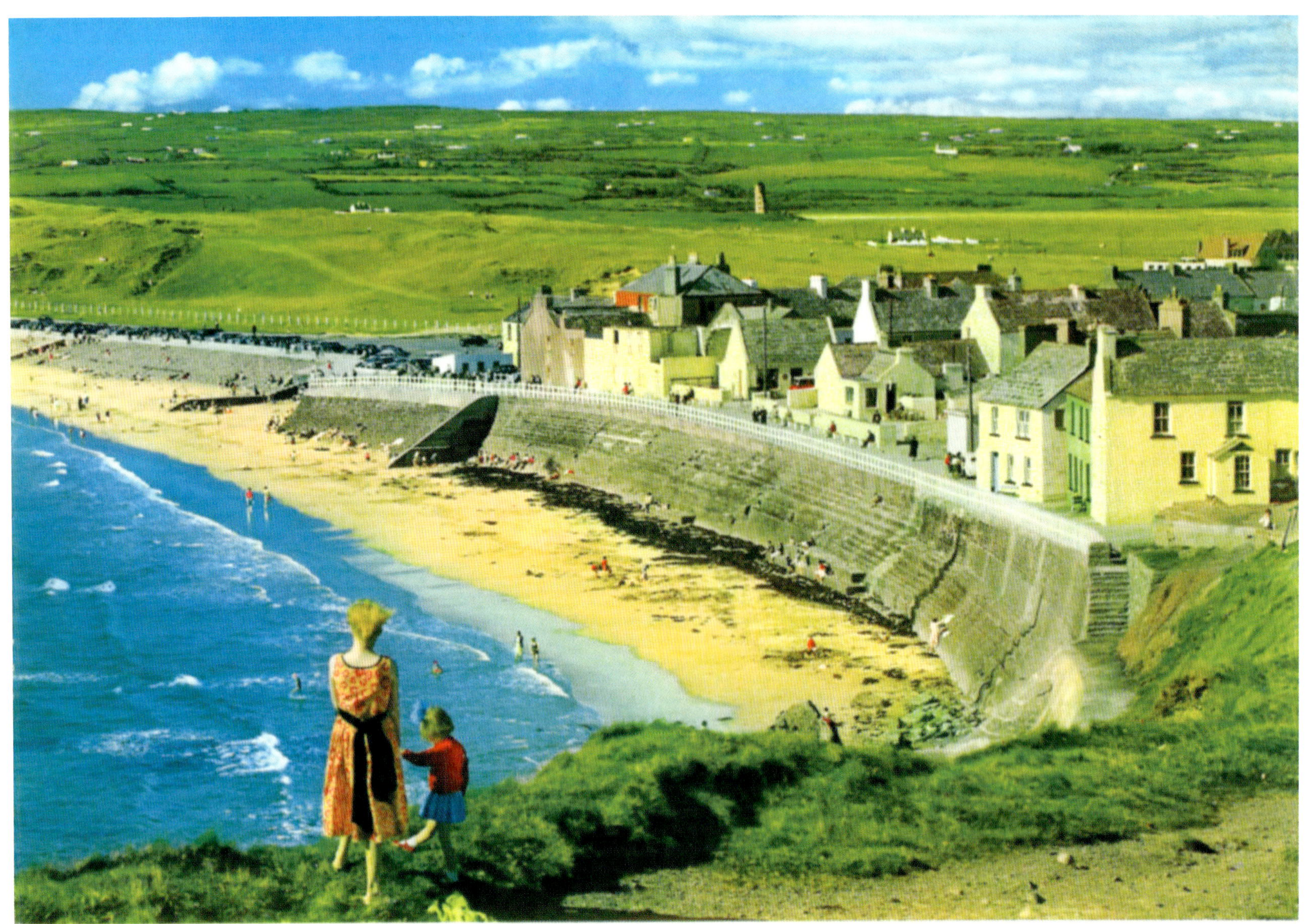

Lahinch, Co. Clare, Ireland.

Colour Photo by John Hinde, F.R.P.S.

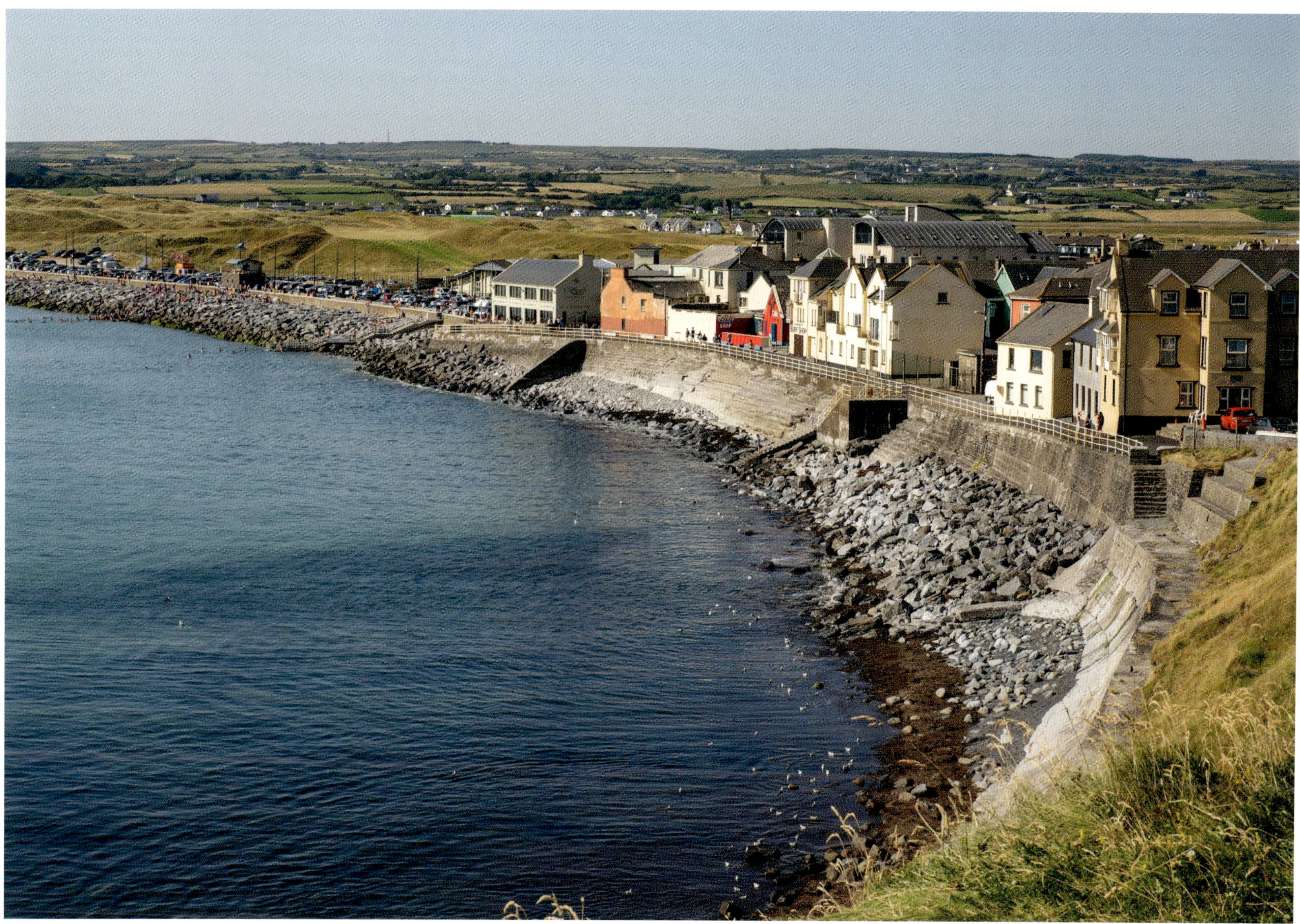

Lahinch might look unchanged, but the cold Atlantic waters lapping this fine Blue Flag beach offer some ultra-modern adventure sports: surfing, kitesurfing and kayaking all benefit from the flooding tide here, and for added drama, it's just a short drive from the Cliffs of Moher.

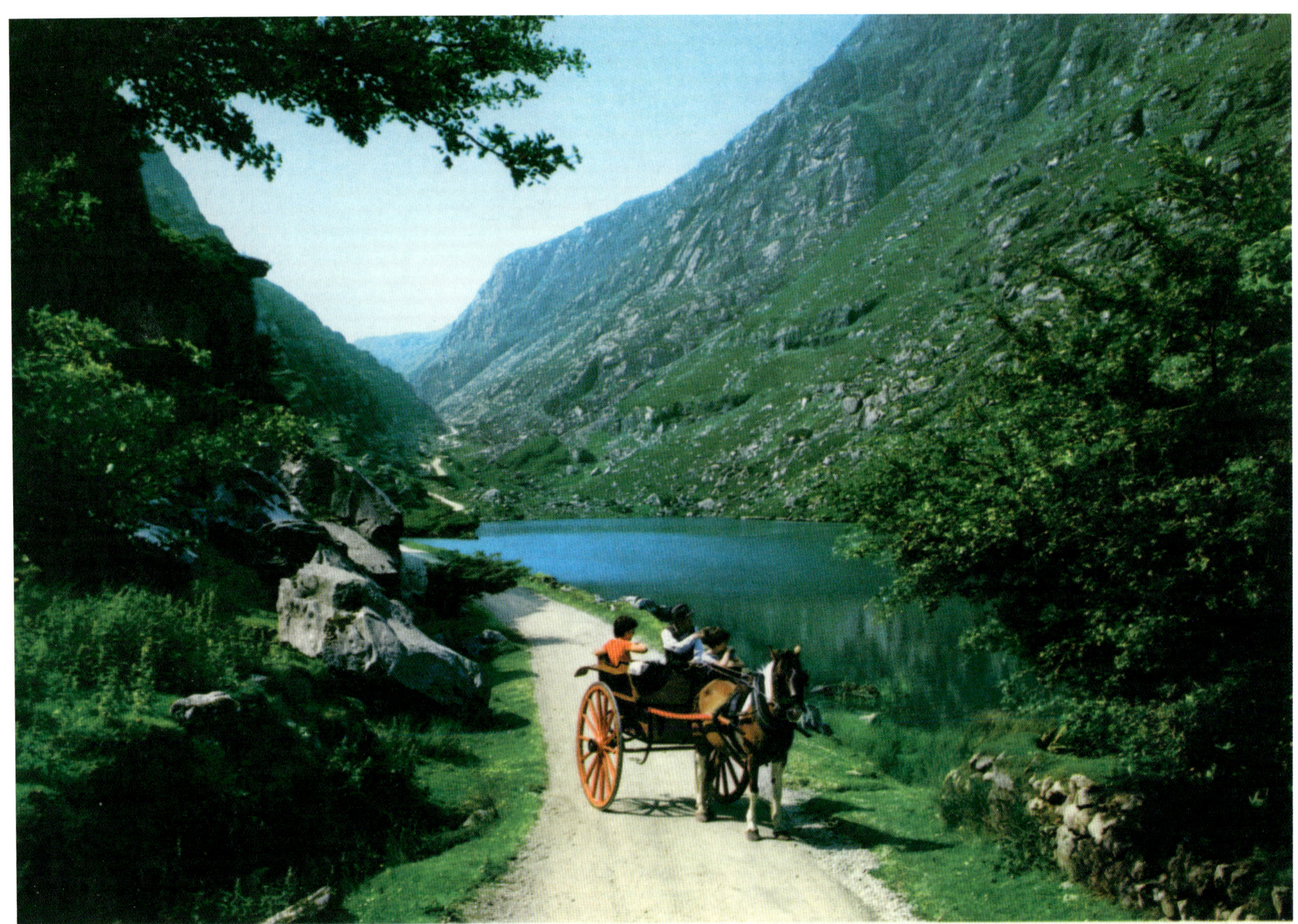

Gap of Dunloe, near Killarney, Co. Kerry, Ireland. *Photo: P. O'Toole, John Hinde Studios.*

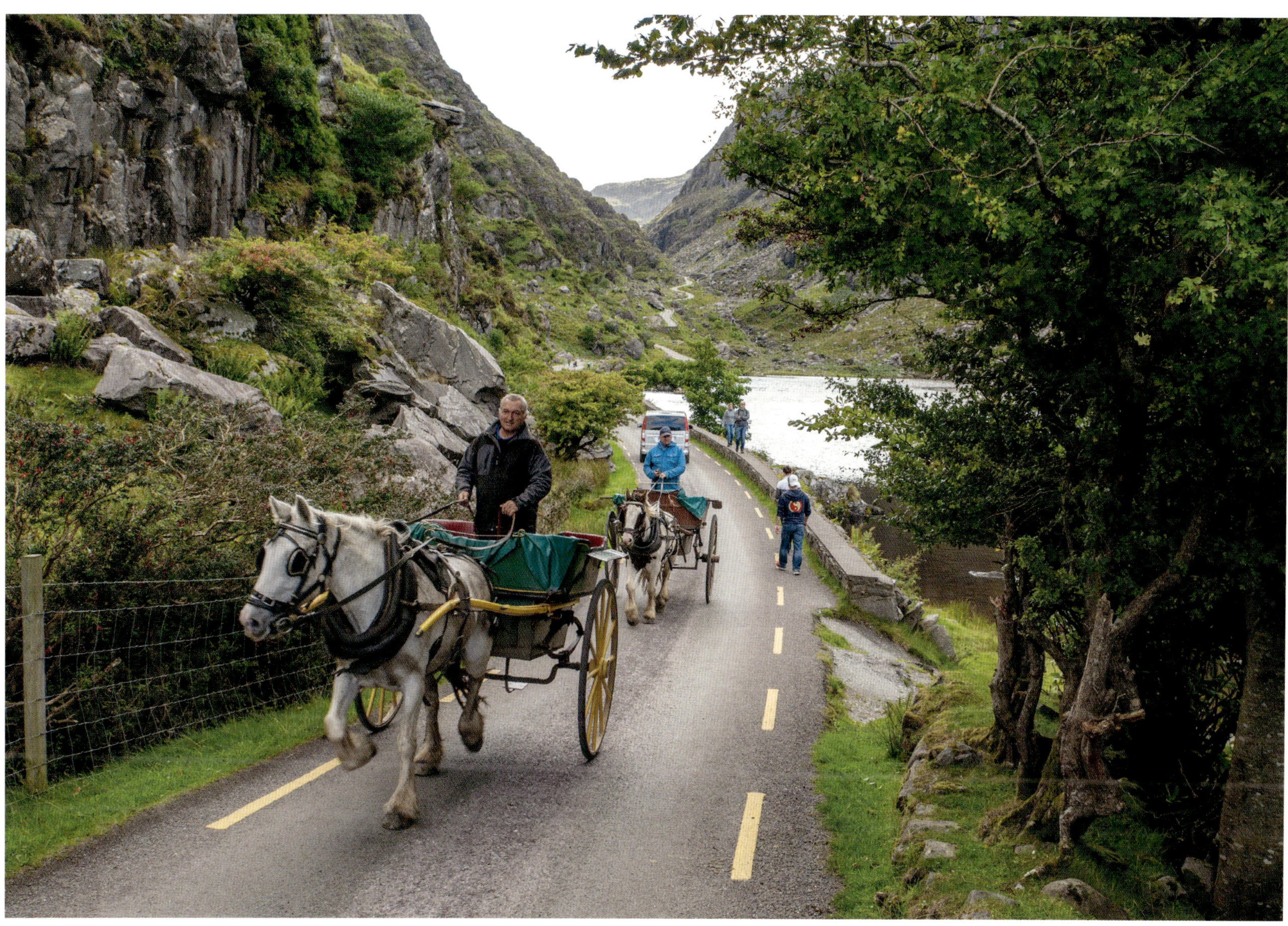

The inscription on the back of this postcard reads: '*Most of the trip is done by the traditional jaunting cart, which nervous visitors find to be much more secure than it looks.*' In scenery so little altered by nature, today's jaunting carts ride on and, for a moment in time, you think nothing has changed at all.

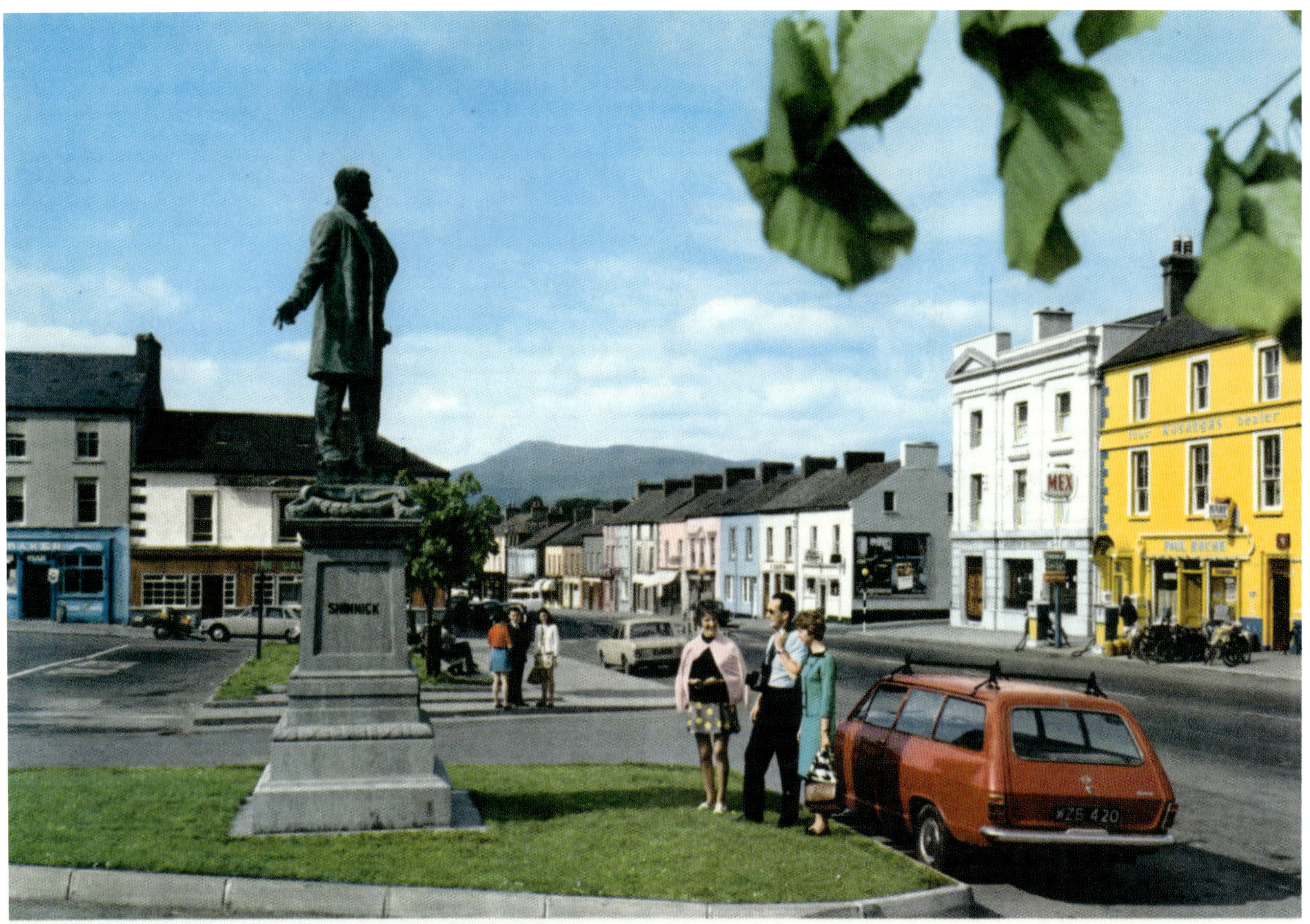

Mitchelstown and Galtee Mountains, Co. Cork, Ireland.

Photo: D. Noble, John Hinde Studios.

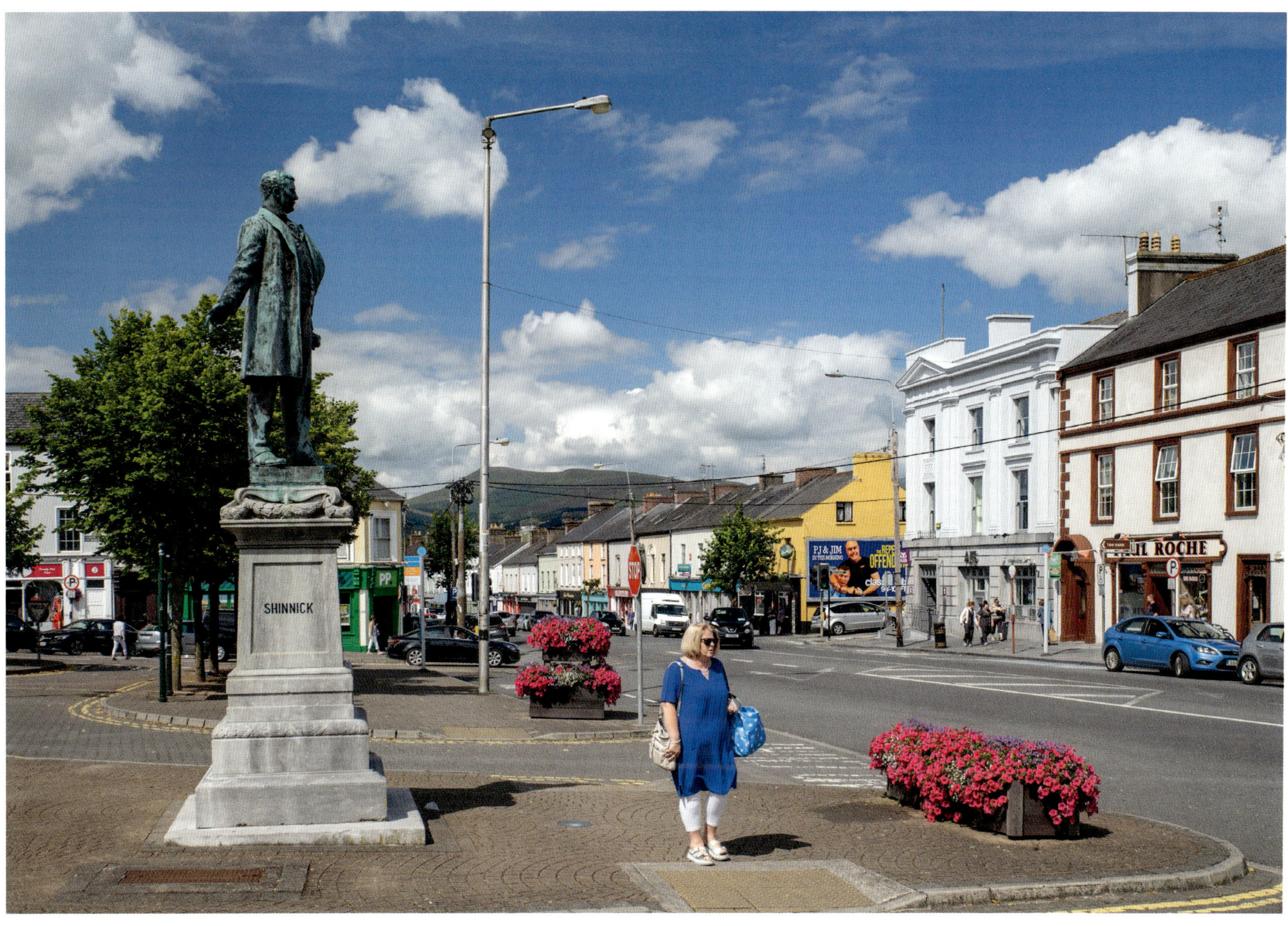

After about an hour of waiting for a red car to pull up and three people to jump out, I was invited into Roche's bar and cycle shop across the street by Mr Roche himself. His grandparents purchased the property around 1956. It's the bright yellow building in the original postcard. On the wall behind his bar was the older postcard, glued to a wooden mount with four hooks for keys.

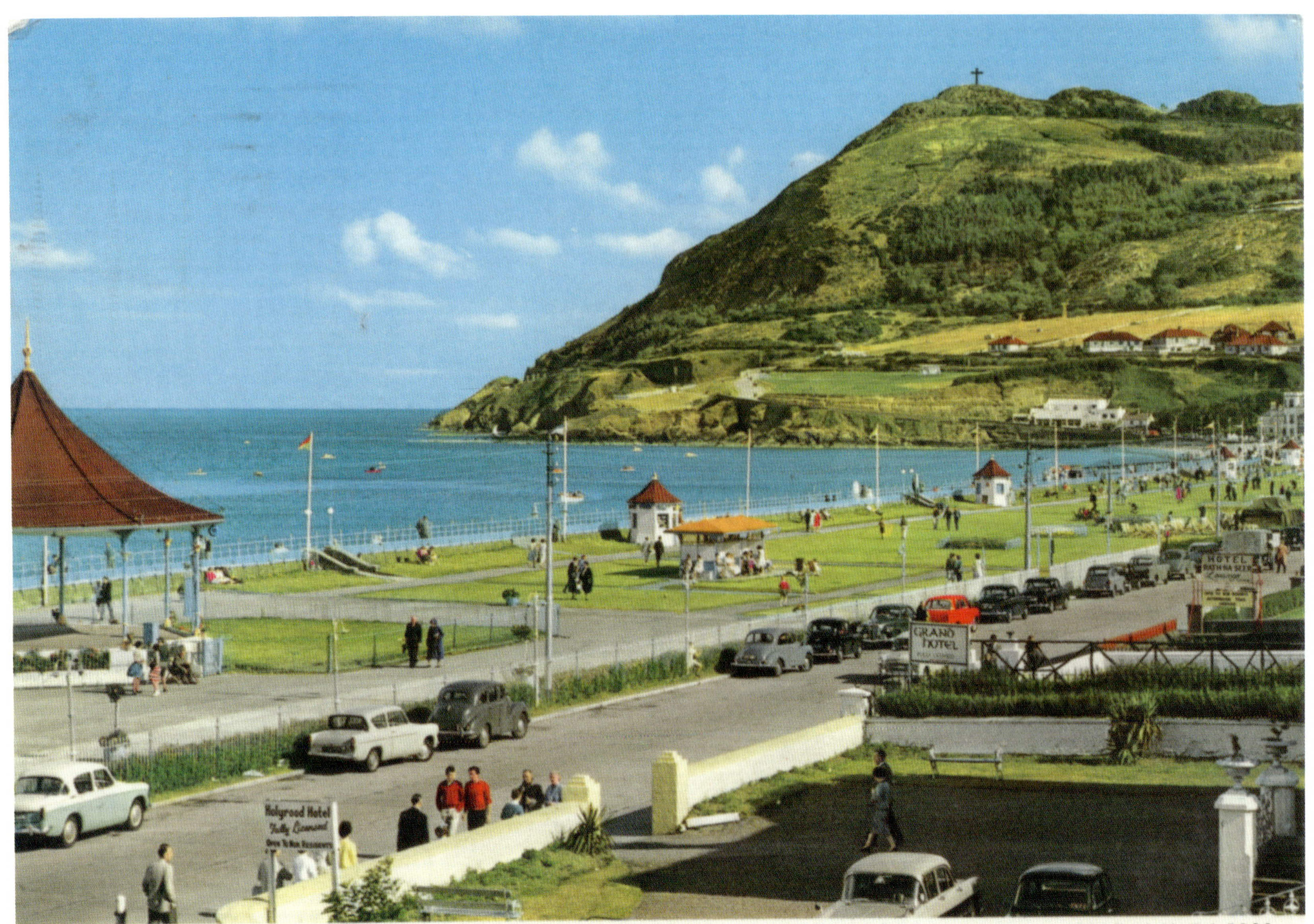
Holyrood Hotel
Fully Licensed
GRAND HOTEL
The Esplanade, Lawns and Head, Bray, Co. Wicklow.
Colour Photo by John Hinde, F.R.P.S.

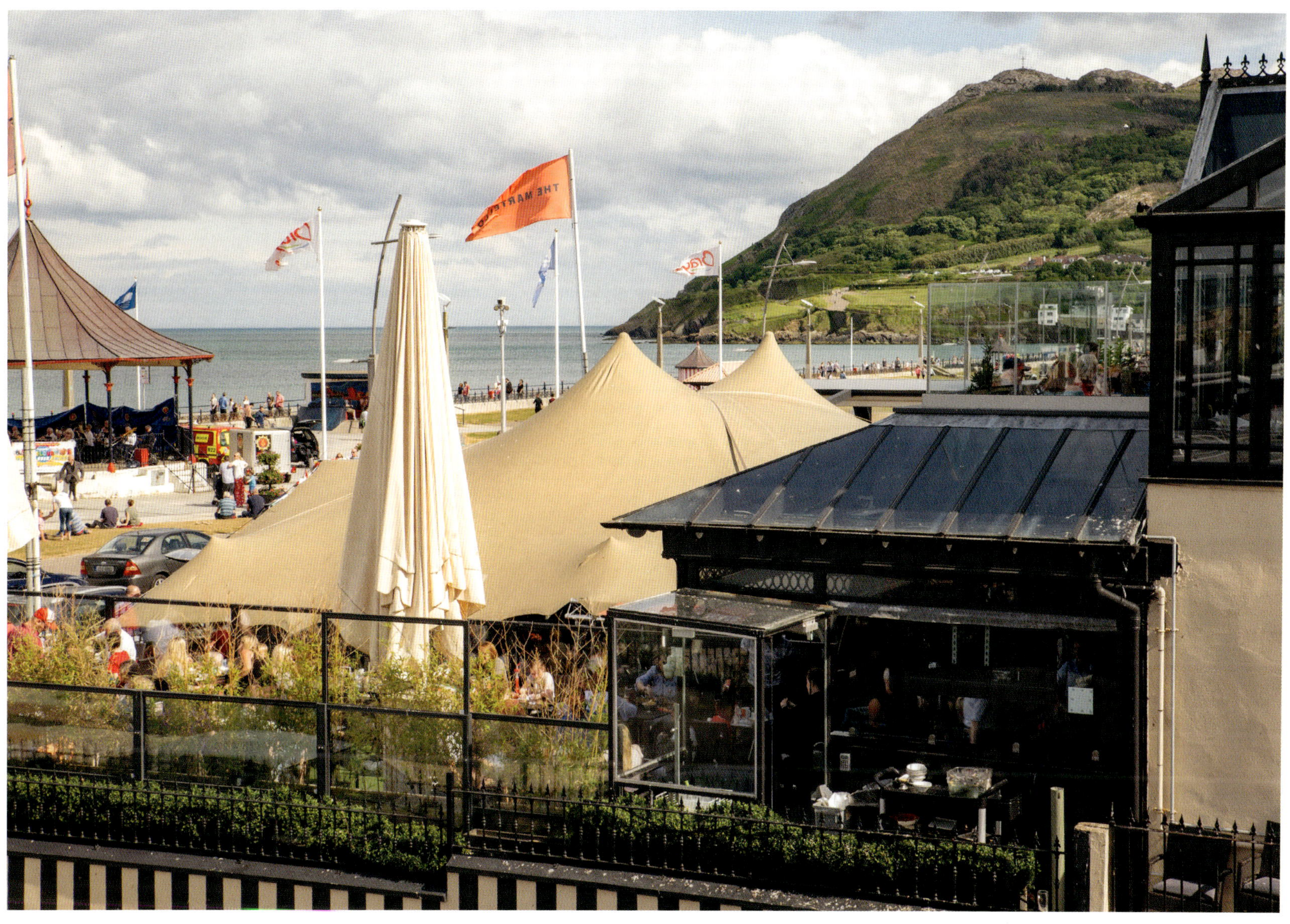

On the Bray promenade in front of what was once the Holyrood Hotel on Strand Road, now the Martello Hotel. The promenade dates to Victorian times when William Dargan, who brought the railway to Bray, aspired to make this town the 'Brighton of Ireland'. Some might say he succeeded.

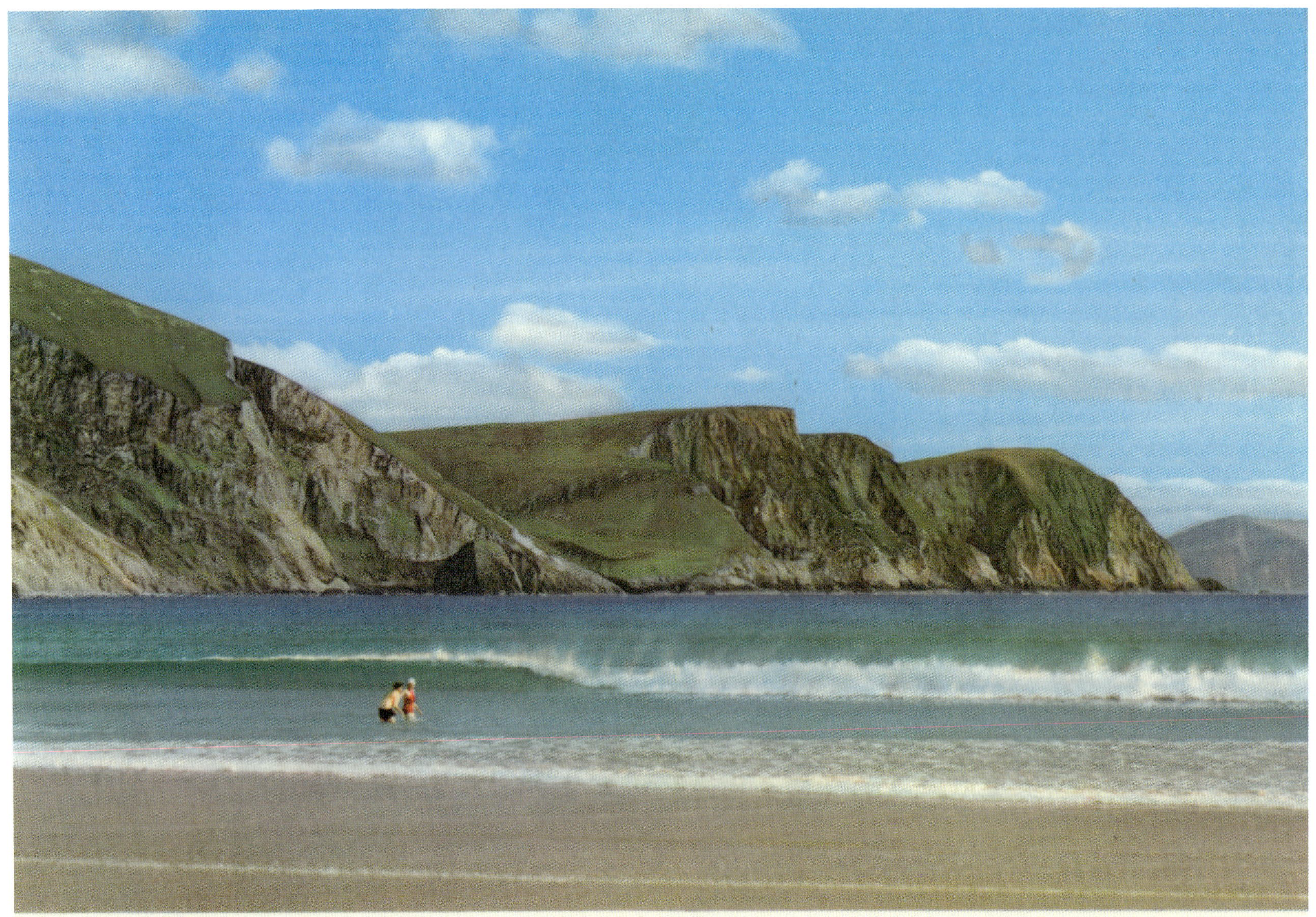

Menawn Cliffs from Keel Bay, Achill Island, Co. Mayo, Ireland. Colour Photo by John Hinde, F.R.P.S.

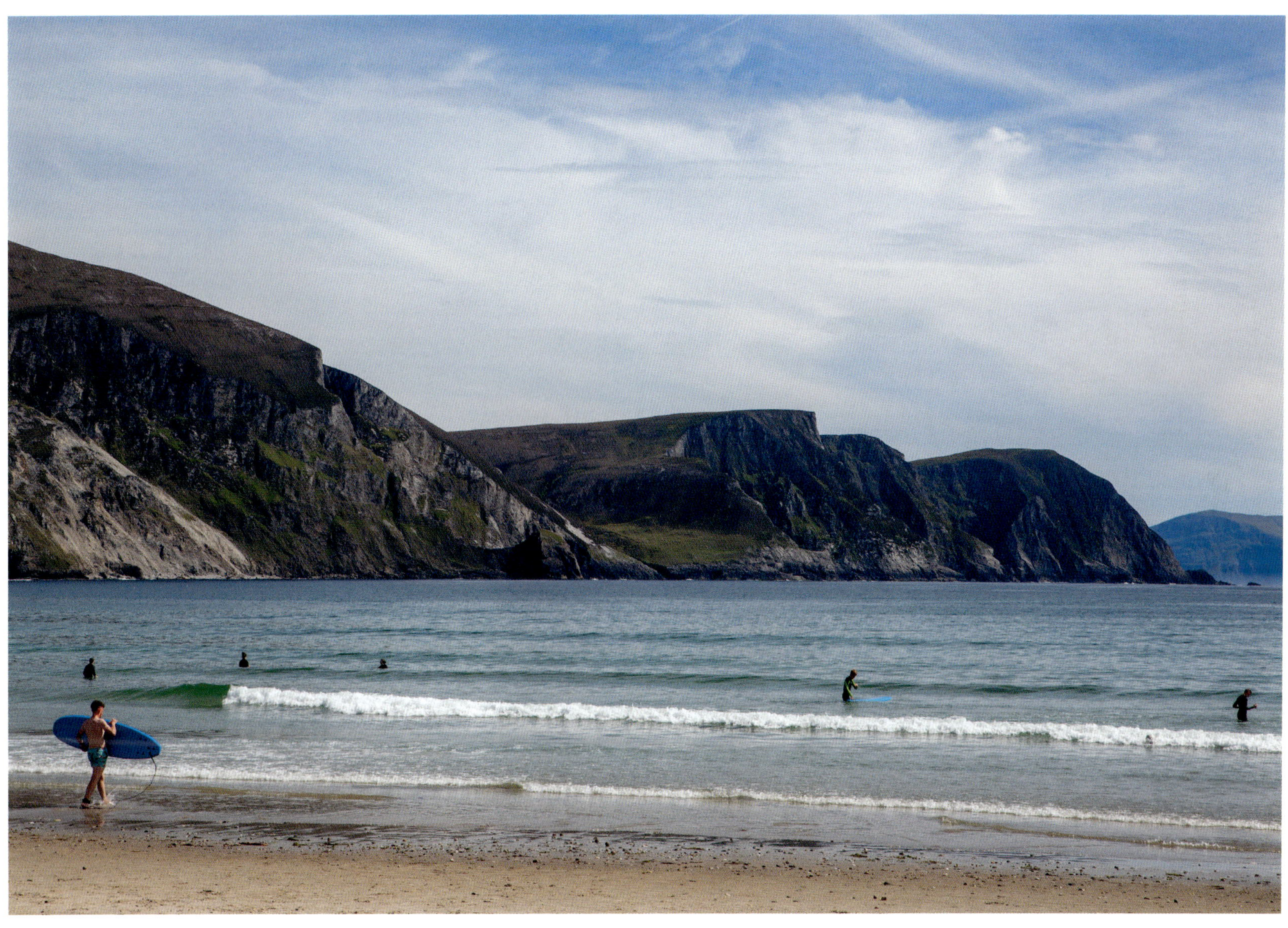

Achill Island's Keel Beach is a three-kilometre-long Blue Flag beach featuring some of the best surfing in Ireland. Achill Island has attracted many artists, writers, playwrights and poets, including Irish painter Paul Henry and British novelist Graham Greene.

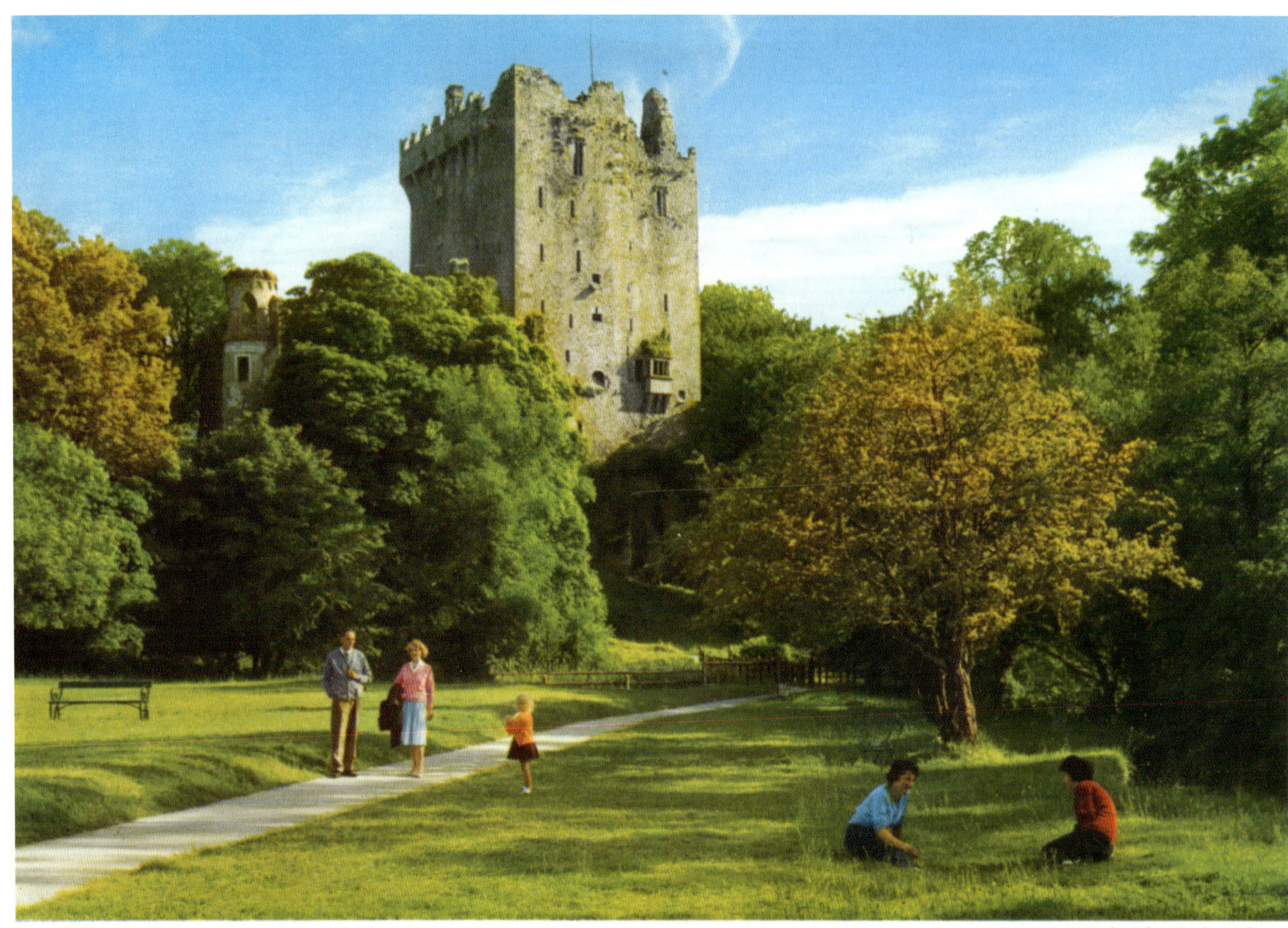

Blarney Castle, Co. Cork, Ireland.

Photo : E. Nägele, John Hinde Studios.

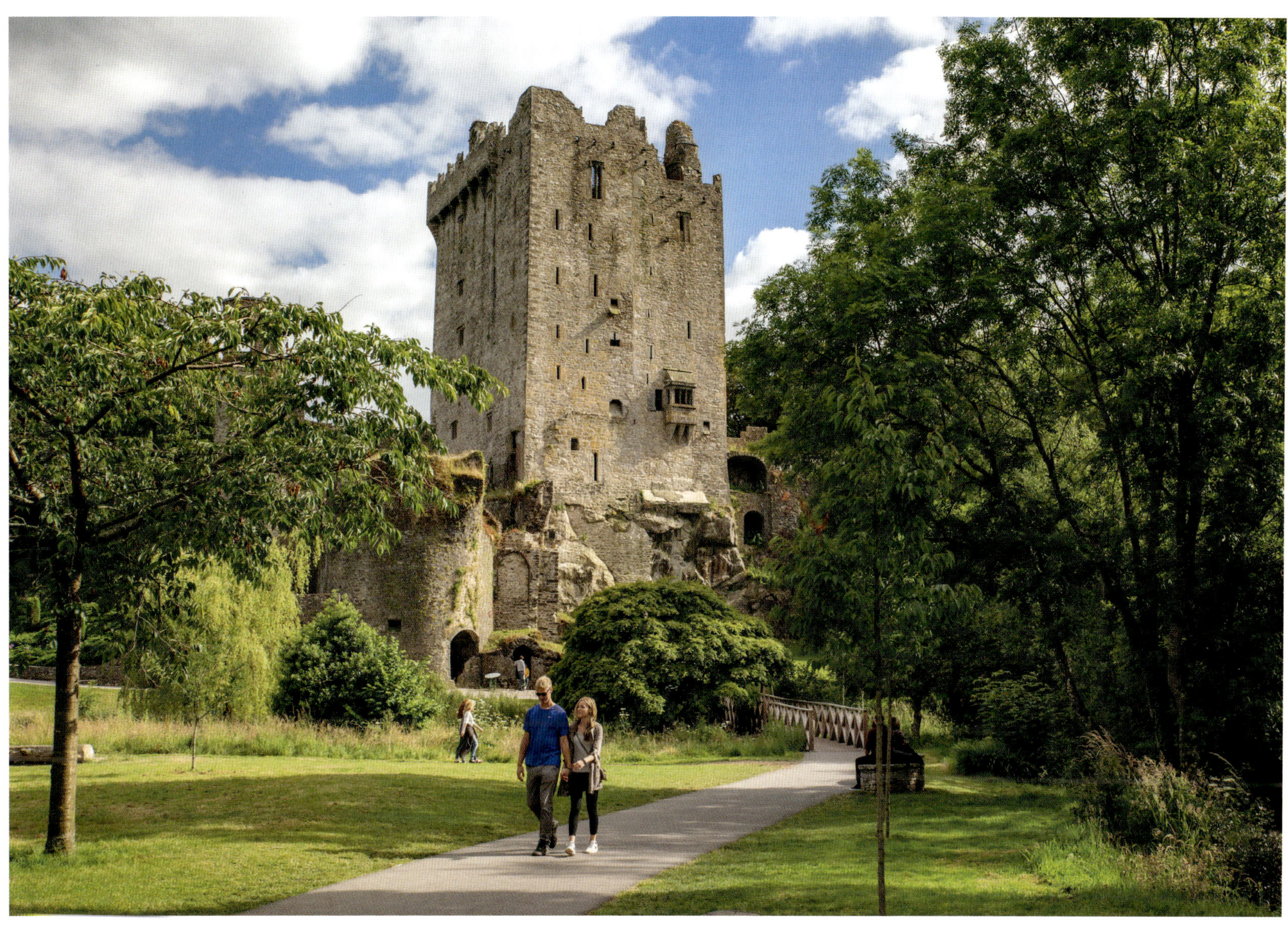

The Stone of Eloquence, or Blarney Stone, can be found atop the castle. Legend says that whoever kisses the Blarney Stone receives the 'gift of the gab', or eloquence. It doesn't come cheap, though. You must climb 127 steps to the top of the 27-metre-high tower. Then, lying upside down, you hold on to two iron railings across a gap in the parapet, before planting your kiss. Eloquence guaranteed.

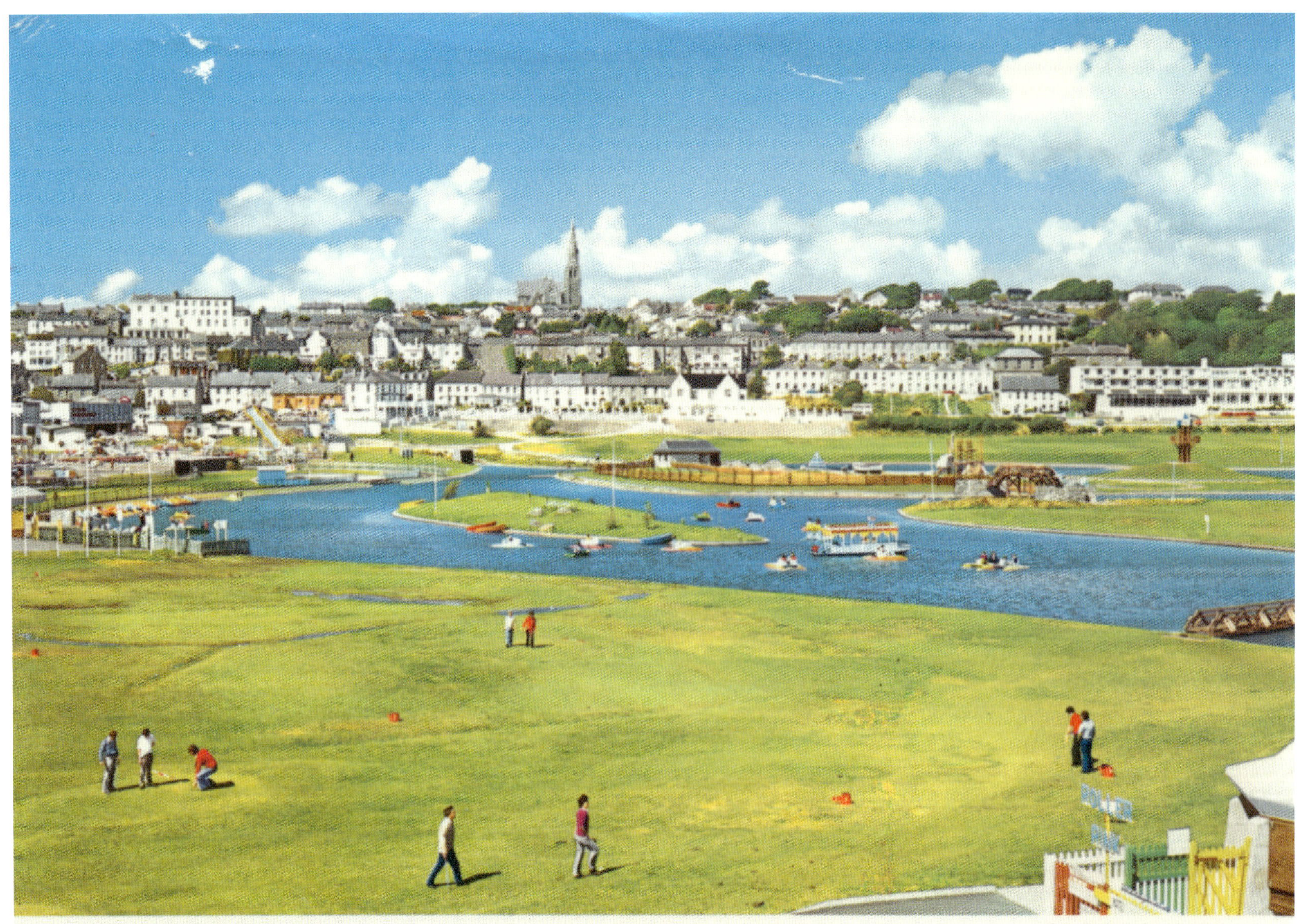

Tramore, Co. Waterford, Ireland. *Photo: P. O' Toole, John Hinde Studios.*

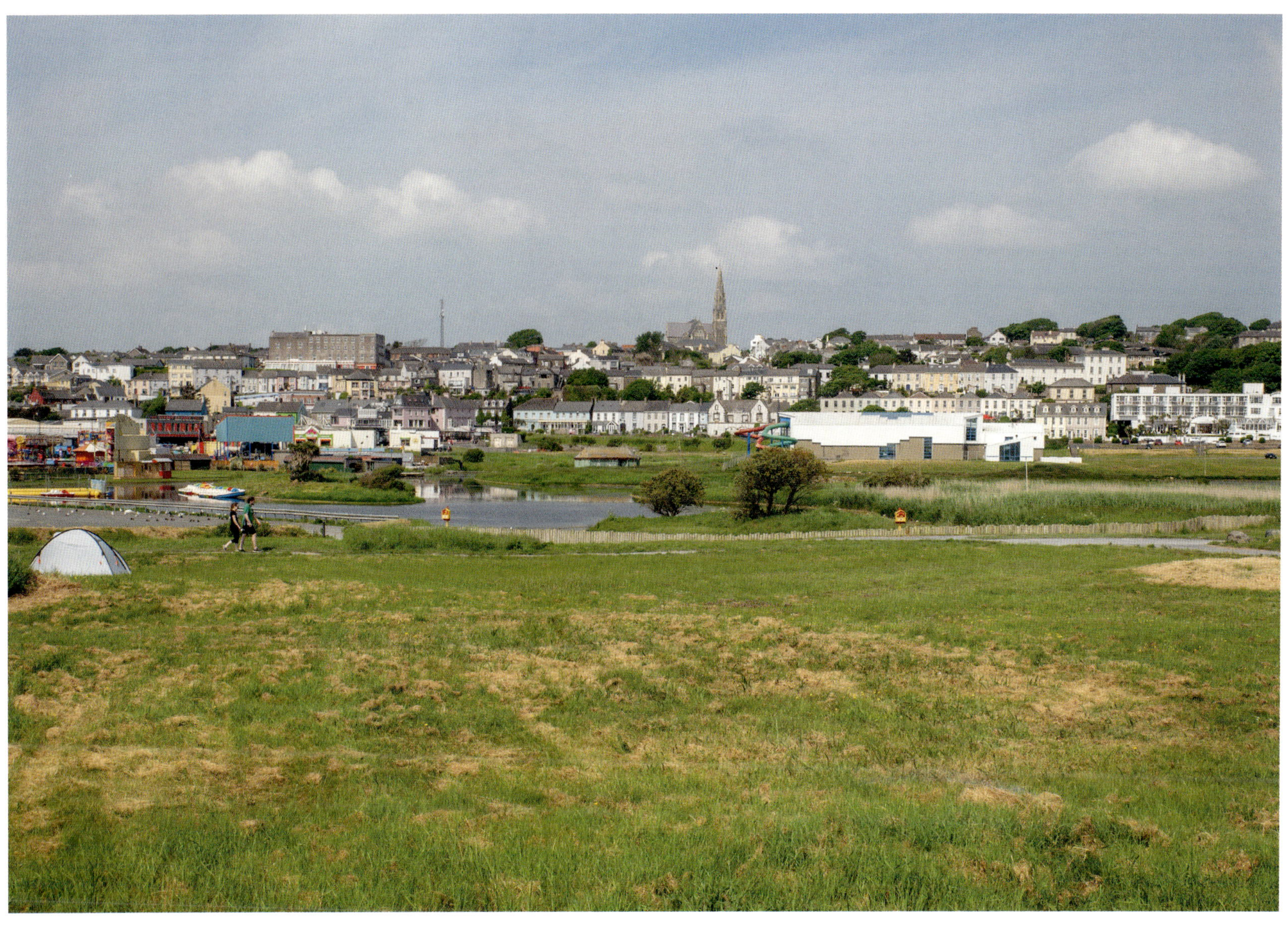

Just to the south of Waterford city is the popular Irish seaside resort of Tramore, resting on the hillside above Tramore Bay. The archetypal tiny fishing village, the railway arrived in 1853 and changed journeys and destinations forever. Today's speed-lovers can choose to accelerate by kitesurfing or windsurfing.

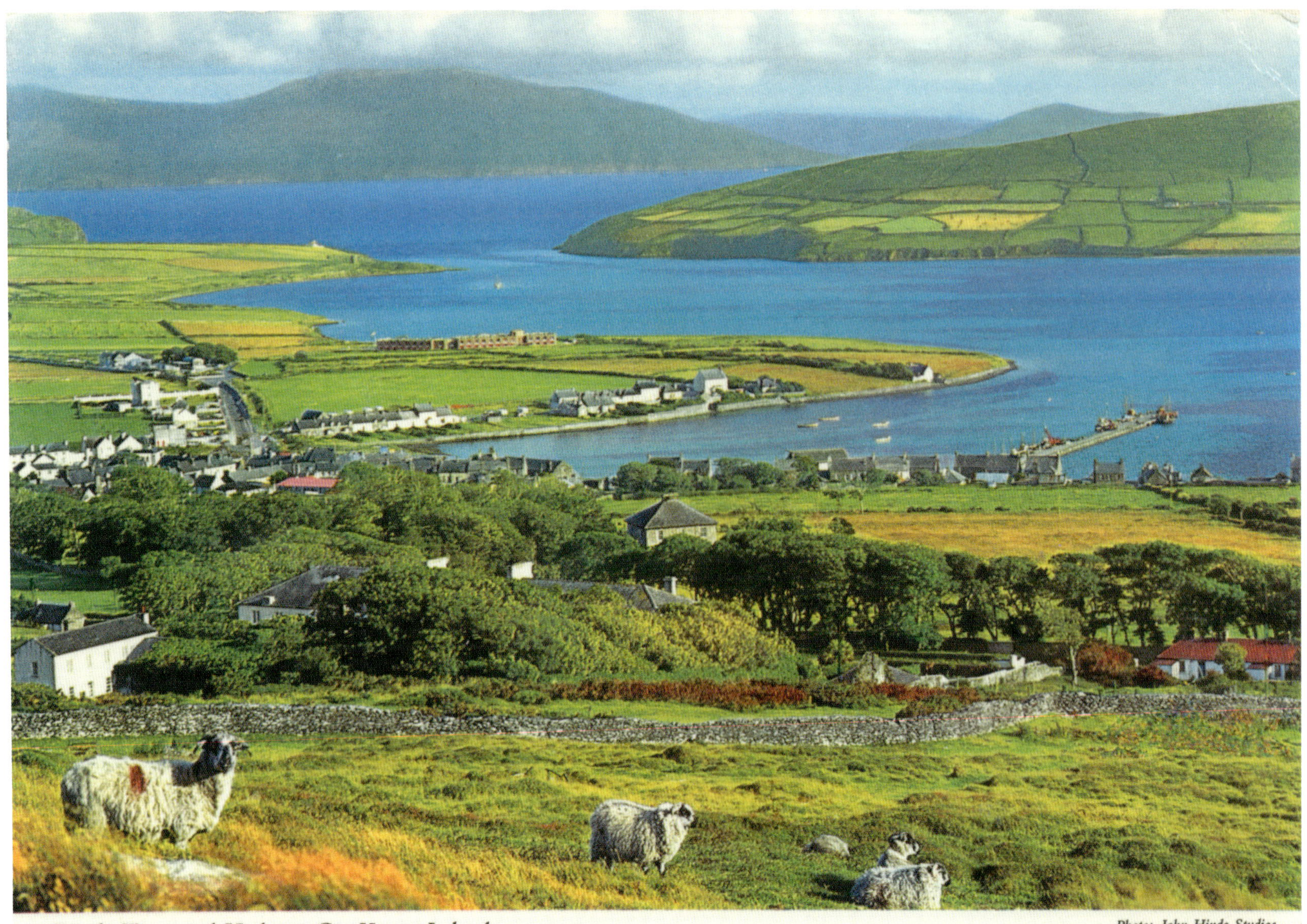
Dingle Town and Harbour, Co. Kerry, Ireland.
Photo: John Hinde Studios.

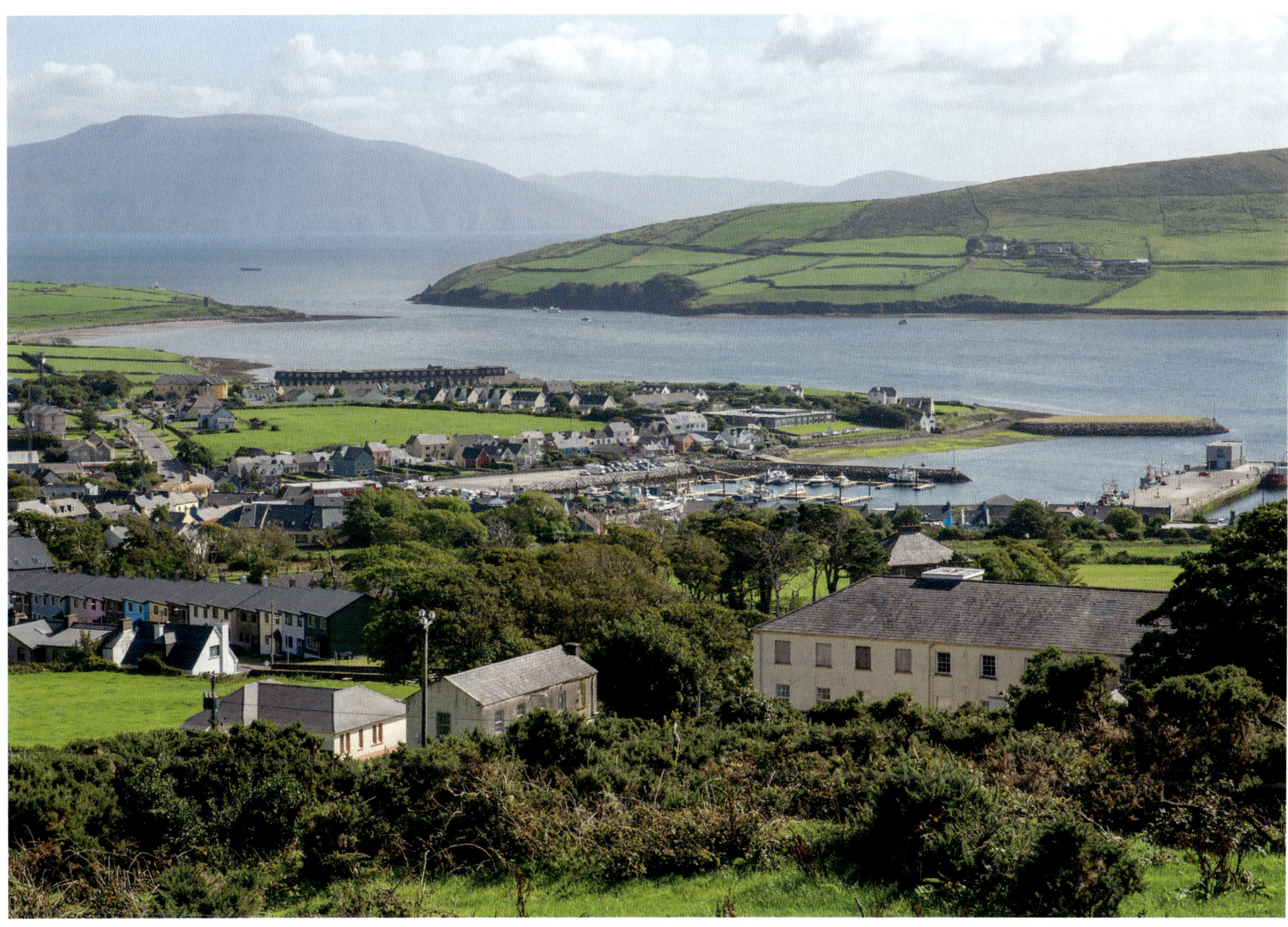

Dingle is a colourful fishing town, full of eclectic cafés, happening restaurants and traditional pubs. The town's most famous resident is Fungie, a friendly bottlenose dolphin who has been living happily in the bay since 1983. Like all true Irish folk, he is known to be of a sociable nature.

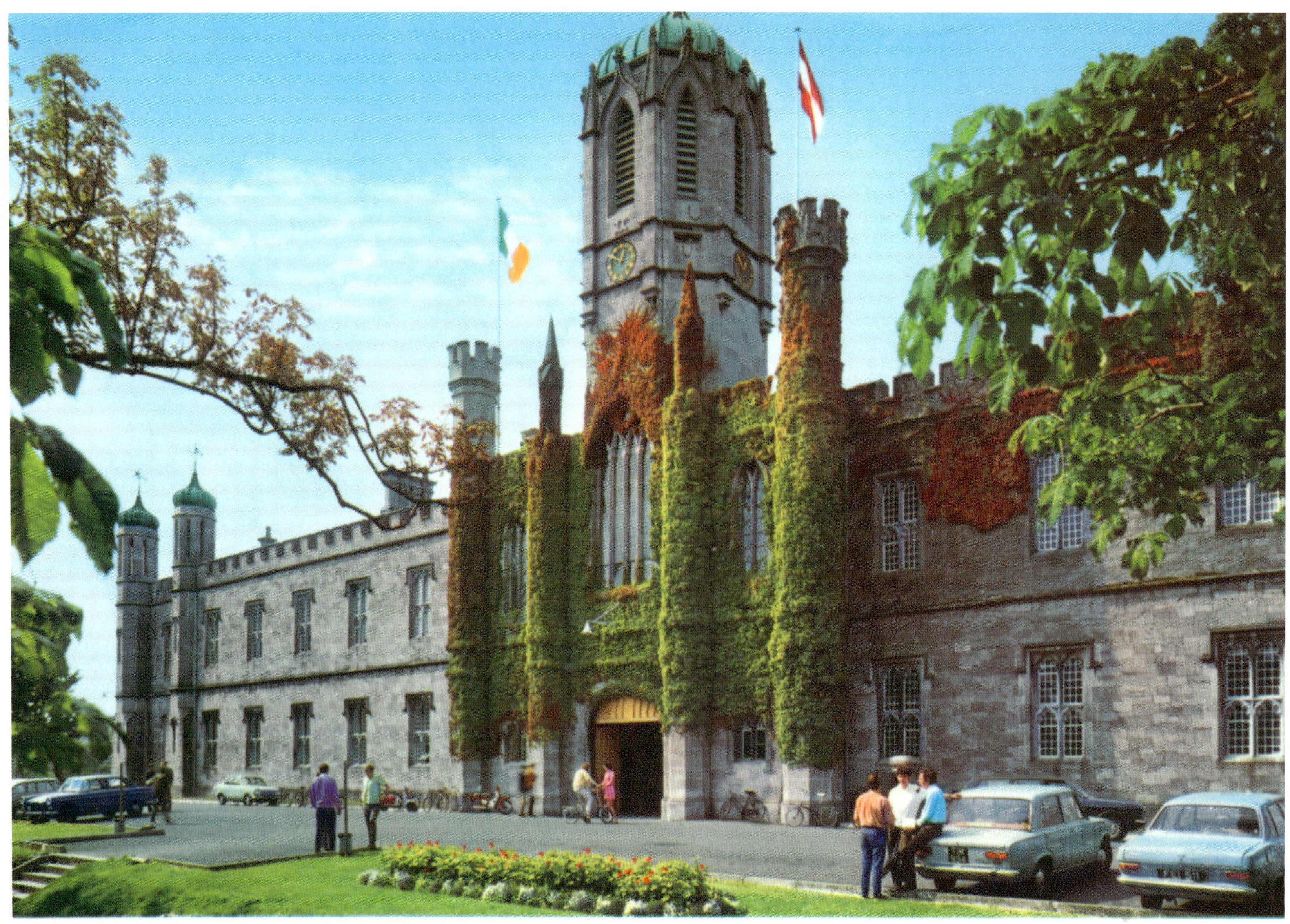

University College, Galway City, Ireland.

Photo: D. Noble, John Hinde Studios.

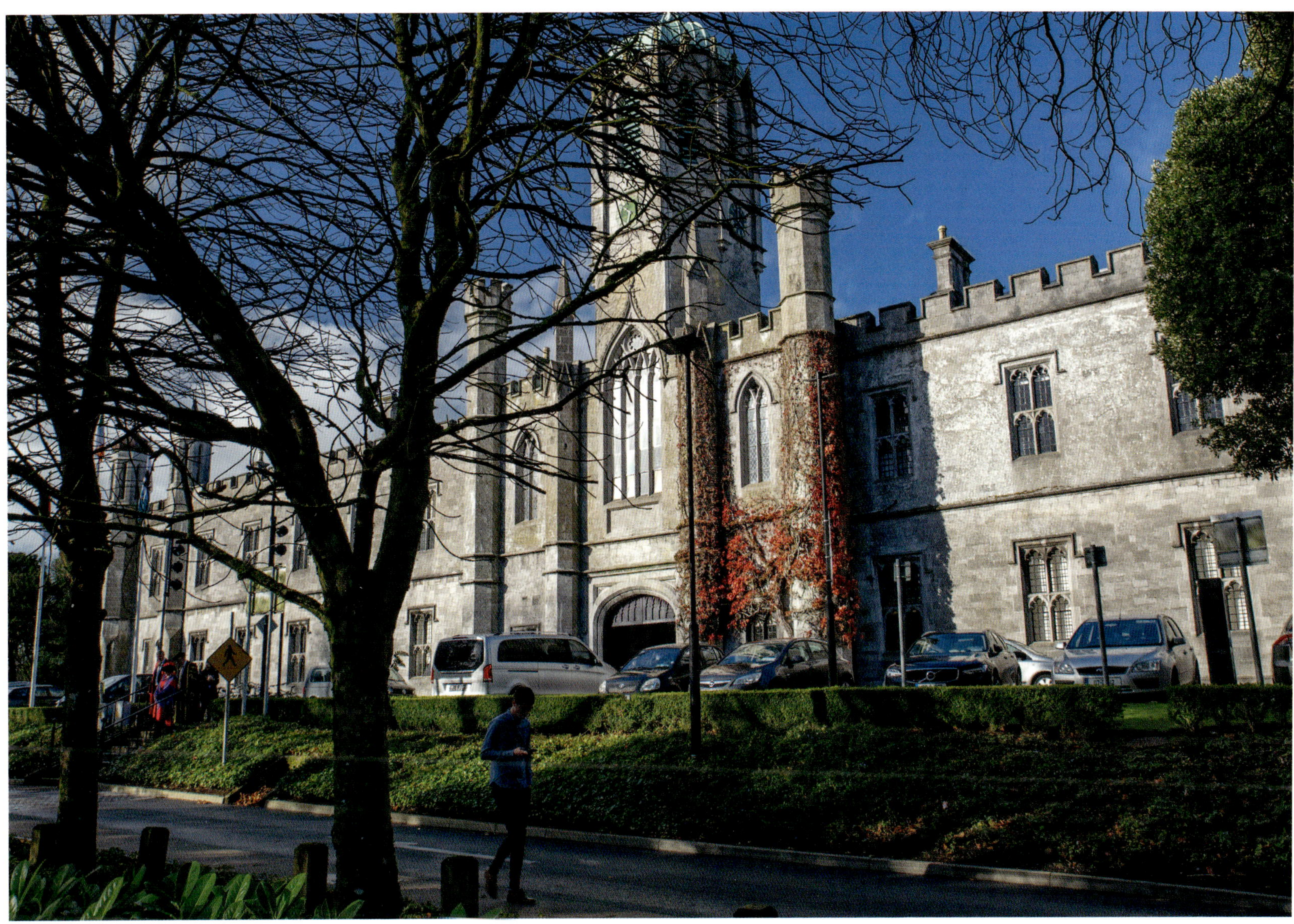

The oldest part of the university, the Quadrangle, with its Aula Maxima, is a replica of Christ Church, one of the colleges of the University of Oxford.

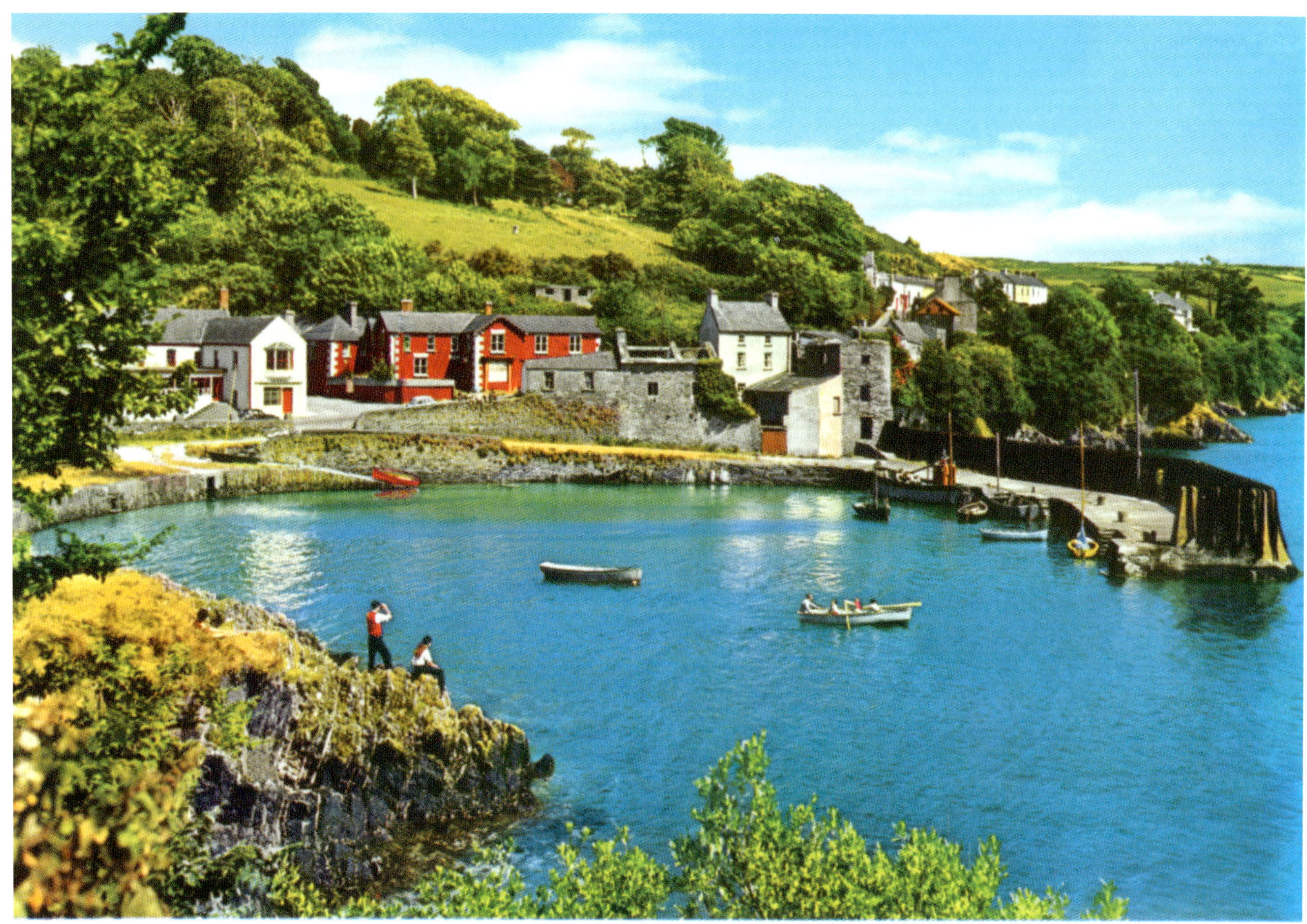

Village of Glandore, West Cork, Ireland.

Colour Photo by John Hinde, F.R.P.S.

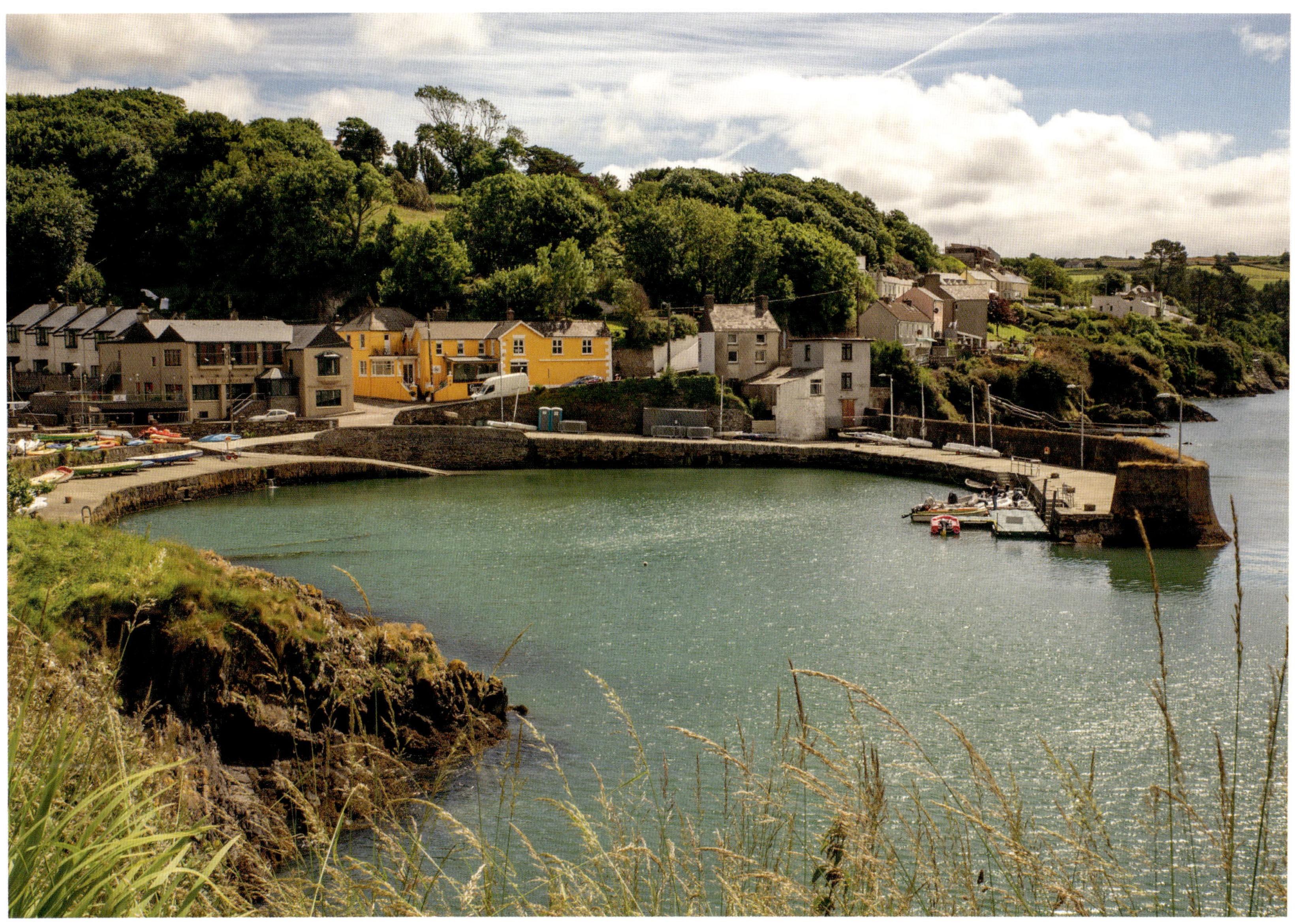

A peaceful, pastoral landscape now, but Glandore and West Cork suffered immensely in the Famine of 1845–49, in which Glandore lost almost half of its population. Today, people walk, cycle, sail and canoe amidst its blooming beauty, bathed by the gentle air of the Gulf stream.

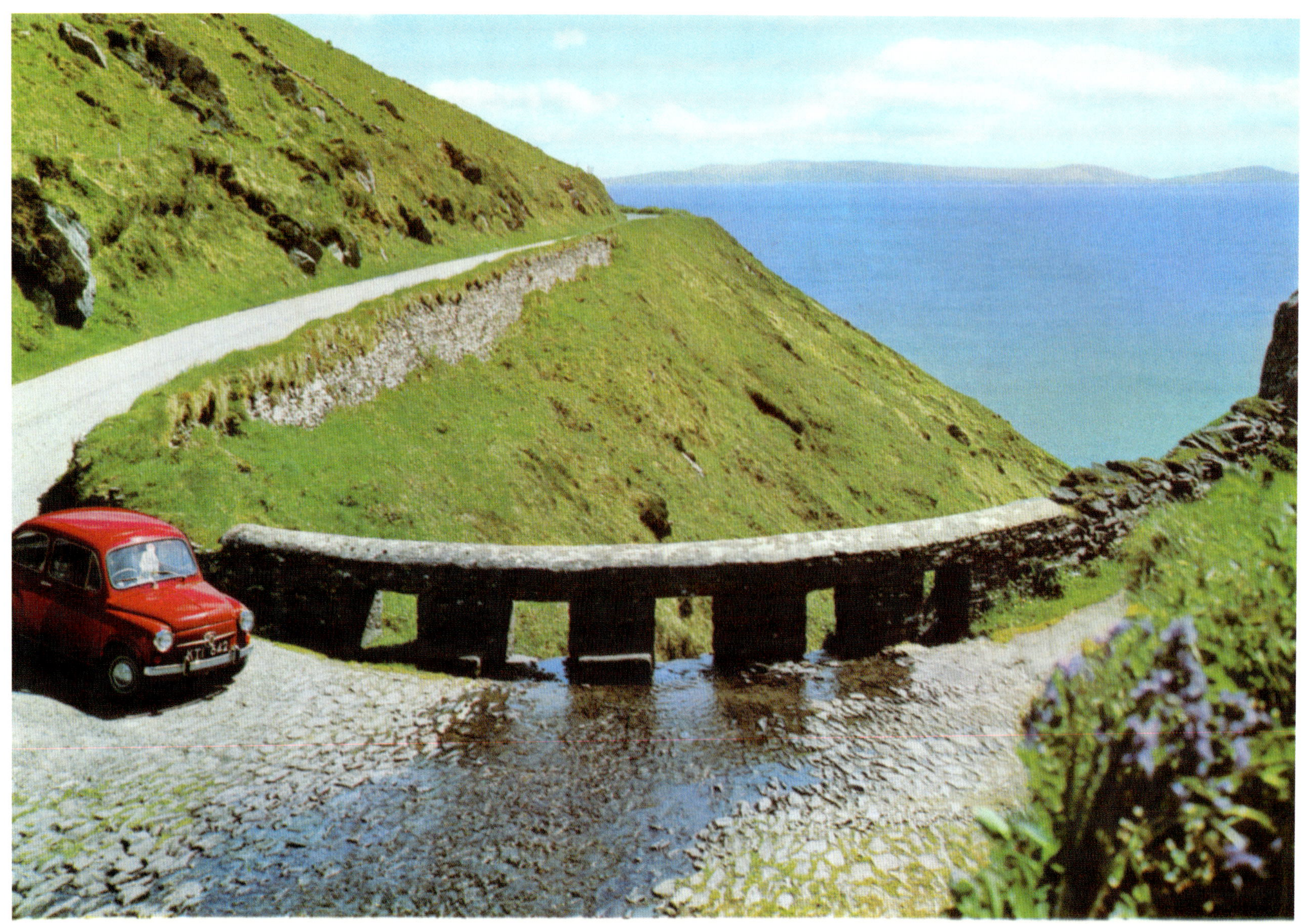

Slea Head, Dingle Peninsula, Co. Kerry, Ireland. Photo: R. Beer, John Hinde Studios.

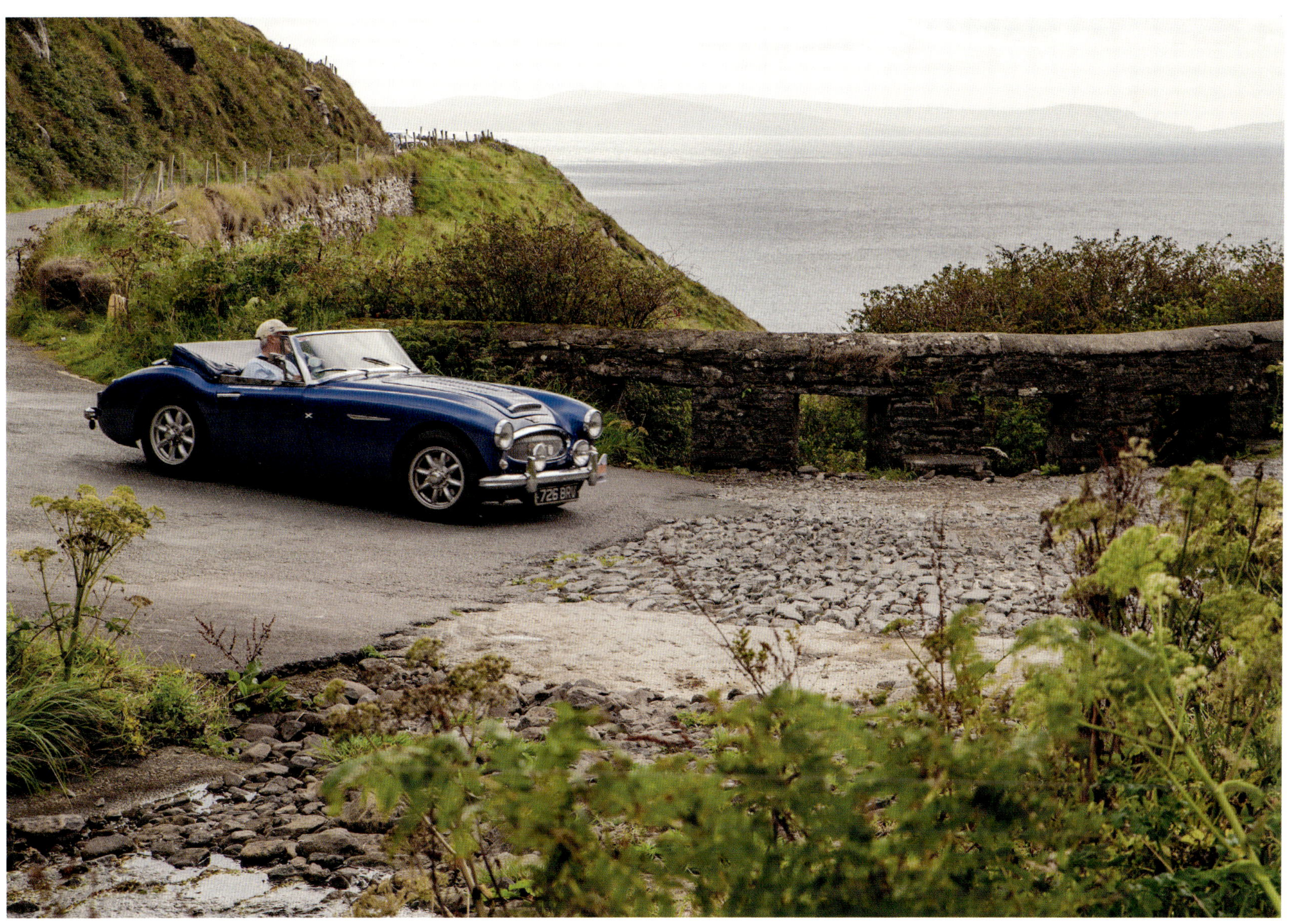

Along the Slea Head Drive, with Valentia Island in the background and a 1963 Austin Healey 3000 turning into the bend. Skies may not always be blue in Ireland, but that day life felt good.

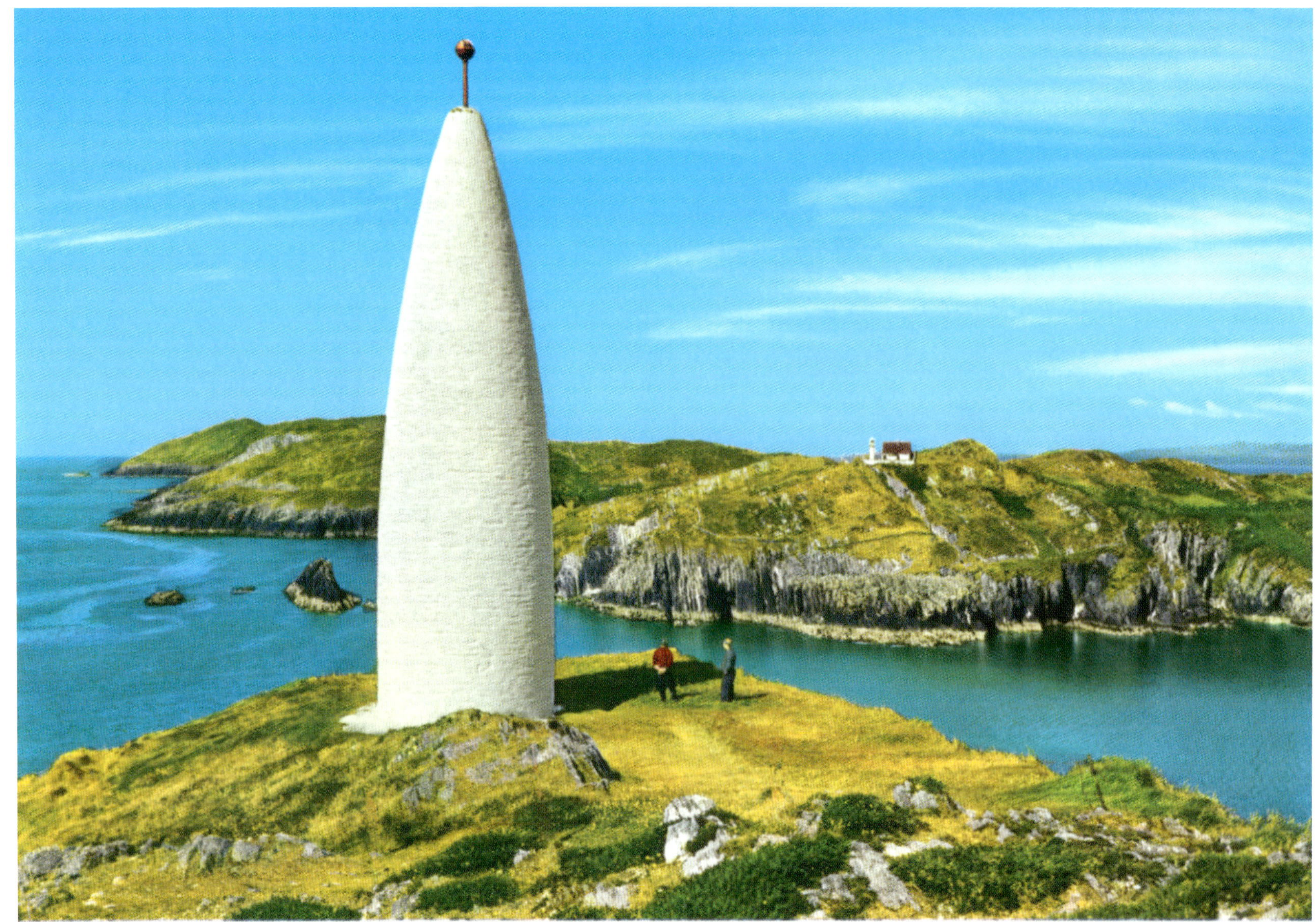

Baltimore Beacon, Sherkin Island and Cape Clear, West Cork, Ireland.

Colour Photo by John Hinde, F.R.P.S.

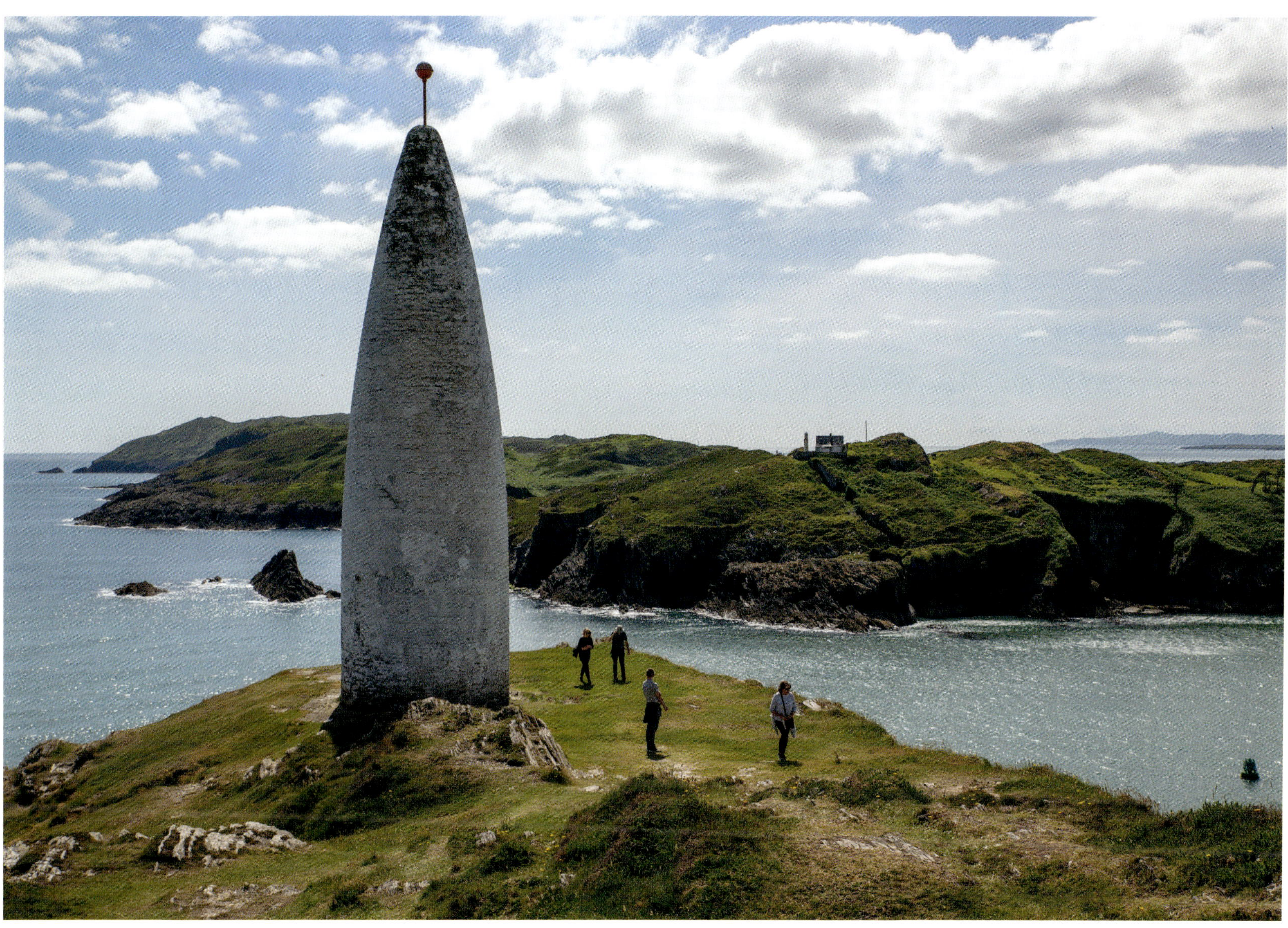

Also known as 'Lot's Wife' by locals, a reference to the Bible story where Lot's sinning wife is turned into a pillar of salt. It was built following the 1798 Rebellion by order of the British government, a grim reminder of power and punishment, now mellowed by time.

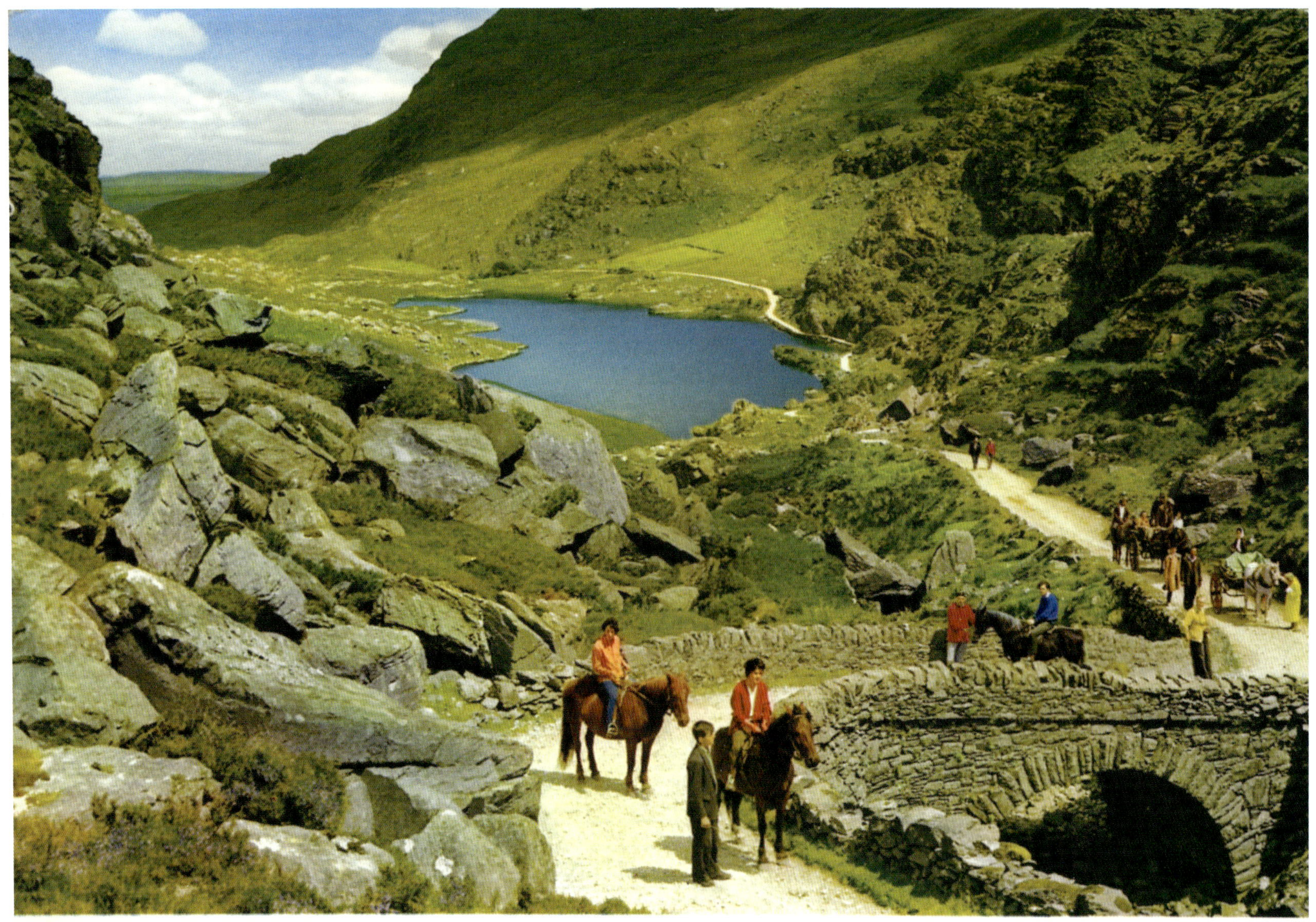

Gap of Dunloe, near Killarney, Co. Kerry, Ireland.

Photo : E. Nägele, John Hinde Studios.

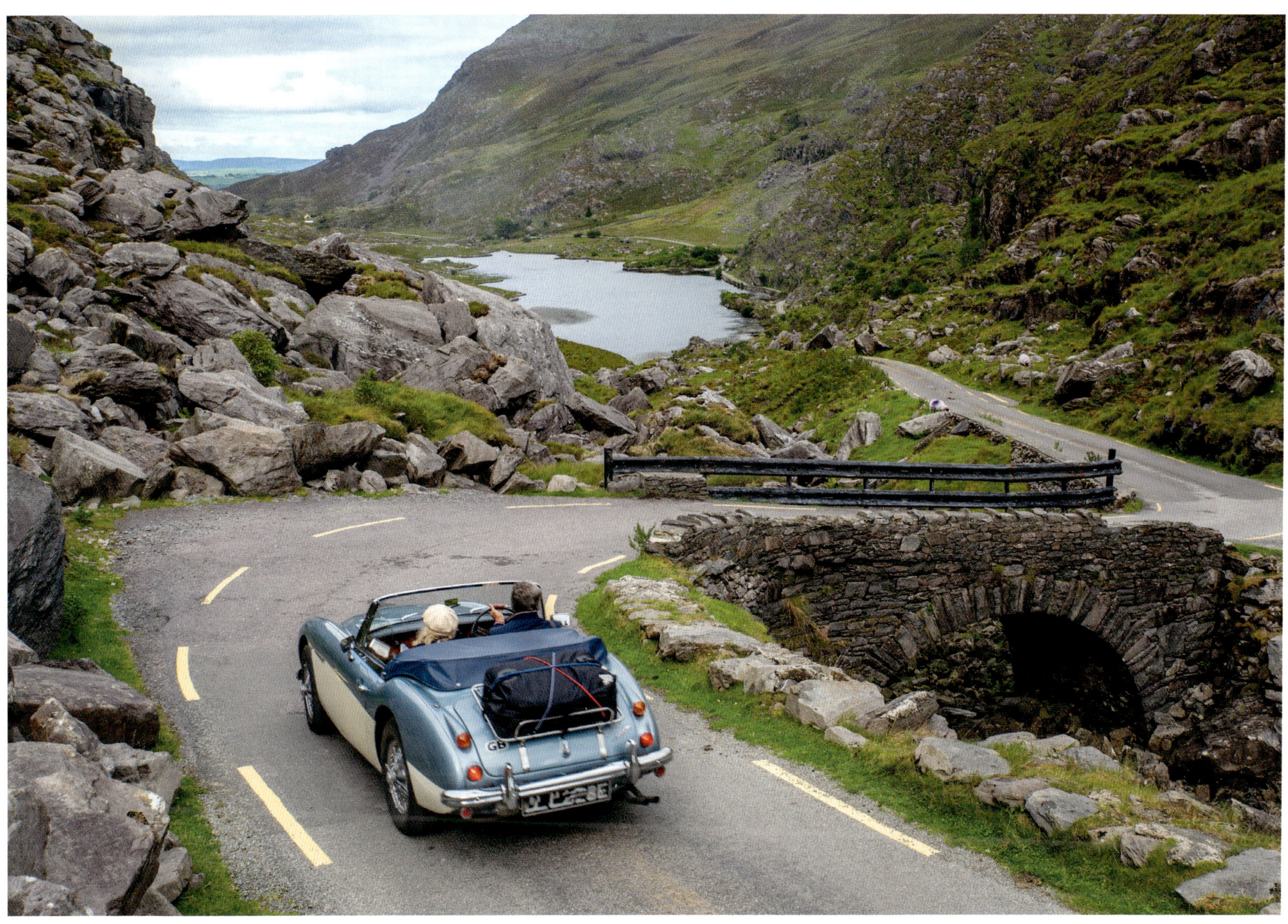

Here, I scrambled up the path strewn with boulders and balanced my tripod precariously between three jagged rocks. Squinting into my viewfinder, I heard a car approaching from behind and captured this curvaceous Austin Healey 3000 threading the Gap. One scene, several decades apart – two classic forms of transport.

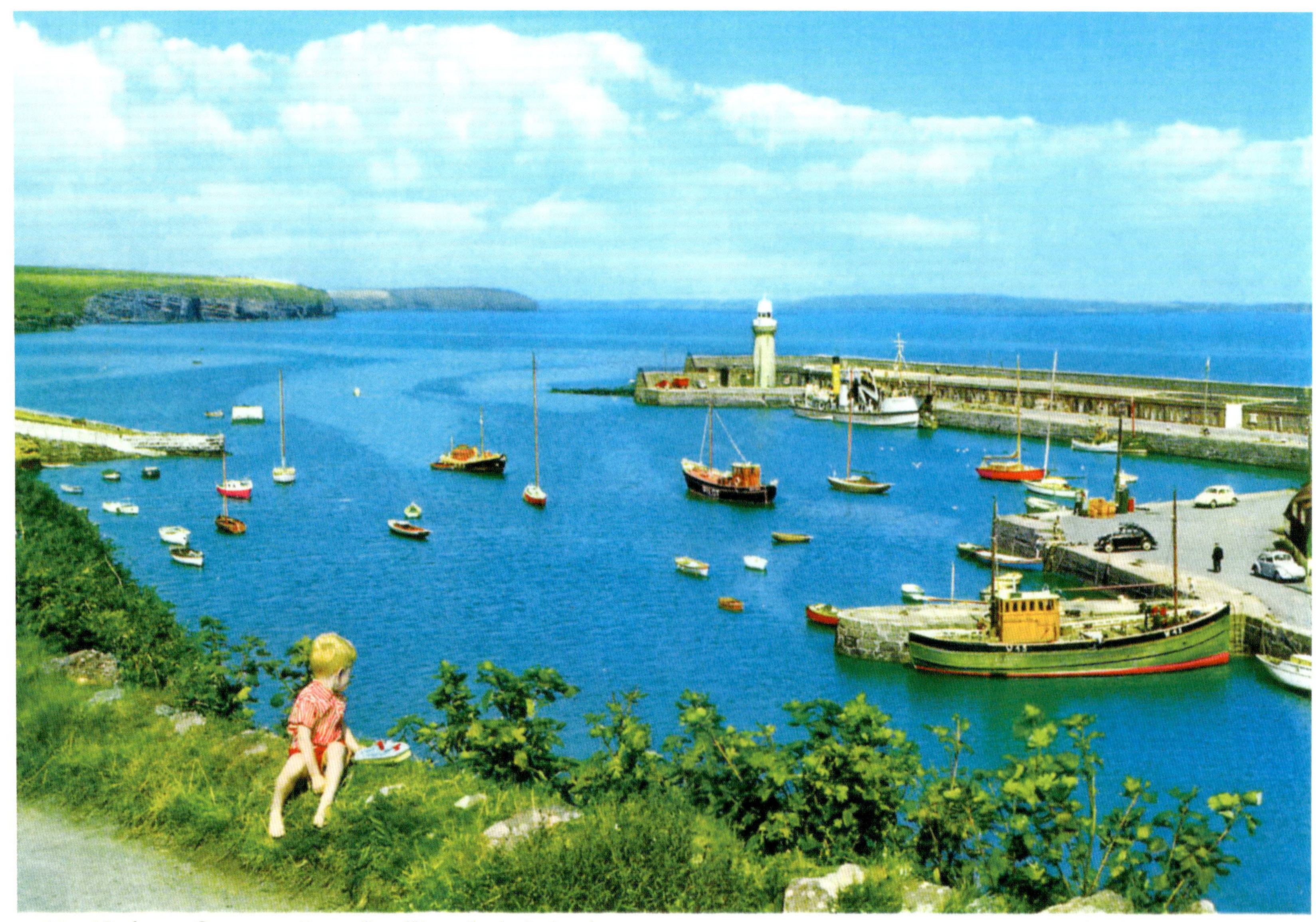

The Harbour, Dunmore East, Co. Waterford, Ireland.

Colour Photo by John Hinde, F.R.P.S.

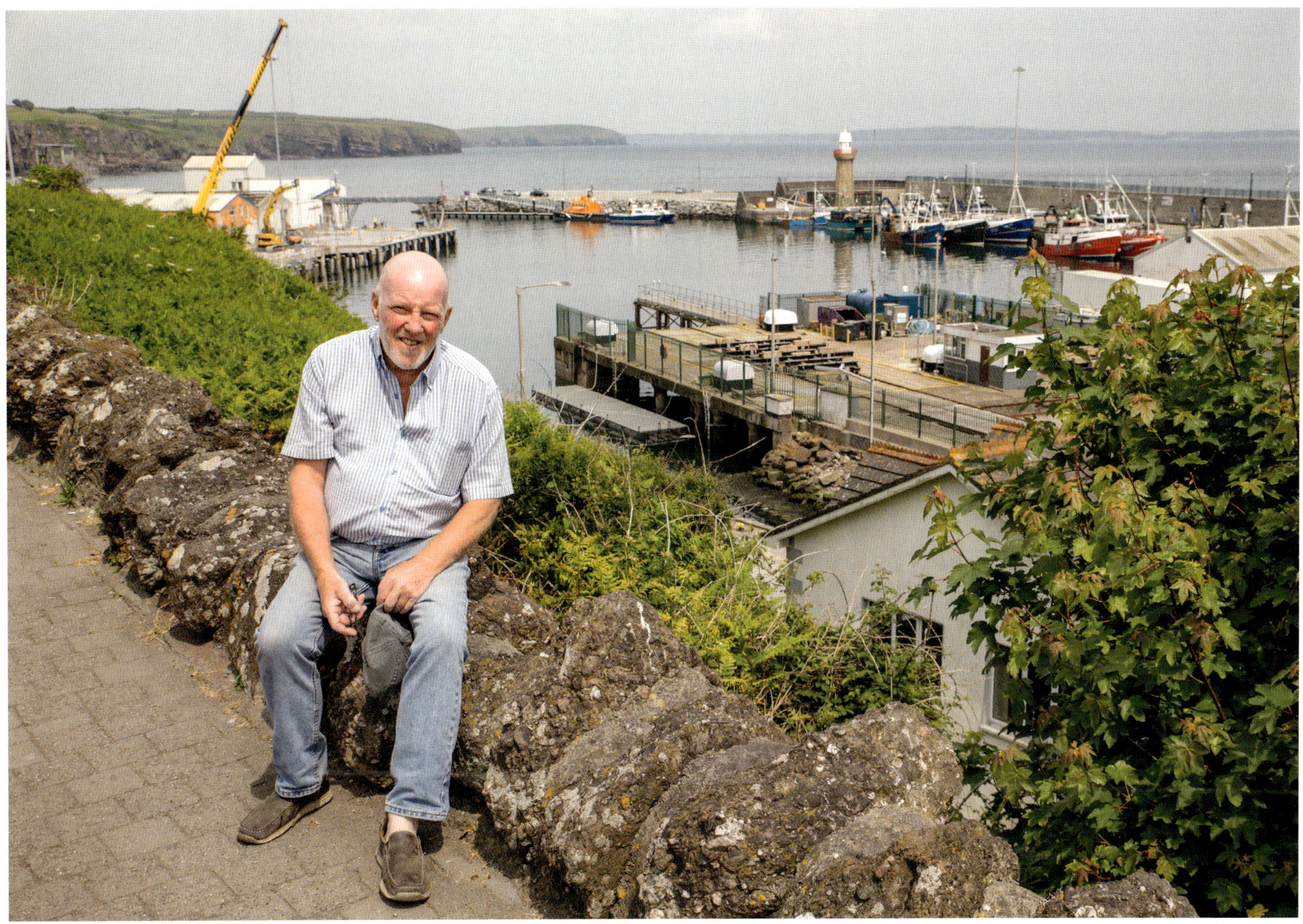

This is David Harris, owner of the Bay café in Dunmore East. In the summer of 1960, a tall man knocked on his door and politely asked his mother if he could borrow her child for a picture postcard. He still remembers that day.

'I was holding this toy boat that squirts water,' he told me as I took this picture. Today he poses in the same spot, just a few steps from his café – a poignant moment.

LIST OF POSTCARDS